Ownership Regimes in the Iberian World (1500–1850)

Max Planck Studies in Global Legal History of the Iberian Worlds

Editor

Thomas Duve

The book volumes in the *Max Planck Studies in Global Legal History of the Iberian Worlds* publish research on legal history of areas which have been in contact with the Iberian empires during the early Modern and Modern period, in Europe, the Americas, Asia and Africa. Its focus is global in the sense that it is not limited to the imperial spaces as such but rather looks at the globalization of normativities within the space related to these imperial formations. It is global also in another sense: The volumes in the series pay special attention to the coexistence of a variety of normativities and their cultural translations in different places and moments, decentring classical research perspectives and opening up for different modes of normativity.

The monographs, edited volumes and text editions in the series are peer reviewed, and published in print and online.

Brill's Open Access books are discoverable through DOAB and distributed free of charge in Brill's E-Book Collections, and through OAPEN and JSTOR.

VOLUME 5

The titles published in this series are listed at *brill.com/mpiw*

Ownership Regimes in the Iberian World (1500–1850)

The Normative Role of Kinship and Community

Edited by

Manuel Bastias Saavedra

BRILL | NIJHOFF

LEIDEN | BOSTON

This volume was prepared as part of the IberLAND project. The project has received funding from the European Research Council (ERC) under the European Union's Horizon 2020 research and innovation programme (grant agreement No. 101000991). For more information, visit https://iberland.eu/.

Cover illustration: Tlaxcalan. *Genealogy and Land Record of Juan Tepetzin* (*Fragmento de las Mujeres*), ca. 1575. © Brooklyn Museum, Charles Stewart Smith Memorial Fund and Henry L. Batterman Fund, 37.361
© Archivum Romanum Societatis Iesu, Goa 22 – I, Antidoto da Inocência – fl. 59r

The Library of Congress Cataloging-in-Publication Data is available online at https://catalog.loc.gov
LC record available at https://lccn.loc.gov/2025002741

Typeface for the Latin, Greek, and Cyrillic scripts: "Brill". See and download: brill.com/brill-typeface.

ISSN 2590-3292
ISBN 978-90-04-72271-2 (hardback)
ISBN 978-90-04-72272-9 (e-book)
DOI 10.1163/9789004722729

This book is printed on acid-free paper and produced in a sustainable manner.

Contents

Preface

The last decade has seen increased interest in questions of land and colonialism, and their contemporary consequences, and this has been reflected in a growing number of publications, publicly funded research projects and international conferences.[1] Traditionally studied within the fields of social and economic history and, especially in Latin America, centred around Marxist theories of development, the field is increasingly giving more attention to legal historical and anthropological perspectives. The idea of these new approaches is to move away from traditional views centred on royal laws, legal doctrine and theories of property. While the traditional focus on legal categories has provided depth and nuance to the ways in which notions of ownership have historically been defined and conceived, it has often ignored the concrete socio-historical conditions that surround these categories and, as such, give them their normative substance. Research on land and colonialism is, however, often still dominated by colonial perspectives and narratives that presume that local populations either did not have any notions of ownership or if they did they were erased and supplanted by the models of the coloniser. American, Asian and African experiences are usually only given a background role as the context and field of action for European agents and legal scholars.

By focusing on case studies from the Iberian world, this volume seeks to provide a new framework for the historical study of the problems of land and colonialism. It looks at the colonial context to show that the holding of land was not only regulated through European doctrine, laws and grace, but was bound to corporate bodies, communities, kinship ties and customs that varied according to the region and the local forms of social and political reproduction. The combination of these diverse orders of normative structuring can be defined as the *Ownership Regime*. Moving from a focus on law to a focus on historical regimes of normativity implies understanding law and juridical normativity as one component within a complex and dynamic ensemble of practices, institutions and social, religious and cultural norms that produced historically efficient and consolidated normative arrangements. Such a perspective demands that historians and legal historians interested in studying land tenure in the different regions of the Iberian world focus more carefully on how the combination of these normative sources produced specific arrangements in the ways

1 For example, the Latin American Association for Rural History (ALAHR) was established last year and held its First Annual Conference this year.

in which land was held, owned, divided and regulated, and how conflicts were adjudicated.

The ten chapters of this volume thus restate the relationship between land and colonialism using this more nuanced perspective. In Chapter 1 (Manuel Bastias Saavedra), I reexamine traditional historiographical views of land ownership, moving away from the typical dichotomy of private and common property to explore the complex, multi-layered normative landscapes of the early modern Iberian world. I argue against the historical narrative that overly simplifies land ownership models by placing them into rigid categories that either reflect European legal traditions or impose colonial legacies on indigenous societies. Instead, a re-evaluation of how historians and legal scholars conceptualise land ownership and its regulation is required, shifting away from Eurocentric and anthropocentric frameworks towards more inclusive, locally sensitive approaches. This reorientation aims to better reflect the complex realities of land relations in the early modern period, emphasising the diversity of practices across different cultures and communities.

One way in which this reorientation may be carried out is by reassessing the ways in which ownership was historically conceived in early modern European society. Alessandro Buono's contribution (Chapter 2) focuses on the semantic and constitutional role played by care and responsibility in organising the distribution of and access to land in early modern Europe and America. He delves into the concept of ownership in early modern Catholic Europe, challenging the conventional anthropocentric view that separates humans from things. He argues that, during this period, things were seen as bearers of rights and capable of representing absent persons, suggesting a deep integration of objects and people into legal and social structures. Buono highlights the idea that ownership was intertwined with responsibilities towards the community and implied stewardship rather than absolute control.

The core of the volume is placed on case studies from Africa, America, and Europe. All the case studies show how, despite the existence of regulation by the Crown, local normativities were central to regulating access to land. Thiago Mota (Chapter 3) examines how Portuguese settlers and traders in Greater Senegambia during the 16th and 17th centuries were subjected to African normative regimes concerning land ownership, rather than imposing their own. Contrary to traditional narratives of European dominion, Mota argues that the Portuguese were essentially dependent on the goodwill and authority of African rulers, revealing a complex interplay of power where local norms governed land control. José Carlos de la Puente Luna (Chapter 4) delves into the intricate relationships between household and community land rights within and between *ayllus* in colonial Peru. The chapter argues for a relational and dynamic understanding of land ownership regimes, where particular and collective rights coexisted and were mutually constitutive. The idea of 'commoning' emphasises how communal and domestic rights were negotiated and redefined over time. Marta Martín Gabaldón (Chapter 5) explores how the indigenous forms of governance and territorial control in colonial Tlaxiaco, which were deeply embedded in the Mixtec political and social systems, continued to influence the region's socio-political landscape. She uses the idea of 'masked' relationships to highlight the subtle or hidden ways in which traditional structures of power and land ownership persisted under colonial rule, even though they were nominally reorganised or subsumed under the new legal frameworks imposed by the Spanish.

These kinds of 'masked' relationships also appear in Carolina Jurado's chapter (Chapter 6), which explores the normative complexities and the implementation of the 1591 Royal Decrees concerning land rights within indigenous communities in colonial Charcas. The chapter shows the importance of detailed archival work, since the intent of the Spaniards to remove power from traditional corporative authorities by placing the holding of land at the domestic level ultimately failed. Through indirect information retrieved from censuses, Jurado shows how the reorganisation of land tenure conducted by Spanish authorities eventually reverted to supradomestic levels of organising land relations as a way to better manage production and resources. Íñigo Ena Sanjuán (Chapter 7) explores the historical management and dispute resolution regarding grassland ownership and use in the Pyrenean valleys of Ansó and Hecho from the 17th to the 19th century. He emphasises the role of local agreements, known as *concordias* and *sentencias arbitrales*, in maintaining communal land rights and resolving conflicts over land use. The chapter details how these agreements, deeply rooted in local customs and historical practices, facilitated sustainable land management and shaped local identities and governance. The historical practices of managing communal lands through local agreements in the Pyrenean valleys represented a form of normative ordering that was effective in maintaining community resources and stability.

However, being rooted in colonial contexts, local normative arrangements did not always stave off dispossession and encroachment on traditional community lands. Alcira Dueñas (Chapter 8) delves into the colonial administration's impact on indigenous land rights in the Andes, particularly focusing on the Vico and Pasco regions during the late 18th century. She examines the shift from the use of *amparos* (legal protections for possession) to the reliance on cartographic evidence in land disputes, highlighting how these changes facilitated the dispossession of communal lands. Dueñas argues that this transition not only altered the means of legal engagement but also reinforced colonial and later aristocratic land grabs at the expense of indigenous communities. Crislayne Alfagali (Chapter 9) examines the land tenure conflicts that emerged from the establishment of an iron foundry in Ilamba, Angola, in the late 18th century. She explores the colonial dynamics of land expropriation and the various strategies employed by local *sobas* (chiefs) to maintain their political power and control over natural resources. Alfagali highlights the complex interplay between colonial exploitation and indigenous strategies of resistance, adaptation and negotiation by showing how colonial demands intersected with local traditions, revealing a complex landscape of normative and cultural negotiation.

Finally, Rosa Congost (Chapter 10) provides an epilogue in which she argues for a de-Westernisation of the models of land ownership used in historical analysis. She challenges the dominant Western-centric historiography, which tends to apply European models of land ownership universally without considering the specific historical and cultural contexts of other regions, particularly Latin America. Congost emphasises the need to recognise and incorporate diverse historical experiences and normative systems to provide a more accurate and nuanced understanding of land ownership across different societies. She calls for more pluralistic and inclusive frameworks that acknowledge the legitimacy of non-Western forms of land ownership and governance. This epilogue, from one of the great European specialists in rural history, is both an invitation and a challenge for the next generation of historians interested in land tenure.

This volume was conceived as early as 2019 as part of the activities of the Glocalising Normativities (GloNo) project at the Max Planck Institute for Legal History and Legal Theory (mpilhlt).[2] That project marked the first coordinated effort at the Institute to move from a Latin American perspective towards one that included all the former territories of the Spanish and Portuguese empires, in what is increasingly referred to as the Iberian world. The aims of this effort, as framed by Thomas Duve, was not to write a legal history of the Iberian empires, but rather to observe normativity from a local perspective in order to write a history of the 'glocalisation of normativity' from a theoretically sensitised history. This volume is partially the outcome of the early years of the above-mentioned joint research project. It has also come out of the work conducted within the IberLAND project,[3] which was initially born at the mpilhlt and is currently hosted at the Leibniz University of Hannover. Most of this volume's chapters were presented at the conference "Ownership Regimes in the Iberian

2 https://www.lhlt.mpg.de/joint-project/glocalising-normativities.
3 https://iberland.eu/.

World", which took place at the mpilhlt in Frankfurt on 1–2 September 2022. I thank the host institution, the speakers and the IberLAND team, who met there for the first time as a group, for their participation and support in making this publication happen. Plans for the second volume of the remaining contributions are already underway.

Finally, I am especially indebted to Camilla de Freitas Macedo for the coordination of this volume. It would not have been possible without her constant support. Leon Charlé was of great assistance in revising the chapters in the last stages of review and Genevieve Beech, as always, did an excellent job shaping the chapters into crisper English. I would also like to thank the anonymous peer reviewers and the colleagues of the IberLAND project for their detailed and insightful comments on the chapters. Finally, I thank Nicole Pasakarnis for her support in the editorial process.

Manuel Bastias Saavedra
Berlin / Goa, August 2024

Illustrations

Charts

Figures

Maps

Notes on Contributors

Manuel Bastias Saavedra
is Associate Professor of Latin American History at Leibniz University Hannover. His research focuses on the legal and institutional history of the Spanish and Portuguese empires. He currently leads the IberLAND project, funded by the European Research Council.

Alessandro Buono
is Professor at the University of Pisa. He focuses on personal identity and ownership in early modern Europe, subject on which he co-edited *Under Guardianship. Properties without Owner and Vacant Successions in a Comparative Perspective, 13th–20th Centuries* (2020).

Thiago H. Mota
is Assistant Professor of African History at the University of California—Santa Cruz. He authored the book *Portugueses e Muçulmanos na Senegâmbia*, and articles published in journals such as Atlantic Studies, Afriques, Slavery & Abolition, and Latin American Research Review.

José Carlos de la Puente Luna
is Professor of History at Texas State University and the author of *Los curacas hechiceros de Jauja* (2007) and *Andean Cosmopolitans* (2018). His research centres on indigenous land tenure and commoner colonization in colonial Andes.

Marta Martín Gabaldón
is a researcher at UNAM's Institute of Historical Research. She studies colonial indigenous territory in Oaxaca and co-coordinates the book *La historia de los pueblos indígenas en México* (2024).

Carolina Jurado
teaches Latin American History at the University of Buenos Aires and she is a researcher at CONICET (Argentina). Her work examines Spanish rule's impact on Aymara leadership and land ownership in Charcas (Viceroyalty of Peru) during the 16th and 17th centuries.

Íñigo Ena Sanjuán
is an Alexander von Humboldt Postdoctoral Fellow at Leibniz University Hannover. He was granted a Marie Skłodowska-Curie Fellowship (2025–2027). His

research interests are state formation and common pastures in the Pyrenean valleys.

Alcira Dueñas
is Professor at the Ohio State University. A specialist in the ethnohistory of colonial state building, she published the award-winning book *Indians and Mestizos in the Lettered City*, several book chapters and articles in Ethnohistory, Colonial Latin American History, The Americas, Histórica, among others.

Crislayne Alfagali
holds a PhD in Social History from UNICAMP, focusing on Colonial Brazil and Africa. She published *Blacksmiths of Ilamba*, detailing labour history at an Angolan iron foundry in the 18th century.

Rosa Congost
is Professor at the University of Girona, directing the Center for Research in Rural History. She has extensively published on property rights, including the monograph *Tierras, Leyes, Historia* (2007).

CHAPTER 1

Beyond Private and Common

Ownership Regimes in the Iberian World (1500–1800)

Manuel Bastias Saavedra

1 Introduction

Land has been at the centre of a global and centuries-old struggle between habitation and resource extraction. Arguably since the beginning of the Spanish and Portuguese imperial expansions in the mid-15th century, defining how land could be used and who could use it has involved and connected diverse peoples and communities across Africa, Asia, Europe and the Americas. The enduring importance of this issue has been brought back into focus by contemporary land grabs, which have seen almost 227 million hectares of land change hands between 2001 and 2011.[1] Most of these land transfers have involved the dispossession and displacement of countless local communities in favour of international corporations dedicated to large-scale farming, forestry, and mining. These conflicts have not only highlighted the importance of competing rights to land, but also the normative value tied to the uses and meanings given to land by different groups. Thus, questions about who has rights to land and how competing interests to land have been reconciled have a long and globally interconnected history, informed by the legacy of empires, nation-state building, and the more recent development of a transnational order.

Though the legacy of empire has connected the regulation of land across different world regions through complex networks of communication since at least as early as the mid-16th century, historical research has tended to view this problem through exclusively national or regional lenses. This has led to the existence of two contradictory narratives for the historical development of private property in land. On the one hand, scholarship has shown that the paradigm of private property in Europe only began to gain ascendancy after the French revolution in the late 18th century.[2] On the other hand, the scholar-

1 Oxfam, "Land and Power".

2 Among others, Beck Varela, *Das sesmarias à propriedade moderna*; Blaufarb, *The great demarcation*; Congost, *Tierras, Leyes, Historia*; Clavero, "Propiedades y propiedad, 1789"; Grossi, *Il Dominio e le Cose*; Grossi and López y López, *Propiedad.*

DOI:10.1163/9789004722729_002

ship on the Iberian territories in Asia, Africa, and the Americas has argued that the paradigm of private property was introduced by European colonisers in the 16th century.[3] More than just reflecting developments in land law, this discrepancy of almost 300 years is the result of a shortcut taken by historians eager to emphasise the cultural distance between colonisers and colonised. Since colonisation was a violent process that involved dispossession of land, the heart of the problem is presented as an issue of fundamentally different conceptions of property: common and private. However well intended, this narrative fails to consider that until the late 18th century land tenure in Europe was not characterised by private property. Moreover, this narrative has not been able to provide a historically accurate account of the different land tenure regimes that resulted from colonisation in the early modern world. Consequences of this still exist today, ultimately shaping the way legal, economic, and political conflicts between habitation and resource extraction are regulated.[4]

At the root of these narratives is a colonial image of the world based on the assumption of a temporal asymmetry that distinguished Europe's experience from those of other world regions: i.e., the idea that all other world regions were developmentally behind Europe. The main contours of this idea can be traced at least as far back as John Locke, who, in his *Second Treatise of Government*, equated the situation in America with the remote past of the world: while England was occupied during the 17th century with the higher problems of civil society and government, American peoples still lived in a state of nature in which "'God had given the earth to the children of men', given to mankind in common".[5] According to Locke, the difference between one and the other could be reduced to the difference between how much land was appropriated and how much had remained in the common. For him, only the English cultivation, enclosure, and improvement of the land could generate property rights.

3 We see this idea represented in different regional historiographies. See, among others, Cushner, *Landed Estates in the Colonial Philippines*; Góngora, *El Estado en el Derecho Indiano*; Graubart, "Shifting landscapes"; Kellogg, *Law and the Transformation of Aztec Culture*; Lynch Jr., "Land Rights, Land Laws, and Land Usurpation"; Mariluz Urquijo, *El Regimen de la Tierra en el Derecho Indiano*; Mariluz Urquijo, "La propiedad en el derecho indiano"; Míguez Núñez, *Terra Di Scontri*; Ots Capdequí, *El régimen de la tierra en hispanoamérica*; Owensby, *Empire of Law and Indian Justice in Colonial Mexico*; Parise, *Ownership Paradigms in American Civil Law Jurisdictions*; Phelan, *The Hispanization of the Philippines*. For a critical overview of the historiography of Spanish America, see: Bastias Saavedra, "The Normativity of Possession".

4 This narrative has not only pervaded the study of Iberian colonialism but has also gained ascendancy in the history of international law. For example, see Koskenniemi, *To the Uttermost Parts of the Earth*.

5 Locke, *Two treatises of government*, 129.

He argued that since Amerindians did not appropriate the common through industriousness and improvement, and rather let the land lay to waste, they could not claim exclusive rights and hence lived as the descendants of Adam had in a distant past: "Thus, in the beginning, all the world was America".[6]

Of course, the fact that this was a theoretical point has not reduced the impact of this idea. In the early 20th century, Caetano Gonçalves, member of the Portuguese Conselho Colonial, in a 1926 article on lands in the Portuguese overseas territories, argued that: "It is well known that among primitive peoples there is no idea of the individual appropriation of land. The way in which such peoples characterise the possession of land is that of agrarian collectivism."[7] Perhaps through sheer repetition, this temporalisation of European and colonial experience has become a pervasive common-sense notion that has even found credence among contemporary historians. Jürgen Osterhammel, for example, when speaking of the expansion towards the American West in his book *The Transformation of the World*, though recognising its simplistic quality, nevertheless believes it useful to stick to the formula: "that European concepts are individualist and exchange related whereas Indian ones are collectivist and use related."[8] And even more recent historical and anthropological research, that argues that indigenous peoples in Africa, Asia, and the Americas did, in fact, possess notions of private property *before* the arrival of the Europeans,[9] remains nonetheless tied to the Lockean premise that access to land in the early modern period could be reduced to a basic dichotomy of private and common property.

This narrative device has, thus, been used by both proponents and detractors of the colonial enterprise to emphasise the cultural distance between Europeans and non-Europeans, presenting the problem, as mentioned, as one of fundamentally different conceptions of property. The problem with this narrative, however, is not that private property is an inadequate category for describing how communities in Africa, Asia and America organised their relations to land during the early modern period; the problem is that, until the 19th century, the category of private property was a fundamentally inadequate way of describing *European* means of organising land relations. Until the late 18th

6 Locke, *Two treatises of government*, 129.

7 Gonçalves, "O regime das terras e as reservas indígenas na colonização portuguesa", 26. All translations in this Chapter are mine.

8 Osterhammel, *The Transformation of the World*, 145.

9 Alan Barnard and James Woodburn, for example, have stated, "Property rights, arguably, are at the foundation of hunter-gatherer society." Emphasis in the original. Quoted in Greer, *Property and dispossession*, p. 64. See also, Greer's discussion on the "anthropology of the hunting grounds", 55–64.

century, land tenure in Europe was organised through different forms of reciprocal obligations between kings and subjects and lords and tenants, as well as being tied to cities and towns, kinship and marriage and various forms of communal usage or ownership. There was, in short, no distinctly *European* manner of organising the relation to the land other than that which functioned within the normative models of traditional society, which did not allow for a clear-cut distinction between public and private law, while usage and ownership were not clearly distinguishable in practice.[10]

This Chapter proposes an analytical framework that goes beyond a narrow focus on 'property' and the private/common dichotomy, to better reflect on the ways in which early modern society organised the relations between people and land. The analytical framework is intended to provide 'lenses' that help historians and legal historians to read the sources in a different light. Instead of focusing on our contemporary conceptions of property and trying to fit early modern notions into distinctions that make sense to us as contemporary observers, the approach suggested here organises the distinctions of the time, as reflected in the sources, into three levels of analysis: the words, the bodies and the spirits. This means focusing on how different institutions or lands are *named* in the sources and highlighting both their place in the imperial framework and the local specificity, as well as the social meanings of these arrangements; highlighting the corporate structure, hierarchies and social positions that determined access to land; and, finally, taking seriously the different spiritual and non-human agencies that were considered relevant to the ways in which different populations could inhabit or use the land.

Such a framework shifts from a culturalist to a functional approach and, therefore, is not based on presumed cultural differences but is rather inductively reconstructed by looking at different institutional practices across a wide range of cases from the Iberian world. In this sense, both European and non-European ways of organising access to land fit into this framework. This kind of approach allows comparison across regions, by looking into the ways in which the question of division and distribution of land was solved through different kinds of institutional mechanisms. This means that the European experience

10 Among others, see, Antoine, "Common land use in the Coutume de Bretagne from the fifteenth to the eighteenth centuries"; Casey, *Family and Community in Early Modern Spain*; Congost, *Tierras, Leyes, Historia*; Dios *et. al.*, *Historia de la propiedad en España*; Goody, Thirsk and Thompson, *Family and Inheritance*; Grossi, *Il Dominio e le Cose*; Grossi, *Un altro modo di possedere*; Neeson, *Commoners*; Neto, *Terra e Conflito*; Robisheaux, *Rural society and the search for order in early modern Germany*; Sabean, *Property, production, and family in Neckarhausen*; Thompson, *Customs in Common.*

should be *provincialised* both by explicitly acknowledging the importance of local African, American, and Asian tenurial systems in the imperial order and by emphatically recognising the pre-modern quality of European modes of tenure.[11] This approach has the potential to push against the temporalisation and the colonial image of the world that have long pervaded the study of land tenure in non-European contexts. Therefore, rather than taking the Lockean myth of property formation and its prescribed categories as a point of departure, this analytical framework strives to recapture the *unfamiliarity* of the relations between people and land in the early modern period—regardless of whether looking at Europe or elsewhere.

2 Which Law? Reassessing the Idea of Law

The implicit or explicit concept of law held by the historian plays a fundamental role in how historical developments are described. The 'narratives of property' discussed in the previous section are a good reflection of this phenomenon. Behind these narratives is a formalistic and legalistic concept in which law is understood as a fixed entity that arises from the legislator's will and can be imposed on, or 'applied' to, different social circumstances. 'Property', within this notion, has atemporal, clearly defined and recognisable contours—often accompanied by the adjectives absolute, individual, private and, even, perfect—and a clearly defined origin—Europe—and, more precisely, a long conceptual tradition dating back to classic Roman law. The opposite side of this notion is the also atemporal notion of 'common property' which encompasses all kinds of (imperfect) experiences that do not fit in with the supposed Roman tradition. The idea of property as well as the notions of private and common are charged with assumptions about law that, as stated above, reflect neither the European nor the colonial experience and, essentially, construct a *black box* that impedes studying the actual institutions as they existed in their local contexts.

Recent legal-historical research has provided a stark re-evaluation of the concept of law; one that helps us move away from atemporal and formalistic conceptions. This reassessment is based on a research approach that does not begin with a predetermined concept of law, instead viewing it as socially rooted and therefore understanding it as subject to both local circumstances and historical change. Carlos Garriga has synthesised the essence of this approach:

11 Bastias Saavedra, "The Normativity of Possession".

"the critical historiography [of law] has always taken seriously the need to define law through its history, without any kind of conceptual apriorism."[12] Defining law through its history signals a predisposition with which the historian approaches his sources, centred on "careful observation, a focus on descriptions, interpretative humility, [and] keeping our own assumptions in check."[13] Law, in this conception, is thus *always* and *only* what is understood as law by the historical actors themselves, and thus cannot be presumed by the historian while also requiring historical reconstruction.[14] This 'emic' perspective pushes against overly relying on essentialist and universalistic concepts of law that focus on its coerciveness, its official quality, its focus on 'justice', and considers it a specific kind of normativity that can be distinguished, a priori, from moral, religious and other kinds of normativity. The socially rooted conception of law ultimately abandons the idea of a radical separation of legal and other forms of regulation. Thomas Duve has sought to give this conception a clearer conceptual and methodological focus through the idea of multi-normativity which should, at once, de-essentialise the category of law and signal an openness to studying law as a complex repository of norms, including their underlying principles and assumptions as well as the norms that are involved in the production of norms.[15]

Following this approach, the idea of law of the European *ancien régime* has been reconstructed in the past four decades by historians who have tried to move away from legalist and statist conceptions of contemporary law to rediscover the alterity and peculiar anthropology of early modern European law.[16] Drawing on the ways in which law was described by early modern jurists, this historiography—inaugurated in the 1970s and 1980s by Spanish, Portuguese, and Italian legal historians—has revealed that law had a deeply religious foundation, giving it a transcendent and ontological role in medieval and early modern European society.[17] Law was perceived as a pervasive presence that preceded human existence: the biblical God created order from chaos and gave a place to everything that was in the world, and thus humans, animals, and things, and the relations between and among them, were governed in sub-

12 Garriga, "¿De qué hablamos los historiadores del derecho cuando hablamos de derecho?", 9.
13 Hespanha, "Histórias do direito".
14 Garriga, "¿De qué hablamos los historiadores del derecho cuando hablamos de derecho?", 16.
15 Duve, "Was ist ›Multinormativität‹?—Einführende Bemerkungen", 93.
16 Clavero, *Antidora*; Hespanha, *La Gracia del Derecho*; Hespanha, "Early Modern Law and the Anthropological Imagination of Old European Culture".
17 Grossi, *El orden jurídico medieval*.

stance by the same rules. Human law was considered part of natural law, and both were thought to derive from divine law, which is why much of human life was understood as participating and fulfilling specific functions in a natural order of things. The notion of status (*estado*) was central to this society and alluded to the place that both humans and things occupied within the order of Creation and the mutual relations and dependencies thereby established.[18] In this sense, because the holder of rights was not the human individual but the status (*estados*), humans, things, and supernatural entities all enjoyed (unequal) rights and obligations according to their position within the larger totality.[19]

Since law was considered to precede human intervention, the generation of norms was not restricted to political rulers, and explicitly formulated laws were not the only norms that composed the corpus of law. Human law was understood to be spontaneously produced through social life; longstanding traditions, conventions, habits and other social norms were understood to derive their validity from the mere fact that they were followed. Practices, social mores and the status quo—as a prevailing factual and, therefore, normative order—were, in and of themselves, considered to have a deep juridical meaning undergirded by their quality of having ultimately derived from divine creation. Explicitly formulated norms were thus not imposed on social reality but derived from it. Jesús Vallejo has elegantly shown how this relation was constructed in early modern doctrine through the distinction between *rudis aequitas* and *aequitas constituta*:

> It was understood that whoever had the power to make laws intervened as an actor in a process of transformation. *Aequitas*, a pre-existent and objective reality available to the legislator, was the raw material from which laws were made. The process of transformation consisted in converting this pre-existent and objective reality, which the legislator could not freely dispose of, into concrete precepts. In this process of transformation, from a *rudis aequitas*—undefined but not for this reason non-existent—we obtain an *aequitas constituta*—a juridical norm, defined and ready to be applied to produce certain outcomes. This *aequitas constituta* reflects the *rudis aequitas* and, as such, cannot contradict it. What the former does with respect to the latter is no more than express it in concrete terms, delimit it, declare it, make it visible.[20]

18 Clavero, *Tantas Personas como Estados*.
19 Hespanha, *Imbecillitas*.
20 Vallejo, "El cáliz de plata", 8.

The distinction between defined and undefined norms did not necessarily mean that there was a substantive difference between them: both kinds of norms had equal expression as law, regardless of whether they were written and explicitly stated or not. Vallejo further indicates that the difference between customs and laws was also one of form, not substance, since even laws were considered to derive from a collective will and hence have a customary origin.[21] Early modern European law was thus a complex repository of both particular and general norms that not only included written laws, edicts, statutes, and ordinances, but also encompassed a wide range of habits, conventions, customs, values, and moral instructions. Due to these features, the *ancien régime* representation of law was essentially pluralistic.

Interpretation (*interpretatio*) was the basic way of transforming the undefined order into explicit norms and juridical and theological opinions. Since all these norms were always concurrently valid—and there were no strict hierarchies between the different orders of norms—rulers, magistrates, officeholders, theologians, and jurists relied on this interpretative capacity for enacting new norms, adjudicating conflicts and finding solutions to juridical and moral problems. Though the hermeneutical capacity of political authorities and scholars was not substantively different, the binding force of the opinions of scholars was only authoritative and persuasive, while rulers, magistrates and officeholders were vested with *iurisdictio*, giving them the power to pass judgement and enact binding norms, and sanction their transgression. *Iurisdictio* endowed its holder with judicial and legislative powers and, since it was bestowed upon the head of the community or holders of public office, it was the basis of and inseparable from political power.

The jurisdictional capacity to enact norms introduces an additional layer of complexity for the historian because law-making capacities in early modern Europe were not restricted to the monarch and his functionaries but were widely distributed across all kinds of communities and corporations. This was tied to the *ancien régime's* corporative image of society. Unlike our contemporary representation of society centred on the individual, early modern society was centred on the idea of the 'body' (*corpora*), as a collective entity, endowed with its own specific ends and functions, and self-organised to achieve the fulfilment of those aims. Society was thus seen as composed of an irreducible multiplicity of collective bodies, each endowed with autonomy and the capacity for self-government, and internally structured by hierarchies and inequalities. Autonomy and self-government meant that each of these *corpora* was naturally

21 Vallejo, "El cáliz de plata".

endowed with *iurisdictio*. In the metaphor of the body, jurisdiction occupied the place of the soul: "just as living beings are governed by a soul, the community has its jurisdiction".[22]

These features of early modern European law, however, does not mean that the sovereign lacked power. Instead, it signals that power was exerted through mechanisms that differ from the contemporary image of an executive state, armed with an administrative apparatus and executing specific policies. The monarch's power, instead, was linked to the notion of *grace*—a concept that is especially relevant to our subsequent discussion. As we have seen, law had an essentially conservative function, seeking to restore peace and harmony, and was not meant to produce transformations in existing states of affairs. The correspondence of the order of things to a divine origin made law and the legislative function look backwards to sustain, and not forwards to modify, existing situations. The monarch, however, was endowed with an extraordinary prerogative—exclusive to popes and kings as God's vicars on earth—of altering the established order through a temporal grace that imitated the heavenly Grace of God. António Manuel Hespanha enumerates the interventions kings could enact through grace as: the capacity to create new norms and revoke existing ones; the capacity to render laws ineffective in specific cases; the capacity to modify the nature of human things ("e.g., emancipating minors, legitimating bastard children, conceding nobility to plebeians, pardoning convictions");[23] and the capacity to modify the 'own' of each through privileges and rewards (*mercedes*).[24] Grace was thus a manner of ordering that—through its capacity to alter the existing order—was essentially distinct from justice.

The socially rooted conception of law of this historiography, of course, has had consequences for writing the history of empires and colonialism, especially in the context of Spanish and Portuguese imperialism from the late 15th century onward, and has generated a fruitful historiographical discussion about how to reinterpret the legal experience in colonial contexts.[25] This reappraisal has questioned the centrality of the empire and royal legislation and high

22 Agüero, "Las categorías básicas de la cultura jurisdiccional", 35.

23 Hespanha, "Porque é que existe e em que é que consiste um direito colonial brasileiro", 71.

24 Hespanha, "Porque é que existe e em que é que consiste um direito colonial brasileiro", 71.

25 Among others, see Duve and Danwerth, *Knowledge of the pragmatici*; Duve, Egío and Birr, *The School of Salamanca*; Hespanha, "Depois do Leviathan"; Hespanha, "Uncommon laws"; Garriga, "¿Cómo escribir una historia "descolonizada" del derecho en América Latina?" For a historiographical discussion see, Bastias Saavedra, "Decentering Law and Empire".

lighted the many ways in which law could operate according to the jurisdictional logic of the *ancien régime*. Power and law-making capacities were thus not only deployed by royal institutions, but were also distributed through the corporate structure of society, tied to the corporations that accompanied the expansion of the Iberian empires—the Church, the Inquisition, brotherhoods, religious orders, *cabildos* and *câmaras*, guilds, cities, provinces, etc.—and to the Native and indigenous corporations that organised local rule—at family, community, or city level, respectively.[26]

Therefore, instead of the transference of a metropolitan model to the colonies, the *ancien régime* logic of law and government of the Peninsula was replicated under new conditions. There was thus not a transposition of European law to the non-European world but rather a 'normative overload', because of the logic of norm-production in the early modern world—in which new norms were created at different levels and did not derogate old ones—which led to an ever-growing accumulation of normative information. Norms accumulated exponentially as the Iberian empires extended their rule: in each new place, kings enacted decrees and bestowed privileges; officials handed down rules; jurists, clerics and theologians—not only in Salamanca and Rome, but also in Goa, Mexico City, Lima and Manila—drew on bodies of law, authorities and classics to produce normative solutions for new situations; magistrates had to reach judgements; and cities, villages and other territorial communities created or sustained their own norms and customs. The critical historiography of law has thus shown that the extension of empire, rather than creating the conditions for voluntary, central rule by the metropolis, supported and reinforced the dispersion of and limitations on law and political power. The localism and contextualisation of the (imperial) conception of law endowed the countless local situations of the empire with a political and juridical autonomy that precluded a pervasive rule and determination from the metropolitan centre. 'Law' was therefore not understood as a stable and objective entity or a concise body of norms that moved across space and superseded other normativities—it was not a 'European conception' that replaced a non-European one. Law was something that happened locally and was shaped not only in the process of conflict resolution, but also in the everyday arrangements of different classes of communities. The consequences of this shift of perspective for ownership and land tenure is that it requires focusing on local cases, revisiting our primary

26 For examples, see de la Puente Luna (Chapter 4), Martín Gabaldón (Chapter 5), Jurado (Chapter 6) in this volume. For how this worked in the European context, see Ena Sanjuán (Chapter 7) in this volume.

sources, changing our analytical frameworks and decentring history by drawing more consciously on the normative representations of different communities and actors.[27]

3 The Lenses: Ownership Regimes

Moving away from traditional narratives towards more complex, local, and decentred representations can certainly entail the possibility of getting lost in endless case studies, where eventually the conclusion is 'everything, everywhere was different'. The proponents of the private/common dichotomy argue that sustaining such distinctions is important due to the supposed comparability that it provides. However, the premises that sustain this dichotomy do not really provide units of comparison but merely allow the classification of 'perfect' and 'imperfect' modes of tenure according to certain abstract standards provided by the theory or categories of property at hand. As we have discussed, in one way or another, all forms of landholding in the early modern world had a collective quality with no clear way of separating overlapping interests and rights claimed over the same lands. Thus, to classify these landholdings as common or private does not really say much one way or another. Comparison, however, remains central to avoiding the inevitable particularisation of each local experience.

The notion of the ownership regime serves this comparative purpose by proposing a way of observing how the relation between people and land was normatively organised. It proposes *the observation of the arrangements of practices, rules, norms and principles and the contingent conditions that were relevant to the construction, mediation and enforcement of expectations that defined the relations between persons and land in specific social and cultural contexts.*[28] Therefore, unlike the notion of property and other similar categories, the idea of the ownership regime is more an observational perspective for historical research than a concept that implies the existence of a specific arrangement. It thus helps study the relation between people and land by taking into account a broader array of norms than merely the legal ones and focusing not only on texts or ideas, but also on practices and tacit or implicit expectations. Moving from a focus on law to a focus on historical regimes of normativity implies

---

27 For further examples on Iberian Asia, see Bastias Saavedra, *Norms beyond Empire*.

28 Regime Theory Working Group, "Historical Regimes of Normativity", Part 1–4. Available at: https://legalhistoryinsights.com/historical-regimes-of-normativity-part-1/. Last seen on 8.7.2024.

understanding law and juridical normativity as one component of a complex and dynamic ensemble of practices, institutions, and social, religious, and cultural norms that produced historically efficient and consolidated normative arrangements.[29]

This Chapter proposes taking this highly abstract notion and operationalising it for the study of ownership regimes in the early modern (Iberian) world. Through a survey of the literature from disparate places in Africa, America, Asia, and Europe, the Chapter highlights three orders of norms that affected the relations between people and land: the words, the bodies, and the spirits. These refer to (4) the names given to specific institutions, and both the relations they created and the practices they involved; (5) the collective bodies that, as social institutions, determined different levels of access to lands; and (6) the supernatural and non-human agencies, and the ways in which they shaped and regulated access to lands and resources. The Chapter, however, does not explicitly address the 'deep grammars' and underlying principles that structured and gave meaning to these different orders of norms, but they are implied and should be carefully scrutinised.[30] Taking the above points together, the ownership regimes perspective goes far beyond the strictly proprietary point of view precisely by pointing to the fact that land relations were polysemic and built upon a broad range of overlapping normative structures that were not exclusively interested in the relationship between individual and thing. Not only that, land relations were built upon rules that regulated interpersonal interactions, relations of dependency, relations with nature and relations with supernatural entities. Ultimately, such a perspective demands that historians and legal historians interested in studying ownership and land tenure in the early modern period focus more carefully on how the combination of these normative representations produced specific arrangements in the ways in which land was held, owned, divided, and regulated, and how conflicts were adjudicated.

4 The Words: Land Tenure in the Iberian World

Research on land tenure in the Iberian world has more traditionally focused on the different institutions that structured land relations during the overseas expansion. Traditionally, these are categories taken from the tradition of the *ius commune* (dominion, possession, emphyteusis, etc.) or from royal legislation

29 Duve, "Legal History as a History of the Translation of Knowledge of Normativity".

30 Conveniently, this is addressed by Buono (Chapter 2) in this volume.

that organised different kinds of relations to land. In this section, I focus on the words that were used to designate different relations between people and land. The objective of the following survey is twofold. First, I seek to dispel the notion that the Portuguese and the Spanish empires imposed homogeneous institutions and land tenure arrangements on their overseas territories. This survey reveals that, even though the Crown could assert its superiority over the holding of land through grace, the categories that organised land tenure across the Iberian world were multilayered and diverse and were adjusted to specific situations and conditions. Second, this survey seeks to draw attention to the possibility of moving beyond the strictly European categories and more systematically drawing on vernacular terms used to describe different kinds of land relations.

The land tenure arrangements that resulted from the global expansion of the Iberian empires were varied and multifaceted. In general terms, however, lands in the Iberian world can be understood to derive from a distinction used by the Crown: granted and not yet granted. The lands that had not yet been granted were considered part of the royal heritage as Crown lands and were understood to be absent of occupants and users.[31] According to the *Ordenações Filipinas*, for example, "all vacant goods for which no rightful lord is found"[32] were considered part of the *património régio* (the royal heritage). Within the Spanish empire these were the *tierras realengas* (royal lands) and *baldíos* (wastelands):

> [...] beyond the lands, meadows, pastures, mountains and waters, which by his [the King's] special grace and favour, *have been granted* to the cities, towns or places of the Indies or to other communities, or to particular persons of them, *everything else* of this genre, and especially what is still unbroken and uncultivated, is and must be from his Royal Crown, and domain.[33]

The main function of these royal lands was to be granted by the Crown for either the founding of towns, villages, and cities or for cultivation.[34] It was thus

31 For the purpose of this discussion, it is irrelevant whether this was the case or not, since the distinction is a fiction that was used by the Crown as an assertion of its superiority. Of course, the question of what 'occupation' means and if lands were effectively occupied, even if not recognised by the Crown, is relevant on a case-by-case basis. But this factual basis does not disprove that the Crown operated using this fiction to both affirm its superiority and secure vassalage.

32 *Ordenações Filipinas*, liv. II, tit. 26, par. 17.

33 Solórzano Pereira, *Politica Indiana*, lib. VI, cap. XII, 991. Emphasis added.

34 A Real Cédula of 1591 stated that all lands that were free of inhabitants and other interests

royal prerogative to have the capacity, through grace, to transform established situations, thus transforming unoccupied lands into occupied lands, taking lands from some to give to others, and shifting the status of land and patrimony. Grace occupied a high order within the arrangement of land relations since, as the above quote shows, even lands already occupied by different groups and communities were thought to be derived from some prior "*particular gracia i merced*" (special grace and favour), which included the possibility of having been granted by previous kings or rulers.[35] Thus, in principle, all occupied lands in the Iberian world were considered to have their origin in a form of grace.

This image of landholding in the Iberian empires was a fiction that was necessary for generating the relations of gift and obligation that were at the basis of political rule in the early modern world. This is what has been called the 'economy of grace' and consists in the ways in which alliances and loyalty were built up between asymmetrical parties through their participation in relationships of exchange of donations and gratitude, which guaranteed that the superior party's benevolence was repaid by the inferior party's services and loyalty. These relations, which were continuously reproduced and renewed, secured power and influence and were the basis of political relations, whether it was at the level of the household or the monarchy. The different obligations tied to the securing of land grants and tributary grants, as well as the tributes and tithes that had to be paid by households, communities, and corporations, reflected these relations of grace and obligation, and placed the Crown at the apex of a series of overlapping interests tied to the land.[36]

---

should be left to the Crown "para hacer merced, y disponer de ella á nuestra voluntad" (to be granted and to dispose of them as we please). *Recopilación de Leyes de los Reynos de las Indias*, tomo II, lib. IV, tit. XII, ley 14, 42.

35 The complete text of the *Politica Indiana*, quoted above, refers to this pre-Hispanic past, which notes the supremacy of previous rulers: "I recogiendome Yo à lo que toca à la de las Indias, hallo que esta mesma Regalia tienen nuestros gloriosos Reyes en ellas, en tal forma, que fuera de las tierras, prados, pastos, montes, i aguas, que por particular gracia, i merced suya, se hallaren concedidas à las ciudades, villas, ò lugares de las mesmas Indias, o à otras comunidades, ò personas particulares dellas, todo lo demas de este genero, i especialmente lo que estuviere por romper, i cultivar, es i debe ser de su Real Corona, i dominio, como antiguamente sabemos que lo era del despotico, i absoluto, que usaban en la Nueva España los Motezumas, i en el Perù los Incas, i à este modo en otras provincias otros Caciques, que de ellas se señorearon, como lo refieren los Padres Ioseph de Acosta, i Fray Iuan de Torquemada, i con mas particularidad Antonio de Herrera, que junta varias consultas, que sobre este punto se hizieron en varios tiempos." Solórzano Pereira, *Politica Indiana*, lib. VI, cap. XII, 991. Italics added.

36 Clavero, *Antidora*; Hespanha, *La Gracia del Derecho*.

Grace was important for how the Portuguese and the Spanish Crowns allocated access to land in their imperial domains. Specific institutions, such as the *sesmaria* and the *merced*, were used to attract Iberian colonists by distributing vacant lands to be used for agriculture or ranching. These grants usually entailed the obligations of raising a family, having residence at the location of the grant, and cultivation and improvement. The *sesmaria* was a common institution in the Atlantic archipelagos, Brazil, and Angola, while the *mercedes de tierra* were ubiquitous across the Spanish empire.[37] The *prazos* and the *encomienda*, on the other hand, were grants or concessions that gave the holders the right to collect payments or tributes from villages or groups of villages encompassed within the concession.[38] These concessions were given where lands were already occupied, and they had the double function of rewarding the grantees for services to the Crown and acculturating the Native inhabitants. While the *encomienda* had an explicit provision requiring the *encomendero* (the *encomienda*-holder) to provide for the indoctrination of the 'Indians', the *prazos* were intended to accommodate the local population to Portuguese rule.

The *prazos* were common in the *Estado da Índia*, the Portuguese empire in Asia, outside of Goa, and were often superposed onto existing institutions, such as the *iqta* in the Northern Province or the *pathu* in Ceylon.[39] The *prazo* system was also the predominant form of access to land in the Zambesi region of Mozambique. The *encomienda* was used across the Spanish empire but was predominantly an institution of the 16th century, after which it was gradually phased out.[40] The *prazos* and the *encomienda*, despite their similarities, were distinct institutions. While the *prazos* sometimes conferred jurisdiction, the *encomienda* was an institution that never entailed jurisdiction. However, since *encomenderos* often held offices with jurisdictional capacity, they sometimes held jurisdiction over the population of their *encomiendas*, as was the case in the early development of the Spanish government in the Philippines.[41] Additionally, unlike the *encomienda*, the *prazos* did not regulate the type of work nor

37 Beck Varela, *Das sesmarias à propriedade moderna*; Alveal, *Senhorios coloniais*; Freitas Macedo, "Sesmarias indígenas na São Paulo colonial"; Mota, "Sesmarias e propriedade titulada da terra".

38 Seminal on the *prazo* system in Mozambique, but also in the broader context of the Estado da Índia, see: Rodrigues, *Portugueses e Africanos nos Rios de Sena*. Also, Newitt, *Portuguese Settlement on the Zambesi.*

39 Rodrigues, *Portugueses e Africanos nos Rios de Sena*, 559–560.

40 On the encomienda, the following seminal text is still relevant: Zavala, *De encomiendas y propiedad territorial en algunas regiones de la América española.*

41 Pérez Zamarripa, "The Principales of Philip II", 85–86.

the relations of the population of the *aldeias* with the Crown. The *prazos* were generally conceded for three generations, while the question of succession of the *encomiendas* was a highly contentious issue, which led to its eventual discontinuation.

The Crown was also considered to be the source of all kinds of corporate lands. Since the process of conquest and colonisation was guided by the principle of grace and favour, reward and punishment were important in determining which of the lands that had been occupied before conquest would remain in the hands of their holders and which would be granted anew. Lands and tribute rights that had been dedicated to Native temples were, for example, generally granted to the Church.[42] Lands held by previous rulers were considered Crown lands, while lands held by conquered elites were generally granted to the incoming elites. In this manner, occupied lands were stripped from their previous holders and granted anew for the benefit of the incoming powerholders.[43] However, this was not the fate of all occupied lands, since it was not uncommon that they were left in the hands of their Native holders under the condition that they become vassals of the Portuguese or Spanish Crown.[44] The *prazo* and the *encomiendas*, for example, were built on the recognition of such preexisting landholdings.[45]

These kinds of Native-held lands, alongside the lands granted to Spanish and Portuguese towns, built up what can be called community lands. When founding a new town, city, or village, the corporation was granted lands that were to be administered by the *cabildo* or the *câmara*. Access to lands in the city,

42 We can see this happening both in Mexico and in Goa during the 16th century. See Lockhart, *The Nahuas after the conquest*, 206, and Xavier, *Religion and empire in Portuguese India*, 70–71.

43 We see this occurring during the foundation of new settlements after conquest: "Standing in open territory and in the presence of notaries when these were available, expedition commanders announced, that under the authority received from the king, viceroy, or governor, they were founding a settlement. They then set the territorial jurisdiction of the community, nominating the local authorities and dividing the land by plots [...]. Similar procedures were carried out where Indian enclaves were already in existence. In all of them—for example, Mexico City, Quito, and Cuzco—the community was reinvented as a Spanish enclave, as though the previous settlement had ceased to exist." Herzog, *Defining Nations*, 43.

44 The literature on this is vast, but the following recent publication is worth mentioning: Candido, *Wealth, land and property in Angola*.

45 On the *encomienda*, for example: "Everything the Spaniards recognized outside their own settlements in the sixteenth century—the encomienda, the rural parishes, Indian municipalities, the initial administrative jurisdictions—was built solidly upon individual, already existing altepetl." Lockhart, *The Nahuas after the conquest*, 14.

town or village was usually conditional on membership—being considered a resident or neighbour—and entitled the member to a series of privileges. In Castile and in Spanish America, neighbours enjoyed "the privilege of using communal property, and in most communities, of voting and being elected to office."[46] The use of common pastures and the granting of urban land plots were some of the central aspects that were regulated by local councils, and this was usually recognised if one was considered *vecino*.[47] *Câmaras* also administered these kinds of lands, which could be distributed to particular families and heads of households, and also administered all kinds of city properties, common pastures and wastelands. Even though they were distributed, these lands ultimately remained as lands of the corporation and its members.

Native-held lands were also considered to be granted by the Crown but were not regulated in the same manner. In Goa, for example, all Native lands were included within the village, composed of an aggregate of family holdings and ruled by a council of the heads of the families of the original settlers of the village, known as gavnkars. The ways in which lands were distributed, apportioned and used within the villages was decided by the gavnkars.[48] In other parts of the Portuguese empire in Asia, the organisation of the villages submitted to the *prazos* is less well known but, whether in the Northern Province, in Ceylon, or in Mozambique, it is commonly assumed that they ruled themselves according to their own traditions. In Angola, the local rulers, known as *sobas*, held lands as was custom, granting it to members of their chiefdoms for cultivation and grazing, and granting settlement rights to whomever they wished.[49] In the Spanish empire, the indigenous populations were organised into *pueblos de indios*, which could either be the result of pre-existing settlements or resettlements carried out by the Crown.[50] *Pueblos* were led by local authorities, both in Spanish America and in the Philippines, and had lands at their disposal that were of the corporation to be divided among family groups, used in common or rented out to generate income.[51] In New Spain, the *cacicazgo*, the estates of the local indigenous elite, became a central institution that had its particular

46 Herzog, *Defining Nations*, 18.

47 Herzog, *Defining Nations*, 18.

48 Souza, "Rural Economy and Life"; Souza, *Medieval Goa*; Xavier, *Terra e Território na Goa de Época Moderna*.

49 See Alfagali (Chapter 9) in this volume; and Candido, *Wealth, land and property in Angola*.

50 See de la Puente Luna (Chapter 4) and Dueñas (Chapter 8) in this volume.

51 Güereca, "La tenencia de la tierra en los márgenes de Mesoamérica"; Okoshi Harada, "Dc lo ajeno impuesto a lo nuestro fundado"; Pérez Collados, "Las tierras comunales en los pueblos de Indios y su trayectoria en el México independiente"; Scott, *Barangay*.

form of land tenure with its lands exempt from tribute, and is often compared to the Spanish *mayorazgo*.[52]

In this kind of analysis, in addition to the particular institutions that were used during the process of colonisation, one could also include the names given to lands. We have just seen how the *cabildos* and *câmaras* had designated lands with specific purposes. These lands included *solares* that were to be distributed to the neighbours; the chacaras destined for agriculture, granted to every neighbour who had *casa poblada* (a household); *ejidos*, *dehesas*, and *potreros* destined for pasture and other common uses; and *propios* and *tierras y montes* reserved for the administration of the *cabildo*, rented or administered to generate income for the community.[53] The Portuguese *câmaras* also had such lands, dedicated to the common usufruct of its members, consisting in *baldios*, *maninhos*, *matos*, *pastos comuns*, etc.[54] The Nahua had different words that reflected the differentiated status of lands, such as the *teopantlalli* (temple lands), *tlatocatlalli* (ruler's land), *tecpantlalli* (palace land), *pillalli* (noble's land), *teuctlalli* (lord's land), *calpollalli* (calpolli lands) and *callalli* (house land).[55] The Mixtec used diverse classifications for lands destined for different uses, among others, the *ñuhu aniñe* (palace land), *ñuhu huahi* (house land) and *ñuhu chiyo* (patrimonial land).[56] The Foral de Goa of 1526 also reveals a differentiated set of landholdings, such as *ortas palmares* (palm groves), *arozaes* (rice fields), *chãos desaproveitados o perdidos* (unused and waste lands) and *arequaes* (areca palm groves).[57] Also in Goa, *namos* or *namoxin* were the names given to the lands under the control of the temple.[58]

We can think of these words as not only having a nominal, but also a normative character, since they did not simply designate how the lands were actually used, but also indicated what could and could not be done on and with those lands. On the one hand, one could tie this normative dimension to the idea of

52 Horn, *Postconquest Coyoacan*; Lockhart, *The Nahuas after the conquest*; Menegus and Aguirre Salvador, *El cacicazgo en Nueva España y Filipinas*. See, also, Martín Gabaldón (Chapter 5) in this volume.

53 Góngora, *El Estado en el Derecho Indiano*, 141–151.

54 Bastião, "O regime dos prazos na Ilha de Moçambique, 1763–1800".

55 Lockhart, *The Nahuas after the conquest*, 156 ff.

56 Terraciano, *Los mixtecos de la Oaxaca colonial*, 320. See, also, Martín Gabaldón (Chapter 5) in this volume. On the *sapçi chacaras* as a specific type of communal lands in the Andes, see de la Puente Luna (Chapter 4) in this volume.

57 Arquivo Nacional da Torre do Tombo, Foral de Goa, 1526, Gavetas, Gav. 20, mç. 9, n. 13. I thank Roger Lee de Jesus for sharing this document with me.

58 Axelrod and Fuerch, "Portuguese Orientalism and the Making of the Village Communities of Goa", 446.

status, as reflecting the social role that linked the land to different entities, such as the community and other lands. In early modern juridical culture, this could be tied to the idea of utility (*utilitas*) as the way in which inanimate objects, in this case lands, served God by fulfilling their purpose in the order of Creation.[59] As such, rights and obligations could be tied to specific types of lands and, through them, bind their holders. José Miguel Lana-Berasain, for example, has shown how sales of specific plots of land conveyed not only rights in the land, but also neighbourhood rights,[60] while certain lands of the *cacicazgo* were exempt from paying tribute. On the other hand, the normative dimension associated with the names given to specific lands requires one to ascertain the precise rules and prescriptions associated with them. This means that not all kinds of lands follow the same rules regarding cultivation, payment of tributes, inheritance, disposition, division, and so on. Once granted to a household, *solares*, for example, could be sold, whereas *ejidos*, *dehesas*, and *potreros* could be used but never disposed of. Each designation is thus not merely nominal but signals the different types of uses and users that certain lands have, and points to implicit rules that are followed—or broken—by the actors interacting with these lands. However, the normative dimension associated with these names cannot be derived from general rules or doctrines but is a question of empirical analysis and careful reading of primary sources.[61]

Finally, the royal origin of land occupation tied all lands to the interest of the Crown, but this did not mean that access to land was limited to royal grants or to distribution within the community. The rights to hold and use land often changed hands through different legal instruments—sales, donations, succession, possession, etc.—which over time modified the original distribution of land. These procedures had a longstanding tradition in the *ius commune* culture and, in the Iberian world, were regulated by Spanish and Portuguese scribal practices.[62] The rights to hold occupied lands could be transmitted

59 Hespanha, *Como os juristas viam o mundo. 1550–1750*, 312.

60 Lana-Berasain, "Forgotten Commons", 147 This is also shown for England by E.P. Thompson, who writes: "The eighteenth century sees this strange period of mixed law in which usages and rights were attached to office or to place and then were regarded as if they were things which commanded human rights in their turn." Thompson, *Customs in Common*, 135–136.

61 For an excellent example, see Jurado's analysis of the application of the term *menester* in the distribution of lands for domestic units in 16th-century Charcas (Chapter 6, in this volume).

62 Beck Varela, *Das sesmarias à propriedade moderna*; Dias Paes, *Esclavos y tierras entre posesión y títulos*; Herzog, "Colonial Law and "Native Customs": Indigenous Land Rights in Colonial Spanish America"; Herzog, *Frontiers of possession*.

through instruments of sale, donation, succession, pawn, and others. Unoccupied lands could be acquired through possession, which usually involved transforming pastures, woodlands, or forests into arable fields, or taking hold of lands that had been forsaken by their owners.[63] While vacant lands were considered to belong to the Crown, occupation and possession were considered legitimate forms of land appropriation and, if the occupation did not infringe on third parties, was usually upheld by courts.[64] These kinds of occupations could be granted after the fact as *mercedes* or *sesmarias*. In the Spanish empire, the conflicting titles between possessors and the Crown could also be regularised through the *composición*, a mechanism that was used variably across the empire.[65]

5 The Bodies: The Institutional Underpinnings of Ownership

The legal categories—the words—used to describe these different kinds of arrangements are condensations of normative information that operate with a certain degree of abstraction. They regulate relations between persons and land, in general, but, at the same time, they regulate relations between persons. Almost all the categories discussed above describe relations established between the Crown and their vassals, reflected in the obligations that were built into these categories. Other categories, such as those of corporate lands, of the Church or belonging to communities, establish relations between members and non-members; others, such as the common use lands, signal who can do what, where, and who cannot. Tributary grants, such as the *prazo* and

63 The principle of first occupation has a long tradition in different regions of the Iberian world, beyond the influence of the *ius commune*. The *ganvkars*, for example, premised their rule over the Goan villages on the fact that they had in an "ancient time [...] taken the island and other wastelands and uncultivated lands which they made useful and fortified". Arquivo Nacional da Torre do Tombo, Foral de Goa, 1526, Gavetas, Gav. 20, mç. 9, n. 13. We also find this idea in Mexico as the founding myths of the *altepetl*. In the primordial title of Cuacuauzentlalpan, claimants argued that their ancestors had gained their lands before the conquest by taking them from the mountain and the lagoon, expelling supernatural forces and defending them against other occupants. López Caballero, *Los títulos primordiales del centro de México*, 229. Also, the *sobas* of Angola justified their landholding as first occupiers. Candido, *Wealth, land and property in Angola*, 39. First occupation was also central to the claims of local lords in Greater Senegambia, as Mota (Chapter 3) shows in this volume.

64 Bastias Saavedra, "The Lived Space"; Bastias Saavedra, "The Normativity of Possession".

65 Among others, see Jurado, "La composición como concierto"; Carrera Quezada, *Sementeras de papel*. Also, see Jurado (Chapter 6) in this volume.

the *encomienda*, however, are restricted to relations between persons: the relation between the grant holder and the Crown and the relations between the grant holder and the populations subjected to the grant. However, since these categories were superposed onto the social institutions that gave them their specific characteristics and regulated their functioning, the specific content of the relations between persons and land cannot be found in their conceptual content, nor in the ways in which they were defined in royal decrees, ordinances or legal doctrine.

In early modern Europe, as we have mentioned, law and legal categories functioned within a society and a worldview centred around collective bodies (*corpora*), not individuals. This worldview presupposed a natural and divine order, gave family units and other collective bodies a central role, was based on a hierarchical image of society and was organised around a combination of moral, affective, and juridical norms. Power—both within and outside the family—was based on these assumptions. Thus, behind the words were bodies, not in the sense of physical or biological bodies, but in the sense of corporate bodies that gave individuals their place in the world, placed them in personal and political relations with others, and defined their roles within the household, the community, and the kingdom. These bodies were not merely the backdrop for individual action. Rather, they were, more importantly, what determined the ways in which individuals could participate in political and legal interactions, and they provided them with the rights, privileges, and obligations that opened or constricted their range of possible actions. In this dimension, the emphasis is placed on the local social structures, hierarchies, and social positions that determined access to land.

Families were considered *corpora* and thus had the capacity for self-government and the capacity to uphold internal order. Authority was vested in the *pater familias*, who governed through domestic discipline and sought the 'common good' of the family group. This family order also provided the key organising principle for the distinction between the private and the public sphere. Outside the family, corporative relations were governed by justice and *iurisdictio*. Here, power was understood as being naturally distributed between different *corpora* and each of these possessed different degrees of self-government. Political power was thus not centralised but polycentric and pluralistic. Finally, this political pluralism was complemented by normative pluralism, and social interaction was regulated by a variety of normative orders, in which royal laws, decrees, and ordinances coexisted and interacted with other sources of normativity, such as custom, morals, and domestic discipline. Each corporation, such as the Church, cities and towns, guilds and others, could have their own particular norms that governed and regulated the collective life of their members.

Seen from this vantage point, the norms that granted access to land were not restricted to those of the Crown but included a variety of normative sources ranging from the domestic *oeconomia*, which regulated the life and economy of the household, to the customs of towns and cities, which meant going through the canon law that regulated ecclesiastical lands. The ways in which peasant and indigenous communities organised land also depended on a further level of norms of kinship groups, lineages, and status, with deep cultural roots and particular ways of regulating division and succession of family and community lands. Some of these norms found expression in the juridical literature and in doctrine, but much of it was neglected, considered as belonging to the natural regulation of the *rustici*. Legal doctrine would generally deal with questions of wealth and patrimony of the high and low nobility and merchants, while 'rustics' were left to do what they wanted ("los rústicos que hagan lo que deseen"),[66] i.e., follow their own customs and uses. Thus, an understanding of how access to land was regulated within these corporate bodies cannot easily be drawn from written law or doctrine but requires shifting the attention towards archival documents and interdisciplinary research to reconstruct how these relations were organised in practice.[67]

The ways in which family lands were accessed, administered and inherited were regulated at the level of the household. In the European tradition, the family was a unity whose members were considered to follow common interests guided by the authority of the father (*pater familias*). This definition extended the idea of the family beyond the spouses and children to include everyone who was subject to the authority of the father. This included extended kinship, servants, slaves, and the public offices and privileges granted by the king, as well as the lands and estates of the household. The family, understood in this broad sense, was ruled by the father through domestic discipline (*oeconomia*). This gave the head of the household ample discretion in regulating the family patrimony, signalling who could have access to the family lands and under which conditions. Lands could be given to members of the kinship group or dependents for their particular use, and lands could be rented out under different kinds of arrangements. As discussed below, we find this regulation at the level of the

66 Dios, *Seis estudios sobre historia de la propiedad*, 53, fn. 126. The phrase is attributed to Saint Bernard, and it was often used by jurists when speaking of the benefits of the *mayorazgo*. The quote used here is from Antonio Padilla y Meneses: "entre los nobles mejor es la dispersión de los hijos que la de los bienes, los rústicos que hagan lo que deseen y es preferible que los mercaderes distribuyan con igualdad sus bienes."

67 For an excellent example of the how the regulatory intentions of the Crown did not supersede the corporative regulation of indigenous communities, see Martín Gabaldón (Chapter 5) and Jurado (Chapter 6) in this volume.

family and household, albeit with other underlying principles, in different parts of the Iberian world. The entails of the Iberian world—*mayorazgos* and *morgadios*, and *capellanías* and *capelas*—highlight the dual regulation that operated between general regulations and those of the household.[68] On the one hand, entails were precisely defined institutions that determined, in general terms, the indivisibility and inalienability of the patrimony, thus subjecting patrimonial lands to a specific regime. On the other hand, these entails were intergenerational acts of regulating a *specific* family patrimony, and transmitting rules of conduct that upheld the name and reputation of the household. At this second level, we find a wealth of normative information that is both regulated within and destined for the family group. The founders of the entails had ample discretion in determining the rules binding the patrimony, by determining the goods that would belong to the entail and determining the lines of succession. While it was common that they were succeeded along male primogeniture, female succession was accounted for under certain conditions. Founders could introduce conditions for succession, such as holding the family name[69] or establishing the condition of marrying a "white man" for the succession of a daughter in the case of a *capela* instituted in 1562 in Cape Verde.[70] *Capellanías* and *capelas* often contained clauses that regulated the amount of masses and charitable donations that had to be secured from the rents derived from the patrimony before the benefactors could receive any rents for the household.[71] These rules and conditions were established in the wills or deeds that instituted the entail, and thus exerted a regulatory function that arose from the head of the household and founder of the entail.

The lands within cities and towns were a diverse arrangement of community and household lands administered by the *cabildos* and *câmaras*, the municipal bodies that represented the neighbours. In the case of the *cabildos*,

> [p]art of this land was used as a municipal commons (*ejido*), from which householders might take firewood, or were in enclosed pastures (*dehesas*) where they might turn their cattle to graze; part was distributed as

68 Seminal studies on the *mayorazgo* in Spain and the *morgadio* in Portugal are: Clavero, *Mayorazgo*; Rosa, *O Morgadio em Portugal, sécs. XIV–XV*.

69 In an example of the constitution of a *mayorazgo* in Jaen, Spain, one condition "established that the successors should carry the coat of arms and last names of Benavides or Valencia, or lose the *mayorazgo*". Porras Arboleda, "Aportación al estudio del mayorazgo", 68.

70 Arquivo Nacional de Cabo Verde, Tombeamento da Capela do Tanque da Nora, Vinculos do Concelho da Praia. I thank Edson Brito for sharing this document with me.

71 Luque Alcaide, "Capellanías (DCH)".

> arable fields to the townsmen; and part, the *propios del consejo*, was rented in plots for gardens and country houses, and became thereby a source of income to the municipality.[72]

The *câmaras* were also endowed with lands which were administered in a somewhat similar fashion. According to the *Ordenações Filipinas*, the aldermen were "to have charge of all the governance of the land and the works of the *concelho* [municipality] [...] so the land and its inhabitants can prosper".[73] One of the main differences between the *cabildo* and the *câmaras* was that residents and neighbours of Portuguese America were subjected to the payment of a *foro* to the municipal body, although some founders requested and received, as a privilege, exemption from this obligation.[74] Anthony John R. Russell-Wood has illustrated how the municipality of Vila Rica was granted a *sesmaria*, from which residents received their plots through the payment of a *foro*, thus generating income for the public offices and other expenditures of the corporation.[75]

Lands held by Native and indigenous inhabitants reflected this order particularly well since, as long as they paid their contributions dutifully, both the Portuguese and the Spanish empire generally let the villages and *pueblos* function according to their own traditions. In the villages of Goa, for example, lands were destined for different uses and their production was meant to sustain different functions of relevance for the community. Cultivated and fertile plains in the river valleys were reserved for the maintenance of the temple, the maintenance of village servants (carpenter, blacksmith, potter, barber, basket-weaver, cobbler, etc.), and for the sustenance of the gavnkars. These lands were considered common and were worked in common and their revenue was also used to pay the tributes to the Crown. The village residences and the family lands of the gavnkars were in the elevated areas of the village, where each family had a plot for the house and orchards. Terraced fields, called *molloi* or *morod*, for the cultivation of cereals were granted by the gavnkari (village council) on temporary (*vanty*) or permanent lease (*kutban*). If an outsider wished to bid on these leases within the village, a *ganvkar* had to bid and vouch for him. The gavnkari could additionally pre-empt sales of land within the village, thus being able to decide who could live, inhabit, and cultivate within the village. Lands could also

72 Haring, "The Cabildo", 12.

73 *Ordenações Filipinas*, I, 66.

74 Damasceno, *Território e propriedade em perspectiva comparada nas Américas Coloniais*.

75 Russell-Wood, "Local government in Portuguese America", 88.

be given as permanent rent-free grants in exchange for services rendered to the village. Finally, every village had common pasture lands.[76]

These communal arrangements can also be observed in the indigenous *pueblos* of the Spanish empire, both in America and in the Philippines.[77] The notion of *pueblo* provided an image of equivalent collective bodies that organised the affairs of the *indios* integrated into the Spanish empire but concealed what were in fact distinct forms of social organisation that had roots in the pre-Hispanic period. In New Spain, for example, the term *pueblo* was superposed on different forms of social organisation depending on the region, such as the *altepetl* in the Valley of Mexico, the *ñuu* among the Mixtec and the *batabil* in the Yucatan Peninsula. These in turn were composed, respectively, of the *calpolli*, the *siqui/siña/dzini* (which varied depending on the Mixtec region) and the cah, extended families or kinship groups that determined the distribution of common and family lands among its members.[78] Access to land was reserved for heads of family through their membership in the broader kinship group.[79] The indigenous *cabildo* administered the distribution of *tierras de común repartimiento* (lands allocated to particular households), the regulation of *pastos y montes* destined for collective uses and the administration of the *propios*, lands that could be cultivated in common, used for animal husbandry, or rented out for the generation of income.[80] The renting of land was regulated in different manners, according to local rules, being only accessible to outsiders under specific conditions, requiring the unanimous consent of the council and by drafting and requiring the rental documents in Nahuatl.[81] In the Philippines, the term *pueblo* was used to designate the pre-Hispanic *bayan*, which grouped several extended families or kinship groups known as *barangay*. Access to land was secured, by family members, slaves, and dependents, through the *barangay*, and rights of succession were also managed at

76 Souza, *Medieval Goa*; Souza, "Rural Economy and Life".

77 A good example can be found in de la Puente Luna's contribution (Chapter 4) to this volume.

78 Lockhart, *The Nahuas after the conquest*; Terraciano, *Los mixtecos de la Oaxaca colonial*; Quezada, *Pueblos y caciques Yucatecos, 1550–1580*; Okoshi Harada, "De lo ajeno impuesto a lo nuestro fundado". A good example of this superposition, and how it 'masked' the underlying relationships, is Martín Gabaldón's contribution (Chapter 5) to this volume. In Peru, they were superposed onto the *ayllu*. See the discussion by de la Puente Luna (Chapter 4), Jurado (Chapter 6), and Dueñas (Chapter 8) in this volume.

79 Menegus, "Cacicazgos y repúblicas de indios en el siglo XVI"; Menegus and Aguirre Salvador, *El cacicazgo en Nueva España y Filipinas*; Quezada, *Pueblos y caciques Yucatecos*.

80 Menegus, *Los pueblos de indios en la Nueva España, siglo XVIII*, 44.

81 Haskett, "Indian Town Government in Colonial Cuernavaca", 557–558.

this level. Father Juan de Plasencia, who wrote on the customs of the Pampangos, described the lands of the *barangay* as being divided among its members, where "each knows his own, especially what is irrigated."[82] Even if the norms of the community were not evident to external observers, its rules were evident to its members.

Of course, conversion and membership of the Christian commonwealth was also an important condition for accessing and retaining lands. The abovementioned local arrangements were sustained—in most, if not all, cases—insofar as the local communities had converted to the Christian faith. In cases, such as Goa, the granting and reinstating of land to converts was a mechanism devised to encourage conversion. Lands that had been abandoned by Muslims after the arrival of the Portuguese were given to converts, and lands that had been given to the Portuguese "could go back to the earlier (or other) local owners if the locals had meanwhile been converted."[83] The Church was also an important landholder, holding not as a monolithic entity, but through different kinds of corporations associated with it, such as religious orders, brotherhoods, convents, hospitals, and *miséricordias*, among others. These lands were often distributed through different kinds of arrangements, such as emphyteutic contracts or *aforamentos*. In Portuguese and Spanish America, ecclesiastical institutions were some of the most important landholders.[84]

Reviewing land relations from this vantage point, thus, shows that the construction of land tenure by the royal economy of grace was built upon a broad array of collective bodies and built up a kaleidoscope of different rules. While the grants made to towns, the Church, and communities are obvious cases in point, the *prazos* and *encomiendas* also, in a certain sense, presupposed the existence of these communities and the self-organisation of their lands. Further, the grants of *sesmarias* and *mercedes*, which have heretofore been considered 'individual' land grants or constituting 'private' property, were actually concessions made to heads of family and were thus linked to households, as shown by the requirement of "tener casa poblada" common to the *mercedes*. Understanding the distribution of lands by the Crown from this vantage point shows that the empire was built on a multilayered system of collective bodies that connected households, communities, and kingdoms through a variety of

82 Scott, *Barangay*, 229.

83 Xavier, *Religion and empire in Portuguese India*, 85.

84 Damasceno, "Território e propriedade em perspectiva comparada nas Américas Coloniais".

relationships that were built up according to various normative orders and tied the organisation of land to different degrees of regulation.[85]

6 The Spirits: Supernatural and Non-Human Dimensions of Land Tenure

To the words and the bodies we can add a third dimension which ordered the relations between persons and land: that of supernatural and non-human entities. This dimension deals with norms that are believed to originate in either supernatural or non-human entities and regulate what can and cannot be done on and with certain lands. This often relates to the qualities attributed to certain lands with important ritual or social functions. On the ritual side, these are lands that often have a 'sacred' quality and are the sites for temples, cemeteries, and all kinds of ceremonies; on the social side, it refers to the ways in which families and communities connect ancestors, lineages, and future generations to the same lands. The idea that people belong to the land—and not the other way around—can be understood as part of this conception. Additionally, one can speak of how 'rights' attributed to supernatural or non-human entities affected the ways in which persons related to the land. While this dimension is often ascribed to indigenous populations, it is possible to find these ways of regulation in Europe as well as in Africa, Asia, and the Americas.

The most obvious point of departure are those lands with ritual functions or those that are considered 'sacred' and, by these very qualities, impose restrictions on how and who can use and appropriate them. The *Siete Partidas*, for example, state that since sacred and religious things are established for the service of God, there can be no dominion over them. The clergy may have them under their power and use them, but they act as custodians and servants: "because they are to keep these things and serve God with them."[86] These things can also not be disposed of and churches and their lands remain sacred—and thus face these restrictions—even if they are razed: "even if some sacred church was demolished, the place where it was founded will always remain sacred".[87] Churches and sacred lands only lose this quality if they fall into the hands of

85 Other arrangements were also possible, such as the relations between main and subordinated towns, or the regulation of the mountain lands by different towns within the valleys. On this see, respectively, Martín Gabaldón (Chapter 5) and Ena Sanjuán (Chapter 7) in this volume.

86 *Las Siete Partidas*, Tercera Partida, Título 28, Ley 12.

87 *Las Siete Partidas*, Tercera Partida, Título 28, Ley 13.

'enemies of the faith', but regain their sacred condition if retaken by Christians. Further, Emanuele Conte has shown how these lands were not only not considered to be disposable but, more importantly, were considered *themselves* to be vested with ownership:

> The centres of late-antique and medieval ecclesiastical organization were often identified by buildings located on burial sites of saints. Because the burial of corpses was considered 'sacred' by Roman law, those locations could not be subject to private ownership. And as Christians believed that the souls of the saints had eternal life, they recurred to Roman law to use those holy places as the true subjects of properties. These non-human, holy subjects attracted vast amounts of donations for centuries, creating economic environments in which profitable goods were permanently tied with places, usually buildings themselves or the altars hosting the saintly relics. Humans entered this permanent relationship by being invested with ecclesiastical authority or as part of the ecclesiastical estate.[88]

Beyond the tradition of the *ius commune*, norms regulating the use and disposition of ritual and sacred lands can be found in different social and cultural contexts. The lands of the Mapuche of southern Chile, for example, were conceived as spaces that were inhabited by communities along with spirits and ancestors, which manifested in different parts of the landscape. Each community was linked to protective hills and mountains, known as *Trentren*, named after the mythical serpent that saved the first peoples from a great flood. Mountains and hills were thus not common places for habitation, but had an important spiritual meaning, acting as safe havens in times of war, sacred burial places for caciques, and places used by healers to collect medicinal plants. The burial grounds of important caciques were also the ritual spaces of the community, essential for organising their relations to the ancestors. The importance of these spaces is that their use was restricted to certain activities and to members of the community—no one outside of the group could make use of these lands.[89]

Insofar as the lands connected communities to their ancestors—as well as to future generations—one could argue that the land belonged to the community as much as the community belonged to the land. In the corporate worldview of the *ancien régime*, the *patrimonium* was essential to the condition of the fam-

88 Conte, "The many legal faces of the Commons", 635.

89 Rojas Bahamonde, Mellado and Blanco-Wells, "Sobrenaturaleza Mapuche".

ily, ensuring its stability beyond the passing of the generations.[90] This notion tied land to blood and structured the ways in which certain families would deal with sales, partitions, and inheritance of land. Richard M. Smith has shown how these patterns were present in medieval and early modern England, where "there was a strong distaste for the selling off of family land or land that descended through blood [...] to the eldest son". The mechanism of keeping land within the family or among closely related kin reflected the idea that land "ought to descend to the blood who held it of old."[91] This notion, also found in the Spanish *mayorazgo* and the Portuguese *morgadio*, sought to secure the intact transmission of the principal holdings of the family from one generation to the next. Within this kind of institutional structure, the holding and disposition of the land was not entirely determined by the head of the family but was rather oriented toward the sustenance of the family group and future generations, as well as sustaining the continuity of an ancestral bloodline.[92]

One can also find this conception in the invocations of immemorial possession that were common to the indigenous populations of Spanish America. While it has often been argued that this was an effective judicial strategy to secure their tenure before colonial magistrates, one must also take the claim seriously as a way of signalling the ancestral bond of the community to the land. In this sense, the claim is not merely that 'the land is ours', but it includes the claim that 'we and our forefathers belong to the land'. One can see this clearly in a 1575 petition by Cacique Don Juan of Suta in Nueva Granada reacting to community lands being taken for the founding of a new town, Villa de Leyva. He argued that "it should not be allowed that our lands and settlements we have of old and were held by our ancestors for more than one hundred years until today be taken" (*no se deve primitir que se no tomen nuestras tierras y açientos que antiguamente tenemos y tuvieron nuestras antepasados de mas de çien años a esta parte*), because great harm would come to his community due to them being "forced to move to strange lands and abandon their nature" (*forçados yrnos a tierras estrañas y dexar nuestra naturaleza*).[93] Other caciques who participated in the proceeding argued that they could not be "dispossessed and

90 See Buono (Chapter 2) in this volume.

91 Smith, "Some issues concerning families and their property in rural England", 14.

92 For all these reasons, it is revealing that the Portuguese in Angola referred to the form of landholding of the *sobas* as "a kind of African morgado". See Alfagali (Chapter 9) in this volume.

93 "Fundación de la Villa de Leiva, disposiciones del resguardo", Fondo: Poblaciones-Boy: SC.46,2, D.10, Archivo General de la Nacíon—Colombia, 380r. I thank Katherine Godfrey for sharing the sources on Villa de Leiva with me.

deprived of our nature and homeland" (*despojar y privarnos de nuestro natural y patria*).[94] The normative quality is given here not by a focus on a narrow conception of property but rather by a relationship with the land that has been consolidated over generations, both granting it familiarity and making it essential to the group's identity. Here we can see how, in some cases, belonging can be closely intertwined with ownership.

Finally, a more widely distributed notion was that rights could be held by all kinds of inanimate objects (houses, buildings, lands), spirits and souls, and even animals. Rights granted to non-humans were perfectly compatible with the legal imagination of the early modern period. We spoke above about how certain lands were themselves endowed with rights and obligations. To add to those examples, easements or servitudes (*servidumbres*) were rights given to specific plots of land in relation to other lands or to persons.[95] When the easement is between two plots of land, such as a right of way, it designates "a limited right permanently attached to the two parcels of land it affects".[96] Rights of citizenship or rights to the use of pastures and other common lands could also be tied to specific houses or lands within a city, parish or village, and these rights remained with the lands and houses and were transferred to the new owners when they were inherited or sold.[97] Buono's chapter in this volume highlights how rights to land could be left to things, and how things "could claim 'the right to be used' and not to be abandoned or destroyed".[98] This conception of tying rights to lands was anathema to the thinkers of the Enlightenment, as reflected in Thomas Paine's protests: "The custom of attaching Rights to *place*, or in other words to inanimate matter, instead of the *person*, independently of place, is too absurd to make any part of a rational argument".[99]

Examples of the extension of 'land rights' to animals can also be found in early modern Europe if we recall the case of Windsor Forest in E.P. Thompson's *Whigs and Hunters*, where the deer were not only "'the principal beauty and ornament of the forest', but the needs of their economy overrode every other need".[100] Thompson describes how a complex system of laws and rules organised the forest dwellers' economy and subordinated what they could do on their

94 Archivo Histórico de Tunja, Legajo 8, Archivo Histórico Regional de Boyacá, 180r.

95 Hespanha, *Como os juristas viam o mundo*, 206.

96 Conte, "The many legal faces of the Commons", 632.

97 Examples can be found in Conte, "The many legal faces of the Commons"; Lana-Berasain, "Forgotten Commons"; Freitas Macedo, "Posesión y propiedad en las disputas por jurisdicción"; Thompson, *Customs in Common*.

98 See Buono (Chapter 2) in this volume.

99 Quoted in Thompson, *Customs in Common*, 136.

100 Thompson, *Whigs and Hunters*, 29.

lands to the needs of the deer's habits and movements for feeding and fawning. Cows, sheep, and horses could not be kept since they competed with the deer for the grass; arable lands could not be fenced so as to impede the deer from passing to their feeding grounds; "[w]hether the land was privately owned or not, no timber could be felled without license from the forest officers"; and, regardless of their owners, "[p]eat and turf could not be cut in preserved grounds".[101] This case, for our purposes, illustrates that the hierarchies of rights to the land could be constructed, within limits, in favour of non-humans. In this way, the use and access of forest dwellers to *their* land and other resources were limited according to the needs of the deer.

Entails (*vínculos*) also raised questions of granting rights to non-humans that did not align with the framework of the Enlightenment. Adam Smith raised his objections to the institution in his infamous *The Wealth of Nations*:

> The earth and the fullness of it belongs to every generation, and the preceding one can have no right to bind it up from posterity; such extension of property is quite unnatural. The insensible progress of entails was owing to their not knowing how far *the right of the dead* might extend, if they had any at all. The utmost extent of entails should be to those who are alive at the person's death, for he can have no affection to those who are unborn.[102]

Smith's critique was primarily directed at the fact that these institutions, by binding the will of present generations to the will of their founders, lacked an economic purpose. The *mayorazgos* and *morgadios* were in effect not merely destined for generating wealth but were rather institutions designed for securing the transgenerational prosperity and reputation of a lineage. As such, they tied the estate to the will of the founder in perpetuity, thus binding the estate and its administration for an indeterminate number of future generations. The *capellanías* and *capelas* were generally created to secure the salvation of the founder's soul, binding the estate's lands and rents to several pious works. In both cases, the will of the founders, once deceased, was carried forth across generations of administrators, possessors and beneficiaries, who could not freely dispose of the estates or change their functions. These institutional constraints were a way of securing the intergenerational rights of those bound by the entail (the 'dead', the lineage, and the yet-to-be-born). Maria Lurdes Rosa

101 Thompson, *Whigs and Hunters*, 29.
102 Smith, *The Wealth of Nations*, 384. Emphasis added.

has explored the ways in which the foundation of *capelas* was conceived not as able to grant rights to the dead—as Smith described—but rather to grant inheritance rights to the founder's soul within a belief system that exalted the "supernatural lives"[103] that existed after the natural death of the body, in recognition of a spiritual world that coexisted with the temporal one.

The rights attached to things (lands, houses), animals, and souls—as non-human entities—in the early modern European tradition aligns with the ways in which a spiritual realm had normative consequences for the human realm in other world regions—even if these appeal to other cosmological hierarchies.[104] Among the Nahua, for example, each *calpolli* viewed their patron saints—as successors to their gods—as residual owners of the land: "Calpollalli [the lands of the *calpolli*] could hence have been primarily and originally land of the gods, and only by extension the land of the corporation."[105] In the lower Gambia, certain spaces were considered to belong to and be occupied by spirits, who inhabited large trees, rocks, swamps, or bodies of water, and were thus not available for human use. "Spirits owned the lands they occupied, and if anyone unwittingly built his house across the pathway of a spirit, he ran the risk of deaths, and illnesses, houses falling down, fires or other disasters."[106] Settling on lands owned by the spirits carried risks, and humans who sought to occupy these lands required spiritual powers to claim them. Within Mapuche cosmology, the figure of the *ngen* serves as a further example. The *ngen* are spirits considered the "owners of the wilderness", which means that any time a person goes into the wilderness, they are required to follow a strict repertoire of actions that includes not raising one's voice, not proffering insults, not causing any unnecessary damage and, if something is used or taken, making an offering in return.[107]

7 Conclusions

This Chapter provides a framework for addressing the question of land tenure in the early modern Iberian world that moves beyond diffusionist narratives that rely on a temporal asymmetry between Europe and other world regions.

103 Rosa, *As Almas Herdeiras*, 12.
104 E.g., see: Castro, *Cannibal metaphysics*.
105 Lockhart, *The Nahuas after the conquest*, p. 152.
106 Sarr, *Islam, power, and dependency in the Gambia River basin*, p. 93. See also the examples provided by Mota (Chapter 3) and Alfagali (Chapter 9) in this volume.
107 Grebe, "El subsistema de los ngen en la religiosidad mapuche".

Instead of dividing the world into peoples who knew of the private division of land and those who, archaically, did not—as depicted in the Lockean and colonial images of the world—the objective has been to show that there is a more fundamental division between the early modern and our own, contemporary, conceptions. We have seen how the division between private and common was inadequate for grasping the many forms in which land was held in the early modern (Iberian) world, where lands were subjected to overlapping rights and interests, were regulated in different collective instances and could be assigned to and regulated by different kinds of non-human entities. Moving away from the narrow focus on 'property' and the dichotomy of private and common helps us better understand these diverse arrangements and the polysemic relationships established between people and land. It also allows for the possibility of reintroducing comparison in a way that avoids *stealing history by imposing our categories and sequences on the past of the world*—to paraphrase Jack Goody[108]—and, instead, offers a way of sensitising the historian to observing the different ways in which the relations between communities and land were normatively constructed.

The issue of time and historical change is also central here. The narrative I have pursued in the preceding pages has a comparative purpose, suggesting ways of comparing different ownership regimes regardless of their regional location—focusing instead on key categories, institutions and social structures, and the belief systems, all of which provide important normative structures for the relationships established between people and land. By creating an analytical framework that spans many world regions for more than three centuries, the temporal dimension has fallen very far into the background, to not overly complexify an already complex undertaking. Leaving the question of time and change in the background was, however, also intentional because it implicitly signals that the main rupture in the conceptions of ownership was not regional or cultural—between Europe and other world regions—but temporal—before and after the 19th century. The casuistic and locally-sensitive conception of law in the early modern Iberian world meant that normative change was ubiquitous—new norms arose from each new case, and innovation, in a way, was a matter of course. The shift away from this model, towards

108 "To affect a valid comparison would involve using not predetermined categories of the kind Antiquity, feudalism, capitalism, but abandoning these concepts to construct a sociological grid laying out the possible variations of what is being compared. That is notably lacking from most historical discourse in the West. Instead, historians have simply claimed desirable and 'progressive' features for themselves. They have stolen history by imposing their categories and sequences on the rest of the world". Goody, *The theft of history*, 304.

the positivistic application of law and the development of jurisprudential reasoning, would signal a major transformation that would require its own analytical framework.

Finally, the narrow focus on property and its dichotomies is not merely problematic in the way it imposes Eurocentric, anachronistic, and anthropocentric perspectives on historical research, but also in the way it places methodological and analytical constraints on the historian. The most important of these is that it constrains the research questions and leads to what we may call *negative* histories: histories that, by taking a strong normative ideal, tend to highlight how social events or realities fall short of these ideals. By departing from an atemporal, clearly defined, and conceptually precise conception of property, it becomes inevitable that the historical accounts end up weighing themselves against these concepts. The accounts are thus *negative* because, when the ways in which land was held in different places and at different times do not fit into the definition, the historical accounts tend to emphasise what these histories and these peoples were *not*: they did *not* have private property and they were *not* modern. This makes the plurality of forms of landholding in the early modern world an impenetrable *black box* because its complexity cannot be addressed through the private/common dichotomy. The approach proposed here takes a different route by not pre-defining the rules surrounding land tenure but instead highlighting different levels of norms that can be explored through the analysis of primary sources and encouraging the exploration of this complexity. The tripartite analytical framework suggested here is intended to draw attention to the ways in which social structures (bodies) and cosmological representations (spirits) were intertwined with the categories (words) that are usually the focus of research on ownership and highlights how all these dimensions played a role in the normative structuring of land relations.

Acknowledgements

This Chapter was written as part of the IberLAND project (see www.iberland.eu) with the support of an ERC-Consolidator Grant (101000991). Previous versions were presented and discussed between 2022 and 2023: in the conference "Ownership Regimes in the Iberian World" at the Max Planck Institute for Legal History and Legal Theory in Frankfurt am Main; at the workshop "Eigentum und Herrschaft" at the University of Duisburg-Essen; in lectures in the law faculties of the State University of Rio de Janeiro (UERJ) and the National University of Brasilia (UNB); in the webinar series of the Institute for History of the Fluminense Federal University (UFF); and at the sixth biennial conference of the European Rural History Organization, held in Cluj-Napoca. I thank the participants of these events for their insights and criticisms. Any shortcomings are, of course, my own.

Bibliography

Manuscripts

Archivo Histórico Regional de Boyacá, Archivo Histórico de Tunja, Legajo 8.

Archivo General de la Nacíon—Colombia, Fondo: Poblaciones-Boy: SC.46,2, D.10.

Arquivo Nacional da Torre do Tombo, Foral de Goa, 1526, Gavetas, Gav. 20, mç. 9, n. 13.

Arquivo Nacional de Cabo Verde, Tombeamento da Capela do Tanque da Nora, Vinculos do Concelho da Praia

Printed Sources

Las Siete Partidas: Tercera Y Cuarta Partida 3–4, Salamanca: Andrea de Portonaris 1555.

Ordenações Filipinas, ed. Mendes de Almeida, Cândido, Rio de Janeiro 1870.

Recopilación De Leyes De Los Reynos De Las Indias, Madrid: Por la Viuda de D. Joaquín Ibarra 1791.

Solórzano Pereira, Juan de, *Politica Indiana*, Madrid: Diaz de la Carrera 1640.

Literature

Agüero, Alejandro, "Las Categorías Básicas de la Cultura Jurisdiccional", in Lorente, Marta (ed.), *De Justicia de Jueces a Justicia de Leyes: Hacia la España de 1870*, Madrid 2007, 21–58.

Alveal, Carmen, *Senhorios coloniais: direitos e chicanas forenses na formação da propriedade na América Portuguesa*, Niterói 2022.

Antoine, Annie, "Common Land Use in the Coutume de Bretagne from the Fifteenth to the Eighteenth Centuries", in Béaur, Gérard (ed.), *Property Rights, Land in Market and Economic Growth*, Turnhout 2009, 71–86.

Axelrod, Paul, and Michelle A. Fuerch, "Portuguese Orientalism and the Making of the Village Communities of Goa", in *Ethnohistory* 45:3 (1998), 439–476.

Bastião, Maria, "O Regime Dos Prazos Na Ilha De Moçambique, 1763–1800", in *Ler História* 76 (2020), 31–53.

Bastias Saavedra, Manuel, "The Lived Space: Possession, Ownership, and Land Sales on the Chilean Frontier (Valdivia, 1790–1830)", in *Historia Crítica* 67 (2018), 3–21.

Bastias Saavedra, Manuel, "The Normativity of Possession: Rethinking Land Relations in Early Modern Spanish America, Ca. 1500–1800", in *Colonial Latin American Review* 29:3 (2020), 223–238.

Bastias Saavedra, Manuel, "Decentering Law and Empire: Law-Making, Local Normativity, and the Iberian Empires in Asia", in Bastias Saavedra, Manuel (ed.), *Norms Beyond Empire: Law-Making and Local Normativities in Iberian Asia (1500–1800)*, Leiden 2021, 1–31.

Bastias Saavedra, Manuel (ed.), *Norms Beyond Empire: Law-Making and Local Normativities in Iberian Asia (1500–1800)*, Leiden 2021.

Beck Varela, Laura, *Das Sesmarias à Propriedade Moderna: Um Estudo de História do Direito Brasileiro*, Rio de Janeiro 2005.

Blaufarb, Rafe, *The Great Demarcation: The French Revolution and the Invention of Modern Property*, Oxford-New York 2016.

Candido, Mariana P., *Wealth, Land and Property in Angola: A History of Dispossession, Slavery, and Inequality*, New York 2022.

Carrera Quezada, Sergio, *Sementeras de Papel. La Regularización de la Propiedad Rural en la Huasteca Serrana, 1550–1720*, Mexico D.F. 2018.

Casey, James, *Family and Community in Early Modern Spain: The Citizens of Granada, 1570–1739*, Cambridge 2007.

Castro, Eduardo Viveiros de, *Cannibal Metaphysics: For a Post-Structural Anthropology*, Minneapolis 2014.

Clavero, Bartolomé, *Mayorazgo: Propiedad Feudal en Castilla, 1369–1836*, Madrid 1974.

Clavero, Bartolomé, *Tantas Personas Como Estados: Por una Antropología Política de la Historia Europea*, Madrid 1986.

Clavero, Bartolomé, *Antidora: Antropología Católica de la Economía Moderna*, Milano 1991.

Clavero, Bartolomé, "Propiedades y Propiedad, 1789: El Derecho Dominical en el Momento Revolucionario", in Dios, Salustiano de, Javier Infante, Ricardo Robledo and Eugenia Torijano (coords.), *Historia de la Propiedad en España, Siglos XV–XX: Encuentro Interdisciplinar, Salamanca, 3–6 de Junio de 1998*, Madrid 1999, 243–295.

Congost, Rosa, *Tierras, Leyes, Historia: Estudios Sobre "La Gran Obra de la Propiedad"*, Barcelona 2007.

Conte, Emanuele, "The Many Legal Faces of the Commons: A Short Historical Survey", in *Quaderni Storici* 168:3 (2021), 625–640.

Cushner, Nicholas, *Landed Estates in the Colonial Philippines*, New Haven 1976.

Damasceno, Claudia, "Território e Propriedade em Perspectiva Comparada nas Américas Coloniais", *Webinários do IHT*, October 27, 2022. Accessed July 14, 2023. https://www.youtube.com/watch?v=yk_NcqHDWkI&list=PLEdpUUGyi9iVFY_W23sKEmm3Btiu_sU1b&index=5&t=234s.

Dias Paes, Mariana, *Esclavos y tierras entre posesión y títulos: La construcción social del derecho de propiedad en Brasil (siglo XIX)*, Frankfurt 2021.

Dios, Salustiano de, Javier Infante, Ricardo Robledo and Eugenia Torijano (coords.), *Historia de la Propiedad en España: Bienes Comunales, Pasado y Presente*, Madrid 2002.

Dios, Salustiano de, *Seis Estudios Sobre Historia de la Propiedad*, Salamanca 2015.

Duve, Thomas, “Was ist ›Multinormativität‹?—Einführende Bemerkungen”, in *Rechtsgeschichte—Legal History* 25 (2017), 88–101.

Duve, Thomas, “Legal History as a History of the Translation of Knowledge of Normativity”, in *Max Planck Institute for Legal History and Legal Theory Research Paper Series* 16 (2022).

Duve, Thomas, and Otto Danwerth (eds.), *Knowledge of the Pragmatici: Legal and Moral Theological Literature and the Formation of Early Modern Ibero-America*, Leiden 2020.

Duve, Thomas, José Luis Egío, and Christiane Birr, *The School of Salamanca: A Case of Global Knowledge Production*, Leiden 2021.

Freitas Macedo, Camilla de, “Sesmarias Indígenas na São Paulo Colonial: Uma Interseção Entre Estatutos Pessoais e Situações Reais”, in *Dimensões* 39 (2017), 112–137.

Freitas Macedo, Camilla de, “Posesión y propiedad en las disputas por jurisdicción (Aralar-Enirio, 1615–1735)”, in *Relaciones, forthcoming.*

Garriga, Carlos, “¿Cómo Escribir una Historia “Descolonizada” del Derecho en América Latina?”, in Jesús Vallejo and Sebastián Martín (coords.), *Antidora: Homenaje a Bartolomé Clavero*, Cizur Menor 2019, 325–376.

Garriga, Carlos, “¿De qué Hablamos los Historiadores del Derecho cuando Hablamos de Derecho?”, in *Revista Direito Mackenzie* 14:1 (2020), 1–24.

Gonçalves, Caetano, “O regime das terras e as reservas indígenas na colonização portuguesa”, in *Boletim Geral das Colônias* 2: 13 (1926), 26–45.

Góngora, Mario, *El Estado en el Derecho Indiano: Época de Fundación 1492–1570*, Santiago 1951.

Goody, Jack, *The Theft of History*, Cambridge 2008.

Goody, Jack, Joan Thirsk, and E.P. Thompson (eds.), *Family and Inheritance: Rural Society in Western Europe, 1200–1800*, Cambridge 1978.

Graubart, Karen B., “Shifting Landscapes: Heterogeneous Conceptions of Land Use and Tenure in the Lima Valley”, in *Colonial Latin American Review* 26:1 (2017), 62–84.

Grebe, María Ester, “El Subsistema de los Ngen en la Religiosidad Mapuche”, in *Revista Chilena de Antropología* 12 (1993), 45–64.

Greer, Allan, *Property and Dispossession: Natives, Empires and Land in Early Modern North America*, Cambridge 2018.

Grossi, Paolo, *Il Dominio e le Cose: Percezioni Medievali e Moderne dei Diritti Reali*, Milan 1992.

Grossi, Paolo, *El Orden Jurídico Medieval*, Madrid 1995.

Grossi, Paolo, *Un Altro Modo di Possedere*, Milano 2017.

Grossi, Paolo, and Ángel M. López y López (eds.), *Propiedad: Otras Perspectivas*, Madrid 2013.

Güereca, Raquel, “La Tenencia de la Tierra en los Márgenes de Mesoamérica: El Caso del Gobierno de las Fronteras de Colotlán, Nueva Galicia”, in Okoshi Harada, Tsubasa,

Julien Michault, and Sarmiento Tepoxtecatl, (eds.), *Recorriendo el Lindero, Trazando la Frontera*, México 2018, 110–130.

Haring, Clarence H., "The Cabildo", in Russell-Wood, *Local Government in European Overseas Empires, 1450–1800*, Aldershot 1999, vol. 1, 1–19.

Haskett, Robert S., "Indian Town Government in Colonial Cuernavaca: Persistence, Adaptation, and Change", in Russell-Wood, A.J.R. (ed.), *Local Government in European Overseas Empires, 1450–1800*, Aldershot 1999, vol. 2, 541–569.

Herzog, Tamar, *Defining Nations: Immigrants and Citizens in Early Modern Spain and Spanish America*, New Haven 2003.

Herzog, Tamar, "Colonial Law and "Native Customs": Indigenous Land Rights in Colonial Spanish America", in *The Americas* 69:3 (2013), 303–321.

Herzog, Tamar, *Frontiers of Possession: Spain and Portugal in Europe and the Americas*, Cambridge 2015.

Hespanha, António Manuel, *La Gracia del Derecho: Economía de la Cultura en la Edad Moderna*, Madrid 1993.

Hespanha, António Manuel, "Early Modern Law and the Anthropological Imagination of Old European Culture", in Marino, John A. (ed.), *Early Modern History and the Social Sciences: Testing the Limits of Braudel's Mediterranean*, Kirksville 2002, 191–204.

Hespanha, António Manuel, "Porque é que Existe e em que é que Consiste um Direito Colonial Brasileiro", in *Quaderni Fiorentini per la Storia del Pensiero Giuridico Moderno* 35 (2006), 59–81.

Hespanha, António Manuel, "Depois do Leviathan", in *Almanack Braziliense* 5 (2007), 55–66.

Hespanha, António Manuel, *Imbecillitas: As Bem-Aventuraças da Inferiodade nas Sociedades de Antigo Regime*, 2008.

Hespanha, António Manuel, "Uncommon Laws: Law in the Extreme Peripheries of an Early Modern Empire", in *Zeitschrift der Savigny-Stiftung für Rechtsgeschichte: Germanistische Abteilung* 130: 1 (2013), 180–204.

Hespanha, António Manuel, *Como os Juristas Viam o Mundo. 1550–1750: Direitos, Estados, Pessoas, Coisas, Contratos, Ações, e Crimes*, Lisboa 2015.

Hespanha, António Manuel, "Histórias do Direito: Anti-Formalismo, Anti-Estadualismo e Anti-Nacionalismo na História Jurídica Contemporânea", in *e-Legal History Review* 29 (2019).

Horn, Rebecca, *Postconquest Coyoacan: Nahua-Spanish Relations in Central Mexico, 1519–1650*, Stanford 1997.

Jurado, Carolina, "La composición como concierto. Prácticas judiciales en espacios rurales durante el primer proceso de visita y composición de tierras y de extranjeros en Charcas. Virreinato del Perú, 1591–1597", in *Prohistoria. Historia, políticas de la historia* 29 (2018), 19–42.

Kellogg, Susan, *Law and the Transformation of Aztec Culture, 1500–1700*, Norman 1995.

Koskenniemi, Martti, *To the Uttermost Parts of the Earth: Legal Imagination and International Power, 1300–1870*, Cambridge 2021.

Lana-Berasain, José-Miguel, "Forgotten Commons: The Struggle for Recognition and Property Rights in a Spanish Village, 1509–1957", in *Rural History* 23:2 (2012), 137–159.

Locke, John, *Two Treatises of Government*, London 1962.

Lockhart, James, *The Nahuas After the Conquest: A Social and Cultural History of the Indians of Central Mexico, Sixteenth Through Eighteenth Centuries*, Stanford 1992.

López Caballero, Paula, *Los Títulos Primordiales del Centro de México: Introducción Y Catálogo* (BA Thesis), México D.F. 2000.

Luque Alcaide, Elisa, "Capellanías (DCH)", in *Max Planck Institute for Legal History and Legal Theory Research Paper Series* 18 (2022), Available at https://ssrn.com/abstract=4239785.

Lynch Jr., Owen J, "Land Rights, Land Laws, and Land Usurpation: The Spanish Era (1565–1898)", in *Philippine Law Journal*, 63 (1988), 82–111.

Mariluz Urquijo, José María, *El Régimen de la Tierra en el Derecho Indiano*, Buenos Aires 1968.

Mariluz Urquijo, José María, "La Propiedad en el Derecho Indiano", in *Revista Chilena de Historia del Derecho*, 6 (1970), 154–157.

Menegus, Margarita, "Cacicazgos y Repúblicas de Indios en el Siglo XVI: La Transformación de la Propiedad en la Mixteca", in Hermann, Manuel (ed.) *Configuraciones Territoriales en la Mixteca: Estudios de Historia y Antropología*, México 2016, 205–220.

Menegus, Margarita, *Los Pueblos de Indios en la Nueva España, Siglo XVIII: El Impacto de las Reformas Borbónicas*, Ciudad de México 2020.

Menegus, Margarita, and Rodolfo Aguirre Salvador, *El Cacicazgo en Nueva España y Filipinas*, México-Barcelona 2005.

Míguez Núñez, Rodrigo, *Terra di Scontri: Alterazioni e Rivendicazioni del Diritto alla Terra nelle Ande Centrali*, Milano 2013.

Mota, Maria Sarita, "Sesmarias e Propriedade Titulada da Terra: O Individualismo Agrário na América Portuguesa", in *Saeculum—Revista de História* 26 (2012), 29–45.

Neeson, J.M., *Commoners: Common Right, Enclosure and Social Change in England, 1700–1820*, Cambridge 1993.

Neto, Margarida Sobral, *Terra e Conflito: Região de Coimbra (1700–1834)*, 2 vols., Coimbra 2018.

Newitt, M.D.D., *Portuguese Settlement on the Zambesi: Exploration, Land Tenure and Colonial Rule in East Africa*, Harlow 1973.

Okoshi Harada, Tsubasa, "De lo Ajeno Impuesto a lo Nuestro Fundado: El Proceso de 'Domesticación' del Espacio en los Pueblos de Indios de la Gobernación del

Yucatán", in Okoshi Harada, Tsubasa, Julien Michault, and Sarmiento Tepoxtecatl, (eds.), *Recorriendo el Lindero, Trazando la Frontera*, México 2018, 14–35.

Osterhammel, Jürgen, *The Transformation of the World: A Global History of the Nineteenth Century*, Princeton 2014.

Ots Capdequí, José María, *El Régimen De La Tierra En Hispanoamérica*, Ciudad Trujillo 1946.

Owensby, Brian, *Empire of Law and Indian Justice in Colonial Mexico*, Stanford 2008.

Oxfam, "Land and Power: The Growing Scandal Surrounding the New Wave of Investments in Land". Available at: https://oxfamilibrary.openrepository.com/bitstream/handle/10546/142858/bp151-land-power-rights-acquisitions-220911-en.pdf;jsessionid=A445F2FE9E7FDA0643A00D667FFFD10B?sequence=32.

Parise, Agustin, *Ownership Paradigms in American Civil Law Jurisdictions: Manifestations of the Shifts in the Legislation of Louisiana, Chile, and Argentina (16th–20th Centuries)*, Leiden 2017.

Pérez Collados, José María, "Las Tierras Comunales en los Pueblos de Indios y su Trayectoria en el México Independiente", in Dios, Salustiano de, Javier Infante, Ricardo Robledo and Eugenia Torijano (coords.) *Historia de la Propiedad en España: Bienes Comunales, Pasado y Presente*, Madrid 2002, 329–390.

Pérez Zamarripa, Abisai, "The Principales of Philip II: Vassalage, Justice, and the Making of Indigenous Jurisdiction in the Early Colonial Philippines", in Bastias Saavedra, Manuel (ed.) *Norms Beyond Empire*, Leiden 2021, 72–101.

Phelan, John Leddy, *The Hispanization of the Philippines: Spanish Aims and Filipino Responses, 1565–1700*, Madison 1959.

Porras Arboleda, Pedro, "Aportación al Estudio del Mayorazgo: Tres Ejemplos Giennenses de los Siglos XIV, XV Y XVI", in *Boletín del Instituto de Estudios Giennenses* 139 (1989), 63–100.

Quezada, Sergio, *Pueblos y Caciques Yucatecos, 1550–1580*, México, D.F. 1993.

Regime Theory Working Group, (Manuel Bastias Saavedra, Gerd Bender, Peter Collin, Thomas Duve, Christian R.J. Pogies, Luca von Bogdandy, Johanna Wolf, and Alexandra Woods), "Historical Regimes of Normativity: Part 1–4", in *Legal History Insights*, Max Planck Institute for Legal History and Legal Theory, 2021. Available at: https://legalhistoryinsights.com/historical-regimes-of-normativity-part-1/

Robisheaux, Thomas Willard, *Rural Society and the Search for Order in Early Modern Germany*, Cambridge 1989.

Rodrigues, Eugénia *Portugueses e Africanos nos Rios de Sena: Os Prazos da Coroa em Moçambique nos Séculos XVII e XVIII*, Lisboa 2013.

Rojas Bahamonde, Pablo, María Amalia Mellado, and Gustavo Blanco-Wells, "Sobrenaturaleza Mapuche: Extractivismo, Seres No-Humanos, y Miedo en el Centro Sur de Chile", in *Revista Austral de Ciencias Sociales* 38 (2020), 7–30.

Rosa, Maria Lurdes de, *O Morgadio em Portugal, Sécs. XIV–XV*, Lisboa 1995.

Rosa, Maria Lurdes de, *As Almas Herdeiras: Fundação de Capela Fúnebres e Afirmação da Alma como Sujeito do Direito* (*Portugal, 1400–1521*) (PhD Thesis) Paris-Lisboa 2005.

Russell-Wood, A.J.R., "Local Government in Portuguese America: A Study in Cultural Divergence", in Russell-Wood, A.J.R., *Local Government in European Overseas Empires, 1450–1800*, Aldershot 1999, vol. 1, 71–115.

Sabean, David Warren, *Property, Production, and Family in Neckarhausen, 1700–1870*, Cambridge 1990.

Sarr, Assan, *Islam, Power, and Dependency in the Gambia River Basin: The Politics of Land Control, 1790–1940*, Rochester 2016.

Scott, William H., *Barangay: Sixteenth Century Philippine Culture and Society*, Manila 1994.

Smith, Richard M., "Some Issues Concerning Families and Their Property in Rural England, 1250–1800" in Smith, Richard M. (ed.), *Land, Kinship and Life-Cycle*, Cambridge 1984, 1–86.

Souza, Teotonio R. de, *Medieval Goa: A Socio-Economic History*, New Dehli 1979.

Souza, Teotonio R. de, "Rural Economy and Life", in Souza, Teotonio R. de (ed.), *Goa Through the Ages: An Economic History*, New Dehli 1989, 78–116.

Terraciano, Kevin, *Los Mixtecos de la Oaxaca Colonial: La Historia Ñudzahui del Siglo XVI al XVIII*, México D.F. 2013.

Thompson, E.P., *Whigs and Hunters: The Origin of the Black Act*, London 1975.

Thompson, E.P., *Customs in Common*, London 1993.

Vallejo, Jesús, "El Cáliz de Plata: Articulación de Órdenes Jurídicos en la Jurisprudencia del Ius Commune", in *Revista de Historia del Derecho* 38 (2009), 1–13.

Xavier, Ângela Barreto, "Terra e Território na Goa e Época Moderna", Unpublished manuscript 2013.

Xavier, Ângela Barreto, *Religion and Empire in Portuguese India: Conversion, Resistance, and the Making of Goa*, Albany 2022.

Zavala, Silvio, *De Encomiendas y Propiedad Territorial en Algunas Regiones de la América Española*, México 1940.

CHAPTER 2

The Rights of Things and the Obligations of the Owner

Exploring the Deep Normative Grammars of the Early Modern Ownership Regime

Alessandro Buono

1 Introduction

The aim of this chapter is to delve into the "deep grammars"[1] that underly the ownership regimes of early modern Catholic Europe. By examining social and institutional practices, it seeks to uncover the implicit principles and ideas shaping these systems. Furthermore, this analysis highlights the profound differences that set the early modern world apart from our contemporary perspective.[2] In the first section, I argue that it is necessary to take seriously how the medieval and early modern juridical thought considered things as bearers of rights and capable of representing absent persons, challenging the sharp distinction between people and things deeply rooted in an anthropocentric view of 'European modernity'. I also discuss the role of things in social aggregation, where early modern corporate bodies were conceived as associations of persons and things. Finally, I state the significance of inheritance transmission in defending and recreating the social order, and the role assigned to things in such a reproduction cycle.

To do so, in the second section, I analyse what could be regarded as a "liminal case": that of vacant inheritances. I will examine the norms and institutions that dealt with vacant estates, beginning with the case of late medieval and early modern Castile, all the way to the so-called Juzgados de Bienes de Difuntos (Tribunals of the Estates of the Deceased), entrusted with the administration of vacant inheritances in the early modern Kingdoms of the Indies. I aim to demonstrate that the task of the just prince and administrator was precisely to prevent both people and things from being isolated, to reincorporate them, and to prevent the resources of the Kingdom from being misused. It was then the

1 See Bastias Saavedra (Chapter 1) in this volume.
2 See Bastias Saavedra (Chapter 1) in this volume.

vulnerability of assets and their need for guardianship that gave rise to a social demand for protection and legitimised the intervention of the King's privative jurisdiction. Ultimately, the goal of the Juzgados was to rejoin assets into local networks and prevent their deterioration, especially in the "New World", where their abandonment could hinder Christianity and civilisation.

In the final section, I explore the conceptual connections between abandoned things and abandoned people in early modern European normative knowledge. By discussing how loneliness and infertility could affect things, and vice versa, I will emphasise the importance of understanding how these societies linked the status of people and things and how these statuses influenced each other. As a result, ownership was always subordinated to the proper use of things and limited by the responsibility that every entity, whether human or non-human, held toward the rest of society. Jurists would eventually qualify this as a genuine servitude (*servitus*) toward the common good that encumbered whatever was considered necessary for the sustenance of the community, primarily the land. Ownership meant, first and foremost, good stewardship, and only useful and stable relationships between people and things could ultimately be accepted. A duty to care rested on every owner: the one who neglected his possessions—akin to a *paterfamilias* who neglected his wife, children, servants and patrimony—had to be compelled to fulfil his duties or face seizure of his assets and being replaced by a more responsible administrator.

2 The *Respublica* as an Association of Persons and Things

In a book devoted to ownership regimes, it might appear contradictory to begin with what could be perceived as a breakdown in the relationship between people and things: the cases of *res nullius* (nobody's things), *res derelictae* (abandoned things), *res nullius in bonis* or *bona vacantia* (vacant inheritance) and *hereditas iacens* (inheritances in abeyance). However, the usefulness of starting from the margins, from the borderline case, in order to grasp the mechanisms underlying the functioning of a society is demonstrated by both Italian microhistory, which has long reflected on the "exceptional-normal" case,[3] and legal history. In particular, scholars like Yan Thomas have effectively demonstrated how the highest level of generalisation in the categories of medieval

3 Starting from Edoardo Grendi's oxymoron "exceptional normal" in Grendi, "Micro-analisi e storia sociale". More recently, see Vallerani, *Sistemi di eccezione*.

and early modern legal thought can be understood precisely through the "stabilization of the exceptional."[4]

Analysing the history of the *persona ficta*, Thomas dwelt on the well-known case of the "disappearing community": what becomes of a (monastic) community when it is reduced to a single member or when all its members vanish? Does the community cease to exist? More importantly, what happens to its rights and patrimony? Should they be considered vacant and therefore open to appropriation? As is well known, medieval juridical thought had worked out solutions that, to a modern mindset, might appear peculiar. One of the most cited theories was that of Moses of Ravenna, according to which, in the absence of the members of the community, possession could be preserved by the monastery building itself, as if the walls could possess the land and the community rights while awaiting the return of the people.[5] The idea that things can possess rights, that they can represent absent persons, that communities are corporate entities made of things and persons (*universitas rerum et personarum*),[6] in which things too have rights and duties and can represent people was, therefore, present in medieval and early modern juridical thought.

Any inquiry into ownership regimes, then, should start from this observation: the status of things and the status of people in the early modern world were not as sharply opposed as in 19th- and 20th-century legal thought. Dealing, then, with the relationship between things and people in this period implies, first and foremost, moving away from the anthropocentrism that has characterised the main historiographical narratives about the birth of the modern world and trying to understand what was to all intents and purposes to be a different anthropology.[7]

According to Paolo Grossi, the early medieval European juridical culture was defined by a profound *reicentrism* and naturalism, an anthropology not characterised by the autonomy of the individual but by a sense of humankind's inferiority to nature and by its participation in the nature of things. As a result, the founding moment of *ius commune* saw a real centrality of things over people and the eclipse of formal ownership: while not disappearing, formal

4 Thomas, "L'extrême et l'ordinaire. Remarques sur le cas médiéval de la communauté disparue", 46.

5 Cortese, "Per la storia di una teoria dell'arcivescovo Mosè di Ravenna (m. 1154) sulla proprietà ecclesiastica".

6 Otaduy, "La universitas rerum como soporte de la personalidad en el derecho canónico".

7 Clavero, *Tantas personas como estados*; Hespanha, *Como os juristas viam o mundo*. The so-called "ontological turn" in anthropology, in fact, seems to be heading in the same direction, see Descola, *Par-delà nature et culture*. For an overview, see Holbraad and Pedersen, *The Ontological Turn*; Mancuso, "La 'svolta ontologica' e le questioni epistemologiche in antropologia".

ownership was perceived as less meaningful than those forms of possession that involved the use and active management of things.[8] Expression of the pronounced *reicentrism* of medieval and early modern normative order was also evident in the tendency to conceive of not only relations to things, but also personal relations (servitude, labour, marriage, kinship, even jurisdiction) as *real* relations, that is "to use servitudes as a model for the technical description of dependency and subordination relationships".[9] Using the tool of analogy, late Middle Ages and early modern jurists did not hesitate to conceive of the right that a lord had over his servant, or that an employer had over a worker, as a right in someone else's thing (*ius in re aliena*), as if they possessed a right 'in' the body of the subordinate, and that might have been claimed in the same manner as a right of way over someone else's land. As an example, the rights acquired by spouses in the body of the partner through marriage were thought of as a *quasi possessio* (*as if* they were possessed),[10] and therefore could have been claimed through petitory and possessory actions, akin to real rights.[11]

Given what we have discussed, it is imperative to heed the insights from the social sciences, which have emphasised the importance of "taking seriously the prerogatives ascribed to things and the burden of rights with which they were invested".[12] This entails, on the one hand, questioning the overly

8 Grossi, *L'ordine giuridico medievale*, 99–100.

9 Madero, "Penser la physique du pouvoir", § 13.

10 Grossi, *Le situazioni reali nell'esperienza giuridica medievale*; Grossi, "*Un altro modo di possedere*". For an enlightening reflection on the relationship between real and personal rights, see Conte, *Servi medievali*. See also Madero, *La loi de la chair*, for marital relations, and Cerutti, *Giustizia sommaria*, for labour relations. The same can be said for personal status and identity in Buono, "Tener persona" and Buono, "Il quasi possesso della consanguineità".

11 I am thinking for example of procedures, such as the so-called *expedientes de vida maridable*, through which an abandoned woman (or, more rarely, a man) could request to regain possession of the spouse's body. Sánchez and Testón, "Mujeres abandonadas, mujeres olvidadas"; Gálvez Ruiz, "Mujeres y "maridos ausentes" en Indias"; Macías and Candau, "Matrimonios y conflictos"; Pascua Sánchez, "'A la sombra' de hombres ausentes".

12 Cerutti and Grangaud (eds.), *Fuori Mercato*, 5. Many scholars, like Daniel Miller, have unveiled the "circular process at which level we cannot differentiate either subjects per se or objects per se" (Miller, *Materiality*, 14). Daniel Miller (*Materiality* and *Stuff*) traces the foundations of such a theoretical stance already well deployed in the Hegelian dialectic. In recent years, however, it can be said that one of the most influential voices in the historiographical literature has been that of Bruno Latour, and Actor-Network Theory (ANT) in general, as pointed out by the leading scholar Frank Trentmann: "things ... recruit us into politics as much as we recruit them" (Trentmann, "Materiality in the Future of History", 300). See a critic of Latour's work in Miller, *Materiality*, 10. In addition to Miller, arche-

sharp distinction between things and individuals and challenging the notion of human subjects as active agents and objects as passive entities. On the other hand, it involves challenging the liberal interpretive paradigm and the tradition of 'European modernity', which has viewed its history as the progressive emancipation of the autonomous will of human beings and their ability and confidence to dominate and transform nature.[13] In essence, things are not mere inert resources but play a crucial role in the processes of social aggregation.

On closer inspection, this is something medieval, and early modern sources tell us. Consider, for example, Jean Bodin's renowned definition of *ménage* (household) and *république* (commonwealth). If "a Familie is the right gouernment of many subiects or persons vnder the obedience of one and the same head of the family; and of such things as are vnto them proper", the "Commonweale is a lawfull gouernment of many families, and of that which vnto them in common belongeth, with a puissant soueraigntie."[14] As can be observed, from the most fundamental social aggregate to the most 'perfect' level of political organisation, the early modern corporate body was conceived as an association of persons *and* things, to the extent that there is no community without some common thing.[15] Just as every family must have a patrimony to be considered

ologists like Ian Hodder (*Entangled* and "The Entanglements of Humans and Things") or Bjørnar Olsen ("Reclaiming Things") have developed a particularly sharp critique, not only of ANT but also of historians who often use only a metaphorical concept of materiality.

13 This is a perspective, it seems to me, to which Paolo Grossi himself is no alien, when he looks somewhat nostalgically at the medieval world, dominated by a relationship that seems to him more authentic with nature (God?). For a critical review of Grossi's interpretation of *L'ordine giuridico medievale*, see Conte, "Droit médiéval". This attitude of rupture between the "medieval" and the "modern" is emphasised, for example, in his analysis of the School of Salamanca's conception of "private property" (Grossi, "La proprietà nel sistema privatistico della Seconda Scolastica"). A less "modernizing" vision can instead be found during the same years in Maccioni, *Il 'dominium altum' nella dottrina di Soto, Molina, Suarez*, or Lalinde Abadia, "Anotaciones historicistas al iusprivatismo de la segunda escolástica".

14 "Ménage est un droit gouvernement de plusieurs sujets, sous l'obéissance d'un chef de famille, et de ce qui lui est propre", (Bodin, *Les Six Livres de la République*, Livre I, chap. II, p. 7) and "République est un droit gouvernement de plusieurs ménages, et de ce qui leur est commun, avec puissance souveraine" (Bodin, *Les Six Livres de la République*, Livre I, chap. I, p. 1). For the first English translation see Bodin, *The six bookes of a commonweale*, Book I, Chap. I and II, pp. 1 and 8.

15 "Le mot de communauté signifie qu'il n'y a point de collège, s'il n'y a rien de commun" (Bodin, *Les Six Livres de la République*, Livre III, chap. VII, p. 333). "And the word communitie, or consociation, signifieth that there ought some thing to be common to all that be fellowes of the colledge or societie: For where there is nothing common, there is no colledge" (Bodin, *The six bookes of a commonweale*, p. 365).

accomplished,[16] to be a *Respublica* means to have a *res publicae*, that is, material matters and things that concern everyone.[17]

Thus, lay and ecclesiastical corporate bodies can be conceived as an association of persons and things, to the point that when all the human beings that compose them disappear it is things that take their place and represent the continuity of the corporate body.[18] As the walls represent the monastery, the *patrimonium* of the family ensures, through the stability of things, the continuity of the lineage beyond the discontinuity represented by people, changing from one generation to the next. Transmission of inheritances can thus be thought of as the primary field in which the social order is defended and continually recreated, precisely because, with each generation, the corporation made up of

16 In the 'natural' association par excellence, the family, human beings and their patrimony almost end up being confused in the eyes of medieval jurists. As Bartolus de Saxoferrato says, "familia accipitur in iure pro substantia", in consonance with the definition given by Ulpianus in the Digest: "'Familiae' appellatio qualiter accipiatur, videamus. Et quidem varie accepta est: nam et in res et in personas deducitur. In res, ut puta lege duodecim tabularum his verbis 'adgnatus proximus familiam habeto'" (D.50.16.195). The reference to the Twelve Tables is precisely to the law concerning *ab intestato* succession: "Si intestato moritur, cui suus heres nec escit, adgnatus proximus familiam habeto", where we see that the term family is translatable as patrimony or even inheritance. On this passage, see Thomas, *La mort du père*, chap. IV.

17 "Mais outre la souveraneité, il faut qu'il y ait quelque chose de commun, et de public: comme le domaine public, le thresor public, le pourpris de la cité, les rues, les murailles, les places, les temples, les marchés, les usages, les loix, les coustumes, la justice, les loyers, les peines, et autres choses semblables" (Bodin, *Les Six Livres de la République*, Livre I, chap. II, p. 10). The reference to Ancient Rome is obviously central to Bodin: "Ce faisant, il fait écho à Cicéron: 'Beaucoup de choses en effet son communes entre eux aux concitoyens: le forum, les temples, les portiques, les rues, les lois, le droit, la justice, les votes, les relations aussi et les amitiés, et pour un grand nombre tous les contrats d'affaires'", in Chrom Jacobsen, *Jean Bodin et le dilemme de la philosophie politique moderne*, 150. In this, the genealogy of the concept of *res* as "cause", "thing under discussion", is illuminating, as Thomas, *Causa*, has shown—there is also an excellent discussion of the issue in Vanuxem, *Les choses saisies par la proprieté*. Not differently, as Heidegger pointed out, the medieval form of the German *ding* (*thing*, *dinc*) also designated "une assemblée réunie pour délibérer d'une affaire, d'un litige" (Vanuxem, *Les choses saisies par la proprieté*, 4).

18 Marcel Mauss' hypothesis is very intriguing: "À l'origine, sûrement, les choses elles-mêmes avaient une personnalité et une vertu. Les choses ne sont pas les êtres inertes que le droit de Justinien et nos droits entendent. D'abord elles font partie de la famille: la familia romaine comprend les res et non pas seulement les personnes. On en a la définition encore au Digeste, et il est très remarquable que, plus on remonte dans l'antiquité, plus le sens du mot familia dénote les res qui en font partie jusqu'à désigner même les vivres et les moyens de vivre de la famille. La meilleure étymologie du mot familia est sans doute celle qui le rapproche du sanskrit dhaman, maison." Mauss, *Essai sur le don*, 178–179.

things and people that is the family faces a discontinuity, as the case of vacant inheritances will show us.

3 Vacant Inheritances in Spain and the Kingdoms of the Indies

Since the Middle Ages, rulers have found a great mass of doctrine on which to build their claim to control successions, in a context in which individuals, seen as imperfect beings, incapable of attaining salvation without guidance, find fulfilment only through insertion in civil and ecclesiastical corporate bodies. It was not desirable for both people and things to remain isolated, infertile or unproductive: each person and each thing had to remain bound to a corporate body (not only a family, but also a local, a professional, a devotional community, etc.). Incorporation would ensure the achievement of the purpose toward which individual entities were destined in the order of creation (primarily reproduction and salvation), limiting potentially destructive individual freedom, first and foremost, through principles of collective responsibility.[19]

It is therefore understandable why the abandonment of inheritance assets was potentially considered a danger to the stability of human associations. Every inheritance had to have an heir to ensure that the rights and obligations inherent to the deceased's social position and estate were satisfied.[20] This is why the social problem of disputed, uncertain and vacant successions led to the emergence of procedures and institutions aimed at filling this possible source of social discontinuity. This is especially true if we consider a distinctive feature of the *ancien régime* society, namely, the extreme uncertainty of the rights associated with ownership: if it is use and possession that take precedence over formal title, if things can 'claim' their right to be used and not be abandoned and destroyed, then abandoned things will 'attract' new possessors to themselves who, through their use, will acquire claims to ownership. But the rupture and reconfiguration of the bond between people and things that such a process of misappropriation entails is not without consequences for the social fabric. It is then the "vulnerability of the things"[21] that produces a social demand for

19 Grossi, *"Un altro modo di possedere"*, 76–80. Herzog, "Terres et déserts, société et sauvagerie".

20 Cerutti, "À qui appartiennent les biens qui n'appartiennent à personne?", 366.

21 On the "vulerabilité des biens", see Cerutti, "À qui appartiennent les biens qui n'appartiennent à personne?", 368.

protection to which multiple instances (communal and corporate, institutional and informal, secular and ecclesiastical) are called upon to respond.

In the early modern societies, and especially in empires extended to a global scale, such as the Spanish and the Portuguese,[22] numerous factors made assets highly vulnerable and in danger of being left without a possessor: on the one hand, high mortality and mobility, on the other, the fact that legal incapacity and lack of autonomy characterised the vast majority of people.[23] Hence the proliferation of guardianship institutions, such as the Juzgados de Bienes de Difuntos (or their Portuguese counterpart, the Provedorias de Defuntos e Ausentes).[24] These institutions served as curators of assets left without a possessor, offering an institutional channel (among many possible ones)[25] for the reintegration of assets into the corporations to which they belonged.

Beneath these institutions, tasked with the reintegration of inheritances in abeyance into their respective corporate bodies,[26] there was a fundamental societal need for guardianship, as if emanating from the assets themselves. As we previously discussed, these assets asserted their right to be utilised and not dispersed, as they served as guarantors of social relationships, rights and obligations linked to their possession. Thus, in the last instance, the goal of these institutions was less the safeguarding of individual ownership rights than the continual and essential upkeep of a society made up of corporate bodies.

As Francisco Tomás y Valiente has shown, during the medieval period, assets left without a successor were subject to a myriad of competing claims, from the local church to the communities and towns in which these were located, all the way to the master of the house in which the heirless individual had died.[27] According to him, with the end of the Roman Empire, the gradual disappearance of testamentary disposition and the influence of Germanic law and ecclesiastical institutions had left vacant inheritances to be primarily claimed

22 But the same can also be said for other states and empires, see Buono, "The King Heir".

23 "[W]ith some exceptions, Spanish laws required married women, slaves, Indians, and minors of age—in short, just about everyone in colonial society—to be represented by powerful adult men in legal matters", Premo, *Children of the Father King*, 6.

24 Costa, "A prática da Justiça na Provedoria de Defuntos e Ausentes de Vil Rica (1711–1808)"; "Das desordens na Provedoria de Defuntos e Ausentes, Capelas e Resíduos na América Portuguesa"; *De cofre não tem mais que o nome*.

25 For the case of the Portuguese empire, for example, the role played by the Misericórdias is well known; Sá, *Quando o rico se faz pobre*; *As Misericórdias Portuguesas de D. Manuel I a Pombal*; *O Regresso dos Mortos*.

26 Cerutti and Grangaud, "Sources and Contextualizations".

27 Tomás y Valiente, "La sucesión de quien muere sin parientes y sin disponer de sus bienes", 194–204.

locally and used for the common good, such as charitable works on behalf of the poor and the souls of the deceased, as well as in public utility work for local communities.[28] The primary concern, therefore, was not so much to safeguard the rights of a purported absentee heir but rather to protect the interests of the community from resource depletion. In fact, the assets left by a foreigner were considered *ownerless*, preventing them from being taken out of the local common pool and appropriated by a foreign heir.[29]

The treatment of assets belonging to foreigners, that is, those who had no local ties,[30] shared the same logic as the management of vacant inheritances. It is not coincidental that the Castilian king's jurisdiction over vacant estates revolved around the concept of *miserabiles personae*, the poor, privileged persons (both 'real' or 'fictitious') in a particularly fragile state who required protection. This jurisdiction provided them with protection precisely to prevent the possible appropriation of their assets by local communities.[31] While it does not appear that a claim on vacant inheritances existed in the early Middle Ages,[32] starting with the *Fuero Real* (1255) and continuing through the *Nueva Recopilación* (1567), the kings of Castile increasingly asserted their claim over vacant assets, initially focusing on those belonging to pilgrims.[33] Gradually—and not without significant fluctuations[34]—the Royal Fisc asserted its claim to vacant assets, although this did not mean an end to competing claims by the church and local communities.[35] The entrenched idea that vacant inheritances, as well

28 Community must be understood not as an abstract "Kingdom's political community" but as the "most direct and immediate form" of local community. Tomás y Valiente, "La sucesión de quien muere sin parientes y sin disponer de sus bienes", 210–211.

29 Tomás y Valiente, "La sucesión de quien muere sin parientes y sin disponer de sus bienes", 215–216.

30 Cerutti, *Étrangers*.

31 Tomás y Valiente, "La sucesión de quien muere sin parientes y sin disponer de sus bienes", 217–218.

32 García González, "La Mañería", 237.

33 *Fuero Real*, lib. IV, tít. XXIV, ley III: "Si romero muere sin manda, los Alcades de la Villa do muriere reciban sus bienes, è cumplan dellos lo que fuere menester à su enterramiento, è lo demás guardenlo, è faganlo saber al Rey, y el Rey mande lo que tuviere por bien" (*El Fuero Real de España, diligentemente hecho por el noble Rey don Alonso IX*, Madrid, Pantaleon Aznar, 1781). *Nueva Recopilación*, I, XII, V (quoted in Tomás y Valiente, "La sucesión de quien muere sin parientes y sin disponer de sus bienes", 222).

34 The *Leyes de Toro* (1505) still established that vacant inheritances were in part to go to spouses and in part to be used for charitable work "for the souls" of the deceased, therefore excluding the Royal Treasury. Tomás y Valiente, "La sucesión de quien muere sin parientes y sin disponer de sus bienes", 228.

35 In addition to the aforementioned Tomás y Valiente, "La sucesión de quien muere sin pari-

as the so-called *bienes mostrencos*[36] (i.e., nobody's things), should somehow benefit the 'public good' was also expressed between the 14th and 15th centuries in the alienation of this right in favour of the *Mercedarios* and *Trinitarios* orders—active in ransoming Christians held captive by Muslims[37]—and later the Commissioners of the Holy Crusade.[38]

We can find similar claims to control over vacant successions beyond the Iberian Peninsula, and indeed they were common in other European polities and in the Ottoman Empire.[39] However, according to Juan de Solórzano y Pereira, "a quite remarkable specificity"[40] characterised the context of the Kingdoms of the Indies: the existence of the so-called Juzgados de Bienes de Difuntos. Unlike in Castile, beginning in the mid-16th century, the Crown had begun to claim privative jurisdiction over the estates of those Spaniards who died without heirs in the so-called New World.

From 1526 onwards, the Crown began addressing what was increasingly seen as an urgent problem; pious provisions and bequests, particularly for the souls of the deceased, were not being fulfilled by the executors of wills.[41] It became immediately apparent that the great mobility triggered by the rise of global empires only increased the uncertainty of hereditary transmissions, now destined to cross the oceans. In the eyes of the Spanish Crown, entrusting the proper transmission of assets solely to the discretion of will executors could not be a solution.

---

entes y sin disponer de sus bienes", see Buono, "The King Heir", and Glesener, "La Cruzada et l'administration des biens vacants en Espagne (XVe–XVIIIe siècles)".

36 Lacruz Mantecón, *La ocupación imposible*.

37 This is no different from what was happening in Portugal. See Luis de Molina's reconstruction in *De Iustitia et Iure Editio Novissima*, Moguntiae 1659, T. I, *Disputatio 53*: "De variis bonorum generibus, quae domino carent. Et quae corum vacantia dicantur, et ad quem pertienant." On Molina, see Alonso-Lasheras, *Luis de Molina's De Iustitia et Iure*.

38 Martínez Millán and Carlos Morales, "Los orígenes del Consejo de Cruzada (siglo XVI)"; Glesener, "La Cruzada et l'administration des biens vacants en Espagne (XVe–XVIIIe siècles)".

39 A reconstruction can be found in Buono, "The King Heir". For the Ottoman Empire, see Grangaud, "Le Bayt al-mâl, les héritiers et les étrangers", and Tamdoğan, "Qu'advenait-t-il aux biens des 'étrangers' après leur décès dans la ville d'Adana au XVIII e siècle?".

40 An *especialidad bien notable*, to use the words of Solórzano Pereira, *Política Indiana*, Lib. 5, Cap. VII, p. 798.

41 Soberanes Fernández, "El Juzgado general de bienes de difuntos", 640–641. On the history of the Juzgados de Bienes de Difuntos, see also González Sánchez, *Dineros de ventura*. For an up-to-date bibliography of work which has made use of the Juzgados sources, see Fernández López, "El procedimiento y los expedientes de bienes de difuntos en la Casa de la Contratación de Indias (1503–1717)"; and Fernández López, *La Casa de la Contratación*.

After the creation of the Reales Audiencias in the Indies, an *oidor* (judge) in each jurisdiction was specifically entrusted with supervising and certifying the work of will executors and more generally with overseeing the protection of the so-called *bienes de difuntos*. The Juez General de Bienes de Difuntos (General Judge of the Estates of the Deceased), therefore, administered as a delegate of the sovereign a privative jurisdiction over the assets of the Spaniards (*naturales de los Reinos de España*) who died in the Kingdoms of the Indies. The Juzgado was to be informed of any Spaniard who died intestate, had to search for possible heirs present in the Indies and, in case of their absence, gather information on the existence of possible heirs on the Iberian Peninsula.[42] In this way, abeyant inheritances of the Spaniards were removed from ordinary jurisdiction and subjected to a special jurisdiction, which was ultimately called upon to defend the assets from misappropriation by the *vecinos* of the Kingdoms of the Indies. Moreover, the Juzgado was also entrusted with ensuring that they did not remain abandoned, and that they quickly found an administrator capable of not leaving them infertile.

Eventually, each Juzgado had to ensure that these assets were transferred to the Spanish Peninsula, where the alleged heirs could claim them in the Sevillian Casa de la Contratación (House of Trade). It is noteworthy that heirs who had not relocated to take possession of their inheritances in the Kingdoms of the Indies would only receive financial compensation.[43] They typically did not

42 As a law promulgated by Philip IV in 1653 said: "Ordenamos, que las causas de abintestados, se traten y conozcan en los Juzgados de bienes de difuntos, aunque no conste de la calidad de que los herederos y interessados estén en estos Reynos de Castilla, ó fuera de donde sucediere la muerte, con tal limitacion, que si el difunto dexare en la Provincia donde falleciere, notoriamente hijos, ó descendientes legitimos, por falta de ellos, tan conocidos, que no se dude del parentesco por descendencia, ó ascendencia, no ha de conocer el Juez general, sino las Justicias Ordinarias, y no constando con notoriedad lo contrario, tocará el conocimiento al Juez general, y faltando herederos, quedarán los bienes vacantes, y tocará el conocimiento al Juzgado de bienes de difuntos, pues el privilegio fiscal excluye a la jurisdicion ordinaria en este caso." Quoted in González Sánchez, *Dineros de ventura*, 36.

43 The typical procedure followed these steps: upon receiving information about a suspected intestate death, the officials of the Juzgados initiated the process by conducting an inventory and making a preventive seizure of the deceased's movable and immovable assets. Subsequently, commissioners were dispatched to gather details about the deceased's identity, investigate whether they had left a will and confirm the presence of potential heirs in the Iberian Peninsula. Eventually, the deceased's belongings were auctioned off to settle all claims and debts, with the first priority being the expenses related to the funeral and requiem masses. The remaining funds were remitted to the Casa de la Contratación, which publicly announced the arrival of the *bienes de difuntos*, inviting legitimate heirs to make their claims. If the inheritance remained vacant the entire sum would be forfeited to the Royal Treasury.

receive the most valuable assets, such as real estate, slaves and animals, which were instead auctioned off. In the vast majority of cases, this procedure therefore involved an economic loss and, unsurprisingly, Spaniards made efforts to avoid the Tribunal's intervention.[44]

These procedures were indeed influenced by practical considerations. Firstly, real estate, being immovable by definition, could obviously not be transferred to the Iberian Peninsula. Additionally, the lengthy duration of these procedures, often spanning decades, necessitated the liquidation of assets that would otherwise remain idle and abandoned and vulnerable to deterioration and ruin. Furthermore, these procedures allowed for the establishment of a cash reserve within the Audiencias' coffers that, while waiting to be sent to Seville, could be utilised in cases of emergency by local authorities (although this practice was prohibited). In any case, the primary goal of the courts was to prevent misappropriation and abandonment and expedite the occupation of those vacant inheritances by legitimate local owners. In fact, the Juez de Bienes de Difuntos was explicitly barred from intervening if the deceased's heirs were present in the Indies.[45] This restriction is evident in several instances where the sale of estates stalled due to claims by local heirs.[46]

To give just one example, we can cite the different outcomes of two hereditary transmissions relating to a father and a son. Baltasar Mexía de la Plaza, a Castilian from Cifuentes (Guadalajara), along with his brothers Melchor and Francisco, ventured to New Spain in the early 17th century, summoned by a letter informing them of a rich inheritance from a deceased relative in Mexico. After crossing the ocean, both he and Francisco married members of the prominent Godoy y Guzmán family in Guatemala. In the mid-1630s the Mexía de la Plaza brothers bought two farms (*haciendas*) with manufacturing enterprises and slaves (respectively, a water-powered sawmill and a *trapiche de azucar*— a sugar mill). Unlike Francisco, who had children in Guatemala, upon his death Baltasar left no direct heir in America. Baltasar's universal heir, Francisco Mexía Garcés, his son from a previous marriage, chose a different path than his father's and decided not to relocate to live on his inheritance in Guatemala: he

44 As shown by Tempère, *Vivre et mourir sur les navires du siècle d'or*; and Soberanes Fernández, "El Juzgado general de bienes de difuntos".

45 Ley de 1° de junio de 1619, Zamora y Coronado, *Biblioteca de legislación ultramarina en forma de diccionario alfabético*, tomo 2, letras B–C, p. 51. See also, *Recopilación de Leyes de los Reynos de las Indias* (L. II, T. XXXII) and Enciso Contreras, *Testamentos y autos de bienes de difuntos de Zacatecas (1550–1604)*.

46 Some cases are analysed in Buono, "'Tratándole como paysano y él a ellos'"; and Buono, "Naturali, vassalli e forestieri".

remained in Madrid and never set foot on Baltasar's *hacienda*, which he entrusted to an administrator.

Following a protracted dispute between the heir in Madrid and the family of María de Godoy y Guzmán (Baltasar's wife), when the administrator appointed by Francisco Mexía Garcés passed away, the local Juzgado de Bienes de Difuntos of Santiago de Guatemala eventually decided to auction off the *hacienda*, qualifying it as abandoned (*ynavitable, sola y tottalmente perdida*) and in ruin (*disipada y arruinada*). The fact that the estate faced the threat of dissolution, that the fields might have been left uncultivated, that the slaves could have died, and that all these assets were in jeopardy of being occupied or, possibly, encroached upon by the neighbouring commons of the indigenous people residing in those valleys, were all dangers exacerbated by the owner's absence. Ultimately, if Baltasar had been able to enjoy his property by moving to the Kingdoms of the Indies, his son Francisco could not do the same: at the end of the procedure, he was *de facto* expropriated and compensated with a meagre sum of money.[47]

What cases like this demonstrate is that the Juzgados de Bienes de Difuntos were tasked not only with safeguarding the Royal Treasury's right to claim vacant assets, but also with ensuring the reintegration of these assets into a local network of economic and human relations, guaranteeing their effective and beneficial utilisation for the common good. Ultimately, an absentee owner was undesirable and untrustworthy. Local wealth should benefit local communities rather than being squandered by an irresponsible owner who did not reside there or oversee its upkeep.[48] This was even more significant in the New World where abandoned assets posed a risk of hindering the progress of Christianity and civilisation by becoming "deserts" and "wastelands".[49]

47 I analysed this case in more detail in Buono, "The danger of ruin and the irresponsible owner".

48 This has been brilliantly illustrated by Bernard Derouet, who speaks of a "principle of locality" (*principe de localité* or *territorialité*), i.e., the idea that a person's rights are linked to the fact that he or she has remained in his or her family and community, and has continued to provide for them. Derouet, "Parenté et marché foncier à l'époque modern", 353.

49 This was pointed out, for the Spanish case, by Tamar Herzog, "Terres et déserts, société et sauvagerie". More generally, see Greer, *Property and Dispossession*.

4 Loneliness, Infertility and the Servitude (*Sèrvitus*) towards the Common Good

We saw that an abandoned and ruined land could be qualified as "lonely" and "lost", but also "sterile" and "infertile". What kind of conceptual constellation does the use of such terms reveal to us? To gain a deeper understanding of how these societies viewed abandoned assets, it is essential to examine how early modern European juridical culture could draw analogies between the status of people and the status of things in a manner that might appear peculiar to a modern perspective and, more importantly, how these statutes influenced each other.

Let us temporarily shift our focus away from the Iberian world and direct it toward France. In 1706, Emmanuel de Gama (probably Portuguese), a lawyer in the Paris Parliament, found himself representing the heirs of Martín de Esnos, a native of Huarte in Navarre.[50] Esnos, who was traveling from Peru to Europe on a French vessel, passed away unexpectedly in Paris. His inheritance, consisting of merchandise and silver bullion, was seized by the French fiscal authorities due to his foreign status and lack of descendants. Indeed, the high court of justice in Paris was enforcing the *droit d'aubaine*, which precisely mandated the confiscation of vacant inheritances of foreigners who passed away on the soil of the French Kingdom. In his defence speech, de Gama tried to prove that this right did not apply generically to foreigners (*étrangers*) passing through the Kingdom, but only to those who intended to permanently settle. Esnos, hence, was a 'mobile' traveller, not an 'immobile' *aubain*, so he could not be subject to confiscation of assets. In other words, his possessions did not belong to that Kingdom, because the traveller had no desire to remain there (he did not have an *animus permanendi*, we may say).

In his favour, de Gama quoted Jean Bacquet, author in the 1570s of the most important early modern treatise on *droit d'aubaine*.[51] Comparable to the English *escheat* and other "special types of inheritance rights" in favour of the Royal Treasury,[52] the *droit d'aubain* stipulated that for all "relics (*épaves*) born out-

50 De Gama, *Dissertation sur le droit d'aubaine*.

51 Bacquet, *Les Œuvres de M. Jean Bacquet*, t. 2. As Peter Sahlins has shown, Bacquet's treatise was the point of reference on *droit d'aubaine* throughout the ancient regime, see Sahlins, *Unnaturally French* and Cerutti, "À qui appartiennent les biens qui n'appartiennent à personne?".

52 The expression by Juan García González (*derecho sucesorio de tipo especial*) is used to distinguish this type of right from the right of reversion (*Heimfallsrecht*). García González, "La Mañería", 224–231. A similar discussion can be found in Tomás y Valiente, "La sucesión de quien muere sin parientes y sin disponer de sus bienes", 211. Indeed, there

side the Kingdom of France, if they have no legitimate heirs procreated by their body in the said Kingdom [...] the King must be their rightful heir."[53] So, according to Bacquet, foreigners (*aubeins*) without descent were "relics"—as if they were shipwrecked[54]—and were associated with a whole other set of figures, such as *bâtards* (bastards) and *manumis* (freed slaves),[55] whose liberty was affected by various restrictions. The right of *aubeine*, the right of *bastardise*, as well as of *mortes-mains* and *formariages*, limited the hereditary transmission of their assets and their right to marry without the lord's consent.[56] Such restrictions affected all these categories of people, who were considered to have no ancestors; the King, then, replaced their ancestors both at the time of their marriage, by granting or denying permission to marry, and, in the event of their death without legitimate descendants in the Kingdom, by becoming their heir.

In fact, what characterised all these individuals was their detachment from a lineage of succession,[57] rendering them both 'orphans' and 'infertile': hindered by royal customs from achieving legitimate descendance, they posed a threat

is debate among early modern jurists about how to regard this right claimed by the king, as witnessed by Peregrinus, *De iure et privilegiis Fisci*, Lib. IV, Tit. 3, or Klock, *Tractatus juridico-politico-polemico-historicus de Aerario*, Lib. II, Cap. 136. See Buono, "The King Heir", § 32–70. For the italian *diritto d'ubena, diritto d'albinaggio* and *leggi di forensità*, see Cerutti, "À qui appartiennent les biens qui n'appartiennent à personne?"; Maifreda, "I beni dello straniero"; Buono, "La manutenzione dell'identità"; Buono, "Anton Bogos Celibì e le eredità ab intestato nella Toscana di fine XVII secolo"; Dani, *Cittadinanze e appartenenze comunitarie*, 37–83.

53 "Tous Épaves natifs de dehors le Royaume de France, [...] s'ils n'ont hoirs legitimes procréez de leurs corps audit Royaume [...] le Roy est leur droit heritier." De Gama, *Dissertation sur le droit d'aubaine*, 37.

54 An association between the "poor" and the "orphan", people with no local ties in need of assistance from the Christian community, and the "shipwrecked" (*naufragis*) is found in Tertullian's *Apologeticum* (39, 5–6), where he discusses who should receive charity from the community's common chest: "All here is a free-will offering, and all these collections are deposited in a common bank for charitable uses, not for the support of merry meetings, for drinking and gormandizing, but for feeding the poor and burying the dead, and providing for girls and boys who have neither parents nor provisions left to support them, for relieving old people worn out in the service of the saints, or those who have suffered by shipwreck, or are condemned to the mines, or islands, or prisons, only for the faith of Christ" (Tertullian, *The Apology of Tertullian*, 110).

55 Bacquet, *Les Œuvres de M. Jean Bacquet*, t. 2, chap. IV, § 1–8, pp. 8–9.

56 They were all required to receive a dispensation from the king if they wished to marry someone of a condition different from their own, as marriage changed their status and that of their assets, incorporating them into a new corporate body. Bacquet, *Les Œuvres de M. Jean Bacquet*, t. 2, chap. IV, See also Steinberg, *Une tache au front*, 57.

57 Cerutti, "À qui appartiennent les biens qui n'appartiennent à personne?", 379 and seq.

to social reproduction.[58] Furthermore, people's sterility was somehow believed to be transmissible to objects. We may say that the assets left by these derelicts were themselves at risk of becoming relics and were a particular type of asset among those who remained without possessor: they were known as *estrayers* or *biens espaves*,[59] *res derelictae* subject to the claims of both local communities and lords, on the one hand, and the sovereign, on the other.

These *relics*, these entities, both people and things, which appear to remain detached from the body of the Kingdom, required a process of reintegration into stable social relations. The term *estraier*, which encompassed both things and individuals, precisely denoting their lack of familial and local rootedness,[60] is defined as follows in a 19th-century glossary: "*Estraier*, wanderer, vagabond [...]. *Estrayer*, [...] the scattered possessions of bastards and strangers",[61] from the Old French *estrai* which also gave birth to the English verb *to stray*, the action of wandering, applicable to both people and animals.[62]

On the one hand, as we have seen, the same constellation of concepts could encompass wandering individuals, stray animals or abandoned livestock isolated from the herd, wandering without an owner. On the other hand, the abandoned assets of a foreigner or a person without descendants, goods 'extracted'

---

58 "*Aubeins* are people whose place of birth is unknown, nor do we know where they came from: as can be said of newborn babies by some young women who wish to remain unknown, and therefore have them placed in front of a church door. [...] or some legitimate children descended from bastards or relics, of whom the King is universal heir when they die, if they have no legitimate children" (*Tous Aubeins sont personnes qui ne sçavent dont ils sont naiz, ne dont ils sont extraits: comme on pourroit dire, enfans nouveauz nasquis, & gaignez par aucunes jeunes femmes desirans estre celées: & pour ce les font mettre aux huys d'aucunes Eglises [...]. Ou aucuns enfans legitimez décendus de Bastards ou Espaves, dequels le Roy est heritier de tout quand ils trépassent, s'ils n'ont enfans legitimez*). Bacquet, *Les Œuvres de M. Jean Bacquet*, t. 2, cit., chap. IV, § 13, p. 10.

59 "Estrayers, sont les biens demeurez de tels Aubeins & Espaves, qui sont demeurans au Royaume, & vont de vie à trépas sans hoir naturel de leurs corps nez au Royayme. Estrayers parcillement sont les biens des Bâtards" Bacquet, *Traité*, cit., chap. IV, § 25, pp. 10–11. French law glossaries contain the definition of *biens estrayers* as "biens espaves" or "les biens des *étrangers* dévolus au fisc, mais par la suite des temps, ce nom a été donné à toutes sortes de confiscations." Ragueau, *Glossaire du droit françois, contenant l'explication des mots*, vol. I, 450.

60 Emmanuel de Gama, in fact, used the example of a tree planted in the earth, casting its roots, to discuss the difference between a passing foreigner and someone who intended to settle permanently in a place: "c'est pourquoi l'Exemple de l'arbre, quoique de la chose à la personne, est applicable". De Gama, *Dissertation sur le droit d'aubaine*, 49–50.

61 "Estraier, errant, vagabond [...]. Estrayer, [...] les biens épars des bâtards et des étrangers." Gachet, *Glossaire roman des chroniques rimées de Godefroid de Bouillon*, vol. III, p. 749.

62 *Oxford Dictionary of English*, ad vocem.

from a genealogical chain, were also, in a certain sense, qualified as "wanderers", "sterile", and "strangers to the land". These possessions were considered as detached from their community, separated and isolated due to their association with incapacitated beings, such as the freed slave, the recently converted to the Christian faith,[63] the foreigner or the bastard. On these things, as on these people, the King of France claimed a right of special protection, qualified as a "right of attraction",[64] in constant competition with local jurisdictions.

Similar claims and analogies between the status of people and things like these are not unique to the Kingdom of France. The same imagery can be found in medieval and early modern Iberian sources. For instance, consider the usage of terms like *yermas*, *hermas* or *ermas*, derived from the Latin *eremus*, meaning solitary or desert, to describe uncultivated lands, found in both Portuguese and Spanish sources. Solitary inheritances (*herdades hermas*) are, for example, those abandoned lands that the king ordered to be returned to sowing and working, as dictated to the Cortes d'Elvas (1361).[65] Especially in frontier regions, the land left uncultivated by labourers who went to reside in Castile was a threat to the common good of the Portuguese communities, who begged the ruler to compel them to return and take care of their inheritances and not to enrich the lands of the neighbouring Kingdom.[66] Accordingly, a 15th-century law prohibited those who owned land in Portugal and left it to live in neigh-

63 Often, the boundaries between these two categories blur. The lord's right to inherit from a manumitted slave, which was already present in Roman Law, is also evident in medieval Spain, where it applied to converted Muslim servants. It can also be observed in the Islamic and the Jewish world, where a neo-convert to Judaism was the only one whose vacant inheritance was subject to escheat since he was conceived as having no ancestral connection to the original twelve tribes of Israel. García González, "La Mañería", 239–240. Aykan, "On Freedom, Kinship, and the Market"; Rackman, "A Jewish Philosophy of Property", 79.

64 "Attrayere, […] qui vient du latin *attrahere*, attirer à soi, signifie, dans quelques coutumes, le droit qu'a le seigneur haut-justicier de s'emparer des biens vacans, à titre de bâtardise, d'épave ou de confiscation", Denisart, *Collection de décisions nouvelles et de notions relatives à la jurisprudence*, vol. 2, 533.

65 "Foi mandado per El Rei nosso Padre em Cortes aos sobredictos que fezessem lavrar e afreutar as herdades e vinhas hermas que tiinham em alghuũas Comarcas dos nossos Regnos que soyam seer lavradas e que nom curarom de o fazer". Santarém, *Alguns documentos para servirem de provas a' parte 2.a*, 4–5.

66 "Grande perda Recebe esta Villa em os lauradores della jrem laurar aos Regnos de castella por cuja cauza as terras que na dita Villa ha se perdem e sam hermas por non sseerem aproueitadas e as terras de castella por serem aproueitadas dos lauradores desta Villa multiplicam cada uez majs e sam mjlhores" (the *Juizes Vereadores* and *procurador* of Elvas to the King, 1498). Santarém, *Alguns documentos para servirem de provas a' parte 1.a*, 85–86.

bouring Castile from cultivating it and extracting its fruits unless they returned to settle in the Kingdom. After a year, these estates could be seized and regranted by the Crown to local owners.[67]

The negligence of people who abandoned their communities to engage in trades that were not deemed "beneficial to the common good" (*proveitosos pera o bem comum*) led to the abandonment of the land, causing great harm to society as a whole.[68] This gave rise to regulations like the so-called laws *das sesmarias*—central to the appropriation and granting of colonial lands, like the Spanish *mercedes* and *composiciones de tierras*[69]—which tied the holding of land to the obligation to work it.[70] In this way, it would have been ensured that "the estates, which are for giving bread, should all be plowed and used" (*as herdades, que som pera dar pam, sejam todas lavradas, e aproveitadas*).[71] Otherwise, the King could recover the lands from these absentee landlords, and grant it to more careful possessors. At the same time, it was not possible for those who were not rooted in the Kingdom to dispose of the fruits of the land and the ownership of those assets could only go to those who were committed to reside in them. The seizure of property and its reassignment were thus justified by the maintenance of the common good.

These ideas were also at the centre of the Castilian *Siete Partidas*, where the King was entrusted with the supreme guardianship over all the people and things of his Kingdom, as well as with the duty to love and care for them:

---

67 "Alguũs moradores nos lugares dos estremos dos Nossos Regnos se vaaõ morar aos Regnos de Castella, e teem seus beẽs em os Nossos Regnos, e d'onde moram e vivem veem adubar seus beẽs, e colher os fructos, e os levam, e fazem delles o que lhes apraz; e quando assy vaaõ, e veem, fazem muitos homezios, e furtos, e outros maleficios, e acolhem-se aos Regnos de Castella, honde moram e vivem: seguindo-se desto aa Nossa terra, e moradores muitos dapnos. [...] Qualquer, que beẽs tever em Nossos Regnos, que venha a elles morar e viver, ou os venda da dada desta nossa Carta ataa hum anno; e qualquer que o contrairo fezer, perderá os beẽs que tever pera Nós, e que os daremos a quem nossa mercee for." *Ordenações Afonsinas*, Livro IV, Título XLIV, *Dos Moradores em Castella, que teem beens em Portugal, que os vendam a tempo certo, ou venham a cá morar*, § 1, 165–166.

68 "As terras e herdades, que soyam a seer lavradas e semeadas, e que som convinhavees pera dar pam, e outros fruitos, per que se os Povoos ham de manter, som desamparadas, e deitadas em Ressios, sem prol, e com grande dapno do Povo." *Ordenações Afonsinas*, Livro IV, Título LXXXI, *Das Sesmarias*, § 1, 282.

69 Herzog, *Frontiers of Possession*, 115–126. Greer, *Property and Dispossession*, 120–121.

70 "Que todos os que ham herdades suas proprias, ou teverem emprazadas, ou afforadas, ou per qualquer outra guisa ou título, per que ajam direito em essas herdades, sejam costrangidos pera as lavrar, e semear." *Ordenações Afonsinas*, Livro IV, Título LXXXI: *Das Sesmarias*, § 2, 282–283.

71 *Ordenações Afonsinas*, Livro IV, Título LXXXI: *Das Sesmarias*, § 2, 282–283.

> The King is not only obligated to love, honour and preserve his people [...] but also the very land over which he rules. For both he and his people derive their sustenance from the things that are in it. And they have everything necessary, as far as they perform all their rightful acts and love, honour and preserve it. [...] The love that the King must have for his land is of two kinds. [...] The first, which is in will, consists of desiring it to be well-populated and cultivated [...]. The second, which is in deeds, involves populating it with good people, primarily his own rather than foreigners, [...] and working it so that men may have its fruits more abundantly. [...] The King should not desire it to remain solitary, nor for it to go uncultivated.[72]

Furthermore, the King had to make sure that the lands, cities and places of the Kingdom were not abandoned, leaving things in danger of ruin, or worse voluntarily damaged:

> The King must be diligent in safeguarding his land in such a way that the towns and other places are not left abandoned, and the walls, towers and other structures are not demolished due to negligence. Likewise, the trees, vineyards and other things that sustain people's lives should not be cut down, burned, uprooted or harmed in any other way.[73]

---

72 "Tenudo es el rey no tan solamente de amar, e honrrar e guardar a su pueblo [...], mas aun a la tierra misma, de que es Señor. Ca pues que el e su gente, biuen delas cosas, que enella son. E han della, todo lo que les es menester, con que cumplen e fazen todos sus fechos derecho es la amen, e la honnren, e la guardem. E el amor que el rey deue auer, es en dos maneras. [...] La que es en voluntad, deue ser cobdiciando, que sea ben poblada e labrada [...]. La segunda, que es de fecho, es en fazer la poblar de buena gente, e ante de los suyos que de los agenos, [...] e labrarla, porque ayan los omes los frutos della mas abondadamente. [...] Con todo esso, non deue el Rey querer que le finque yerma, ni por labrar" (*Las Siete Partidas glosadas por el Licenciado Gregorio López*, P. II, T. XI "Qual deue el Rey ser a su tierra", ley I "Como el Rey deue amar a su tierra"). In the *Bocados de Oro*, one of Aristotle's teachings to Alexander the Great read like this, "Por tres cosas se onran los reyes: por poner fermosas leyes, e por conquerir buenas conquistas e por poblar las tierras yermas." Guadalajara Salmerón, *Bocados de oro: edición crítica y estudio*, 476 (*Dichos de Aristóteles*, XXIII, § 34).

73 "Acucioso deue ser el Rey en guardar su tierra, de manera que se non yermen las villas, nin los otros logares, ni se derriben los muros, ni las torres, ni las casas, por mala guarda. E otrosi, que los arboles, ni las viñas, ni las otras cosas, de que los omes biuen, ni los corten, ni los quemen, ni los derrayguen, ni los dañen de otra manera" (*Las Siete Partidas glosadas por el Licenciado Gregorio López*, P. II, T. XI, ley III "Como el Rey deue guardar su tierra").

It was therefore just to seize land to ensure that its lack of use or misuse did not cause harm to the land and its inhabitants, causing things and people to fall into ruin. These ideas remained relevant during the early modern age to the extent that we find them discussed with particular attention in the theological and legal debates among the leading scholars of the School of Salamanca. Since all things were originally created for the common benefit of mankind,[74] ownership (*dominium proprietatis*)—while firmly anchored in a 'faculty' (*facultas*) and a 'power' (*potestas*) inherent to human beings as images of the supreme Lord and *dominus*[75]—nonetheless remained constrained by the original purpose of using all things for the satisfaction of the common good.

As Francisco Suárez stated, although the King did not have an arbitrary power to dispossess an owner, it was as if, after things had been distributed through the *ius gentium* or positive law, they retained an servitude towards the fulfilment of the common good (*quasi servitutem respectu boni publici*), permitting their reassignment in the event of use contrary to the original intended purpose.[76] This was what Suárez called the *dominium altum*, superordinate and more 'general' to the ownership rights of the 'particular' owners (*dominium particularis*), that belonged to the Prince, as the head and father of the Kingdom, its supreme administrator and bestower of its resources, as well as more generally to each and every corporate body.[77] This power of the supreme administrator (*potestas supremi dispensatoris et administratoris bonorum reipublicae*), which was the responsibility of the representative of the body politic, was in fact inherent to the *Respublica* itself.

In effect, if the sovereign claimed to be the supreme guardian,[78] each body exercised the same power over its resources and produced regulations for this

74 On the efforts made by the Iberian early modern scholastics to reconcile the de facto existence of private ownership with the theological principle of the primitive communism of goods, see Gómez Camacho, *Economía y filosofía moral*, chap. 3.

75 Paolo Grossi insists on seeing in the School of Salamanca, despite different positions and gradations, the prodromes of the birth of *homo oeconomicus* and of the modern anthropology of the subject that resolves the relationship between persons and things "more into a power over things than into a relationship between subjects relative to a thing". Grossi, "La proprietà nel sistema privatistico della Seconda Scolastica", 218–219.

76 "Nam de iure gentium est, ut nullus privetur possessione sua [...] consuetudo inducere potest modum, et conditionem domini, atque adeo potest introducere, ut dominia particularia includant illam conditionem, et quasi servitutem respectu boni publici". Francisco Suárez, *De Legibus ac Deo Legislatore*, (1612) l. 7, c. 4, n. 6 (quoted in Maccioni, *Il 'dominium altum' nella dottrina di Soto, Molina, Suarez*, 54).

77 Quoted in Maccioni, *Il 'dominium altum' nella dottrina di Soto, Molina, Suarez*, 50.

78 From this perspective, Luca Mannori's paradigm of the 'sovereign guardian' (*sovrano tutore*) review by Bartolomé Clavero is very interesting. Clavero pointed out that through-

purpose, as is evident in cities' statutes. For instance, the statutes and ordinances concerning the "tilled land and outer commons"[79] (*huertas y montes*) of Zaragoza collected in 1593, and republished in 1799 and 1861, prescribe as follows:

> Those who have fallow inheritances (*erdades yermas*) within [...] the boundaries of this City, although they can be irrigated, since they were formerly outer commons (*montes*): it is ordained and established that any persons who have left such lands fallow [...] uncultivated for more than ten years, within three years from today, must cultivate, sow or plant them, under penalty that if they do not do so within that time, after that, any citizen (*vezino*) of the present City may take them, plant and cultivate them without any penalty or blame, in accordance with the ancient statutes of the City's tilled lands and outer commons. And the vineyards that become fallow from this day onwards, their masters and owners must replant, cultivate or sow them within ten years [...] under penalty that if they do not do so, and leave them fallow [...], any citizen of the present City may take such fallow vineyards, and plant, cultivate and sow them for their own benefit and profit, without any penalty or blame. And if it should happen that someone cultivate such fallow lands and then three years pass without them having planted, cultivated or sown vineyards on them; in that case, the citizens of the present City may take them in the same way as if those lands (*erdades*) were in the outer commons (*montes*) of the present City.[80]

out the early modern age, not only did supreme powers legitimise their intervention in this manner, but so did any power within that pluralistic system. Mannori, *Il sovrano tutore*; Clavero, "Tutela administrativa o dialogos con Tocqueville". On closer inspection, even Súarez asserted that this 'high power' belonged to the "prince or commonwealth" (*in principe, vel in republica*). "Respublica etiam per potestatem altiorem, quam habet ad regendos homines, potest ex iuxta causa (ut in poenam) hominem privare sua libertate", Maccioni, *Il 'dominium altum' nella dottrina di Soto, Molina, Suarez*, 50 and 52.

79 I take this definition from Alan Greer: "areas on the periphery of a village's croplands where resources were collectively owned and communally managed". Greer, *Property and Dispossession*, 249. "Areas shared by several communities (*mancomunales*), also defined as *montes*, or 'uplands,' [...]. Communities had usage rights over them and their management provided a framework for political action at the local scale that, despite its weak level of formalization, was effective". Viso, "Communs et dynamiques de pouvoir dans l'Europe du Sud médiévale", 17.

80 "Los que tuvieren erdades yermas en los términos [...] de la presente Ciudad, aunque se puedan regar, por quanto han sido antes Montes: se ordena y estatuye, que qualesquiere

Thus, the goal of avoiding abandonment not only concerned the Prince and his laws, but also the normative regimes produced by the self-organisation of the local territorial bodies.[81] We find here the same concerns toward the productivity of community resources, toward the avoidance of the loneliness of the lands, toward their reintroduction into a reproduction cycle that is both economic and genealogical. The lands we are discussing, originally qualified as commons, were indeed "inheritances" allocated to families to be passed down in a genealogical chain, ideally indefinitely, thus perpetuating both the 'native' families and the community. So, acquisitive prescription merely reaffirmed the *reicentrism* and "servitude towards the common good" mentioned above.[82] It is the inherent nature of things that gives rise to these norms, not mere human will. Lands that were created by God to provide sustenance for human beings and its social associations must ultimately be placed in a condition to fulfil that purpose.

---

personas que tuvieren yermos algunos […] que no los ayan culturado por tiempo de más de diez años, que dentro de tres años, del día de oy adelante, los ayan de labrar, sembrar, o plantar, so pena, que si dentro dicho tiempo no lo hizieren, pasado aquel, qualquiere vezino de la presente Ciudad se los pueda tomar, plantar, y labrar sin pena ni calonia alguna; conforme a los Estatutos antiguos de los Escalios, y montes de la Ciudad. Y las Viñas que del presente día en adelante se hizieren yermas, los señores y dueños dellas las ayan de bolver a plantar, labrar, o sembrar, dentro tiempo de diez años […] so pena, que si no lo hizieren, y las dexaren yermas […] qualquier vezino de la presente Ciudad pueda tomar las tales Viñas yermas, y plantar, y labrar, y sembrarlas para su utilidad y provecho, sin pena ni calonia alguna. Y si caso fuere que algunos labraren dichos yermos, y después pasaren tres años que no uvieren sembrado, labrado, o plantado Viña en ellos; en tal caso los vezinos de la presente Ciudad se los puedan tomar, de la mesma manera como si fuesen dichas erdades en los Montes de la presente Ciudad". The spelling has been partially normalised to aid reading. *Estatutos y ordinaciones de las guertas y montes de la Ciudad de Çaragoça, De los Montes*, cap. 11, *De los yermos de los terminos de Miralbueno, y Planos de Fuentes*, fol. 1^{r}.

81 See Bastias Saavedra (Chapter 1) in this volume.

82 It is worth noting that prescription ceased if the owner had built a brick house on the abandoned land because it is then presumed that "the house holds possession of said lands" (*que la tal Casa está en la posesión con las tales tierras*). In these cases, the time during which the lands can be abandoned is extended from three to ten years (*Estatutos y ordinaciones de las guertas y montes de la Ciudad de Çaragoça, De los Montes*, cap. 11, *De los yermos de los terminos de Miralbueno, y Planos de Fuentes*, fol. 2^{r}). The presence of a stable building continues to represent the absentee lord, creating a presumption of possession and reducing the chances of a challenge due to abandonment. As can be seen, the theory of Moses of Ravenna remained in operation throughout the early modern age and beyond. In Italy it was actively used in courts by the mid-20th century, as Ennio Cortese has shown. Cortese, "Per la storia di una teoria dell'arcivescovo Mosè di Ravenna (m. 1154) sulla proprietà ecclesiastica".

The task of the good ruler, therefore, was to ensure all the human or non-human entities under his care were incorporated into a chain of reproduction, mainly because both 'fertility' and 'stability' of persons and things influenced each other and depended on their active contribution to the community life.[83] In the *Ordenamiento de Menestrales* (1351), the King Pedro I of Castile and León sought to limit beggars and vagrancy, ordering that "no men or women who are fit to work should wander as vagrants (*baldíos*) through my lordship, neither begging nor seeking charity, but all should work and live from the labour of their hands."[84] Vagrant people could produce "vagrant things", such as the Spanish *bienes baldíos* or the Portuguese *bens vagos*.

Once again, we see the same concepts being applied to things and people. The discussion concerning the nature of *bens vagos* can be found within the broader context of the *disputationes* regarding the forms of acquiring ownership. For instance, Luis de Molina, attentive to the interplay of Roman law and the Iberian *ius proprium*, distinguished between various categories of things without an owner (ranging from items that never had a master to those that have not been possessed since time immemorial, from abandoned items to actual *bona vacantia* or vacant inheritances). The Spanish Jesuit states that there were numerous disputes over the right to occupy, claim, and use these assets, including claims by the first occupant, their use for the redemption of captives or other charitable purposes, all the way to their incorporation into the Crown domain. Anyway, he had to note that in the Ordinances *bens vagos* basically meant vacant inheritances and that they were claimed by the King.[85] In the mid-18th century, Antonio Cortez Bremeu,[86] while still assessing Molina's doubts and distinctions, reported under the term *bens vagos* "all

83 "E el Rey que desta guisa, que sobredicha es, amare e touiere, honrrada e guardada su tierra: sera el, e los, que y biuieren, honrrados, e ricos, e abondados, e temidos por ella. E si de otra guisa lo fiziesse venir le ya el contrario desto". (*Las Siete Partidas glosadas por el Licenciado Gregorio López*, P. II, T. XI, ley III).

84 "Tengo por bien e mando que ningunos omes nin mujeres que sean e pertenescan para labrar, non anden baldíos por el mío sennorío, nin piden mendigando; mas que todos labren e vivan por labor de sus manos", quoted in Iglesia García, "El debate sobre el tratamiento a los pobres durante el siglo XVI", 7. "Dans la Castille de l'époque moderne, on appelait *baldíos* (sans feu ni lieu) aussi bien les vagabonds qui 'allaient de par le monde sans raison ni profit' que les friches inhabitées ou le bétail errant", in Herzog, "Terres et déserts, société et sauvagerie. De la communauté en Amérique et en Castille à l'époque moderne", 532.

85 Molina, *De Iustitia et Iure Editio Novissima*, T. I, *Disputatio 53*, "De variis bonorum generibus, quae domino carent. Et quae corum vacantia dicantur, et ad quem pertienant."

86 António Cortez Bremeu, *Universo Jurídico*, 400 et seq. "Tit. XXIV, Como se adquire o dominio de alguns outros bens, que não tem proprietario §.1. Varios bens, que carecem de proprio dono."

things without an owner" (*bens que não tem dono propio*) and particularly "those which someone leaves when they die without disposing of them and have no heirs."[87] These inheritances that remained 'useless' and somehow 'vagrant', both according to the *ius commune* and according to the *Ordenaçoes* of Portugal, had to be incorporated into the Crown patrimony, and the supreme administrator would redistribute them again for the sake of the public good.[88]

A stable presence, local commitment, and care were what ultimately ensured fertility, which was among the ultimate purposes and duties of every being created by the Biblical God. Infertile people and barren lands were to be discouraged: the rights of *mañería* and *maninhadengo* affected childless people whose infertility could be transmitted to the land, by imposing on them and their patrimony "a kind of punishment against infertility" (from the seizure of one-third of the assets, up to the confiscation of the entire estate).[89] The parallel Catalan *exorquía* (from *aixorch axorch, exorch*, sterile), derived from the Latin word *esterilitas*,[90] the Spanish *mañería* or the Portuguese *maninhado*, in all their forms derived from the Hispanic Latin *manninus* (corresponding to *sterilis, infoecundus*),[91] was used from the 12th century onwards to qualify both people without descendants and uncultivated land. The *bens maninhos* was used as synonymous with the previously mentioned *bens vagos*.[92] Ultimately, the mobility of the people who left their things unattended, as well as their barrenness that would leave them outside a chain of succession, was dangerous in that it could transmit those same qualities to the things of the Kingdom, making them unrooted and sterile, preventing them from performing their intended function in service of the common good.

---

87 "Aquelles, que algum deixa quando morre sem delles dispor, e naõ tem herdeiros." Cortez Bremeu, *Universo Jurídico*, 401.

88 Ordenações Afonsinas 2,24,12, "§ 3. Disserom as Leys Imperiaaes, que Direito Real he [...] § 12, Item. Todolos beẽs, a que non he achado certo Senhor". Ordenações Manuelinas 2,15,16, "§ 6. Item Direito Real he poder o Principe tomar [...] § 16. Item todos os bens vaguos, a que nom he achado certo senhorio". *Ordenações Filipinas* 2,26,17 "§ 7. Direito Real he poder o Principe tomar [...] § 17. [...] todos os bens vagos, a que não he achado senhor certo". Quoted in Magalhães "O Estado como herdeiro legítimo", 2375.

89 García González, "La Mañería", 252.

90 García González, "La Mañería", 253.

91 Oliveira, "Dissertaçam particular, que examina que são Maninhos", 203.

92 "Assim foram chamados os bens, que ficavam por morte do homem, ou mulher casados que morriam sem filios, e sem fazer testamento, não tendo parente atè o decimo gráo: estes costumava o Almoxarife d'El-Rei tomar para a coroa." Santa Rosa de Viterbo, *Elucidario das palavras, termos e frases que em Portugal antigamente se usaram*, t. 2, 76.

5 Conclusion: The Owner as Administrator and Its Constitutional Role

In this Chapter, I have analysed the underlying principles that characterise the early modern ownership regimes building on the extreme case of vacant and abandoned estates. It is important to note that 'abandoned things' are not an entity: there is no such a thing as *wastelands* in nature.[93] What we have been discussing are, in fact, qualifying operations performed on things by actors.[94] These operations are aimed at legitimising actions, creating statuses and relationships between such things and the people interested or tied to them. However, it is by reading through these operations that we gain insight into ownership as a system of relationships,[95] understanding the principles and stakes at play behind them.

What I have argued is that to gain a better understanding of practices and norms concerning the relationships between things and people in the early modern Iberian worlds, certain assumptions are crucial. First and foremost, it is essential to take seriously the perspective of a worldview dominated by a *relational* and *reicentric* concept of the relationship between people and things.[96] In such a juridical culture, which thought of social bodies as communities of things and people, the rights emanating from things, specifically their right to be used according to intrinsic purposes inscribed within their nature, still had their place in the normative regime. Furthermore, social relations between things and people, as well as among people themselves, were ultimately conceived in terms of possession,[97] and persons and things (both material and immaterial) in this normative regime seem to have been entirely interchangeable entities whose statuses mutually influenced each other. It is likely, although it was not this chapter's aim to prove this, that other societies beyond Europe shared some of these traits, starting with corporate rather than individualistic types of social organisation.[98]

93 Herzog, "How Did the Commons Become Terra nullius?".

94 Cayla, "La qualification ou la vérité du droit".

95 See the anthropological conception of "property relations" discussed in Hann (ed.), *Property relations*.

96 In a sense, it can be said, with Baptiste Morizot, that the ancient regime's ontology is still largely pre-humanistic, relational and "chosiste". Morizot, "L'écologie contre l'Humanisme", § 34.

97 See Conte, *Servi medievali*; Madero, *La loi de la chair*; and Madero, "Penser la physique du pouvoir".

98 To cite a comparative work that I have personally conducted with my colleague Luca Gabbiani, see Buono and Gabbiani (eds.), *Sous tutelle*. More generally, a vast ongoing anthro-

Secondly, these same relations, along with the rights and obligations that arose from them, were closely associated with a duty of care. Only those who actively engaged and sustained these relations through consistent, undisputed and responsible use were ultimately deemed worthy of possessing them.[99] Absence[100] delegitimised possession vis-à-vis the corporate bodies ultimately entrusted with the administration (*administratio*) and allocation (*dispensatio*) of all material and immaterial resources belonging to (or claimed by) them. Responsible use and care toward things, therefore, formed the foundation for building trust. Only the faithful (*fideles*), in the sense of individuals worthy of trust (*fides*), were ultimately deemed reliable and legitimate owners of these relationships.[101] Being a trustworthy member meant shouldering local burdens, such as paying taxes, attending assemblies, cultivating the land and residing permanently. Therefore, the privilege of enjoying rights associated with membership (such as ownership of real estate,[102] access to public offices, charity,[103] and even to the labour market[104]) was closely tied to the demonstration of love

pological reflection tends to see in *ancien régime* Europe something profoundly different from Western modernity, as Descola has shown in *Par-delà nature et culture*. To give just two examples, consider how in medieval times not only the Cartesian mind-body opposition, but also the supposedly dualistic opposition body-soul were not actually as clear-cut as one might think, as Jérôme Baschet has shown in *Corps et âmes*; or consider the extraordinary air of familiarity noted by António Manuel Hespanha between traditional European and Chinese legal-political thought: Hespanha, "Incursión en el pensamiento jurídico político chino".

99 On the link between ownership rights and rights of citizenship, see in particular the work of Simona Cerutti, and more generally the work of the research group she directed. Bargaoui, Cerutti and Grangaud (dir.), *Appartenance locale et propriété au nord et au sud de la Méditerranée*.

100 This has been shown to us by Bernard Derouet in "Territoire et parenté"; "Les pratiques familiales, le droit et la construction des différences (XVe–XIXe siècles)"; and "Parenté et marché foncier à l'époque moderne". For an anthropological reflection, see Ferguson, *Give a Man a Fish*; and Ferguson, *Presence and Social Obligation*.

101 Todeschini, *I mercanti e il tempio*, 21.

102 Bargaoui, Sami, Simona Cerutti and Isabelle Grangaud (dir.), *Appartenance locale et propriété au nord et au sud de la Méditerranée*.

103 Cerutti, *Giustizia sommaria*; Torre, *Il consumo di devozioni*; Torre, "Cause Pie"; Colombo, *Carità*; Buono, "La manutenzione dell'identità"; Buono, "'Tratándole como paysano y él a ellos'".

104 During the *ancien régime*, labour itself was regarded as "a *local* resource, rooted in a specific location, and primarily intended for those belonging to that locality". The labour market, like the land market, in other words, was conceived as a "corporate market" to which only members of the body corporate had access. Trade guilds, therefore, rather than merely regulating standards of production, were channels of access to this restricted-access market. Cerutti, "Lavoro e cittadinanza", 236.

and care for the community, as much as was being *natural* to a place and originating from a *native* family.[105] In other words, only the care towards things inscribed in the community demonstrated what jurists called an *animus permanendi*, a will to remain, which transformed a foreigner into a responsible member of both a family and a locality, to whom local rights and duties could be entrusted.

Lastly, all entities within this ownership regime were ideally bound to specific functions. Every being, whether human or non-human, whether living or deceased, had an established role within the natural order established at the moment of creation. The task of the owner and rightful possessor is that of a *pro tempore* guardian, a shepherd who guides things toward the fulfilment of their purposes. Therefore, he bears responsibilities not only to his family, community, and the *Respublica* but, above all, to the things themselves (and again this resonates with what can be seen in other societies both past and present).[106] From this perspective, it could be said that the entailment of an estate for the purpose of reproducing a family or a corporate body (such as the *fideicommissum* and its various medieval and early modern European manifestations, but also any other form of *inalienable possession* like the Islamic *waqf*, East Asian *ritual property*, etc.)[107] is not the exception but the ideal in these societies. Both people and things circulated within closed 'corporate markets' whose access was linked to membership.[108] In conclusion, this is why abandoned things were perceived as so dangerous in these societies: their infertility was not only economic but also constitutional. Ensuring continuity and reproduction appears to be among the primary concerns of the early modern societies discussed here.[109]

105 On the fact that it ultimately makes no sense to contrast *ius soli* and *ius sanguinis*, but that the two principles are always interpenetrated, see the seminal works of Herzog, *Defining Nations*; and Cerutti, *Étrangers*.

106 And this seems not to be specific of Indigenous American societies only, but also African ones. See, for example, what Liberski-Bagnoud, "Les Gardiens de la Terre" discusses regarding the figure of the *guardian of the land*. Comparable logics are also evident in the contemporary world, as illustrated by Emilia Schijman's sociological and ethnographic work on Argentina and France—in Schijman, *Vivir de prestado*, and in Schijman, "From abandoned properties to commons"—or by Claire Herbert who analyses the "rise of property informality" and "ethos of care" in 21st-century Detroit: Herbert, *A Detroit Story*.

107 Deuchler, *Under the Ancestors' Eyes*; Bargaoui, Cerutti and Grangaud (dir.), *Appartenance locale et propriété au nord et au sud de la Méditerranée*; Buono and Gabbiani, *Sous tutelle*.

108 Cerutti and Grangaud (eds.), *Fuori Mercato*.

109 Fundamental, in this regard, are the works of the anthropologist Annette Weiner, "Reproduction: A Replacement for Reciprocity"; and *Inalienable Possessions*. Weiner's work is a critical reading that starts from the famous *The Gift* by Marcel Mauss, who already in the

Acknowledgments

Many of the reflections in this chapter would not have been possible without the discussions I had with Simona Cerutti and Emilia Schijman, to whom I am grateful (for the outcome of this collaboration see Buono, Cerutti and Schijman "Responsibility and Presence"). Furthermore, this chapter was developed within the framework of the project "Propriété et citoyenneté au nord et au sud de la Méditerranée (XVIe–XIXe siècles)" (financed by the French Agence Nationale de la Recherche, 2017–2021, convention N°ANR-16-CE41-0006-01) (https://procit.hypotheses.org). The results of this collective effort have been published in Cerutti, Glesener, and Grangaud, *La Cité des Choses*. In addition, this research has been supported by the project "Constructing Intergenerational Ties: Charity and Welfare in Italy and the Iberian World (16th–19th Centuries)" (Next-GenerationEU—Piano Nazionale di Ripresa e Resilienza (PNRR)—Missione 4 Componente 2, Investimento N. 1.1, Bando PRIN 2022 D.D. 104 del 02-02-2022—CUP N. I53D23000160006).

Bibliography

Printed Sources

Bacquet, Jean, *Les Œuvres de M. Jean Bacquet* [...], Lyon 1744: Chez les Frères Duplain.

Bodin, Jean, *Les Six Livres de la République* [...], Lyon 1580: Par Iacques du Puys.

Bodin, Jean, *The six bookes of a commonweale* [...], London 1606: Impensis G. Bishop.

Cortez Bremeu, António, *Universo Jurídico, ou jurisprudência Universal Canonica e Cesaria regulada pelas disposições de ambos Direitos commum e pátrio*, Lisboa, por Domingos Rodrigues, 1749.

De Gama, Emmanuel, *Dissertation sur le droit d'aubaine* [...], Paris 1706: C. Moette.

Denisart, Jean-Baptiste, *Collection de décisions nouvelles et de notions relatives à la jurisprudence*, Paris 1783: chez la Veuve Desaint.

Estatutos y ordinaciones de las guertas y montes de la Ciudad de Çaragoça, Zaragoza 1593.

early 20th century had understood the similarities between the way Polynesian or North American peoples owned and exchanged things, their understanding of the interpenetration between persons and things, and certain concepts of Roman law, such as that of the *immeubles par destination* or of the entanglement between family and patrimony, between persons and things, in archaic Roman juridical thought. See, for example, the enlightening paragraph on "Droit personnel et droit réel (droit romain très ancien)", in Mauss, *Essai sur le don*, chap. 3, § 1.

Gachet, Émile, *Glossaire roman des chroniques rimées de Godefroid de Bouillon, du Chevalier au Cygne et de Gilles de Chin*, Brussels 1859: M. Hayez.

Klock, Kaspar, *Tractatus juridico-politico-polemico-historicus de Aerario* [...], Norimbergae 1671: Sumptibus Johannis Andreae, et Wolfgangi Endteri Junioris, Haeredum.

Las Siete Partidas glosadas por el Licenciado Gregorio López, Salamanca 1555: Por Andrea de Portonariis.

Molina, Luis de, *De Iustitia et Iure Editio Novissima*, Moguntiae 1659.

Oliveira, Domingo Nunes de, "Dissertaçam particular, que examina que são Maninhos", in Id., *Discurso Juridico econômico-político em que se mostra a origem dos Pastos que neste Reino chamão Communs*, Lisboa 1788: Na Typografia Morazziana.

Ordenações Afonsinas, ed. By the Fundação Calouste Gulbenkian, Lisboa 1999.

Peregrinus, Marcus Antonius, *De iure et privilegiis Fisci* [...], Coloniae Agrippinae 1663: Sumpt. Andreae Bingii Bibliopolae.

Ragueau, François, *Glossaire du droit françois, contenant l'explication des mots* [...], Paris 1704: chez J. et M. Guignard.

Recopilación de Leyes de los Reynos de las Indias [...], Madrid 1681: Por Iulian de Paredes.

Santa Rosa de Viterbo, Fr. Joaquim de, *Elucidario das palavras, termos e frases que em Portugal antigamente se usaram* [...], Lisboa 1865: A.J. Fernandes Lopes.

Santarém, Manuel Francisco de Barros e Sousa de, *Alguns documentos para servirem de provas a' parte 1.a das Memorias para a historia e theoria das Cortes geraes* [...], Lisboa 1828: na Impressão Regia.

Santarém, Manuel Francisco de Barros e Sousa de, *Alguns documentos para servirem de provas a' parte 2.a das Memorias para a historia e theoria das Cortes geraes* [...], Lisboa 1828: na Impressão Regia.

Solórzano Pereira, Juan de, *Política Indiana* [...], Madrid 1647: en la Officina de Diego Díaz de la Carrera.

Tertullian, *The Apology of Tertullian, Translated and Annotated by W. Reeve* [...], London and Sydney 1889: Griffith, Farran, Okeden & Welsh (online edition: https://www.tertullian.org/articles/reeve_apology.htm).

Zamora y Coronado, José María, *Biblioteca de legislación ultramarina en forma de diccionario alfabético*, Madrid 1844–1849: Impr. de Alegria y Charlain.

Literature

Alonso-Lasheras, Diego, *Luis de Molina's De Iustitia et Iure. Justice as a Virtue in an Economic Context*, Leiden-Boston 2011.

Aykan, Yavuz, "On Freedom, Kinship, and the Market. Rethinking Property and Law in the Ottoman Slave System", in *Quaderni storici* 154:1 (2017), 13–39.

Bargaoui, Sami, Simona Cerutti and Isabelle Grangaud (dir.), *Appartenance locale et propriété au nord et au sud de la Méditerranée*, Aix-en-Provence 2015.

Baschet, Jérôme, *Corps et âmes: Une histoire de la personne au Moyen Age*, Paris 2016.

Buono, Alessandro, "La manutenzione dell'identità. L'identificazione degli eredi legittimi nello Stato di Milano e nella Repubblica di Venezia (secoli XVII e XVIII)", in *Quaderni storici* 148:1 (2015), 231–266.

Buono, Alessandro, "'Tratándole como paysano y él a ellos'. Pertenencia local, redes supralocales y transmisión de bienes entre el Nuevo y el Viejo Mundo (siglo XVII)", in *Tiempos Modernos* 39 (2019), 128–152.

Buono, Alessandro, "The King Heir. Claiming Vacant Estate Succession in Europe and in the Spanish World (13th–18th Centuries)", in Buono, Alessandro and Luca Gabbiani (eds.), *Sous tutelle. Biens sans maître et successions vacantes dans une perspective comparative, XIIIe–XXe siècles—Under Guardianship. Properties without Owner and Vacant Successions in a Comparative Perspective 13th–20th Centuries*, monographic issue of *L'Atelier du Centre de recherches historiques* 22 (2020) (online edition https://journals.openedition.org/acrh/10893).

Buono, Alessandro, "Naturali, vassalli e forestieri. La presunzione di estraneità e la reincorporazione degli individui nelle cause per eredità giacenti (Italia spagnola e Nuovo Mondo, sec. XVII)", in Meriggi, Marco and Anna Maria Rao (eds.), *Stranieri. Controllo, accoglienza e integrazione negli Stati italiani (XVI–XIX secolo)*, Napoli 2020.

Buono, Alessandro, "Tener persona. Sur l'identité et l'identification dans les sociétés d'Ancien Régime", in *Annales HSS* 71:1 (2020), 75–111.

Buono, Alessandro, "Il quasi possesso della consanguineità. Le registrazioni parrocchiali di antico regime come trascrizione di atti di possesso di stato", in Andrea Addobbati and Matteo Giuli (eds), *Genealogie credibili. Scritti di storia in onore di Roberto Bizzocchi*, Pisa 2023.

Buono, Alessandro, "The danger of ruin and the irresponsible owner. Inheritance disputes in the Spanish Empire (Kingdom of Guatemala, 17th century)", in Buono, Alessandro and Emilia Schijman (eds.), *Neglected Properties*, special issue of *Quaderni Storici* 174:3 (2023), 585–615.

Buono, Alessandro, "Anton Bogos Celibì e le eredità ab intestato nella Toscana di fine XVII secolo", in Dyble, Jake, Alessandro Lo Bartolo and Elia Morelli (eds.), *Un Mare connesso. Europa e mondo islamico nel Mediterraneo (secoli XV–XIX)*, Roma 2024.

Buono, Alessandro and Luca Gabbiani (eds.), *Sous tutelle. Biens sans maître et successions vacantes dans une perspective comparative, XIIIe–XXe siècles—Under Guardianship. Properties without Owner and Vacant Successions in a Comparative Perspective 13th–20th Centuries*, monographic issue of *L'Atelier du Centre de recherches historiques* 22 (2020) (online edition https://journals.openedition.org/acrh/10893).

Buono, Alessandro and Emilia Schijman (eds.), *Neglected Properties*, special issue of *Quaderni Storici* 174:3 (2023).

Buono, Alessandro, Simona Cerutti and Emilia Schijman, "Responsibility and Presence in Early Modern and Contemporary Societies: On the Limits of Property and Membership", in *Historische Anthropologie* 2 (2024), 206–223.

Cayla, Olivier, "La qualification ou la vérité du droit", *Droits, revue française de théorie juridique* 18 (1993), 3–16.

Cerutti, Simona, *Giustizia sommaria. Pratica e ideali di giustizia in una società di Ancien Régime (Torino XVIII secolo)*, Milano 2003.

Cerutti, Simona, "À qui appartiennent les biens qui n'appartiennent à personne? Citoyenneté et droit d'aubaine à l'époque moderne", in *Annales. HSS* 62:2 (2007), 353–383.

Cerutti, Simona, *Étrangers. Etude d'une condition d'incertitude dans une société d'Ancien Régime*, Montrouge 2012.

Cerutti, Simona, "Lavoro e cittadinanza", in Ago, Renata (ed.), *Storia del lavoro in Italia. L'età moderna: Trasformazioni e risorse del lavoro tra associazioni di mestiere e pratiche individuali*, Roma 2018, 235–269.

Cerutti, Simona and Isabelle Grangaud, "Sources and Contextualizations: Comparing Eighteenth-Century North African and Western European Institutions", in *Comparative Studies in Society and History* 59:1 (2017a), 5–33.

Cerutti, Simona and Isabelle Grangaud (eds.), *Fuori Mercato*, special issue of *Quaderni Storici* 154 (2017b).

Cerutti, Simona, Thomas Glesener, and Isabelle Grangaud (dir.), *La Cité des Choses. Une nouvelle histoire de la citoyenneté*, Toulouse 2024.

Chrom Jacobsen, Mogens, *Jean Bodin et le dilemme de la philosophie politique moderne*, København 2000.

Clavero, Bartolomé, *Tantas personas como estados. Por una antropología política de la historia europea*, Madrid 1986.

Clavero, Bartolomé, "Tutela administrativa o dialogos con Tocqueville", in *Quaderni fiorentini per la storia del pensiero giuridico moderno* 24 (1995), 419–468.

Colombo, Emanuele C. (ed.), *Carità*, special issue of *Quaderni Storici* 162:3 (2019).

Conte, Emanuele, *Servi medievali. Dinamiche del diritto comune*, Roma 1996.

Conte, Emanuele, "Droit médiéval. Un débat historiographique italien", in *Annales. HSS* (2002), 1593–1613.

Cortese, Ennio, "Per la storia di una teoria dell'arcivescovo Mosè di Ravenna (m. 1154) sulla proprietà ecclesiastica", in Kuttner, Stephan and Kenneth Pennington (eds.), *Proceedings of the Fifth International Congress of Medieval Canon Law*, Città del Vaticano 1980, 117–155.

Costa, Wellington Júnio Guimarães da, "A prática da Justiça na Provedoria de Defuntos e Ausentes de Vil Rica (1711–1808)", Anais do XIX Encontro regional de história 2014 (online edition: http://www.encontro2014.mg.anpuh.org/site/anaiscomplementares#G).

Costa, Wellington Júnio Guimarães da, "Das desordens na Provedoria de Defuntos e Ausentes, Capelas e Resíduos na América Portuguesa", Anais do XXVIII Simpósio

Nacional de História 2015 (https://anpuh.org.br/index.php/documentos/anais/category-items/1-anais-simposios-anpuh/34-snh28?start=1700).

Costa, Wellington Júnio Guimarães da, *De cofre não tem mais que o nome. A Provedoria das fazendas dos defuntos e ausentes no Brasil colonial (séculos XVI–XVIII)* (Ph.D. thesis), Mariana 2018.

Dani, Alessandro, *Cittadinanze e appartenenze comunitarie. Appunti sui territori toscani e pontifici di antico regime*, Roma 2021.

Derouet, Bernard, "Territoire et parenté. Pour une mise en perspective de la communauté rurale et des formes de reproduction familiale", in *Annales. HSS* 50:3 (1995), 645–686.

Derouet, Bernard, "Les pratiques familiales, le droit et la construction des différences (XVe–XIXe siècles)", in *Annales. HSS* 52: 2 (1997), 369–391.

Derouet, Bernard, "Parenté et marché foncier à l'époque moderne: une réinterprétation", in *Annales. HSS* 56: 2 (2001), 337–368.

Descola, Philippe, *Par-delà nature et culture*, Paris 2005.

Deuchler, Martina, *Under the Ancestors' Eyes. Kinship, Status, and Locality in Premodern Korea*, Cambridge—Massachusetts 2015.

Enciso Contreras, José, *Testamentos y autos de bienes de difuntos de Zacatecas (1550–1604)*, Zacatecas 2000.

Ferguson, James, *Give a Man a Fish. Reflections on the New Politics of Distribution*, Durham and London 2015.

Ferguson, James, *Presence and Social Obligation: An Essay on the Share*, Chicago 2021.

Fernández López, Francisco, "El procedimiento y los expedientes de bienes de difuntos en la Casa de la Contratación de Indias (1503–1717)", in *Tiempos Modernos* 8:30 (2015).

Fernández López, Francisco, *La Casa de la Contratación. Una oficina de expedición documental para el gobierno de las Indias (1503–1717)*, Sevilla-Zamora (México) 2018.

García González, Juan, "La Mañería", in *Anuario de Historia del Derecho Español* (1951–1952), 224–299.

Gálvez Ruiz, María Ángeles, "Mujeres y "maridos ausentes" en Indias", in Morales Padrón, Francisco (ed.), *XIII Coloquio de Historia Canario-Americana; VIII Congreso Internacional de Historia de America:* (1998), 1162–1173.

Glesener, Thomas, "La Cruzada et l'administration des biens vacants en Espagne (XVe–XVIIIe siècles)", in Buono, Alessandro and Luca Gabbiani (eds.), *Sous tutelle. Biens sans maître et successions vacantes dans une perspective comparative, XIIIe–XXe siècles*, monographic issue of *L'Atelier du Centre de recherches historiques* 22 (2020) (online edition: https://journals.openedition.org/acrh/10893).

Gómez Camacho, Francisco, *Economía y filosofía moral: la formación del pensamiento económico europeo en la Escolastica española*, Madrid 1998.

González Sánchez, Carlos Alberto, *Dineros de ventura. La varia fortuna de la emigración a Indias (siglos XVI–XVII)*, Sevilla 1995.

Grangaud, Isabelle, "Le Bayt al-mâl, les héritiers et les étrangers. Droits de succession et droits d'appartenance à Alger à l'époque moderne", in Bargaoui, Sami, Simona Cerutti and Isabelle Grangaud (dir.), *Appartenance locale et propriété au nord et au sud de la Méditerranée*, Aix-en-Provence 2015.

Greer, Allan, *Property and Dispossession. Natives, Empires and Land in Early Modern North America*, Cambridge 2018.

Grendi, Edoardo, "Micro-analisi e storia sociale", in *Quaderni Storici* 35:2 (1977), 506–520.

Grossi, Paolo, *Le situazioni reali nell'esperienza giuridica medievale*, Milano 1968.

Grossi, Paolo, "La proprietà nel sistema privatistico della Seconda Scolastica", in Grossi, Paolo (ed.), *La Seconda Scolastica nella formazione del diritto privato moderno*, Firenze 1973.

Grossi, Paolo, *"Un altro modo di possedere". L'emersione di forme alternative di proprietà alla coscienza giuridica postunitaria*, Milano 1977.

Grossi, Paolo, *L'ordine giuridico medievale*, Bari-Roma 2005 (1st ed. 1995).

Guadalajara Salmerón, Sergio, *Bocados de oro: edición crítica y estudio*, PhD Thesis, Universidad Complutense de Madrid, Madrid 2020.

Hann, Chris (ed.), *Property relations. Renewing the anthropological tradition*, Cambridge 1998.

Herbert, Claire, *A Detroit Story. Urban Decline and the Rise of Property Informality*, Oakland 2021.

Herzog, Tamar, *Defining Nations. Immigrants and Citizens in Early Modern Spain and Spanish America*, New Haven 2003.

Herzog, Tamar, "Terres et déserts, société et sauvagerie. De la communauté en Amérique et en Castille à l'époque moderne", in *Annales. HSS* 62:3 (2007), 507–538.

Herzog, Tamar, *Frontiers of Possession. Spain and Portugal in Europe and the Americas*, Cambridge 2015.

Herzog, Tamar, "How Did the Commons Become Terra nullius? Contextualising Colonial Debates and Asking About Their Consequences", in *Quaderni storici* 168:3 (2021), 607–623.

Hespanha, Antonio Manuel, "Incursión en el pensamiento jurídico político chino", in Hespanha, Antonio Manuel, *La gracia del derecho. Economía de la cultura en la edad moderna*, Madrid 1993.

Hespanha, Antonio Manuel, *Como os juristas viam o mundo. 1550–1750. Direitos, estados, pessoas, coisas, contratos, ações e crimes*, Lisboa 2015.

Hodder, Ian, *Entangled. An Archaeology of the Relationships between Humans and Things*, Southern Gate (UK) 2012.

Hodder, Ian, "The Entanglements of Humans and Things: A Long-Term View", in *New Literary History* 45 (2014), 19–36.

Holbraad, Martin and Morten Axel Pedersen, *The Ontological Turn. An Anthropological Exposition*, Cambridge 2017.

Iglesia García, Jesús de la, "El debate sobre el tratamiento a los pobres durante el siglo XVI", in Javier Campos, Francisco and Fernández de Sevilla (coord.), *La Iglesia española y las instituciones de caridad*, San Lorenzo de El Escorial 2006.

Lacruz Mantecón, Miguel L., *La ocupación imposible. Historia y régimen jurídico de los inmuebles mostrencos*, Madrid 2011.

Lalinde Abadía, Jesús, "Anotaciones historicistas al iusprivatismo de la segunda escolástica", in Grossi, Paolo (ed.), *La Seconda Scolastica nella formazione del diritto privato moderno* in *Quaderni fiorentini per la storia del pensiero giuridico moderno* 1 (1973), 303–375.

Liberski-Bagnoud, Danouta, "Les Gardiens de la Terre. La notion de responsabilité dans les systèmes rituels voltaïques," in Supiot, Alain and Mireille Delmas-Marty (dir.), *Prendre la responsabilité au sérieux*, Paris 2015.

Maccioni, Giampiero, *Il 'dominium altum' nella dottrina di Soto, Molina, Suarez. Studio per un ridimensionamento della dottrina scolastica sulla proprietà privata*, Roma 1966 (Excerpta ex dissertatione ad Lauream in Facultate Philosophica Pontificiae Universitatis Gregorianae).

Macías, Alonso Manuel and María Luisa Candau, "Matrimonios y conflictos: abandono, divorcio y nulidad eclesiástica en la Andalucía moderna (Arzobispado de Sevilla, siglo XVIII)", in *Revista Complutense de Historia de América* 42 (2016), 119–146.

Madero, Marta, *La loi de la chair. Le droit au corps du conjoint dans l'œuvre des canonistes (XIIe–XVe siècle)*, Paris 2015.

Madero, Marta, "Penser la physique du pouvoir. La possession de la juridiction dans les commentaires d'Innocent IV et d'Antonio de Budrio à la décrétale Dilectus", in *Clio@Thémis* 11 (2016).

Magalhães, David, "O Estado como herdeiro legítimo: velhas soluções para novos problemas (ou mais um exemplo da inevitabilidade do direito romano)", in Murillo Villar, Alfonso and María Olga Gil García (eds.), *Fundamentos Romanísticos del Derecho Contemporáneo*, Tomo VIII, *Derecho de Sucessiones*, Madrid 2021.

Maifreda, Germano, "I beni dello straniero. Albinaggio, cittadinanza e diritti di proprietà nel Ducato di Milano (1535–1796)", in *Società e Storia* 129 (2010), 489–530.

Mannori, Luca, *Il sovrano tutore Pluralismo istituzionale e accentramento amministrativo nel principato dei Medici (secc. XVI–XVIII)*, Milano 1994.

Mancuso, Alessandro, "La 'svolta ontologica' e le questioni epistemologiche in antropologia", in *Rivista di antropologia contemporanea* 1 (2020), 55–89.

Martínez Millán, José and Carlos Javier Carlos Morales, "Los orígenes del Consejo de Cruzada (siglo XVI)", in *Hispania* 51:179 (1991), 901–932.

Mauss, Marcel, *Essai sur le don. Forme et raison de l'échange dans les sociétés archaïques*, Florence Weber (ed.), Paris 2007.

Miller, Daniel (ed.), *Materiality*, Durham (NC) 2005.

Miller, Daniel, *Stuff*, Cambridge UK 2010.

Morizot, Baptiste, "L'écologie contre l'Humanisme", in *Essais* 13 (2018), 105–120.

Olsen, Bjørnar, "Reclaiming Things: An Archaeology of Matter", in Carlile, Paul R., Davide Nicolini, Ann Langley and Haridimos Tsoukas (eds.), *How Matter Matters. Objects, Artifacts, and Materiality in Organization Studies*, Oxford 2013.

Otaduy, Javier, "La universitas rerum como soporte de la personalidad en el derecho canónico", in *Ius canonicum* 55 (2015), 47–89.

Oxford Dictionary of English, Oxford 1998.

Pascua Sánchez, María José, ""A la sombra" de hombres ausentes: mujeres malcasadas en el Mundo hispánico del Setecientos", in *Studia Historica: Historia Moderna* 38: 2 (2016), 237–285.

Premo, Bianca, *Children of the Father King: Youth, Authority, and Legal Minority in Colonial Lima*, North Carolina 2005.

Rackman, Emanuel, "A Jewish Philosophy of Property: Rabbinic Insights on Intestate Succession", in *The Jewish Quarterly Review* 67:2/3 (1976–1977), 65–89.

Sahlins, Peter, *Unnaturally French. Foreign Citizenship in the Old Régime and After*, Ithaca-London 2004.

Sánchez Rubio, María Rocío and Isabel Testón Núñez, "Mujeres abandonadas, mujeres olvidadas", in *Cuadernos de Historia Moderna* 19 (1997), 91–119.

Sá, Isabel dos Guimarães, *Quando o rico se faz pobre: Misericórdias, Caridade e Poder no Império Português, 1500–1800*, Lisboa 1997.

Sá, Isabel dos Guimarães, *As Misericórdias Portuguesas de D. Manuel I a Pombal*, Lisboa 2001.

Sá, Isabel dos Guimarães, *O Regresso dos Mortos: Os Doadores da Misericórdia do Porto e a Expansão Oceânica (Séculos XVI–XVII)*, Lisboa 2018.

Schijman, Emilia, *Vivir de prestado. Deudas, derecho y pobreza*, Buenos Aires 2022.

Schijman, Emilia, "From abandoned properties to commons. Houses in post-industrial France", in Buono, Alessandro and Emilia Schijman (eds.), *Neglected Properties*, special issue of *Quaderni Storici* 174:3 (2023), 695–721.

Silva, Teresa Rebelo da, "Maninhos," in Serrão, José Vicente, Márcia Motta and Susana Münch Miranda (dir.), *e-Dicionário da Terra e do Território no Império Português*, Lisboa 2014 (CEHC-IUL, online edition: doi:10.15847/cehc.edittip.2014v007).

Soberanes Fernández, José Luis, "El Juzgado general de bienes de difuntos", in *Revista Chilena de Historia del Derecho* 22 (2010), 637–660.

Steinberg, Sylvie, *Une tache au front: La bâtardise aux XVIe et XVIIe siècles*, Paris 2016.

Tamdoğan, Işık, "Qu'advenait-t-il aux biens des 'étrangers' après leur décès dans la ville d'Adana au XVIII e siècle?", in Bargaoui, Sami, Simona Cerutti and Isabelle Grangaud (dir.), *Appartenance locale et propriété au nord et au sud de la Méditerranée*, Aix-en-Provence 2015.

Tempère, Delphine, *Vivre et mourir sur les navires du siècle d'or*, Paris 2009.

Thomas, Yan, *Causa. Sens et fonction d'un concept dans le langage du droit romain*, Paris 1976.

Thomas, Yan, "L'extrême et l'ordinaire. Remarques sur le cas médiéval de la communauté disparue", in Passeron, Jean-Claude and Jacques Revel (dir.), *Penser par cas*, Paris 2005.

Thomas, Yan, *La mort du père. Sur le crime de parricide à Rome*, Paris 2017.

Todeschini, Giacomo, *I mercanti e il tempio. La società cristiana e il circolo virtuoso della ricchezza tra Medioevo ed Età Moderna*, Bologna 2002.

Tomás y Valiente, Francisco, "La sucesión de quien muere sin parientes y sin disponer de sus bienes", in *Anuario de historia del derecho español* 36 (1966), 189–254.

Torre, Angelo, *Il consumo di devozioni. Religione e comunità nelle campagne dell'Ancien Régime*, Venezia 1995.

Torre, Angelo, "Cause Pie. Riflessioni su lasciti e benefici in antico regime", in *Quaderni Storici* 154:1 (2017), 155–180.

Trentmann, Frank, "Materiality in the Future of History: Things, Practices, and Politics", in *Journal of British Studies* 48 (2009), 283–307.

Vanuxem, Sarah, *Les choses saisies par la proprieté*, Paris 2012.

Vallerani, Massimo (ed.), "Sistemi di eccezione", special issue of *Quaderni storici* 2 (2009).

Viso, Rao, "Communs et dynamiques de pouvoir dans l'Europe du Sud médiévale. Une comparaison entre l'Italie du Nord et le plateau du Duero (viie–xve siècle)", in *Annales HSS* 77:3 (2023), 511–542 (english edition).

Weiner, Annette, "Reproduction: A Replacement for Reciprocity", in *American Ethnologist* 7:1 (1980), 71–85.

Weiner, Annette, *Inalienable Possessions. The Paradox of Keeping-While-Giving*, Berkeley-Los Angeles-Oxford 1992.

CHAPTER 3

Guests in Foreign Lands

Land Control and Ownership in Greater Senegambia in the Face of the Portuguese Presence (16th and 17th Centuries)

Thiago H. Mota

1 Introduction

On 22 March 1626, King Philip, ruler of Portugal and Castile, increased the Bishop of Cape Verde's salary through a letter of grace that began as follows: "*Dom* Philip, by the grace of God, King of Portugal, and of the Algarves on this side and beyond the sea in Africa, Lord of Guinea, and of the Conquest, navigation, trade of Ethiopia, Arabia, Persia and India, etc.".[1] Such a preamble was quite common in Portuguese official documents. This discursive construction suggests the subjugation of various parts of the world under direct Portuguese control through concepts like "lord" and "conquest", which, in the political vocabulary of the time, expressed ownership and dominion, especially over lands.[2] In the early 17th century, the term "Guinea" no longer referred to the entire land south of the Maghreb, as it had before, but took on more specific contours related to the region south of the Senegal River, which became known in Portugal as Guinea of Cape Verde.[3] Therefore, the expression "Lord of Guinea" as a qualifier for the King of Portugal represented him as an authority over an African region, even though its boundaries were still in the process of definition.

In Lisbon, government institutions, such as the Council of India, actively worked to incorporate the African coast in front of the Cape Verde archipelago into the so-called Portuguese Empire. Thus, in the *Relation of the Coast of Guinea*, circa 1606, this Council defined "that 'the Captaincy of Cape Verde comprises the Island of S. Tiago with the adjacent ones', [and] later admitted that

1 Brásio, *Monumenta Missionaria Africana, África Ocidental*, serie 2, vol. 5, document 40. Original: "Dom Felipe, por graça de Deus rei de Portugal e dos Algarves, daquém e dalém mar em África, senhor da Guiné e da conquista, navegação, comércio de Etiópia, Arábia, Pérsia e Índia, faço saber …". All translations are mine.

2 Bluteau, Rafael. *Vocabulario portuguez, e latino* …. See: "Conquista"; "Senhor".

3 Horta, "*A Guiné do Cabo Verde*", p. 41 et *passim*.

'the district of this captaincy along the mainland coast begins at the Sanaga River and ends at the Casses River, where the district of Sierra Leone begins'", which characterised the Coast of Guinea.[4] As Zelinda Cohen argues, the incorporation of this region as a district of the Captaincy of Cape Verde aimed to highlight the ability of the island authorities to intervene in what was happening on the continental portion, where the Portuguese monarchy faced significant resistance—both from local rulers and its own vassals—in implementing its administrative mechanisms.[5] Therefore, based on official documentation from the Portuguese Crown, one can see Portugal's desire for lordship and control over this point of the African coast.

However, on the ground, the reality was more complex. In the annual letter written on 1 January 1610, on the island of Santiago, Cape Verde, the Jesuit Father Baltasar Barreira reported the conditions in which Portuguese traders lived on the West African coast between present-day Senegal and Sierra Leone. The Jesuit lamented that "the Portuguese living in these ports are in great submission, and they suffer tyrannies from kings and others who govern the land, just to live there at their will and leave the land rich, even at the risk of losing everything in one day".[6] A few years later, in 1623, an English merchant reiterated this observation, stating that "the conditions that [the Portuguese *lançados*][7] live subject unto, under the black kings, make it appear they have little comfort in any Christian country".[8] Such findings raise questions about the early Portuguese presence in West Africa, inviting us to analyse the forms

4 Cohen, "Administração das ilhas de Cabo Verde e seu distrito no segundo século de colonização (1560–1640)", 193. Original: "que 'a Capitania do Cabo Verde compreende a Ilha de S. Thiago com as mais adjacentes' [and] admitia mais à frente que 'o distrito dessa Capitania pela costa firme começa no Rio Sanagá e acaba no Rio dos Casses, onde começa o distrito da Serra Leoa'".

5 Cohen, "Administração das ilhas de Cabo Verde e seu distrito no segundo século de colonização (1560–1640)", 192–194.

6 Annual letter from Father Baltasar Barreira to the Provincial of Portugal, in Brásio, *Monumenta Missionaria Africana, África Ocidental*, serie 2, vol. 4, 383. Original: "é grande a sujeição em que vivem os portugueses destes portos, e as tiranias que sofrem dos reis, e dos mais que governam a terra, só por viverem à sua vontade e por sair dali ricos, ainda que a risco de perder tudo em um dia".

7 *Lançados* were those who had removed themselves from the Portuguese jurisdiction and unofficially settled in African lands, without legal authorisation from the Crown. The features of Portuguese *lançados* are a hot topic in the historiography concerning the early Portuguese presence in West Africa. See Soares, "Os Lançados nos Rios da Guiné: século XVI–meados do século XVII"; Nafafé, "Lançados, Culture and Identity: Prelude to Creole Societies on the Rivers of Guinea and Cape Verde" and Cook, "The Silent Tangomão", 24–62.

8 Jobson, *The Golden Trade*, 98.

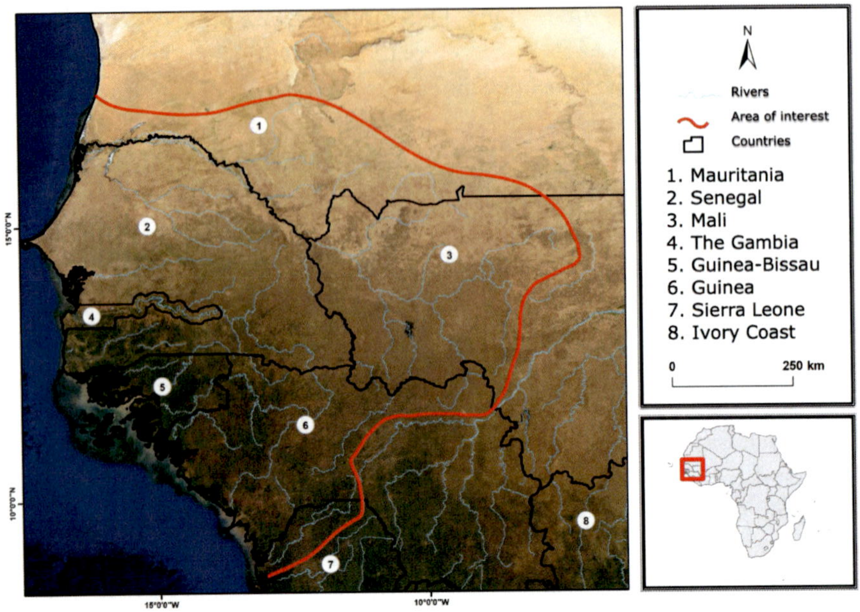

MAP 3.1 Greater Senegambia. Greater Senegambia, formed by the basin of the Senegal and Gambia rivers and, to the south, the Kolonté river, whose headwaters are in the same region as the two rivers that flow to the north.
Note: Mota, "O Islã na África Atlântica: transformações no significado de comportamentos religiosos".
MAP BY THE AUTHOR

of access, control and use of African lands made available to European foreigners, against the idea of Portuguese lordship over them.

In this Chapter, my goal is to demonstrate how the Portuguese who settled on the African coast were subjected to local African normative regimes, related to the ownership and control of land, and the implications of this for other kinds of properties held by foreigners during the 16th and 17th centuries. The area under study comprises the basin of the Senegal and Gambia rivers, extending from the south of present-day Mauritania to the north of Sierra Leone, the "Greater Senegambia", as shown in Map 3.1. Contrary to the idea of Portuguese lordship or conquest in this portion of Africa in the Early Modern period, my argument builds on previous scholarship about dependency and reciprocity between African landlords and their guests.[9] Methodologically, this investiga-

9 On reciprocity, see Brooks, *Eurafricans in Western Africa*; Green, *The rise of the Trans-Atlantic Slave Trade in Western Africa*, 84; Mark and Horta, *The Forgotten Diaspora* 61; Malacco, *A Senegâmbia e o Atlântico*, 75–79.

tion is based on the examination of oral and written sources. The former comes from African oral traditions, available at the *National Center for Arts and Culture*, an important archive of oralities in the Republic of The Gambia. The latter includes several textual genres produced by Europeans and Portuguese descendants from Cape Verde.

This Chapter is placed at the intersection of African and Portuguese Empire historiography. Its contribution involves an analysis of the Portuguese presence in West Africa emphasising intercultural relations in a bottom-up historical approach. Through such methodology, my main goal is to demonstrate the significance of recognising local normative cultures for a better understanding of ownership regimes in the Iberian empires, revealing the role of African agency. My point is that the key element for comprehending the norms governing Portuguese properties in Africa should be sought within African normative cultures, rather than Portuguese or broader European laws. This argument states that foreign agents were entirely subjected to the control exercised by local rulers. European merchants and practical connoisseurs of African societies in the period used to state that the Portuguese were guests in foreign lands, as asserted by the Cape Verdean merchant Francisco de Lemos Coelho, in the mid-17th century.[10] Thus, their relationships were imbalanced in favour of African powers, which authorised a European presence through rights concessions that could be revoked at any time.

This observation differs from the notion of "conquest", which granted rhetorical and political legitimacy to the concept of "Portuguese Empire". Of course, the idea of an empire ruled from Lisbon and able to impose its will over peoples on several continents is no longer accredited, and historians have more sophisticated tools to approach the relationship between Portuguese agents and local powers, traders, religious authorities, and common folks along the extension of the Portuguese presence across the world. However, these understandings are most often brought to debate by the historiography concerned with the empire's periphery, like Africanist, Brazilianist, and Asianist historians.[11] The longstanding influence of Charles Boxer's *The Portuguese Seaborne Empire*, first published in 1969 and based on an approach that neglects the role African societies had during the building of such an empire, reinforces the need for this Chapter. In Portuguese-written scholarship, for instance, the argument intro-

10 Lemos Coelho, *Discripção da Costa de Guine e Situação de todos os Portos e Rios dela …*, 92–93.

11 For example, see Candido, *Wealth, Land, and Property in Angola*; Bastias Saavedra, "Decentering Law and Empire".

duced here is far from hegemonic. The fact that Boxer's book was re-edited in Portugal in 2018 illustrates how a Luso-centric perspective is as strong as ever.[12]

My approach begins with the question: how were Portuguese merchants, clergy, administrators, and *lançados* incorporated into African societies regarding property custody, housing, concession, and land use? To answer this, I first address theoretical questions concerning land and labour studies in precolonial Africa. I then present local agrarian regimes considering West African oral traditions. Following that, I explore the interplay between justice and orality in Greater Senegambia. Finally, I use the insights gained from the latter topics to provide a fresh perspective on European-written sources, particularly regarding the Portuguese presence in the region. Such an approach leads to my contribution, which states that understanding the ownership regime applied to Europeans on the African coast is contingent on knowledge of African normative cultures on its own terms, available by crisscrossing written and oral information.

This Chapter thus analyses how land ownership regimes in Senegambia were intertwined with local norms. This approach is relevant in recognising the primacy of local institutional forms of land control in regions colonised by Portugal worldwide. I propose that studies on land tenure in Africa be framed within local normative categories rather than exclusively relying on European colonial legislation. By decentring Iberian jurisdictions as the only lens through which to view ownership regimes in Africa and elsewhere, we open new avenues for addressing a latent issue in societies of colonial origin: the appropriation of indigenous lands, continually legitimised by a historiography focused on the dynamics of European legislation to the detriment of indigenous political and normative cultures. As demonstrated in the introductory chapter of this volume, this system of ideas is based on the principle of European exceptionalism and is a rhetorical device used to justify the expropriation of indigenous lands in the Americas, rooted in ideas proposed by John Locke.[13] Overcoming this paradigm is an urgent task.

12 Boxer, *O Império Marítimo Português 1415–1825*.

13 See Bastias Saavedra (Chapter 1) in this volume.

2 Labour Control and Land Ownership in Africa

In the field of Africanist historiography during the Early Modern period, also known as precolonial African history, studies on land ownership and control occupy a marginal position. The exploration of agrarian issues in Africa largely emerged from European colonial policies on the continent that started in the 1880s.[14] In his seminal study of economic transformations in precolonial Africa, with a focus on Senegambia, Philip Curtin extensively examined trade, its routes, agents, products and currencies, as well as its internal and external dimensions. While the economic dynamics of the region, including land usage, are central to Curtin's argument, he did not delve into land control as a pivotal element of economic production. This absence can be traced back to the assumption that the abundant availability of land would have driven African social and political systems to prioritise labour control. Once land was considered by historians as abundant, communal and widely accessible, dominance over people became the primary factor in generating wealth.[15]

Building on this premise, John Thornton posited that, before the 19th century, access to land in Africa had a communal characteristic, making the control of labour the primary driver of wealth production. Thornton argued that European records of the time reflected land ownership in Africa because European chroniclers could not conceive of any other arrangement.[16] He acknowledged "state ownership or at least corporate control by the state",[17] arguing that those who were introduced in European sources as landowners were indeed dependent on the political authority. Thornton concludes, "hence, rather than being private estates where tenants were charged rents, the nobles' 'lands' in Sierra Leone were revenue assignments".[18] He makes his point clear: "we have good reason to believe that Africa did not have a small property, that is, plots

14 Berstein, "Rural Land and Land Conflicts in Sub-Saharan Africa".
15 Curtin, *Economic Change in Precolonial Africa.*
16 Thornton, *Africa and Africans in the Making of the Atlantic World*, 76: "Sixteenth- and seventeenth-century European observers were fully aware that African societies were both politically and economically inegalitarian and that these inequalities were represented in social and legal structures. But their understanding of those social and legal structures was usually shaped by European terms and the institutions they represented. Thus, although some recognized the absence of landed private property, many made Africans into landholders in spite of themselves. […] European witnesses, after all, came from an area where the concept of landownership and income based on its lease to tenants was the fundamental starting point of law."
17 Thornton, *Africa and Africans in the Making of the Atlantic World*, 80.
18 Thornton, *Africa and Africans in the Making of the Atlantic World*, 81.

of land owned by cultivators or let out to rent by petty landlords, just as it did not have great property".[19] Connecting the dots, Thornton addresses the role of slavery:

> It is precisely here, however, that slavery is so important in Africa, and why it played such a large role there. If Africans did not have private ownership of one factor of production (land), they could still own another, labor (the third factor, capital, was relatively unimportant before the Industrial Revolution). Private ownership of labor therefore provided the African entrepreneur with secure and reproducing wealth.[20]

In the historiography he engaged with, this conception of land justified a slave-based system of production, where ownership of a product did not correspond to the owner of the land but rather to the one controlling the labour force. The principle of "control over people" is widespread among scholars and, as highlighted by Assan Sarr, has its roots in colonial officials and anthropologists. Along with the colonial science on Africa, this interpretation was supported by an analytical framework developed to address the Russian territorial expansion and spatial control. In Russia, the abundance of land purportedly motivated servitude systems as a means of adding labour to the land, thereby ensuring agricultural productivity, tax collection, and social control over productive space. In Africa, this model was adapted by replacing servile relationships with slavery, due to anthropological scepticism regarding land's inherent ownership.[21]

Thornton embarked on this idea to find a better explanation for slavery in Africa. Thus, he asserted that African law accepted the property of enslaved people instead of the ownership of land. This was seen as a norm that, while distinct from the European system where land ownership was allowed, still made room for the private ownership of products resulting from labour. However, European travellers and chroniclers were not oblivious to the realities they observed, nor were they exclusively influenced by a European environment where land was always privately owned. As Manuel Bastias Saavedra has discussed, land ownership in Europe was not universally characterised by private property until the late 18th century. Both in Europe and Africa, land management was governed by a complex web of social ties and local rights, ensur-

19 Thornton, *Africa and Africans in the Making of the Atlantic World*, 84.
20 Thornton, *Africa and Africans in the Making of the Atlantic World*, 85.
21 Sarr, *Islam, Power, and Dependency in the River Gambia Basin*, 3–5.

ing various forms of communal land use and tenure.[22] Then, the idea that European documentation imposed a particular land ownership regime onto African contexts primarily stems from a misinterpretation of contemporary land ownership regimes in Europe. Even if written sources were merely projections of European perceptions onto Africa, they would still allow for the description of various forms of social relations regarding land.

Thornton's point about land as state ownership aims to make a case that opposes individual and communal use of land. He argues that those presented in European sources as landowners "did not obtain their territorial jurisdictions by heredity, could not sell or alienate it, and could not pass it on to their progeny (so it was clearly not 'theirs'). Instead, it was given to them by the kings as a source of income while they served him as officials."[23] However, other scholarships lead to another direction. Robert Baum's research among Diola people in Greater Senegambia reveals that "paddy land was individually owned but was often worked by brothers, together with their wives and children. Most rice paddies were passed down from a father to his sons, though a small number were inherited by daughters from their mothers".[24] Also, Walter Hawthorne cross referenced contemporary data with 17th-century documents to argue that though fathers used to give land to their sons when they married, the inheritance system favoured the elder son. Hence, patterns of migration and the opening of new fields could emerge when disputes could not be settled by consensus.[25] Both of these reveal that land could be transmitted within a familyhood and was an important economic resource. As Sarr posits, there was no contradiction between individual/family use and communal/state control over land.

Engaging with these viewpoints, recent scholarship has thickened the challenge against the prevailing narrative. Crislayne Alfagali, through her examination of land conflicts in 18th-century Angola, demonstrates how control over land was a significant concern for local leaders and how local norms in Central West Africa were acknowledged by Portuguese agents at the time. In the context of establishing an iron factory in the Ilamba region of Angola's hinterland, Portuguese records indicated that the land "belonged, in the political and economic sense",[26] to local rulers who held the title of *soba*, according to Alfagali.

22 Bastias Saavedra (Chapter 1) in this volume.
23 Thornton, *Africa and Africans in the Making of the Atlantic World*, 81.
24 Baum, *Shrines of the Slave Trade*, 29.
25 Hawthrone, *Planting Rice and Harvesting Slaves*, 47–48.
26 Alfagali, "Conflito de terras nos sertões de Angola", 8. Also see Alfagali (Chapter 9) in this volume.

She reveals how Portuguese interests were directed towards lands belonging to others and managed in accordance with local norms. Consequently, disputes arising from claims over these lands demanded consideration of local African justice.

Alfagali also illustrates Portuguese administrators' acknowledgment of Ambundo people's customs by documenting instances where the Governor of Angola doubted settler residents who asserted they had purchased land from the *sobas*. This doubt stemmed from the fact that "no *soba* could have carried out this negotiation because 'commonly the *sobas* cannot sell their land because they are a kind of *morgado*'",[27] as acknowledged by Governor Francisco de Sousa Coutinho. Alfagali argues that the term "morgado" was used by the Governor due to its similarity to the notion of kinship and the transmission of titles among the Ambundo people. In Portugal, *morgados* were "tied assets that the successor possesses precisely without the ability to alienate or divide, in the same form and order as declared by the founder". The use of this term to describe the situation in Angola indicates that "the Governor believed that land ownership was governed by kinship rules in a sort of African *morgado*".[28]

Although Portuguese strategies in the regions of Senegambia and Angola differed considerably and underwent transformation between the 16th and 18th centuries, local African elites played significant roles in both realms.[29] The concessions of land rights, resistance to Portuguese interests and occupations and various negotiations all unfolded within the framework of local normative cultures and in adherence to local African customs. Therefore, it is imperative to revisit primary sources to challenge the paradigm that relegated land to a secondary position in the West African political and economic system. Drawing inspiration from Alfagali's work, this Chapter illustrates how an understanding of juridical systems in Greater Senegambia and its local norms related to land ownership is imperative to comprehending the Portuguese presence in the region, which was only made possible through concessions by local authorities.

27 Alfagali, "Conflito de terras nos sertões de Angola", 9.

28 Alfagali, "Conflito de terras nos sertões de Angola", 14.

29 This Chapter addresses cases from Greater Senegambia, including Guinea-Bissau. For Mozambique and Angola, see Rodrigues, *Portugueses e Africanos nos Rios de Sena*, Carvalho, *Sobas e homens do rei*, Candido, "Conquest, occupation, colonialism and exclusion: land disputes in Angola", 223–235.

3 Land Control in West African Oral Traditions

Oral traditions serve as crucial historical records for various regions of Africa.[30] In the field of professional historiography, Jan Vansina's 1961 *De la tradition orale: Essai de methode historique* broke new ground by positing the oral tradition among credible sources for history through sophisticated methodology that considered its nature, forms of transmission, textual framework and symbolisms and poetics, the role played by memory and, of course, its limits.[31] However, oral sources differ substantially from written sources, which originate from the past and bear witness to it. Oral historians generally agree that these oral documents are not dormant in the archives of memory, awaiting someone's interest. Instead, they are actively produced during the act of narration, even though they draw upon cultural learning and memory.[32] Narrated traditions imbue the past with meanings closely connected to the present. Nevertheless, societies organised around orality have structures that adapt to innovations, embracing change when necessary but avoiding it when possible. For instance, the public context of narration and the social validation of the narrated events are crucial elements to consider when analysing this type of documentation.

However, the primary motivation for turning this chapter toward oral traditions is not merely a desire to extract factual African information about the past; the reliance on orality is driven by the need to identify categories native to African societies for the purpose of reflecting upon and constructing their own historical narratives. Concerning land control and ownership, I am looking for local tenets and institutions transmitted orally that set local normative regimes. Far from being mere repositories of the past, these traditions are intellectual productions aimed at guiding the present by drawing on connections to the past. These connections are often conveyed through the organised and systematic transmission of knowledge from one generation to the next and are conventionally referred to as tradition. Thus, the application of this knowledge helps us to understand the agrarian structure in Greater Senegambia and provides us with insights guided by African social norms that allow a re-reading of early European written sources.

Oral documents used in this chapter are available at the National Center for Arts and Culture (NCAC), an oral archive located in Fajara, The Gambia. A similar archive once existed in Guinea-Bissau but was tragically destroyed during the civil war of 1998–1999. Today, the NCAC is a pivotal institution for preserving

30 Ba, "A tradição viva".

31 Vansina, *Oral Tradition: A Study in Oral Methodology*.

32 Ferreira and Amado, "Apresentação", xiv.

the historical memory of Greater Senegambia, as its collection of oral traditions encompasses not only the history of The Gambia but that of the entire region. While most of the oral documents available originate from The Gambia, there are narratives from Senegal and Guinea-Bissau as well. The collection comprises traditions gathered mostly between the 1950s and 1980s.

Today, the original oral texts were recorded and transcribed. They are often bilingual as the interviews were conducted in the languages of the interviewees (Mandingo, Wolof, Fula, among others) and subsequently translated into English. The collection has been digitalised and is expected to be available online in the coming years.[33] Access to this archive enables historians to re-evaluate European sources in light of African perspectives, offering fresh approaches to writing the history of Africa and for the Portuguese presence in Africa, thereby moving beyond the myth of "five centuries of colonisation"[34]—which continues to frame non-specialists' historical imagination about the relationship between Portugal and its former African colonies.

For the writing of this Chapter, I have methodically analysed nine narratives, orally collected in The Gambia between 1972 and 1978, using transcripts from the NCAC collection. These texts were selected from the catalogue available at the NCAC, focusing on narratives related to the political history of precolonial states in the region, such as Kaabu, Fulado, Kombo, Wuli, and Chadu. Through an intensive examination of this *corpus*, several categories linked to local agrarian law were identified, including the conditions for land occupation and the social relationships associated with land tenure. These categories emphasise the central role of territory in the oral traditions, be it a category for state political power or a domain held by local families and communities.[35]

Land as state territory and as socially defined political and economic resources are intertwined categories. In Mandingo oral traditions, the 13th century emerges as a transformative period as most Mandingo people, the predominant people in present-day Gambia, reference it as the moment of their migration from the Mali Empire towards the east. In the official ethnic memory, they were led by the renowned Mandingo conqueror Tiramakang Traore—an event seen as seminal, marking Mandingo presence in Greater Senegambia. Conversely, many family oral traditions suggest a gradual movement of

33 https://ncac-national-digital-archive.blogs.uni-hamburg.de/. Accessed 11 August 2022. I would like to thank Hassoum Ceesay and all his team working at NCAC, Fajara.

34 Pélissier, *História da Guiné*, 23.

35 I would like to thank Maria Raquel Morais Fernandes, a History student at the Federal University of Viçosa, who received a CNPq scholarship in a Scientific Initiation project and whose final conclusions supported the analysis in this section.

Mandingo families occurring long before Tiramakang's conquests. These early "settlers" established homes among pre-existing communities, likely the Bainunk people, engaged in interethnic marriages and forged novel relationships with neighbouring communities well before the military conquests deemed as foundational.[36]

These narratives display distinct meanings for land ownership legitimacy. The first one argues that a military conquest made the governorship possible, settling a territory under Mandingo rule. However, Mandingo rulers were unable to dispossess local settlers, as they did not have rights over land, which was managed by local institutions. The second tradition states that land rights were achieved through social ties, like marriage, which integrated some Mandingo migrants into local societies and, hence, allowed them to access land through local institutions.

This context explains why encounters between Mandingo populations and the indigenous peoples of Greater Senegambia, particularly in the Gambia River region to the south, are depicted in oral narratives as fraught with disputes over land dominance. Expressions, such as "we own the land",[37] "this land is our inheritance",[38] or "we are the owners of the land",[39] manifest local concerns with constructing a historical narrative that secures present-day land usage. The legitimacy of this usage is rooted in the history of land occupation and its disposal as an important economic resource. The term "settled" describes those who initially occupied a particular place, whether by founding villages or developing family lineages associated with territorial dominance.

Oral traditions indicate that the legitimacy of land ownership can be the result of social, political, and military conquest. The granting of land use to others and its access through inheritance, marriages, or other social mechanisms signify the acquisition of the resource as a social conquest. This elucidates why Mandingo family traditions advocated for a peaceful migration to Senegambia, highlighting how Mandingo people intermingled with local inhabitants and gradually gained land ownership rights. The topic of military conquest by Tiramakang's army remains a prevalent memory, as the rhetoric of African imperial power and the legacy of ancient Mali hold deep and extensive roots in West Africa, portraying Mandingo people as possessing noble origins.[40] Nev-

36 Sidibé, *A Brief History of Kaabu and Fuladu (1300–1930)*, 14.

37 National Center for Arts and Culture/Oral History and Antiquities Division, Research and Documentation Division, (hereinafter NCAC), Folder 3346B, 52.

38 NCAC. Folder 487B, 17.

39 NCAC. Folder 163A, 12.

40 Gomez, *African Dominion*.

ertheless, land domain and its legitimacy derive more from social conquest, recognised according to local norms, than from military acquisition.

Narratives that explore the life of Alieu Malali, the father of Alpha Molo, the Fulani leader who established the Fulado State between Upper Casamance and Guinea-Bissau, reflect conflicts related to the legitimacy of land control through conquest. These narratives suggest that the Fula people from Futa Jalon, in present-day Guinea-Conakry, feared losing their governing rights due to the lack of public acknowledgement of their land ownership.[41] In essence, they conquered the territory politically and militarily but recognised that the land did not belong to them, in accordance with widely accepted local customs. Given that the Fula military conquests occurred between the 18th and 19th centuries, their social legitimacy had not yet been firmly established through integration with indigenous peoples in the late 19th and early 20th centuries, in contrast to the Mandingo political expansion in the 13th century which was well-integrated in local norms by the 18th century, when Fula newcomers obtained power.

The local norm that governs these perceptions regarding land legitimacy before the Mandingo and Fula peoples is based on the conditions that allow a foreigner, whether European or African, to settle in a particular location. In this process, two elements assume central importance in oral traditions: access to unoccupied land, often described as "turning the bush into land", and permission granted by a local authority for the foreigner to settle there. In the first case, the act of "clearing the land" represents the cornerstone of the right to occupy a location through prior claim. In the second case, recognition of the local authority, who possesses the socially acknowledged prerogative of managing the territory and its resources, plays a pivotal role in granting or denying land access to others.

The phrase "clearing the land" signifies a method of appropriating natural space, establishing territorial claims and thereby subjecting it to local norms. This concept is evident in narratives of the occupation of places, such as Bakau, Gambia: "the way they found [the space], people formed their places, they also settled in that way, everyone cut their bush", that is, they cleared a space which became theirs.[42] Similar stories emerge regarding Basee Tenda, where the entire area was once wilderness, but the act of clearing and settling transformed it into a habitable space: "at that time, the whole place was a bush. Basee Tenda was a bush. Our father cleaned Basee Tenda. When he cleared, he

41 NCAC. Folder 490A-02, 14.

42 NCAC. Folder 419A, 16.

settled in Basee Tenda."[43] This concept also applies to the narratives concerning the Sanneh and Manneh family lineages, marking the expansion of the Mali Empire: "when Tiramakang arrived in this land, he raised it into a village, [...] Until then, it was just a bush".[44] The underlying idea is that the land belongs to those who first occupy it.

Authorisation from a local power plays a vital role when foreigners wish to establish themselves in an already inhabited land. Such permission must align with the norms of the community. This aspect is particularly relevant to the arrival of Europeans who sought to settle in African lands during the 16th and 17th centuries. Identifying the legitimate owner of the land or the authority responsible for the community, to whom the foreigner should make contact and form a bond, is a recurring theme in several narratives. The trajectory of Malali serves as an enlightening example, as he journeyed through various places but faced rejection until reaching a region located between The Gambia and Guinea-Bissau known as Chadu, where he was *permitted* to settle.[45]

Numerous oral accounts describe how the head of a community grants land to foreigners, either permitting or forbidding the occupation of specific land parcels. The criteria for granting or denying access to land can encompass physical or metaphysical aspects, indicating various forms of interaction, coexistence and segregation between humans and non-humans. For instance, in Basee Tenda, Gasamma-Jimintee prevented Arfang Musa from occupying certain land due to the presence of a spirit, redirecting him to an area free from spiritual restrictions.[46] Therefore, oral traditions assert that non-human agency can substantially influence the right to occupy a particular place. Moreover, this recognition requires careful consideration to prevent the categorisation of lands inhabited by spiritual entities as unproductive or unoccupied. The rights attributed to non-human beings integrate them deeply into local social and political dynamics, as well as into the land they inhabit.

In his work on land control in the Gambia River basin, Sarr highlights that human occupation in some regions was restricted due to spiritual prohibitions. Although these areas were fertile and resource-rich, human occupation was prohibited because they were inhabited by spirits, which were to be avoided due to the potential for dangerous interactions. However, with the spread of Islam in the region, Sarr argues that these forbidden lands were eventually occupied through spiritual battles waged by Muslim preachers, known as *mar-*

43 NCAC. Folder 346B, 4–5.
44 NCAC. Folder 553, 43.
45 NCAC. Folder 490A-02.
46 NCAC. Folder 346B, 6–8.

abouts, against the spirits inhabiting those areas. After the Muslims' victory and the expulsion of the spirits, new villages were established in formerly forbidden forests.[47] Building upon Sarr's argument and the example cited earlier, it is evident that interactions between humans and non-humans form an integral part of the local norm in West Africa, necessitating their consideration in the analysis of land ownership regimes and their implications on the local normative culture.[48]

In addition to the spiritual conquest of land facilitating the expansion of Islam in Greater Senegambia, the concession of territories by local rulers played a fundamental role in the establishment of the Islamic State of Bundu, located along the upper Senegal River in the late 17th century. Malick Dauda Sy was a prominent Tuculor ruler and a key figure in the *jihad* that founded Bundu as an imamate in 1695. Sy, whose known biography is mostly derived from oral tradition, is depicted as a distinguished *marabout*, surrounded by disciples and recognised for his religious devotion. Born to a Muslim leader, he received his initial Islamic education from his father.[49] Later, he attended the madrassa or Koranic school in Pir, near present-day Tivaouane, Senegal, and left for Mauritania, where he finished his Islamic training.[50]

Upon returning to Bundu, Sy dedicated himself to Islamic teaching and founded a community on a parcel of land granted by the *tunka*, the ruler of the Gajaaga polity in the upper Senegal River.[51] By surrounding himself with *talibes* (disciples), Sy sought to consolidate his political strength and create a network of dependency relationships centred around the land he had been granted.[52] He achieved this position by attracting *talibes* to whom he would teach the Koran and Islamic tenets. Thus, they would live with him and farm on his land, which made it more productive and allowed Sy to accumulate a surplus, further applied in overpassing the Gajaaga's ruler through a *jihad* declared in 1695.[53] Sy distinguished his new cluster from the *tunka*'s network, where he held a subordinate position. In this example, land conquering was legitimate if there was a local Muslim community to appreciate it due to the newly introduced Islamic norms.

47 Sarr, *Islam, Power, and Dependency in the River Gambia Basin*, 89, 102.
48 On the different ways in which non-human agencies affect ownership, see also Bastias Saavedra (Chapter 1) in this volume.
49 Curtin, "Jihad in West Africa: Early Phases and Inter-Relations in Mauritania and Senegal", 18.
50 Ka, *École de Pir Saniokhor*, 96–98.
51 Ka, *École de Pir Saniokhor*, 96–98.
52 NCAC. Tape 132/A, 3–4.
53 Klein, "Social and economic factors in the Muslim Revolution in Senegambia", 110–112.

At the state level, land ownership also played a significant role in granting rights to pass through the land, settle, or collect resources. According to oral traditions, when a territory served as the sole or primary access point to other locations, people—particularly traders—needed authorisation, often involving payment, to traverse it. These dynamics influenced conflicts and alliances formed in the region. Traders travelling through West Africa—as recounted by Muso Singhate, an 81-year-old man knowledgeable on The Gambia's history—paid taxes, the amount of which "depends on the type of wealth, and who orders them to pay is the owner of the village".[54] Similarly, land productivity and territorial resources, such as water, were subject to taxation, as described by Mbalefele Janneh, a resident of Bakau, The Gambia, well-versed in the region's history. Residents of Banjul, for instance, were required to pay tribute to Mansa Kabu for the founding of the island. In Niumi, a cluster of villages at the mouth of the Gambia River, dwellers "paid Mansa of Niumi for the river. [...] for the bounties of the river".[55] Here, "Mansa" is a title for the ruler.

In conclusion, African oral traditions clearly demonstrate that land, even if not treated as personal property that could be bought or sold, was held under someone's control. These narratives acknowledge land ownership and show that it was a resource entwined in political networks and governed by local laws. Either as a territory ruled by a sovereign or as an economic resource controlled by community, family, or local potentates, the land was under local ownership regimes. Consequently, access to it by explorers, be they European or African, fundamentally depended on their engagement with this complex web of social, political, and economic relationships, and their submission to local normative culture.

4 Justice and Orality in Greater Senegambia

The most basic questions concerning how West African societies functioned during the first centuries of contact with Europeans involve their juridical systems. How was justice produced? How was it limited? Could despotic rulers apply their will without any constraints? What normative context did the Europeans get into? To address them, we must recognise that most West African societies have cultivated normative cultures rooted in orality, as shown above. Consequently, grasping how justice operates through local traditions and insti-

54 NCAC. Folder 163A, 81.

55 NCAC. Folder 419A, 05.

tutions, passed down orally across generations, becomes essential for comprehending the dynamics related to the ownership of movable assets and land.

Portuguese sources about West Africa show how oral administration of justice was closely intertwined with gerontocracy. As described by the chronicler and merchant André Álvares de Almada, who extensively documented the societies of Greater Senegambia in the 1590s, governance in the region's political entities was overseen by chiefs supported by the elders of the land, "who are much obeyed by all the nations of the black people and to whom they always give a hand".[56] Among the Mandingo people of Casão, present-day Kasang on the northern shore of the Gambia River, Almada noted that "the judgements of this land of the Casangas are made the same way as on the Coast, before the King or Lord of the land, with some old men who serve as judges, and then they verbally give their sentences; the parties state their reasons and give witnesses without any delay".[57] It is their knowledge of local norms that empowers these elderly individuals to dispense justice effectively.

Within the Wolof communities, the predominant ethnic group in Senegal and widespread throughout Greater Senegambia, Almada emphasised the pivotal role of elders as custodians of order and actors in the administration of justice: "among these people in this nation, like the others we have discussed, there are judges, who are determined by the Kings with the elders, who are like judges, or by the governors of the places, always assisting with them the old and ancient men."[58] Similarly, on the Bijagós Islands in present-day Guinea-Bissau, people also "obey their elders".[59] By virtue of the roles they assumed, elders exercised direct influence over community decisions and the evolution of social interactions. In the region encompassing present-day Sierra Leone, as noted by the Jesuit priest Manuel Álvares in his memoir penned between 1607 and 1615, all people were "obstinate in following the example of their par-

56 Almada, "Tratado Breve dos rios da Guiné do Cabo Verde …", 235–236. Original: "pelos velhos da terra, os quais são muito obedecidos de todas as nações dos negros e lhes dão sempre a mão".

57 Almada, "Tratado Breve dos rios da Guiné do Cabo Verde …", 293. Original: "os juízos desta terra dos Casangas fazem-se como na Costa de que já tratamos, diante do Rei ou Senhor da terra, com alguns velhos que servem como desembargadores, e logo verbalmente dão suas sentenças; as partes alegam suas razões e dão testemunhas sem dilação nenhuma".

58 Almada, "Tratado Breve dos rios da Guiné do Cabo Verde …", 262. Original: "entre estes desta nação, como os mais de que tratamos, há juízes, os quais são determinados pelos Reis com os velhos, que são como desembargadores, ou pelos governadores dos lugares, assistindo sempre com eles os homens antigos e velhos".

59 Almada, "Tratado Breve dos rios da Guiné do Cabo Verde …", 316. Original: "dão obediência aos mais velhos".

ents; and so they say: I'm going where my father walked, fulfilling the journey of life".[60]

Regarding the formalisation of normative proceedings, the Cape Verdean merchant André Donelha provided a significant account of the justice system in the village of Casão. In his memorial dedicated to the Governor of Cape Verde, Francisco Vasconcelos da Cunha, dated 1625, Donelha painted a vivid picture of the venue where justice was administered—the house of the *sandeguil*, or Duke of Casão in Iberian terminology. The place was a "square house, made of adobes, very white, with a fence around it",[61] built in the Mandingo style in a predominantly Muslim region.[62] More than 50 men patiently awaited their audience at the entrance, seeking a resolution for their disputes from the ruler and his aides. Guided by Gaspar Vaz, a Mandingo man acting as a local intermediary, Donelha made his way into the enclosure. As he moved among the litigants, he eventually reached the *sandeguil*.

Within the audience area, Donelha recounted that "only the duke was in the house, sitting on a three-step platform".[63] Then, "alongside him, on the second step, two old men were sitting, one on his right and one on his left, who were judges; on the first step were two other old men, one on one side, one on the other, who served as lawyers".[64] The *sandeguil* invited the foreign trader to sit directly opposite him, marking the commencement of the proceedings. Donelha vividly described the proceedings:

> Two litigants entered, plaintiff and defendant, each bowing with his right hand on his chest and his turban in his left, without saying a word. An old man, the author's lawyer, spoke with his eyes on the duke; the defendant's lawyer soon replied; the plaintiff's lawyer and the defendant's lawyer spoke again, and they fell silent. The duke, very still, turned to the judge who was on his right and this one said what he thought, and he turned

60 Álvares, *Etiópia Menor e Descrição Geográfica da Província da Serra Leoa*, 63. Original: "são ferrados muito do exemplo de seus progenitores; e assim dizem eles: vou por onde caminhou meu pai, cumprindo a jornada da vida".

61 Donelha, *Descrição da Serra Leoa e dos Rios de Guiné do Cabo Verde*, 150. Original: "casa quadrada, feita de adobes, mui alva, com um poial ao redor".

62 Mark, *"Portuguese" Style and Luso-African Identity*, 51–53.

63 Donelha, *Descrição da Serra Leoa e dos Rios de Guiné do Cabo Verde*, 150. Original: "não estava na casa mais que o duque, assentado em um poial de três degraus".

64 Donelha, *Descrição da Serra Leoa e dos Rios de Guiné do Cabo Verde*, 150. Original: "a par dele, no segundo degrau estavam assentados dois velhos, um à sua direita e outro à esquerda, os quais eram juízes; no primeiro degrau estavam outros dois velhos, um a uma parte, outro a outra, que serviam de advogados".

> to the other judge, who gave his opinion. The duke pronounced his sentence, without the lawyers or the parties saying a word. The parties, as they were, with their hands on their breasts, bowed. The winner went out through the door he had entered, telling how he had won; the loser went out through the opposite door and left. And two more went in, and the rest likewise, until the audience was ended.[65]

Donelha's accounts illustrate how justice was efficiently administered in Casão in the early 17th century. This model, however, was not unique to this locale, as evidenced by the observations of Álvares and Almada. It exemplifies a system of justice grounded in local norms, passed down orally and presided over by the community's eldest members, who were renowned for their profound knowledge of local customs, often referred to as tradition. The legitimacy of the verdict is universally acknowledged because it hinges on the recognition of those who dispense justice as bearers of expertise in local norms. This underscores the institutionalised nature of how these societies resolved disputes, the roles allocated to those responsible for justice, and the accepted legitimacy of this process—recognised by litigants who sought these forums to address their concerns. Within this framework of normative institutions, grounded in local norms, one must seek the local interpretations of ownership, control and land concession in Senegambia.[66]

5 Reframing Ownership Regimes

In 1610, Porto d'Ale (now Saly Portudal, Senegal) was under the administration of a Muslim *alcaide* (mayor). During this time, Jesuit priest Barreira visited the

65 Donelha, *Descrição da Serra Leoa e dos Rios de Guiné do Cabo Verde*, 152. Original: "Entraram dois litigantes, autor e réu, fazendo ambos cada um sua mesura, com a mão direita posta no peito e o turbante na da esquerda, sem falarem palavra. Falou um velho, advogado do autor, com os olhos para o duque; logo respondeu o advogado do réu; tornou a falar o advogado do autor, e o do réu, e calaram-se. O duque, mui quieto, virou para o juiz que estava a sua direita e disse o que lhe parecia, e se virou para o outro juiz, o qual deu seu parecer. O duque pronunciou sua sentença, sem os advogados nem as partes falarem palavra. As partes, assim como estavam, com a mão no peito, fizeram sua mesura. O vencedor saiu pela porta por onde entrara, contando como vencera; o vencido saiu pela porta contrária, e se foi embora. E entraram outros dois, e da mesma maneira os mais, até se acabar a audiência."

66 As stated by António Correia e Silva, African powers remained largely independent of European ones during the period studied. Silva, "Cabo Verde e a geopolítica do Atlântico", 11.

region, and he was warmly received by the local ruler. The *alcaide* embraced Barreira, "declaring that he was no less happy with [the visit] than the Portuguese".[67] Porto d'Ale was a bustling commercial centre inhabited by Portuguese, English, French, and Dutch traders. It was a place marked by religious tolerance, where Barreira found the opportunity to conduct public sermons and even organise a procession.[68] As he noted, "because the King of that land and those who govern it and the natural inhabitants are Moors [i.e., Muslims], and [as] among them there are many Bexerins [preachers of the Koran], there was some human fears and opinions against [the procession]".[69] Despite these reservations, Barreira went ahead with his plan, asserting that he was accompanied and respected by the Muslim community. His presence in the region was made possible by the local ruler's permission, who benefited from the foreigner's presence in his land. Barreira's staying there, therefore, was a concession.

This story of local hospitality is also echoed in the account of Spanish Franciscan Mateo de Anguiano. When discussing the missionary work of Friar Serafim and his colleagues near Porto d'Ale, Anguiano mentions that the local ruler, after listening to the sermons of the religious, remained "determined in his sect of Mahoma".[70] Despite this, this ruler "offered of his own free will to give them domicile in his court, lands to sow on and other things of the land."[71] Despite demonstrating the Muslim's resistance to the proposal of converting to Catholicism, Anguiano exposes the local receptivity to foreign missionaries, who were granted housing and land to stay on and other facilities throughout the region.

Similarly, Donelha documented the open-mindedness of Wolof rulers in Atlantic coastal ports, including Porto d'Ale, regarding the presence of foreigners and religious diversity. In 1625, he stated that in that village lived "Por-

---

67 Annual Letter from Father Baltasar Barreira to the Provincial of Portugal, Brásio, *Monumenta Missionaria Africana, África Ocidental*, serie 2, vol. 4, 363. Original: "declarando que não se alegrava menos com [a visita] que os portugueses".

68 Roteiro da Costa da Guiné (1635), Brásio, *Monumenta Missionaria Africana, África Ocidental*, serie 2, vol. 5, 288.

69 Annual Letter from Father Baltasar Barreira to the Provincial of Portugal, Brásio, *Monumenta Missionaria Africana, África Ocidental*, serie 2, vol. 4, 375. Original: "o Rei daquela terra e os que a governam e os moradores naturais são Mouros [i.e. muçulmanos], e [como] entre eles há muitos Bexerins [pregadores do Alcorão], não faltaram alguns temores humanos e pareceres em contrário [à procissão]".

70 Anguiano, *Misiones Capuchinas en Africa*, 72. Original: "determinado em sua seita de Mahoma".

71 Anguiano, *Misiones Capuchinas en Africa*, 72. Original: "ofereceu de sua própria vontade a dar-lhes domicílio em sua corte, terras em que semear e outras coisas da terra".

tuguese Jews and Portuguese Christians, who are *lançados* there, to rescue [or trade in people], and French traders, but [the ruler] does not consent that there is a dispute about which of the laws [religions] is better".[72] This liberal approach by the ruler showcased the region's acceptance of European presence and the coexistence of diverse religious practices, as the ruler declared that "each one should benefit from it, and live as they wish according to the law they have, and there should be no dispute, because they will be punished in his kingdom".[73] The ruler, therefore, was lenient with the European presence, but demanded respect for the local free fair, where religious diversity was not allowed to be a problem.[74]

In all these instances, the underlying reason for such hospitality, land grants, and rights extended by African rulers to European missionaries and merchants was primarily economic and aligned with local customs. It was not a case of European conquest along the African coast; rather, Europeans were reliant on the established local authorities. This pattern of relationship has been debated across the historiography based on what George Brooks called a sociocultural paradigm: the landlord-stranger reciprocity. Lost in antiquity, this pattern of behaviour guaranteed that "travelers were provided food, lodging, and security of possessions".[75] On the other hand, Brooks continues:

> [...] the behavior of strangers was conditioned by all of the foregoing; by the dread of spending a night in the bush bereft of the protection of a community; by dependence on hosts for food, shelter, access to commercial networks, land, and other resources; and by respect for the occult powers wielded by landlords through their associations with the spirits of an area, especially through the mediation of ancestors.[76]

Considering the nature of this relationship, I do not agree that it is based on landlord-stranger *reciprocities*. Brooks' statement, contrary to the concept of reciprocity that he bears, makes clear a *dependence* of strangers upon landlords. Even if those landlords profited from the benefits brought about by strangers,

72 Donelha, *Descrição da Serra Leoa e dos Rios de Guiné do Cabo Verde*, 128. Original: "judeus portugueses e portugueses cristãos, que andam lá lançados, a resgatar, e franceses, mas [o governante] não consente que haja disputa sobre quais das leis é melhor".

73 Donelha, *Descrição da Serra Leoa e dos Rios de Guiné do Cabo Verde*, 128. Original: "cada um faça seu proveito, e vivam como quiserem na lei que tiverem, e não haja porfia, porque serão castigados no seu reino".

74 Mark and Horta, *The Forgotten Diaspora*, 20.

75 Brooks, *Eurafricans in Western Africa*, 29.

76 Brooks, *Eurafricans in Western Africa*, 29.

there was only one direction in this relationship, which means the power was concentrated in the hands of the one with political control.

For instance, in 1610, Barreira reported a significant challenge faced by Portuguese traders: when a foreign trader died, the ruler of the territory where they had settled became the heir to their possessions. He noted:

> When someone falls ill, if they understand that the disease is dangerous, they immediately surround the house, so that nothing is taken from it. And as soon as he expires, everything is immediately laid hold of, whether it be his, or belonging to absent people who had company with him. That's what happened to a rich man I met there, he died and was soon robbed not only of what he had at home, his own and parts of others, but because at that time a ship of his, which was very important, had arrived at the port, they soon seized it and everything it carried.[77]

In 1625, merchant Donelha reiterated this narrative, noticing that "the *lançado* Christian and the Jew and the French who die, the king is his heir, and as soon as one of the said ones falls ill, if the illness is serious, then the mayor, who is called *falfa* there, surrounds his house and puts it under guard so that nothing can be taken from it".[78] These accounts highlight that the permissions, land concessions and ownership rights of Europeans in African societies were under the local norm, which establishes that foreigners were dependent on rulers and these, in turn, were heirs of the former. Such a custom was under the watchful control of African rulers. The fact that the local ruler had the right to possess the goods of dead Europeans demonstrates how the territory control belonged to him. He had the right to welcome foreigners, grant them land for temporary use, be responsible for them and, finally, inherit the goods they left behind.[79]

---

77 Annual Letter from Father Baltasar Barreira to the Provincial of Portugal, Brásio, *Monumenta Missionaria Africana, África Ocidental*, serie 2, vol. 4, 383. Original: "Em adoecendo algum, se entendem que a doença é perigosa, logo lhe cercam a casa, para que não se tire dela coisa alguma. E tanto que expira, imediatamente logo lhe lançam mão de tudo, ora seja seu, ora seja de ausentes que tinham companhia com ele. Assim aconteceu a um homem rico que eu ali conheci, morreu e foi logo esbulhado não somente do que tinha em casa, seu e de partes, mas porque naquele tempo acertou de chegar ao porto um navio seu, que importava muito, logo lhe lançaram mão dele, e de tudo quanto trazia".

78 Donelha, *Descrição da Serra Leoa e dos Rios de Guiné do Cabo Verde*, 128. Original: "o cristão lançado e o judeu e o Francês que morre, o rei é seu herdeiro, e tanto que adoece um dos ditos, se a doença é grave, logo o alcaide, que lá chamam falfa, lhe cerca a casa e lhe põe guarda para dela não se tirar nada".

79 Buono's discussion (Chapter 2 in this volume) on vacant inheritances and the treatment of the assets of deceased foreigners, shows how this was also a common doctrine in Europe.

This is a paramount point because what is at stake is the very nature of the Portuguese Empire. When the region of Greater Senegambia, described at the time as Guiné, was put under the administration of Cape Verde and requested as part of that empire, the control over properties owned by Portuguese subjects deceased on the coast was claimed by Portuguese institutions. As showcased by Zelinda Cohen, quoting a 1567 regulation, "it was the duty of the governors and treasurers of Cape Verde to appoint 'an individual each year to go to the Rivers of said Islands, accompanied by another person acting as a scribe, to collect the estates of the deceased who had passed away in those rivers'".[80] It is arguably acknowledged that Portugal was unable to impose any rule over African authorities. Moreover, it is clear now that such an empire could not control its own subjects' properties either once they fell under local law.

These customs were not limited solely to Europeans traversing African territories. In the early 16th century, chronicler Valentim Fernandes recounted a technique employed in elephant hunting, elucidating the ceremonies that accompanied the triumph of successful hunters. This technique involved using a poisoned harpoon to wound the elephant and then tracking it to the location where it ultimately succumbed. However, a significant challenge arose in this practice: the elephant's final resting place could often be situated at considerable distance from the site of the initial injury, potentially leading it into the jurisdiction of a different ruler. According to Fernandes, once an elephant had been wounded, "the black man follows it for a league, or two or more, to where it goes to die. And if the animal is going to another jurisdiction, the elephant might be taken, the hunter has to pay for it or they go to war for it".[81] In essence, this meant that if the elephant met its demise within the territory of another ruler, the hunter was obligated to remunerate that ruler for the rights to claim the killed animal on his land. Failure to do so could result in the elephant being seized or even trigger a conflict between the two groups.[82]

Land ownership played a critical role in asserting control and rights over goods within that land. In the 1590s, Almada reiterated the report by Fernandes 100 years earlier, explaining that when hunting elephants, part of the meat of

80 Cohen, "Administração das ilhas de Cabo Verde e seu distrito …", 193–194. Original: "Aos provedores e tesoureiros de Cabo Verde competia ordenar 'uma pessoa que em cada um ano vá aos Rios das ditas Ilhas com outra pessoa por escrivão, a fazer a arrecadação das fazendas dos defuntos que nos ditos rios falecerem'".

81 Brásio, *Monumenta Missionaria Africana*, África Ocidental, serie 2, vol. 1, 735. Original: "o negro lhe segue uma légua, ou duas ou mais, até onde vai a morrer. E se vai ter a outra jurisdição, tomam-lhe o elefante ou o pagam ou põem guerra por isso".

82 Freitas, *Desenterrando mortos e enterrando vivos em suas entranhas*, 91.

the slaughtered animal should be given to the king who had rights over the land.[83] Similarly, in 1610, Father Barreira complained about the way in which African laws disadvantaged foreigners. He said that "if any ship sinks off the coast, it is immediately taken for the king, with all the goods that it carries, and for the kings to do the same with those who are sitting in the village, it is enough for them to pretend they commit some guilt they call *chay*."[84] The prevailing local understanding was that anything within a ruler's territory became their property. Whether it was the possessions of a deceased individual, a sunken ship, or animals hunted within their domain, rulers had the rights to them.

In Greater Senegambia, adherence to local social norms was essential to secure ownership of various assets. Goods could be confiscated if foreigners committed (or were blamed for) crimes under the local customs, known as *chays*. Barreira lamented that it was sufficient for local rulers to accuse the Portuguese of wrongdoing and to seize their belongings. However, other sources suggest that foreigners often disregarded local customs. Almada narrated that, in the region of Rio Grande, present-day Guinea-Bissau, there were some birds as big as turkeys, which, "by the laws of the kingdom, cannot be killed, nor does anyone kill them, because there are heavy penalties placed on it".[85] The reason for this was the local belief that "these birds are the souls of their ancestors",[86] corroborating oral sources regarding the rights attributed to non-human agencies, seen above. Despite these prohibitions, Almada explains that "our people, finding them in hidden places, where they cannot be seen, kill and eat them".[87] Although the hunting of these birds was prohibited locally, it was practiced by foreigners who did not recognise the legitimacy of the prohibition. However, once discovered, they were subjected to justice in accordance with the local regulatory regime. Perhaps it was *chays* like this that Barreira was referring to when he considered them feigning a crime.

83 Malacco, "Novas aproximações sobre o comércio, produção e uso do marfim", 62.

84 Annual Letter from Father Baltasar Barreira to the Provincial of Portugal, Brásio, *Monumenta Missionaria Africana, África Ocidental*, serie 2, vol. 4, 383. Original: "se algum navio dá à costa, é logo tomado para el-rei, com toda a fazenda que nele acha, e para fazerem isso mesmo aos que estão de assento na povoação, basta fingirem alguma culpa que cometera a que chamam chay".

85 Almada, "Tratado Breve dos rios da Guiné do Cabo Verde …", 328. Original: "por leis do reino, não se podem matar, nem ninguém as mata, porque há grandes penas postas sobre isso".

86 Almada, "Tratado Breve dos rios da Guiné do Cabo Verde …", 328. Original: "são estas aves as almas dos seus antepassados".

87 Almada, "Tratado Breve dos rios da Guiné do Cabo Verde …", 328. Original: "os nossos, achando-as em lugares escusos, donde não sejam vistos, as matam e as comem".

From the point of view of local norms, based on common knowledge about the family lineages that had first occupied the land and subsequent rights arising from the establishment of social ties, there was no Portuguese land ownership in Greater Senegambia. Land could not be purchased and the right belonging to a family line could not be transferred. For this reason, Portuguese merchants were invariably subject to local government, which sometimes protected them and sometimes, legitimately under local norms, stripped them of their goods. In the first decade of the 17th century, Father Barreira said indignantly that, in Porto d'Ale, there was "a village of one hundred Portuguese who follow the law of Moses, and the king defends them from anyone who wants to stop them. This port is the most important for the rescue of [or the purchase of enslaved people by] foreigners".[88] If the protection of Portuguese Jews revolted the Jesuit, this did not happen when they were Portuguese Christians who were under the protection of the local sovereign, as in Bissau: "the king of Bissau shelters the Portuguese, and there they have houses and a large ransom [or trade]".[89]

All these dynamics of use, control, and concession of land were under customs that are compatible with those expressed through oral traditions, as discussed above. At the beginning of the 17th century, Father Álvares described how the Mandingo presence had become naturalised in the region of the Gambia River, to the point that the territory began to be recognised as the land of the Mandingo, to the detriment of the indigenous people who had preceded them. In the writings of the Portuguese Jesuit, the distinction between Mandingo and Soninque (Sonequi in early Portuguese documents) was based on the legitimacy of land control. The Mandingo were newly arrived foreigners; the Soninque were those who already inhabited the region. However, the process of naturalisation of the Mandingo people made it confusing for Europeans to recognise who were the holders of rights over the land. Alvares narrated:

> The land of the Sonequi heathen is today confused and is so connected with the Mandingo that it is named after them. But dealing specifically, it is the river of Gambia and that hinterland, which the common people call

88 Letter from Father Baltasar Barreira to Father João Álvares, Brásio, *Monumenta Missionaria Africana, África Ocidental*, serie 2, vol. 4, 165. Original: "uma aldeia de cem portugueses que seguem a lei de Moisés, e el-rei os defende de quem os quer impedir. Este porto é o mais importante para os resgates dos estrangeiros".

89 Letter from Father Baltasar Barreira to Father João Álvares, Brásio, *Monumenta Missionaria Africana, África Ocidental*, serie 2, vol. 4, 168. Original: "o rei de Bissau agasalha os portugueses, e ali têm casas e grande resgate".

> Mandingo's, the very heritage of the idolatrous heathen Sonequi; because the Mandingo comes from Mande Mansa.[90]

In other words, the Mandingo come from Mali, and they were not native at the coast. When explaining that the land was "heritage of the heathen Sonequi", the Jesuit recognises the local custom based on oral traditions, which guarantees that the control of the land rests with the one who first occupied it. Social practice, however, seemed confusing to him, once the Mandingo, a people of foreign origin, had seemingly come to dominate the region. To better understand this transition, we need to go back to the previous section to remember that the first occupation of a space—to clean the bush—was the main way to legitimise the later domain. However, the establishment of social bonds, mainly through marriages with members of the family lineages that owned the land, allowed, generation after generation, control over the land to pass from one social group to another. In view of this, the fact that the sources demonstrate that the Mandingo people came to have control over the land reveals the impact of social dynamics in Senegambia.

It was in the second half of the 17th century that the trader Lemos Coelho explained what was going on, once again recognising the importance of oral traditions. On the Bintang River, a tributary of the southern bank of the Gambia River, Lemos Coelho observed that the Mandingo peoples dominated the territory and explained that such dominance derived from two facts: on the one hand, it originated from ancient migration accompanied by new links with the local population, through which the Mandingo became naturalised; on the other hand, it stemmed from the fact that the indigenous peoples had adopted the culture brought by the Mandingo, that is, they became Mandingo. Lemos Coelho reports: "from one side to the other [of the Bintang river], they are Mandingo, a nation that, coming from the land of Mandimança as local guests, became naturalised here, or the inhabitants of the land, taking their rites, also took the nickname of Mandingo, being all Mohammedans", i.e., Muslims.[91] In

90 Álvares, *Etiópia Menor e Descrição Geográfica da Província da Serra Leoa*, 9. Original: "está a terra do gentio sonequi hoje confusa, e tão ligada com os mandingas, que deles se denomina. Mas tratando especificamente, é o rio de Gâmbia e aquele sertão, a que chama o vulgo de mandingas, próprio patrimônio do sonequi gentio idólatra; porquanto o mandinga traz sua origem de Mande Mansa".

91 Lemos Coelho, Francisco, Discripção da Costa de Guine e Situação de todos os Portos e Rios dela …, 117. Original: "de uma banda como de outra [do rio Bintang], são Mandingas, nação que vindo por hóspedes da terra de Mandimança se naturalizaram aqui, ou os povoadores da terra, tomando os seus ritos, tomaram também o cognominamento de mandingas, sendo todos mahometanos".

both cases, it turns out that control over the land in the vicinity of the Gambia River, at that time, belonged to the Mandingo.

The processes of naturalisation of the Mandingo and the 'Mandingusation' of the natives resulted from the establishment of family ties between the newcomers and those already there. This was also the resource used by several Europeans to access goods, land, and commercial networks in West Africa: to marry, according to local customs, women from family lines that held political power in the region. There are already several cases documented by the historiography. Regarding the Portuguese presence, among the most famous are the rich merchants of Cacheu, Crispina Perez and Bibiana Vaz.[92] These women's marriages to European men or men of European descent gave them access to the Atlantic market and gave the husbands access to internal commercial networks and land belonging to the women's family lines, in accordance with local law.

The wealth of West African elites derived precisely from their control over the land, exercised through the collection of taxes for the use of natural resources: land for planting or grazing, logging, hunting, fishing or drawing water from rivers. In the previous section, we saw how oral traditions explained the collection of taxes for the use of the territory's resources. The written documentation supports these records.[93] However, we also saw that political power was not a despotic will played by local rulers. The existence of a court justice system based on orality and the elderly explains how the resources were locally distributed, including land and property rights related to land ownership. In 1610, Barreira considered abusive "the rights that [the Portuguese] pay for the goods they bring in or take out, and the rigor with which [local rulers] make some pay what others owe, with no other reason than being from the same nation".[94] In 1731, the Englishman Francis Moore pointed out the need to pay tribute to land holders in Senegambia: if foreign traders refuse, "the king will not allow them to have either wood or water in their country",[95] making everything more or less impossible. In highly fiscal political organisations, such

92 Havik, *Silences and Soundbytes*; Santos, "Mulheres africanas nas redes dos agentes da inquisição de Lisboa …" 72–76.

93 Malacco and Gonçalves, "Entre Senegâmbia e Angola", 66.

94 Annual Letter from Father Baltasar Barreira to the Provincial of Portugal, Brásio, *Monumenta Missionaria Africana, África Ocidental*, serie 2, vol. 4, 383. Original: "os direitos que [os portugueses] pagam das mercadorias que metem ou tiram, e o rigor com que [os governantes locais] fazem pagar a uns o que outros deviam, sem outro fundamento mais que serem da mesma nação".

95 Moore, *Travels into the Inlands parts of Africa*, 20.

as the Senegambian States,[96] local control of land, territory, and political power were complementary spheres that fed back to one another.

6 Conclusions

At the beginning of this Chapter, we saw that Father Barreira lamented the vulnerability of Portuguese traders in African territories. Since many of them did not have social ties that would guarantee them protection under local law, the rulers acted with great liberality over their possessions. At the end of the 16th century, Almada was exasperated with the treatment received by the Portuguese who lived in the village of Buguendo, in present-day Guinea-Bissau, saying:

> These blacks from the village of Buguendo were so mean to our people, and they treated them so badly that they couldn't suffer [more]. And a black man was not seen as an honourable man if he didn't take their hats off and give them some punches and slaps. And there were many blacks from the King's house called Reinaldos, and others Roldoes, and other names of this quality. And when they came to this village, they brought a squadron of black rogues and loafers in front of them, who came saying to our people: "Here comes Reinaldo, here comes Roldão", so that they would prepare for them and arrange what they would be given. And if they didn't have it, they treated the Portuguese very badly. And with all these things the blacks make them suffer.[97]

A few years later, Barreira reported that when a potentate needed money, he sent one of his representatives to the Portuguese house to demand it. "This one comes with great accompaniment and enters their houses so freely and with such authority, as if the inhabitants of them were their slaves, with no one

96 Green, *A fistful of shells*, 16; chap. 7.

97 Almada, "Tratado Breve dos rios da Guiné do Cabo Verde …", 304–305. Original: "Eram tão maus estes negros da aldeia do Buguendo para os nossos que os tratavam tão mal, que se não podia sofrer, E não se tinha por honrado negro que lhes não tomava os chapéus, e dessem bofetadas e pancadas. E havia muitos negros da casa do Rei chamados a uns Reinaldos, e outros Roldoes, e outros nomes desta qualidade. E quando vinham a esta aldeia traziam uma esquadra de negros velhacos e vadios de diante deles, que vinham dizendo aos nossos: "Lá vêm Reinaldo, lá vem Roldão", para que lhes fizessem prestes e aparelhassem o que lhes haviam de dar. E tanto que não havia[m] isto os tratavam muito mal. E com todas estas cousas sofriam aos negros".

to tackle them, or dare to deny what they ask or want".[98] That is why, in 1684, Lemos Coelho recommended that other Portuguese or Cape Verdean traders who ventured along the African coast should realise that they were "guests and pilgrims, and that they are in foreign lands, which the blacks prevented them from controlling".[99] And Lemos Coelho continued, elaborating what I called the "handbook about how to be a foreigner":

> Treat well the black who takes [you] as a guest, who is always one of the nobles of the land. Do not deny kings and their officials anything that you have, as it is in their power and will to ask or take from you, it is not discretion to go to extremes. In their disgusts and in their parties, visit them and accompany them, that in this way, wherever you live, you will preserve yourselves with love and quietness, and will take advantage of the interests of the land and will do business more comfortably, and will sleep your nights rested.[100]

As demonstrated throughout this Chapter, Europeans in Africa found themselves guests in foreign lands. They were, therefore, as much subject to the local sovereigns as to the justice practiced in those lands, according to established customs. In view of this, the ownership regime that applied to them was not the one established by the law in force in Portugal. Rather, to understand the formation of the Portuguese empire in a global range, given the plurality of norms in force, it is essential to recognise how the law was applied in the lands where the Portuguese settled, through concessions by local powers. Those who controlled the land, understood both as a resource for production and as a political territ-

98 Annual Letter from Father Baltasar Barreira to the Provincial of Portugal, Brásio, *Monumenta Missionaria Africana, África Ocidental*, serie 2, vol. 4, p. 383. Original: "Este vem com grande acompanhamento, e entra pelas suas casas tão livremente e com tanta autoridade, como se os moradores delas fossem seus escravos, sem haver quem lhe vá à mão, ou se atreva a lhe negar o que pede, ou deseja".

99 Lemos Coelho, Francisco, Discripção da Costa de Guine e Situação de todos os Portos e Rios dela …, 92–93. Original: "hóspedes e peregrinos, e que estão em terras alheias, das quais os negros os privaram do domínio delas".

100 Lemos Coelho, Francisco, Discripção da Costa de Guine e Situação de todos os Portos e Rios dela …, 92–93. Original: "Tratem bem ao negro que [os] tomarem por hóspede, que sempre é um dos fidalgos da terra. Aos reis e seus oficiais não neguem coisa alguma do que tiverem, que pois está na sua mão e vontade pedir-lhe ou tomar-lhe, não é discrição chegar ao extremo. Em seus nojos e em suas festas, visite-os e acompanhe-os, que deste modo em qualquer parte que viverem se conservarão com amor e quietação, e se aproveitarão dos interesses da terra e farão o negócio com mais comodidade, e dormirão seus sonos descansados".

ory, were those who *de facto* had legitimacy to apply justice and, hence, extend their power over foreigners' property rights, revealing the centrality of African agency within the so-called Portuguese Empire.

The ownership regime of Europeans on the African coast must thus be understood from the point of view of local norms, and no longer from European ones. Therefore, I consider it essential that studies on land ownership in the Portuguese empire advance toward understanding the local justice of the societies where this empire intended to establish itself. The history of European regimes is not the history of property laws. Local customs, as a way of interpreting laws, are fundamental. In Africa, the Portuguese were subject to a regime of possessions different from the one prevailing in Portugal. Although they also responded to the Portuguese Crown, and the metropolitan archives document this process well, the daily life in Greater Senegambia was permeated, in all aspects, by African customs. These findings demand that greater attention should be given to the regimes of norms experienced in African local contexts, instead of conceiving the European presence in Africa as a sufficient reason to universalise European justice as a norm that was applied to European subjects everywhere.

Acknowledgments

This Chapter was conceived during the Spring Term/2022 at the University of Pennsylvania (USA) during my time as a Fulbright visiting scholar. This chapter resulted from the research projects "Islamic expansion and retraction in the region of present-day Guinea-Bissau: Contours of a West African exceptionality"—Grant Term FAPEMIG/DAP nº. 36527059/2021; and "Islam, agrarian culture and politics in pre-colonial Guinea-Bissau", funded by CNPq Call No. 09/2022—Bolsa de Produtividade em Pesquisa—PQ No. 303208/2022-8. I am grateful to all the funding institutions.

Bibliography

Manuscripts

Álvares, Manuel. *Etiópia Menor e Descrição Geográfica da Província da Serra Leoa composta pelo Padre Manuel Álvares da Companhia de Jesus estando assistente na mesma província da Serra Leoa que não concluiu nem pôs a limpo por causa do seu falecimento no ano de 1616*. Copiada do próprio original que se conserva no Real Convento de São Francisco da Cidade de Lisboa. S.d. Sociedade de Geografia de Lisboa (SGL), Res.3 E-7.

National Center for Arts and Culture/Oral History and Antiquities Division, Research and Documentation Division (NCAC), Folders: 3346B, 163A, 419A, 487B, 490A-02, Tape 132/A, 346B, 553.

Printed Sources

Almada, André Álvares de, "Tratado Breve dos rios da Guiné do Cabo Verde dês do Rio de Sanagá até os baixos de Santa Ana de todas as nações de negros que há na dita costa e de seus costumes, armas, trajos, juramentos, guerras. Feito pelo capitão André Álvares d'Almada natural da Ilha de Santiago de Cabo Verde prático e versado nas ditas partes. Ano 1594", ed. Brásio, Padre António, *Monumenta Missionaria Africana, África Ocidental*, 2.ª série, vol. 3, Lisboa 1964.

Anguiano, Mateo de. *Misiones Capuchinas en Africa*, Tomo II: Misiones al Reino de la Zinga, Benín, Arda, Guinea, y Sierra Leona, por el P. Mateo de Anguiano, O.F.M. CAP., ed. Carrocera, P. Buenaventura de, Madrid 1957.

Bluteau, Rafael. *Vocabulario portuguez, e latino, aulico, anatomico, architectonico, bellico, botanico ...: autorizado com exemplos dos melhores escritores portuguezes, e latinos; e offerecido a El Rey de Portugal D. Joaõ V*, Coimbra, Collegio das Artes da Companhia de Jesu: Lisboa, Officina de Pascoal da Sylva, 1712–1728. 8 v; 2 Suplementos. Available in https://www.bbm.usp.br/pt-br/dicionarios/vocabulario-portuguez-latino-aulico-anatomico-architectonico/. Accessed on 12 June 2023

Brásio, Padre António (ed.). *Monumenta Missionaria Africana, África Ocidental*, serie 2, vol. 1, (1341–1499), Lisboa, 1958.

Brásio, Padre António (ed.), *Monumenta Missionaria Africana, África Ocidental*, serie 2, vol. 4, (*1600–1622*), Lisboa 1968.

Brásio, Padre António (ed.), *Monumenta Missionaria Africana, África Ocidental*, serie 2, vol. 5, (*1623–1650*), Lisboa 1979.

Donelha, André, *Descrição da Serra Leoa e dos Rios de Guiné do Cabo Verde* (*1625*), ed. Mota, Avelino Teixeira da, Lisboa 1977.

Jobson, Richard, *The Golden Trade. Or, A Discovery of the River Gambia*, ed. Gamble, David; Hair, P.E.H., London, 1999.

Lemos Coelho, Francisco, *Discripção da Costa de Guine e Situação de todos os Portos e Rios dela, e Roteyro para se Poderem Navegar todos seus Rios. Feita pelo Capitam Francisco de Lemos em Sam Thiago de Cabo Verde, no Anno de 1684*, ed. Peres, Damião, *Duas Descrições seiscentistas da Guiné*, Lisboa 1990.

Moore, Francis, *Travels into the Inlands parts of Africa*, London: Edward Cave, at St John's Gate, 1738.

Literature

Alfagali, Crislayne, "Conflito de terras nos sertões de Angola. Estudo de caso da disputa pelas terras de Ilamba, século XVIII", in *Revista de História* 178 (2019).

Ba, Amadou Hampatê, "A tradição viva", in Ki-Zerbo, Joseph (ed.), *História Geral da África I. Metodologia e pré-história*, Brasília 2010.

Bastias Saavedra, Manuel, "Decentering Law and Empire: Law-Making, Local Normativities, and the Iberian Empires in Asia", in Bastias Saavedra, Manuel (ed.), *Norms beyond Empire. Law-Making and Local Normativities in Iberian Asia, 1500–1800*, Leiden 2022, 1–31.

Baum, Robert M., *Shrines of the Slave Trade. Diola Religion and Society in Precolonial Senegambia*, New York 1999.

Berstein, Henry, "Rural Land and Land Conflicts in Sub-Saharan Africa", in Moyo, Sam and Paris Yeros (eds.), *Reclaming the Land. The Resurgence of Rural Movements in Africa, Asia and Latin America*, London 2005, 67–101.

Boxer, Charles R., *O Império Marítimo Português 1415–1825*, Lisboa 2018.

Brooks, George, *Eurafricans in Western Africa. Commerce, Social Status, Gender, and Religious Observance from the Sixteenth to the Eighteenth Century*, Athens (OH) 2003.

Candido, Mariana. "Conquest, occupation, colonialism and exclusion: land disputes in Angola", in Serrão, José Vicente, Bárbara Direito, Eugénia Rodrigues and Susana Münch Miranda (eds.). *Property Rights, Land and Territory in the European Overseas Empires*, Lisboa 2015, 223–234.

Candido, Mariana, *Wealth, Land, and Property in Angola. A History of Dispossession*, Slavery, and Inequality, New York 2022.

Carvalho, Flávia Maria de, *Sobas e homens do rei. Interiorização dos portugueses em Angola (séculos XVII e XVIII)*, Maceió (AL) 2015.

Cohen, Zelinda, "Administração das ilhas de Cabo Verde e seu distrito no segundo século de colonização (1560–1640)" in Santos, Maria Emília Madeira (ed.), *História Geral de Cabo Verde* (Vol. 2), Lisboa 2001, pp. 189–224.

Cook, Lexie, "The Silent Tangomão. Fictions of Intermediation along the Rivers of Guinea", in *Journal for Early Modern Cultural Studies* 21:4 (2021), 24–62.

Curtin, Philip, *Economic Change in Precolonial Africa. Senegambia in the Era of the Slave Trade*, Madison 1975.

Curtin, Philip, "Jihad in West Africa. Early Phases and Inter-Relations in Mauritania and Senegal", in *The Journal of African History* 12:01 (1971), pp. 11–24.

Ferreira, Marieta de Moraes and Janaína Amado, "Apresentação" in Ferreira, Marieta de Moraes and Janaína Amado (eds.), *Usos e abusos da História Oral*, Rio de Janeiro 2006, pp. vii–xxv.

Freitas, Roberth. *Desenterrando mortos e enterrando vivos em suas entranhas. Uma história social dos Sapes na Serra Leoa (1506–1615)* (M.A. Thesis), Belo Horizonte 2022.

Gomez, Michael A. *African Dominion. A New History of Empire in Early and Medieval West Africa*, Princeton 2018.

Green, Toby. *The Rise of the Trans-Atlantic Slave Trade in Western Africa, 1300–1589*, New York 2012.

Green, Toby, *A Fistful of Shells. West Africa from the Rise of the Slave Trade to the Age of Revolution*, Chicago 2019.

Havik, Philip, *Silences and Soundbytes. The gendered Dynamics of Trade and Brokerage in the pre-colonial Guinea Bissau Region*, Munster 2004.

Hawthrone, Walter, *Planting Rice and Harvesting Slaves. Transformations along the Guinea Bissau Coast 1400–1900*, Portsmouth (NH) 2003.

Horta, José da Silva. *A, "Guiné do Cabo Verde". Produção textual e representações (1578–1684)*, Lisboa 2011.

Ka, Thierno, *École de Pir Saniokhor. Histoire, Enseignement et Culture arabo-islamique au Sénégal du XVIIIe au XXe siècle*, Dakar 2002.

Klein, Martin, "Social and Economic Factors in the Muslim Revolution in Senegambia", in *Journal of African History*, 13:3 (1972), pp. 419–441.

Malacco, Felipe, *A Senegâmbia e o Atlântico. Espaço e Agência Local (1580–1700)* (Ph.D. Thesis), Belo Horizonte 2023.

Malacco, Felipe and Ivan Sicca Gonçalves, "Entre Senegâmbia e Angola. Comércio atlântico, protagonismo africano e dinâmicas regionais (séculos XVII e XIX)", in *Afro-Ásia*, 62 (2020), 46–97.

Malacco, Felipe, "Novas aproximações sobre o comércio, produção e uso do marfim", in Santos, Vanicléia Silva, Eduardo França Paiva and René Lommez Gomes (eds.), *O comércio de marfim no Mundo Atlântico. Circulação e produção* (séculos XV ao XIX), Belo Horizonte, 2017, pp. 41–64.

Mark, Peter, *"Portuguese" Style and Luso-African Identity. Precolonial Senegambia, Sixteenth–Nineteenth Centuries*, Bloomington 2002.

Mark, Peter and Jose da Silva Horta, *The Forgotten Diaspora. Jewish Communities in West Africa and the Making of the Atlantic World*, New York 2011.

Mota, Thiago H., "O Islã na África Atlântica: transformações no significado de comportamentos religiosos (séculos XVI–XVII)", in Reginaldo, Lucilene and Roquinaldo Ferreira (eds.), *África, margens e oceanos. Perspectivas de História Social*, Campinas 2021, pp. 181–216.

Nafafé, José Lingna, "Lançados, Culture and Identity: Prelude to Creole Societies on the Rivers of Guinea and Cape Verde", in Havik, Philip J. and Malyn Newitt (eds.), *Creole Societies in the Portuguese Colonial Empire*, Cambridge 2015, pp. 65–91.

Pélissier, René, *História da Guiné. Portugueses e Africanos na Senegâmbia (1841–1936)*, Lisboa 1989.

Rodrigues, Eugénia, *Portugueses e Africanos nos Rios de Sena. Os prazos da Coroa em Moçambique nos séculos XVII e XVIII*, Lisboa 2013.

Santos, Vanicléia Silva, "Mulheres africanas nas redes dos agentes da inquisição de Lisboa. O caso de Crispina Peres em Cacheu, século XVII", *Politeia. História e Sociedade* 20:1 (2021). 67–95.

Sarr, Assan, *Islam, Power, and Dependency in the River Gambia Basin. The Politics of Land Control, 1790–1940*, Rochester 2016.

Sidibé, Al Haji Bakary, *A Brief History of Kaabu and Fuladu (1300–1930). A Narrative Based on Some Oral Traditions of the Senegambia (West Africa)*, Torino 2004.

Silva, António Correia e, "Cabo Verde e a geopolítica do Atlântico", in Santos, Maria Emília Madeira (ed.), *História Geral de Cabo Verde* (Vol. 2), Lisboa 1995.

Soares, Maria João, "Os Lançados nos Rios da Guiné. Século XVI–meados do século XVII", *Revista STUDIA*, 56/57 (2000).

Thornton, John K., *Africa and Africans in the Making of the Atlantic World, 1400–1800*, Cambridge 1998.

Vansina, Jan, *Oral Tradition. A Study in Oral Methodology*, Chicago 1965.

CHAPTER 4

A Widow's Tale

Shifting Land Regimes and the Interplay between Household and Community in Colonial Peru

José Carlos de la Puente Luna

1 Introduction

On 22 September 1586, indigenous city authorities executed Francisca Colloc's last will and sold portions of her estate at public auction. Among the belongings of this resident of the semiurban parish of El Hospital in Cuzco was "a ball of yarn to measure plots" which one María Pasña bought on the spot for a tiny fraction of a peso.[1] We do not know what made this particular string suitable for that specific purpose. Nor do we know of any occasions on which Francisca may have laid the yarn over her fields or those of others. Perhaps she sold such balls of yarn to other parish residents, for her relatively small estate included wool and pieces of cloth. Whether Francisca and María were relatives or neighbours is not specified either but, based on the former's possession of the ball of yarn and the latter's wish to purchase it, presumably for her own use, it is fair to say that measuring, and thus delimiting, agricultural tracts was of some importance for these two women, and surely many others. While our limited understanding of the mechanisms available to Native Andean women like Francisca and María for exerting control over particular plots—that were, in most cases, also subject to varying degrees of familial and communal oversight—does not allow us to say much more about Francisca's mysterious measuring string, in this Chapter, I explore the relationship between women like Francisca and the land ownership regimes of the *pueblos de indios* of their time.

Much has been written about indigenous land tenure in the colonial Americas. Regarding the Andes region and, until recently, the debate has lingered on a twin set of opposites: the private versus the communal dimension, on the

1 "with Vn obillo de cabuya para medir chacaras." "Auto de prosecución de la almoneda pública de los bienes de Francisca Colloc", Cuzco, 22 September 1586. Archivo Regional del Cuzco, Protocolos Notariales, 4 (Pedro de la Carrera Ron/Pedro Quispe), fol. 695r. I thank Gabriela Ramos for sharing this precious information with me.

DOI:10.1163/9789004722729_005

one hand, and permanent and exclusive ownership versus temporary use, on the other. These basic oppositions have generally informed past historiographical assumptions about pre-Hispanic agropastoral communities, particularly the premise that such collectives held all pasture and farmland "in common" and, therefore, novel forms of exclusive (i.e., private or individual) control over land and its products were introduced only in the aftermath of the Iberian conquest.[2] A new agrarian history has started to challenge these long-held assumptions by noting that earlier views tended to overstate the importance, and in fact the very existence, of private land regimes in early modern Spain, creating a stark contrast between the Spanish and Andean worlds of the 16th century, one that simply did not exist. In fact, as Alan Greer and others have recently noted, "Spain stood out in the European context as the kingdom par excellence of public lands, municipal commons and extensive grazing privileges."[3] Thus, ironically, the emphasis on usufruct and possession over firm property rights, as applied to Andean ownership regimes, is also largely applicable to the 16th-century Iberian world.[4] A parallel critique of old paradigms has pointed out that a diversity of land ownership regimes, as defined in Manuel Bastias Saavedra's Chapter in this volume, existed in the Andes at the time of contact

2 Pease G.Y., "La noción de propiedad entre los Incas", 11; Hernández Astete, "La historiografía andina y la idea de propiedad"; Ramírez, "El concepto de 'comunidad'", 183–184; Ramírez, "Land and Tenure in Early Colonial Peru", 10; Ramírez, "Despedazando lo común", 288, 299; Noejovich Chernoff, *Los albores de la economía americana*. Although the use of the term *property* in Andean ethnohistory has been common, it is partially anachronistic. 16th- and 17th-century jurists would have understood tenure in terms of domain (*dominio* or *señorío*), which encompassed property and other related legal regimes, such as *dominio directo, dominio útil, posesión* and *detentación*. Bastias Saavedra, "The Normativity of Possession"; Gonzales Escudero, "Una aproximación procesal a la defensa de la tierra indígena". An early critique of the alleged incompatibility between widespread practices found within Andean peasant communities, such as labour exchanges among households and collective labour recruitment and self-interest and calculation survival, can be found in Guillet, "Agro-Pastoral Land Use", 14–15.

3 De Dios et al., *Historia de la propiedad en España*; Greer, *Property and Dispossession*, 16 [quote]; Herzog, *Frontiers of Possession*; Izquierdo, *El rostro de la comunidad*.

4 On land held as commons in Spain and other parts of Europe, see also Arguedas, *Las comunidades de España y del Perú*; Conte, "The Many Legal Faces of the Commons"; Greer, *Property and Dispossession*, 249–250; Herzog, "How did the Commons Become Terra nullius?"; Vassberg, *Land and Society in Golden Age Castile*, 26–64. On the type of farming known as sectoral fallowing or common-field agriculture, found in the Central Andes and the Iberian Peninsula, see Godoy, "The Evolution of Common-Field Agriculture". For poignant critiques of these assumptions, see Bastias Saavedra, "The Normativity of Possession"; Godoy, "The Evolution of Common-Field Agriculture", 401, n. 5; Graubart, "'*Ynuvaciones malas e rreprouadas*'", 160; Graubart, "Shifting Landscapes", 67; Greer, *Property and Dispossession*, 16, 95.

and after. Karen Graubart has argued, for instance, that, "[b]eneath the archival appearance of standardized descriptions of land tenure were a whole gamut of actual relationships to property, both in terms of tenure and use."[5] From these studies, a different picture, one with a plurality of pre-Hispanic and post-conquest landholding regimes—bundles of practices, rules, norms and principles mediating the relationship between people and land—is beginning to emerge.[6]

In this Chapter, I take on this second line of inquiry by reassessing communal ownership regimes and village customs regarding land management and inheritance through the lens of Andean colonial forms of commoning. I propose that, while it is true that ideal dichotomies and an excessive emphasis on law, doctrine, and legal theory have limited our understanding of indigenous land regimes within the context of European colonialism, the distinction between individual and collective remains methodologically relevant for our understanding of how mid-colonial Native communities held, used, and regulated land at the village level. The 'individual', in this context, refers to the particular; it is situational, relational, and embedded. It is, for that reason, never exempt from a social dimension, because particular historical actors were inscribed in household, *ayllu* (kin group), village, and colonial power dynamics. As I will show, however, the 'individual' exists as an aspiration, a sense of entitlement, a matter of judicial rulings, and perhaps even a distinct normative subjectivity that, by strategically shifting the emphasis from the whole to the part, aimed to lessen, and in some specific instances even reduce to the minimum, temporary or permanent extended family and communal control over people, labour, and land. This is the status that the documents discussed below identify as being the *dueño* or owner of household fields, often termed *heredades* or *hacienda propia* in the sources, as opposed to plots considered properly communal (*tierras de comunidad*).[7] Just as important, the particular—someone's 'own', which usually takes the form of a hereditary claim associated with a single household—is a necessary component of the commons, since 'community' can be thought of as an aggregate of distinct households and *ayllus* that try to regulate each other's landholding rights. In his sweeping overview of 'property formations' in

5 Graubart, "Shifting Landscapes", 78.

6 Most notably, see Graubart, *Republics of Difference*. For New Spain, for which this topic has been thoroughly addressed, see Gibson, *The Aztecs under Spanish Rule*, 257–299; Lockhart, *The Nahuas after the Conquest*, 141–202; Villella, "'For So Long the Memories of Men Cannot Contradict It'". For Spanish and Portuguese America, see Herzog, *Frontiers of Possession*. For North America more broadly, see Greer, *Property and Dispossession*.

7 Medelius and Puente Luna, "Curacas, bienes y quipus"; Puente Luna, "Customs Apart".

North America, Greer argues that "the opposition of 'communal' and 'private' property (or 'collective' versus 'personal') seems inadequate, if not meaningless."[8] He suggests instead that we treat these terms, "not as poles of a dichotomy, but as different aspects of a single regime."[9] Pushing Greer's argument further, I contend that family and collective aspects of land within Native communities were not opposite ends of a spectrum but instead coterminous and historically contingent ways of acting on—that is, exerting power and control over—the same resources, even after death. By way of a case study based on rare intracommunal records, I show that a dynamic, mutually constitutive relationship existed between the two. In other words, my argument is not one of mere coexistence, but of dialectical opposition. By documenting the simultaneous existence of common fields alongside plots held in severality by specific households,[10] I hope to advance an alternative model for thinking relationally *and* dynamically about land regimes in relation to the local normative orders that regulated them.

Several formative bodies of literature have shaped my approach to communal land tenure.[11] Spanning three decades, the work of John Murra was instrumental in renewing our views about indigenous understandings of territory, land tenure, and land use prior to the Spanish conquest. Drawing on recently published colonial administrative inspections, Murra highlighted the existence of multiple, overlapping regimes at the household, community, and state levels, offering one of the first classifications of a wide range of holdings. Regarding peasant subsistence and tributary ownership regimes—my focus in this Chapter—Murra emphasised the importance of kinship for organising labour and granting community members "universal access" to both labour and, indirectly, plots and pastures, but did not delve much into the local normative orders regulating them. Murra also outlined the tension between individual and collective rights at the core of communal life, though he postponed

8 Greer, *Property and Dispossession*, 53–54.

9 Greer, *Property and Dispossession*, 34–35.

10 Serulnikov, "The Politics of Intracommunity Land Conflict". Anthropologists doing fieldwork in the Andes in the 1970s and 1980s thoroughly documented this coexistence. Albó, *La paradoja aymara*, 18; Benavides, "Tenencia de tierras agrícolas en el valle del Colca", 62; Cadena, *Economía campesina*, 33–35; Cadena, "Cooperación y mercado en la organización comunal andina", 44–43; Gálvez, Ansión, and Degregori, "Lo individual y lo colectivo en la comunidad andina"; Guillet, *Agrarian Reform and Peasant Economy*; Mayer and Cadena, *Cooperación y conflicto en la comunidad andina*, 29; Ossio A., "La propiedad en las comunidades andinas", 36, 56–57.

11 Readers interested in a more detailed assessment of the literature can see an earlier version of this study, published as Puente Luna, "Of Widows, Furrows, and Seed".

a more in-depth discussion of community-level land tenure patterns until additional archival findings had come to light.[12]

Numerous studies developed Murra's insights, although the processual aspects of his viewpoint gradually faded from the scholarship. A 1644 municipal trial involving a widow from the village of Santiago de Carania and her written claims to land can help us examine the tensions between the individual and the collective that Murra's pathbreaking analysis 40 years ago left unresolved. This file is one of only a handful surviving records that document the inner workings of Andean municipalities as courts of justice prior to 1700.[13] The dossier provides a series of village stories that would be otherwise inaccessible. This record places into focus land and the regulation of the community, allowing us to think about this relationship, as others have done, as social process.[14] The analysis also foregrounds the interplay between community and family holdings, allowing us to probe into what these categories and the local normativities that informed them meant to Native Andeans not only when crafting arguments with their attorneys for presentation to a judge, but also in their everyday lives outside the colonial courtroom.

To unlock ownership regimes within Andean commons, I take up Murra's suggestion to focus on energy in flux, and I draw inspiration from Joseph Bastien's conceptualisation of communal land rights as "flexible, reciprocal, and periodical [...] intimately linked to the ecological, corporate, and cultural structure of the *ayllu*."[15] Moreover, I build on theorisations, particularly Marisol de la Cadena's, of the *ayllu* as a mutually constitutive relation between individuals and the group, thus refraining from imposing too drastic a distinction

12 Murra, "Waman Puma", 14. See also Murra, "Derechos a las tierras en el Tawantinsuyu"; Murra, "Una visión indígena del mundo andino".

13 For two examples of Andean *cabildos* acting as courts of law, see Mumford, "Las llamas de Tapacarí"; Puente Luna and Honores, "Guardianes de la real justicia". A handful of novel cases is presented in Puente Luna, "Customs Apart". Using late-colonial records, Sergio Serulnikov offers an excellent discussion of intracommunal strife between *ayllus* and nuclear families in 18th-century Chayanta (Charcas). Serulnikov, "The Politics of Intracommunity Land Conflict". Graubart adds yet another case to the growing corpus, this time from the Lima countryside, in *Republics of Difference*, 170–171.

14 Kosiba and Hunter, "Fields of Conflict".

15 Bastien, "Land Litigations", 115. Murra emphasised the negotiation and regulation of human energies after eventually moving away from a focus on formal claims to land, because without regimented access to other people's labour, formal claims to land, water and pastures in this context were ultimately hollow. Murra, "Derechos a tierras en el Tawantinsuyu", 305–306. On property rights as "obligations owed between persons in respect of things", see the classic study by Gluckman, *Politics, Law, and Ritual in Tribal Society*, 46.

between part and whole.[16] Although this Chapter has a single case study at its heart, I have supplemented my findings for the *corregimiento* (judicial district) of Yauyos, where Carania is located, with examples from other midsize north central and central Andean societies, including those in the neighbouring *corregimiento* of Huarochirí, to highlight the significance of my conclusions. These societies shared basic cultural practices and historical features, such as organisation into strong, semiautonomous *ayllus* that endured the Inca and Spanish conquest, formal resettlement of their populations in nucleated villages between the 1560s and 1580s, steep competition for pastures and periodic land disputes between households and *ayllus* and, as far as we can tell, similar agricultural traditions and land management systems. In reconstructing the relationship between people and their fields in the village of Carania, I also draw inspiration from a body of ethnographic observations about land and tenure, mainly produced in the 1970s and 1980s, and largely overlooked by colonial Andeanists. This fieldwork, especially that devoted to Yauyos, noted that communal "productive zones" were in fact delimited through varying degrees or levels of individual and collective oversight and authority over labour, infrastructure, agropastoral cycles, and surplus. All these zones were crisscrossed by tensions among individual households, extended families and the community.[17]

Moreover, to overcome the static portrait of land regimes inherited from earlier community and ethnohistorical studies, I highlight practices and strategies of commoning, uncommoning, and recommoning through individual and collective action. As Silvia Federici notes, commoning activities "require, as well as produce, community."[18] Indeed, by shifting the emphasis from the com-

---

16 Cadena, *Earth Beings*, 12, 26, 57, 258, 274. Catherine Allen has also recently suggested that people in-*ayllu* "bring about each other within a relation." Allen, "Final Commentaries", 339.

17 Benavides, "Apuntes históricos y etnográficos del valle del río Colca", 18–19; Cadena, "Cooperación y mercado en la organización comunal andina", 46; Guillet, *Agrarian Reform and Peasant Economy*; Izko, "Comunidad andina", 63–66; Mayer, *The Articulated Peasant*; Mayer and Cadena, *Cooperación y conflicto en la comunidad andina*; Orlove and Godoy, "Sectoral Fallowing Systems in the Central Andes"; Orlove, Godoy, and Morlon, "Sistemas de barbecho sectorial"; Ossio A., "La propiedad en las comunidades andinas", 45–48; Stein, "La práctica de la antropología económica en los Andes peruanos", 557–561.

18 Federici, *Re-enchanting the World*, 166. Wesley Chaney's analysis of commons governance in the Tao River watershed (Northwest China) similarly shows that, "in regulating access to depletable resources, *gong* [commons] regimes delineated, and perhaps even played a role in defining, the boundaries of a community." Chaney, "Threats to Gong", 47. See also Herzog's reflections regarding use of land and community membership in *Frontiers of Possession*, Part II.

mons as a noun to commoning as an action, a view that resonates with recent conceptualisations of the commons as movement, process, and relation, I take the analysis beyond legal definitions of property and dominion, the appropriation of indigenous lands, and the recognition of the entangled nature of land tenure systems in villages and towns throughout the colonial world.[19] Insofar as it expressed shifting social relations, commoning could be enacted, reversed, and reinstated through community and household norms and practices that necessarily took place over time and involved multidirectional shifts, regardless of whether the resulting tenure regimes found correlates in the language and genres of colonial law. This type of processual approach to land tenure claims and disputes brings the shifting realities of Andean collectives to the fore. At play in the story that follows (and likely those of many other mid-colonial Andean villagers whose disputes were never committed to writing) was the ebb and flow of the commons and its self-reproduction and regulation through practices of commoning and uncommoning.

2 The *Rayas* at Cancaurco

The events unfolded in an ordinary *pueblo de indios* (village) and *común* (community) named Santiago de Carania, located southeast of Lima in the upper Cañete watershed at roughly 3,800 metres above sea level.[20] A colonial foundation near an old settlement, Carania sat, like most villages in the area around Huarochirí and Yauyos, in a high mountain valley.[21] Surrounded by snow-

19 Blaser and Cadena, "The Uncommons", 190; Harvey, "The Future of the Commons", 105; Linebaugh, *The Magna Carta Manifesto*, 44–45. I am also influenced by Maria Ågren's verb-oriented approach to early modern women's work and by the story of Tsuneno, a 19th-century Japanese woman, as beautifully told by Amy Stanley. Ågren, "Making Her Turn Around"; Stanley, "Maidservants' Tales".

20 The literature on colonial Andean *comunes de indios* (Indian communities), a classic subject that bridges ethnohistories about Inca and early colonial times with histories and ethnographies about modern peasant communities, is too voluminous to cite fully. Some of the landmark works include Abercrombie, *Pathways of Memory and Power*; Rasnake, *Domination and Cultural Resistance*; Spalding, *Huarochirí*; Stern, *Peru's Indian Peoples and the Challenge of Spanish Conquest*. A recent, excellent example is Penry, *The People Are King*. Frank Salomon's important ethnographic work has critically expanded our knowledge of communal practices and infrastructures for managing collective resources and the legal and moral frameworks governing their use, reproduction and transfer since colonial times. Salomon, "Collca y *Sapçi*"; Salomon et al., "Los khipus de Rapaz en casa"; Salomon et al., "*Khipu* from Colony to Republic"; Salomon, "Guaman Poma's *Sapçi* in Ethnographic Vision".

21 An old road still connects Carania with the archaeological site of Huamanmarca, with

capped peaks and grasslands and contained within a relatively narrow ravine (*quebrada*), the Carania valley was created by the river of the same name, a tributary of the Cañete that still transports meltwater from a nearby lake into the ravine and across the valley. Prized terraced and unterraced farmlands for maize, potatoes and other tubers clustered around the settlement, along the riverbanks and on the steep mountain slopes that encase the valley (see Figure 4.1).[22]

In August 1644, María Jamarca, a widow in the village, appeared before municipal authorities to denounce *Ayllu* Chacallongo for "usurping" two of her *rayas* (boundary lines), threatening her livelihood and that of her two children.[23] As was customary in Carania and other places in the Andes, the *rayas*, named Chacasmarca and Chilcasonique, demarcated a segment of a much longer terrace (*andén* or *tabla*), one of several patches of productive land composing an agricultural sector; María's was of unspecified size.[24] Such toponyms, which Carania residents started recording in painstaking detail in their wills around this time, generally applied to both the *rayas* and the plots enclosed within, and were the primary means for distinguishing sectors and plots, distributing irrigation water and making landholding claims.[25] The fields associated with these toponyms did not belong to Chacallongo, María protested. Rather, they had been earmarked for "her" great-grandfather *Apu* (Lord) Caxauarco back "in the time of the Inca."[26] His direct descendants had

---

signs of prehispanic and early colonial occupation. Enríquez Tintaya, "Resultados preliminares", 86.

22 Spalding, *Huarochirí*, 13. Upper Yauyos and Lower Yauyos (Huarochirí) had been moieties of a single Inca administrative unit. Their inhabitants claimed a common ancestor, Pariacaca mountain. Dávila Briceño, "Descripsion", 65–66.

23 "Pues no es justo ni razon que me las usurpen." "Autos que siguen", fols. 11ʳ–11ᵛ. Here I use the style for naming *ayllus* that appears in the original document ("ayllo Chacallongo", "ayllo Pelle"), which follows traditional Spanish word order. In other parts of the dossier, María Jamarca's name appears as "María de la Concepción" and as "María Pachanxamarca".

24 On the use of *rayas* (literally "lines" in Spanish) as *mojones* (boundaries, landmarks) in a 1595 map of nearby Santo Domingo de Cochalaraos, see Beyersdorff, "Covering the Earth", 158, n. 58. The original Quechua expression in this map reads "raya mojonichic". "Titulación de la comunidad". For modern *surcos* (furrows, another meaning of *rayas*) and their role in distributing water evenly within plots, see Soler Bustamante, "La agricultura", 93, 111. Soler's ethnography also includes songs and sayings regarding the ploughing of these *rayas* in the neighbouring village of Huancayre. The original Quechua term being translated was probably 'suyu'. Itier, *Palabras clave de la sociedad y la cultura incas*, 263–268.

25 Wernke, Negotiated Settlements, 260.

26 "Autos que siguen", fols. 11ʳ⁻ᵛ. As early as 1566, Indigenous lords and others were making similar claims about inheriting tracts of land from their ancestors. Herzog, "Colonial Law and 'Native Customs'", 305–306; Ramírez, "Despedazando lo común", 296–298.

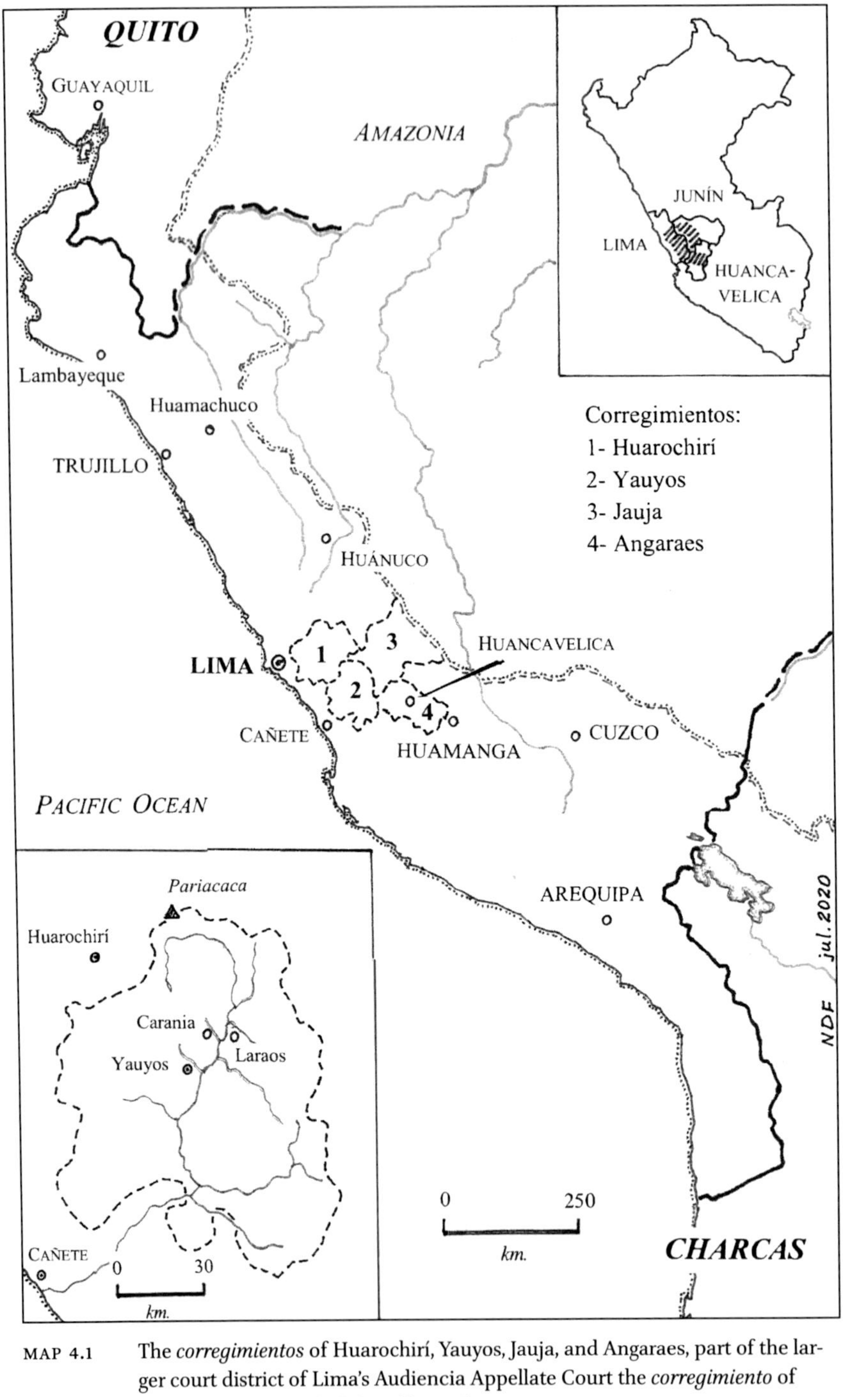

MAP 4.1 The *corregimientos* of Huarochirí, Yauyos, Jauja, and Angaraes, part of the larger court district of Lima's Audiencia Appellate Court the *corregimiento* of Yauyos, which included the village of Carania
MAP BY NICANOR DOMÍNGUEZ

been ploughing these fields for four generations uninterrupted. *Apu* Caxaurco likely presided over his fields, albeit in lithified form, for María referenced a stone staked in the ground as the critical marker of her ancestors' rights to the land.[27]

In her petition, María argued that, to justify seizing control of the plot, Chacallongo had resorted to a recent viceregal decree (not included in the dossier) secured in Lima after the filing of a previous petition, ostensibly by its members. The decree had recognised communal control over a presumably large agricultural sector named Cancaurco (Canca mountain), a well-delimited mountainside known to all parties that included the terraced fields in dispute. The decree had allocated it for "the benefit of the community." María detailed in her suit that Cancaurco had eight *tablas* in total: seven were to be tilled as commonage, but the eighth was hers to sow.[28] She beseeched the *alcalde* (municipal judge) to protect her right to support her family until her son turned of age by not "suspending" the fields, as had been done in previous years (she was likely referring to the decision to leave the fields fallow).[29] The municipal judge ruled in her favour, ordering Chacallongo to abstain from trespassing the boundary markers, "of which Diego Caxauarco [her son] is the *dueño*."[30] Put simply, the ruling meant that the judge (and likely others) considered Diego, the grandson of one Felipe Caxauarco, presumably *Apu* Caxauarco's son or grandson, the current owner (*dueño*) of the fields.[31] The judge ordered Chacallongo to plant and cultivate the *ayllu*'s seven terraces in Cancaurco collectively without invading other terraces or risk harsh punishment. The local Spanish *corregidor* upheld the verdict.

Even so, the following year, amidst the new agricultural cycle, María found herself before the next *corregidor*, again to defend the same fields and boundary lines (*chacras y rayas*) from Chacallongo's attempts at domaining. Echoing the gendered aspects of the *persona miserabilis* status generally afforded by colonial courts to indigenous women, particularly widows, María pleaded that

---

27 "El mojonado con una piedra." "Autos que siguen", fol. 11r. On the ongoing cult of the "antiguos dueños" (ancient owners) of important landmarks around Laraos (across the river from Carania), those who turned into lakes, springs and "piedras toscas sin figura alguna", see "Carta del Padre José de Arévalo".

28 Notice that "Cancaurco" is the name of a *raya* as well as the eight *tablas*.

29 "Hasta que mi hijo aya en hedad no suspenda como en los años passados." "Autos que siguen", fol. 11r.

30 "ques dueño del Diego Caxauarco nieto." "Autos que siguen", fol. 11v.

31 "Autos que siguen", fols. 11r–v. María refers to *Apu* Caxauarco as her grandfather ("mi besaguelo"), but the succession presented thereafter suggests a shorter genealogical distance between her husband and this ancestor.

her rivals were taking advantage of her being a "destitute and wrong-headed woman."[32] Furthermore, Chacallongo had resorted to the revealing strategy of scattering two *almudes* (about 16 kilograms) of seed over her fields. This was not ordinary but communal seed (*semillas de comunidad*), a crucial point to which I will return. The quantity of unidentified seed (very likely maize) is a clue as to the field's size. It also speaks to the type and amount of labour needed to till it. María had probably completed the land-preparation phase or *barbecho* by then, which was nothing short of hard work, which made the situation all the more aggravating.[33] On 3 March 1644, the Spanish magistrate sided with "this Indian woman", ordering Carania's Native municipal judge to uphold María's claims and to stop Chacallongo.[34] Four days later, Don Francisco Fernández Yauriuacho, the municipal judge tasked with enforcement, passed his own, lengthier judgement supporting the widow's claims.

Much more knowledgeable than his Spanish counterpart about inter-*ayllu* relations, local rules of inheritance, and customary regulations regarding land and labour, the Native judge protected (*amparar*) María's guardianship of her minor son's rights, confirming her possession of the *rayas* and, indirectly, the fields that they enclosed. However, he warned María not to let the seed enter the ground but to return it in full to Chacallongo.[35] Rather puzzlingly to an external observer, the judge reminded Chacallongo, with several *principales* (lineage heads) of some of the *ayllus* of Carania present, not to meddle in "the communal *rayas* of Ayllu Pelle" and that anyone who did so would be lashed in the pillory and shamed by having their hair cut short.[36] The judge's mention of *Ayllu* Pelle, one of the kin groups settled in Carania in the 1570s and 1580s, revealed that, at the municipal level, María's fields, inherited by three gener-

32 "pobre muger desatenado." "Autos que siguen", fol. 12^{r}.

33 Ethnographic work conducted in the 1950s in the villages of San Pedro de Huancaire and Santiago de Anchucaya (Huarorchirí; former Lurin Yauyos), related to the cultivation of potatoes, maize, and other crops, confirms that fieldwork was divided by sex and age. While adult men generally handled the ox plough (where available), women of different ages performed equally demanding tasks, including the planting of seed and their selection and categorisation after the harvest. Other, almost exclusively female tasks included hilling, watering and weeding. Matos Mar, *Las actuales comunidades*, 290; Soler Bustamante, "La agricultura en la comunidad de San Pedro de Huancaire", 111–122. On the contribution of women to Andean household and communal economies in general, see Brush and Guillet, "Small-Scale Agro-Pastoral Production", 25.

34 "esta Yndia." "Autos que siguen", fol. 12^{r}.

35 An entire sentence, probably detailing what was to happen with the communal seed, is torn from the original document.

36 "no se entremitan el ayllo Chacallongo en las rrayas de comunidad del ayllo Pelle." "Autos que siguen", fol. 12^{v}.

ations of her husband's patriline, also belonged to this *ayllu*. Could the fields now be Chacallongo's as well? The difference seemed one of perspective.

3 Carania's Communal Sector

To untangle the bundle of rights over Cancaurco, we must start by defining the type of land under dispute and the nature of María's claims to it. María had filed her complaint long after the first round of *reducción general* (general forced resettlement) undertaken in Yauyos by a diligent *corregidor* named Diego Dávila Briceño. Indeed, 60 years earlier, Dávila Briceño had boasted of having resettled more than 300 scattered hamlets into 39 newly founded villages, razing most of the old settlements to the ground.[37] Undoubtedly, the aggressive redistribution of the population and its forced resettlement was to contribute to the tensions surrounding farm and pastureland over the next 300 years. Despite deep social, political, and religious transformations caused by the *reducciones*, however, its effects on land tenure should not be overstated. While new villages, often near roads, rivers, and ravines were to dot the colonial landscape, others were founded again on older, pre-Hispanic sites where friars had established the first *doctrinas* (benefices) a few decades earlier.[38] Moreover, Dávila Briceño had to admit in 1586 that, given the harsh topography of the province and the scarcity of farmland, most fields had remained right where they were before, irrespective of the location of the new villages: on or around the old settlements.[39] After Dávila Briceño departed the province, Native peoples themselves abandoned some officially established villages and created multiple others. Households and *ayllus* (but not so much municipalities, as we will see) remained paramount in exerting power over internal decisions concerning the status, allocation, and classification of a village's core holdings.[40]

Cancaurco was where household, *ayllu*, and community met. At the time of María's filing, it was under the jurisdiction of the nearby hamlet (*asiento*) of San

37 Glave, "La cuadratura del círculo y las rendijas del encierro", 106–107; Spalding, *Huarochirí*, 178–180.

38 Schmitt Perea, "San Agustín de Guaquis".

39 "Residencia: Diego Dávila Briceño", fol. 313r. Forced resettlement, in Spalding's view, "did not affect the landholding patterns of the social groups [in Huarochirí] to any significant degree." Spalding, *Huarochirí*, 179.

40 My research on this point aligns with Serulnikov's findings for 18th-century Pocoata, a village in Northern Potosí. According to this author, "collective possession and repartition of land seems to have been mostly vested at the ayllu level." Serulnikov, "The Politics of Intracommunity Land Conflict", 122.

Bartolomé de Vaichana, a tiny settlement without municipal government, subject to Carania but not part of the original forced resettlement. Interestingly, 80 years later, San Bartolomé de Guaychana, along with Santa Ana Cancabilco (Cancaurco?) and San Antonio de Ache were included in a partial list of Carania's common fields, probably signalling their gradual absorption into the larger village endowment.[41] In Carania and elsewhere, so-called communal sectors, such as Cancaurco, were composed of parcels of variable size and productivity, often dependent on a combination of rain and irrigation, and sometimes scattered over one or more ecological niches. Such fields were subject to meticulous rotational fallowing and, between harvest and planting, even unimpeded grazing of family and community herds.[42] These communal lands were subdivided into sectors, known until recently across the Peruvian and Bolivian Andes as *suyu*, *aynuga*, *laymi*, *manay*, *muyuy*, and *moya*, among other names. Each sector was in turn broken down into clearly bounded and individually named fields, delimited by stones, ridges and other markers, such as the ones that María mentioned in her petition. But these boundaries were not fixed or permanent. What anthropologist Ricardo Godoy called "boundary ephemerality" was a necessary attribute of this type of common-field agriculture, as well as a mechanism for adapting to demographic and fiscal changes.[43]

Thus, Cancaurco mountainside fell within a specific productive zone available to some Carania residents, one where the boundaries among household, *ayllu*, and community use rights to land and labour not only coexisted but were also constantly shifting. Based on need and custom, and without relinquishing the community's rights, local authorities periodically reassigned or confirmed some of these fields to domestic units, extended families, and *ayllus*, with the lands often remaining in their control for several generations.[44] Caciques and

41 "Juan Agustín Vargas contra Sebastián Rojas", fol. 40^{v}. Huaychana is recognised as one of the peasant community's agricultural sectors today.

42 Brush and Guillet, "Small-Scale Agro-Pastoral Production", 26; Guillet, *Agrarian Reform and Peasant Economy*, 54, 72; Guillet, "Land Tenure, Ecological Zone, and Agricultural Regime", 140–141; Godoy, "The Evolution of Common-Field Agriculture", 403; Godoy, *Mining and Agriculture in Highland Bolivia*, 40–41.

43 Godoy, *Mining and Agriculture*, 46. As Serulnikov reminds us, "the question in the Andes is not the absence of boundaries but their flexible nature." "The Politics of Intracommunity Land Conflict", 132. "Fixed and stable boundaries" between plots were introduced in the Bogotá region during the latter half of the 18th century. Castro Benavides, "The Enclosure of the Ejidos of Bogotá", 8–9.

44 Murra, "Derechos a tierras en el Tawantinsuyu", 300–301; Murra, "Una visión indígena del mundo andino", liii. Detailed information on these distributions within the town of Sumaro's communal sector in the 1590s can be found in Amado Gonzales, "Reparto de tierras indígenas", 201–204.

principales were, in that sense, some of the greatest commoners in the Andean world. Other fields within the same sectors, generically called *sapçi chacara* or *tierras de comunidad*, were collectively but proportionately ploughed, taking turns, by *ayllu* members and assigned for the putative benefit of the larger commons, as will be discussed later. In both cases, the community—that is, an aggregate of households, and the local caciques on their behalf—retained a significant (but not total) degree of oversight over labour, surplus, crop choice, and the rhythms of the fallowing cycle.[45]

More importantly, for our understanding of land ownership regimes, such divisions were not static. Previously described as a "gradient" of divisible and indivisible use rights, a "myriad of unenclosed and inter-mixed parcels", or as a "tissue" connecting particular and collective rights and customs,[46] communal sectors, such as Carania, were in fact the commons in motion. Over time, and occasionally within a single cycle, specific plots and even sectors transitioned in and out of the *sapçi chacara* category, as the social relationships behind community, *ayllu*, and household rights shifted due to internal and external forces. In other words, the entangled web of household and communal claims that constituted the commons was subject to expansion, contraction, segmentation, and, in some cases, disintegration through uncommoning and recommoning.[47]

As such, these fields were also ripe for conflict. Ethnographic work undertaken in the South and Central Andes by David Guillet, Ricardo Godoy and others shows that fallowing of communal sectors is critical to maintaining both soil fertility and the productive capacity of households over extended periods. Therefore, decisions—regarding which crops to sow and which fields to fallow and for how long—must be taken at the supra-household, often *ayllu*

45 This rotation of cultivated and fallowed patches is documented for the early colonial period. Falcón, "Representación", 465; Garcilaso de la Vega, *Primera parte de los comentarios reales*, Bk. 5, Chapter 1, 101; Ondegardo, "Las razones", 238.

46 Guillet, "Land Tenure, Ecological Zone, and Agricultural Regime", 140–141 (gradient); Campbell and Godoy, *Commonfield Agriculture*, 5, 11–12 (inter-mixed parcels), Linebaugh, *Stop, Thief!*, 55 (tissue). On the commons as "neither romantic nor static", see also Chaney, "Threats to *Gong*", 47.

47 This was true of Carania's sectoral fallowing system in the 1970s. Mayer and Fonseca Martel, *Sistemas agrarios*. For the better-documented case of Laraos, across the Cañete River from Carania, see Brunschwig, "Sistemas de producción de laderas de altura"; Mayer and Cadena, *Cooperación y conflicto en la comunidad andina*, 31; Mayer, *The Articulated Peasant*, 252; Orlove and Godoy, "Sectoral Fallowing Systems". For neighbouring Huarochirí, see Matos Mar, *Las actuales comunidades de indígenas*, 70–71. For the Mantaro valley between the 16th and 20th centuries, see Adams, *A Community in the Andes*, 18–21.

and village levels.[48] Cultivating out of sequence, ignoring calls for coordination and cooperation and generally breaking other arrangements regarding cropping and fallowing are "a major source of conflict" and "can have disastrous effects."[49] Moreover, while periodic reallotting of land can have an equalising effect (by granting people access to lands of different quality and allowing have-nots to meet their tribute quotas), the irregular layout of holdings means that each year some families will be forced to leave a disproportionate amount of their plots uncultivated.[50] Recall here María's plea that her fields at Cancaurco not be "suspended"—left fallow—as in previous years.

In sum, simultaneous claims over the *rayas* of Chacasmarca and Chilcasonique and the land that they enclosed, made by María as well as the *ayllus* Pelle and Chacallongo, especially applied to communal sectors, such as Cancaurco, where, due to inheritance practices, common field and family holdings would eventually be found next to each other, and thus particular rights coexisted with collective ones at any given time. In a way, as we will see, the widow's court case was triggered by the viceregal decree rezoning Cancaurco as part of the larger, multi-*ayllu* Carania commons, which included both *ayllus* Pelle and Chacallongo. But María's predicament had begun earlier when, upon the death of her husband, the elder Diego Caxauarco, around 1640, her status changed from married woman ascribed to her husband's *ayllu* to that of widow with two minors. This shift unleashed the dialectic of uncommoning and recommoning, discussed in the next section.

4 Widows and the Law of *Sapçi*

In his expanded ruling, Carania's Native municipal judge revealed some of the local, contingent norms by which the widow had remained in control of the fields for three or four years. He highlighted how, as we have already seen, Diego, son to María's late husband, was a direct descendant of the apical ancestor, *Apu* Caxauarco. It is important to note that the name of María's daughter was never mentioned in the trial, which suggests that, for the issue of securing continued access to the fields, María's ancestry and kinship affiliation, as well as her

48 For an example of this coordination in 16th-century Charcas, see Jurado (Chapter 6) in this volume.

49 Guillet, "Agrarian Ecology"; Guillet, *Agrarian Reform and Peasant Economy*, 76–79 [quotes].

50 Godoy, "The Evolution of Common-Field Agriculture in the Andes", 400, note 4; Campbell and Godoy, *Commonfield Agriculture*, 16–17.

female line of descent, mattered less than her male child's patrilineage and her late husband being in-*ayllu* with Pelle.[51] As discussed in the previous section, information first mined by Murra from the Huánuco and Chucuito inspections of the 1560s sheds some light on the inheritance principles likely at play: the elder Diego Caxauarco and his ancestors had probably enjoyed continuous possession of their plot within Pelle's domain somewhat freely—that is, with minor communal oversight over land, labour, and product—perhaps because the plots were not considered to be *in* Carania originally.[52] From the perspective of *Ayllu* Pelle, the lineage's control over Chacasmarca and Chilcasonique rested on a discommoning of sorts—a partial disentanglement of certain fields from the nominally collective domain for several generations—due to a land distribution said to have occurred more than a century before.[53]

After Diego's demise, *Ayllu* Pelle had regained control of the plot. Instead of dividing up this portion of the *tabla* among Diego's close relatives, members of his lineage or his *ayllu* in common, as seems to have been the general custom, Pelle had decided to let it pass undivided to María. A crucial point to understand is that, despite the semblance of continuity in family possession since time immemorial, Pelle had communalised the land anew, placing it under much tighter communal oversight, only to give it back to María, not to her husband's kin, under a different regime. María, now a widow, was to enjoy the fields, though as part of a new regime, that of Pelle's *tierras de comunidad* or *sapçi chacaras*, until her son came of age and married. At that point, both the *rayas* and the obligation to support an elderly María would probably be conveyed to him and his wife.[54] The field would then be removed from the collective domain—communal supervision over labour and surplus would

51 Evidence for a later period suggests that men in Carania could lay claim to the family lands of their wives' *ayllu* of origin; others found such claims problematic and contested them. "Juan Agustín Vargas contra Sebastián Rojas", fols. 1^{r-v}.

52 Murra, "Derechos a tierras en el Tawantinsuyu", 299–300.

53 Guillet, "Land Tenure, Ecological Zone, and Agricultural Regime", 142; Long and Roberts, "Introduction", 28. In his ethnographic work in the Mantaro Valley in the 1950s, Richard Adams described decision-making mechanisms for the one-time and gradual division of communal sectors among families and institutions, offering evidence of processes of discommoning dating back to the 16th and 17th centuries. Adams, *A Community in the Andes*, 18–21.

54 In the 1970s, in the highland community of Santa Lucía de Pacaraos (in Canta province), communal authorities still customarily gave preference to widows and sons when reassigning plots within sectoral fallowing lands. Degregori and Golte, *Dependencia y desintegración estructural*, 46–48. On the reabsorption of family fields into communal parcels in Huancayre (in Huarochirí province) in the 1950s, see Matos Mar et al., *Las actuales comunidades de indígenas*, 190–191.

decrease—as Diego reclaimed it for his own household.[55] That, along with the family's own labour and enhanced control over the land and its surplus, would redefine this segment of the *tabla* as a household plot within the Cancaurco sector. Until then, the plot would remain a special category of *sapçi chacara*.

Likely the centrepiece of a larger conceptual universe, the Quechua term *sapçi*, as it applied to certain land holdings, appears scattered in a series of interrelated contexts. To our knowledge, the Jesuit priest and missionary Diego González Holguín offered the first textual codification of *sapçi* in his 1608 Quechua vocabulary, where it appears as a feature of certain nouns meaning "that which is common to all" (*cosa común de todos*), perhaps the most famous shorthand for the Native Andean commons. The lexicographer also presents *sapçichacra*, or "communal plot", and *sapçiñam*, or "communal road", resources that resulted from the type of social relations embedded in *sapçi*: assets built, maintained, and controlled by people who saw themselves as part of a given community. Additional Spanish and Quechua expressions related to *sapçi* place communal endowments at the forefront, as in *sapçi ymampas* or *hazienda de comunidad*, which roughly translate as "commonwealth" or "that which belongs to the community".[56] Other uses include references to *sapçi* infrastructure built and maintained by community members, such as common granaries (*collca*) and corrals (*cancha*).[57]

At any given time, *sapçi* fields, where they existed, were only a portion of a community's holdings. In 1644, for example, the lords of Luringuanca, a polity in the Jauja Valley, immediately to the east of Yauyos and Huarochirí, described a rather meagre communal endowment. The Luringuancas' *bienes de comunidades* (notice the plural, communities) was composed of some liens of which the commons, as the corporate lender, was the beneficiary, as well as "some parcels and *sabsis*" categorised as such at the time. The *sabsis* (*sapçi* plots) differed from others, particularly in that they were worked "communally" and in equitable turns by all able *ayllu* members to help pay the Luringuancas' trib-

55 Bianca Premo cites the declaration of the *principales* of Acora (in Chucuito) to a colonial inspector in 1566: a man became an adult when he "took a woman, received his chácara, and made a home [where they would live] until they were old people." Premo, "From the Pockets of Women", 71.

56 González Holguín, *Vocabulario*, 324. See also Guaman Poma de Ayala, *El primer nueva corónica*, 977. The Spanish term *comunidad* appears in colonial documentation almost exclusively in relation to these holdings. Zagalsky, "El concepto de 'comunidad' en su dimensión espacial".

57 Salomon and Urioste, *The Huarochirí Manuscript*, 103; Murra, "Una visión indígena del mundo andino", lii; Guaman Poma de Ayala, *El primer nueva corónica*, 977; González Holguín, *Vocabulario*, 324, 333; Ramírez, "Land and Tenure in Early Colonial Peru".

ute in specie.[58] As noted by Guillet and others, communally ploughed plots embodied a labour regime wherein collective oversight due to fiscal exigencies was paramount. As in Carania, these properly communal fields were interspersed with, but clearly distinguishable from, family-controlled ones within the same sectors. The community contributed both seed and labour to these communal fields, making them *sapçi*. Through ritual and political mechanisms, the community also maintained control over these fields' surplus, which could be stored in monetary form in the famous community lockboxes, and regulated planting and harvesting as well as the crop to be grown in any given year within the rotational cycle. Produce was often earmarked to meet communal obligations—fiscal, religious, or otherwise. Common fields were also worked collectively to support those serving in positions of authority and their families (who the Spanish reimagined as the cacique class) or those rendering their labour elsewhere on behalf of the commons.[59]

Reciprocity extended to other groups within the community. *Yxmauarmi chacran* were plots of the *sapçi* type, but they could be set aside from the collective domain for assignment to widows, such as María, to be worked by them or others on their behalf.[60] Relief of the poor was, in fact, an important communal obligation, which made the use of *sapçi chacaras* even more appropriate. This was not a mere hand-out, however, for, as Bianca Premo has demonstrated for Chucuito, a region heavily impacted by a gender imbalance occasioned by the Potosí *mita*, women played a central role as tribute producers in their community and were, often heads of households, like María.[61]

Some of the gendered dimensions of *sapçi* that shaped María's claims in Carania can be grasped through another extremely rare document, this one pertaining to Ananguanca, a central Andean polity comprising several *ayllus* that neighboured Luringuanca to the immediate south. In the 1570s, the Anan-

58 "Residencia: Diego de Escobar", Concepción, 1644, BNP, MS B1482, fols. 220ᵛ–221ʳ. For a description of *comun kallpas* or tribute common fields in present-day Bolivia, see Godoy, *Mining and agriculture in Highland Bolivia*, 42–44.

59 Benavides, "Grupos de poder en el valle del Colca", 160; Serulnikov, "The Politics of Intracommunity Land Conflict", 122; Zagalsky, "El concepto de 'comunidad' en su dimensión espacial", 78–79. Ricardo Godoy suggests, in this sense, that the fiscal advantages which *ayllus* confer on villagers help explain why this form of social organisation has survived into the present day. Godoy, "The Fiscal Role of the Andean Ayllu".

60 Guaman Poma de Ayala, *El primer nueva corónica*, 897 [911]; Murra, "Una visión indígena del mundo andino", lii; Trelles, *The Integration of an Andean Ethnic Group into the Early Encomienda System*, 68–69.

61 Premo, "From the Pockets of Women", 68, 70–72, 84. On widows as heads of households, around 20 percent of the total number of women in Sacaca and Acasio—Chayanta, northern Potosí—in 1614, see Tandeter, "Teóricamente ausentes, teóricamente solas".

guancas had received a restitution of 8,000 pesos—a recommoning of illegitimately appropriated surplus by their *encomenderos*. The interest was earmarked for tending to the sick and destitute as well as providing a dowry to help impoverished, orphaned girls marry well. In the 1660s, almost a century later, the Ananguancas had not yet collected on the revenues accrued by this now sizable investment fund, totalling some 45,000 pesos and administered by distant authorities in Lima.[62]

To determine how to best apportion these proceeds, local priests, Native municipal authorities, caciques, and commoners gathered in 1664 and prepared a comprehensive census register of the poor and needy among the Ananguancas. The list of 342 people, broken down by village and *ayllu*, includes 195 poor men (57 percent of those listed), all of tributary age (between 18 and 49) and presumably unable to meet their tribute quota; and 145 poor orphaned maidens (42 percent), all between 11 and 46 years of age but mostly in their mid to late teens and early 20s.[63] While no further information is provided for the men, the list includes information about the parents of the 145 poor orphaned maidens (*solteras güerfanas*). These 103 additional individuals (22 fathers and 81 mothers) raise the total number of people included in the list from 342 to 445.[64] Women (all listed as "poor" or "very poor") now represent more than half (51 percent) of the sample. Moreover, some of those listed as poor single "orphans" in fact lived with their two parents (11.7 percent), but these couples were always described as destitute, elderly, or disabled. Equally telling, while 40 percent of the young single women classified as poor and orphaned had both parents missing, the majority (41.4 percent) were fatherless and had a poor or very poor widowed mother. This was perhaps to be expected within Ananguanca's villages, where years of failed crops and unattended fields, compulsory work in nearby mercury mines and onerous tribute obligations translated into high mortality and absentee rates for local men, which made it hard for impoverished women to find a partner.[65] Nonetheless, destitute widows with at least

62 "Provission real de los yndios de Hananguanca en rason de su renta", fols. 679^{r}–718^{v}. Thanks to Víctor Solier for sharing this document with me.

63 The two others listed were women, aged 25 and 46, respectively, of unknown marital status and listed alongside poor men. For men whose ages were recorded, the average is 30 and the mode 25. For women, these figures are 17 and 15, respectively.

64 Since no kinship relation is stated for poor single orphans, some sisters may have been counted twice.

65 The number of poor men of tributary age (195) is particularly high, considering that the male tributary population of Ananguanca between 1683 and 1687 oscillated between 427 and 1032 individuals. "Autos originales que se han seguido contra don Martín de Zamudio", fols. 2^{r}–3^{v}. A census conducted c. 1617 listed 3140 young (*mozos*) and tributary men

one dependent daughter represented 29 percent of the total poor and more than half (56 percent) of the total women listed in the census. At the very least, these numbers suggest that although failure to meet tribute quotas (for which caciques were ultimately responsible) was likely the most urgent concern behind the Ananguancas' efforts to collect the money then sitting in Lima, widows with young children, like María, were among the main recipients of *sapçi* aid.

Thus, much like María, elders, orphans, and the infirm in Carania, and those who, in the words of Murra, "[did] not have enough relatives to really make in loud tones and in an assertive way the claim to the reciprocity which [was] due them",[66] depended for their livelihood on continuous forms of land and labour commoning, so much so that for the Native colonial author Felipe Guaman Poma de Ayala, supporting the *ayllu's* "poor and destitute" was the utmost reason for the existence of the agropastoral commons.[67] An earlier ecclesiastical inspection in Carania had revealed 26 *reservados* (individuals exempt from tribute) out of a population of 407 villagers (about 6 percent of the total).[68] Now reclassified as a widow, María had joined this category, gaining access to Pelle's commons in the form of an *yxmauarmi chacran*. Letting a seemingly destitute widow enjoy the product of *sapçi* fields more autonomously, thereby loosening communal oversight over surplus, was how the whole planned to honour its duty toward one of its constituent parts.

Things did not turn out that way, however. Widowhood, possible need, and in-*ayllu* relationships only tell part of María's story in Carania. Labour contributions and other obligations became equally significant in validating María's possession of the fields at Cancaurco, especially under the new agreement. María's contractual duties toward *Ayllu* Pelle are not spelled out, but they can be surmised from the precious little that we can gather from similar examples. Although specific *ayllu* expectations depended on age, gender, able-bodiedness and, ultimately, kinship network, widows, single women and elderly men were often required to work communal fields.[69] María was likely able to till the fields, either alone or with the aid of close relatives, in which case no additional help from *Ayllu* Pelle would be required. In neighbouring Huarochirí, a *tabla* was

---

(*tributarios*) as opposed to 5145 women. Vázquez de Espinosa, *Description of the Indies*, 457.

66 Murra, *Reciprocity and Redistribution in Andean Civilizations*, 27.

67 Guaman Poma de Ayala, *El primer nueva corónica*, 247. On Guaman Poma de Ayala's multiple engagements with *sapçi*, see Salomon, "Guaman Poma's *Sapçi*"; Puente Luna, "That Which Belongs to All".

68 *Libro de visitas de Santo Toribio Mogrovejo*, 214.

69 Zagalsky, "El concepto de 'comunidad' en su dimensión espacial", 78–79.

understood as a piece of land that a single person could cultivate in a single day.[70] Custom dictated, moreover, that she and her children contribute other age and gender-based tasks, such as weaving or guarding communal herds, for the overall benefit of the collective.[71] Only if no direct descendants outlived María would the Cancaurco lands remain communal, to be reassigned by the heads of *Ayllu* Pelle.[72]

By enacting the law of *sapçi, Ayllu* Pelle had renewed its commitment to one of its members, though not for long. Ultimately, María was to reject this agreement, instead entering a written claim before the municipal court and thus placing herself partially outside *ayllu* norms as well as recruiting other legal paradigms about land and tenure to her cause. Before we discuss María's choices, however, let us turn to Chacallongo, the collective behind the request for a new land distribution, and its stake in this matter. Considering the recent viceregal decree rezoning Cancaurco, Pelle's previous confirmation of María's exclusive rights looked like an attempt by this *ayllu* to discommon a resource from the newly defined multi-*ayllu* Carania commons for the sake of a single household. Chacallongo's voice was never heard during María's complaint, yet the *ayllu* spoke loudly through its attempts at recommoning.

5 Whose Commons?

The viceregal decree had reserved the eight terraces of the Cancaurco sector for "the benefit of the community." The intertwined issues of who could benefit from the commons and in exchange for what were now coming to the surface. For three generations, María's fields had also been recognised as part of Pelle's domain. Nevertheless, by virtue of some negotiated agreement predating María's initial complaint, Chacallongo now enjoyed rights over seven of the eight subdivisions at Cancaurco, and Pelle enjoyed rights over the eighth. There

70 Spalding, *Huarochirí*, 179.

71 Widows of tributaries sometimes paid tribute to maintain their parcels. Penry, *The People Are King*, 222n26; Serulnikov, "The Politics of Intracommunity Land Conflict", 138. Murra recounts the 1562 case of Xeque, a poor and disabled elderly widow from Huánuco. In exchange for having her fields laboured by neighbours, she contributed ten balls of cotton yarn and a hen to her *ayllu's* annual tribute obligation. Murra, "Derechos a tierras en el Tawantinsuyu", 304.

72 In a strikingly similar case from 1619, the leaders in Macha (in the district of Charcas, in present-day Bolivia) petitioned a Spanish magistrate to have three plots of land that had sustained three elderly widows for several years reinstated to *ayllu* Sulcahavi's domain. Jurado, "Tierra, estatus y viudez".

was likely a proportional relationship among the parcels controlled by each *ayllu*, reflecting *ayllu* size, seniority and available resources outside Cancaurco, among other variables constitutive of inter-*ayllu* rank and prominence. Indeed, at least four other *ayllus* cohabited in Carania at this time. Under the nominal authority of the municipality, these collectives shared the village's municipal land reserve but probably held farm and pasture lands beyond as well.

Viceregal decree in hand, Chacallongo now wanted to see the whole of Cancaurco defined as commons. There were at play, however, interlocking understandings of the definition of *communal*. Although *comunes de indios* could share access to resources with other groups and individuals, simultaneously or sequentially, any commons is meaningful only in relation to that which is not part of it. In other words, the commons "is always governed", and it is rarely a synonym for open, unregulated access.[73] Colonial *sapçi* regimes, though widespread, required some degree of enclosure and administration even if customary rights of common usage for certain individuals and collectives were preserved or negotiated anew. Although open or unclaimed resources could coexist with collectively held ones, they were not one and the same. Colonial reserves of *comunes de indios*, such as Carania, were exclusive to individuals within a collective. Their boundaries, however, were relational; that is, they depended on the shifting arrangements that bound old and new *ayllus* together for the reproduction of a specific commons.[74] A 1657 loan brings the many levels through which these relationships were mediated into sharper focus. Upon lending 10,000 pesos to a Spanish resident of a nearby city, Native authorities in Luringuanca asked that an unusual proviso be added to the contract: although on paper and for legal purposes the money would be owed to the whole of Luringuanca, the funds belonged to the individual communities (*comunidades*) of each of its seven villages. The individual *ayllus* operated as the main keepers of Luringuanca's nominal endowment.[75]

Susan Ramírez's detailed analysis of petitions for land brought before Supreme Justice Gregorio González de Cuenca in 1566 illustrates relational definitions of *common* and adds temporal depth to María's mid-17th-century claims.

---

73 Linebaugh, *Stop, Thief!*, 147. See also Harvey, "The Future of the Commons", 103; McCay and Acheson, "Human Ecology", 7–8. Blaser and De la Cadena make a similar point: "Both commoning and enclosures involve domaining, and the domains thus delineated have variable reach and scope." Blaser and De la Cadena, "Uncommons", 190. For forests as regulated commons in colonial Mexico, see Woolley, "The Forests Cannot Be Commons", 44–45.

74 As Murra has shown, moreover, multiple *comunes* intercommoned resources, such as the coca fields of Quivi, in the upper Chillón River, in the 1550s. Murra, *Formaciones políticas y económicas del mundo andino*, 93.

75 "Venta que hace la comunidad de indios de Lurin Huancas", fols. 140^{r}–141^{v}.

The leader of the community of Guaman, in the Chimu Valley near Trujillo, described a type of open, apparently unclaimed land as “a common thing and open to all and of which no one could have nor acquire possession.”[76] While Ramírez interprets the cacique’s statement as applying to pre-Hispanic land in general, other petitions filed during the same inspection underscore narrower definitions of *common*. Miguel Cerquen, of *Ayllu* Ferreñafe, complained that, to support his family, he had been toiling in “some lands that are held in common.” However, large irrigation infrastructure was *sapçi*, and his caciques had denied him access to water, making cultivation impossible. Thus, he asked the judge to ease communal oversight by ordering the caciques to grant him access to the canals that watered the fields, “for they are held in common.”[77] The plots in question fell within the canals’ reach, which indicates that the plots, while of Miguel’s exclusive use, were also in-*ayllu* and thus subject to commoning and recommoning. These lands were not open to the same degree as were the lands mentioned by the lord of Guaman in his 1566 petition. Properly speaking, the lands were not common but communal—that is, exclusive to Ferreñafe.

In a similar case from the same year, Felipe Filmirref, a head of *Ayllu* Ferreñafe, expressed his need of a plot to pay tribute and to support his wife, four children and many destitute relatives. Although Felipe had “no known lands of my own”, the caciques had denied him the right to toil “in the communal lands that have no recognised *dueño* and are uncultivated.” Thus, he asked to be allowed to work a portion of the communal sector, then fallow or barren.[78] Again, while the fields were untilled, they were not common to the point of being open range or up for grabs. Felipe’s *ayllu* had domained them, establishing social boundaries to claim them as *tierras de comunidad*. Felipe, like María in Carania, wanted the judge to intervene and secure his discommoning of the fields through family labour. Although Felipe’s petition refers to these fields ambiguously as “communal lands”, they were different from *sapçi* lands. Rather than being set aside and laboured communally to fulfil collective obligations, they were to be worked and managed by a household or extended family, under varying degrees of communal oversight. Felipe’s complaint shows that, as in the case of María, individual work performed in common fields was supposed to guarantee access to and continued use of house plots. In referring to this social contract, which he claimed had existed before the conquest,

76 Ramírez, “Land and Tenure in Early Colonial Peru”, 38n24. See also Ramírez, “Despedazando lo común”, 288.

77 Ramírez, “Despedazando lo común”, 295. For irrigation and the commons, see also Ramírez, “Land and Tenure in Early Colonial Peru”, 39.

78 Ramírez, “Despedazando lo común”, 295.

colonial magistrate Polo Ondegardo differentiated between these two types of "land". His 1561 report to the Crown explained that individuals agreed to honour supra-household demands to work in common, mainly in the form of tilling communal tracts destined to satisfy labour tribute quotas, only so their remaining time could be used to satisfy their individual needs: labouring their fields, tending their herds and weaving their clothes. Tribute in labour (and, after the conquest, in labour and specie) was supposed to be given *de comunidad*—that is, by labouring the communal fields, but never from the household's estate (*hacienda*).[79]

6 The Casting of Communal Seed

After this necessary detour into the bundle of landholding rights that shaped the relationship between part and whole, we can now return to Carania village, Chacallongo, and the fields at Cancaurco. Already by the court case's starting date, Chacallongo had come to perceive the discommoning of Chacasmarca and Chilcasonique, formerly within Pelle's domain, on behalf of Caxauarco's descendants as a form of temporary uncommoning, rooted in a prior enclosure of collectively claimed resources at the multi-*ayllu* level. Pelle's decision seemed arbitrary—that is, intra- rather than inter-*ayllu*. As Frank Salomon suggests, the commons is also a matter of perspective. Indeed, the dynamics of commoning and uncommoning fully emerge when grasped as multileveled phenomena: as social actions that link, in descending order of inclusiveness, community, *ayllu*, extended family, and household. Referring to present-day *sociedades* in Tupicocha (located in Huarochirí province), lineage-based groupings that mediate between household and *ayllu*, Salomon suggests that "when an asset of putative *ayllu* commons is put in use by one component *sociedad*, from the viewpoint of nonbeneficiaries it is privatized, but (so to speak) *sapçichasqa* [or] 'sapsified' from the sociedad members' viewpoint."[80] María's predicament not only makes sense in this light but also illuminates the importance

79 Ondegardo, "Informe del licenciado", 151–156. See also Trelles, "The Integration", 68–69. On the penuries of early-colonial households who, on the contrary, had to sacrifice hours of work in their family fields to meet increasing tribute quotas, see Mayer, "Los atributos del hogar", 582. Significantly, Guaman Poma de Ayala claims that caciques earmarked excess lands for "la comunidad y sapçi" only after confirming or reassigning household plots. Guaman Poma de Ayala, *El primer nueva corónica y buen gobierno*, 250.

80 Frank Salomon, in an email to me, 19 April 2020. See also Salomon, "The Long Afterlives of Central-Peruvian Khipu Patrimonies".

of individual and collective labour as well as communal oversight in setting the shifting boundaries between ownership normative regimes at any given time.

Indeed, alongside the more static definitions of commons discussed earlier, generally reproduced in the specialised literature, González Holguín's Quechua vocabulary describes open-ended activities performed on behalf of a collective, including "communal tasks" and "communal work" (*trechos* or *faenas*).[81] Pertinent here is Peter Linebaugh's insight that "commoning is embedded in a labor process."[82] This explains why Native authors deeply familiar with *sapçi* regimes extended the notion of *sapçi* to mills, vineyards, textile workshops, tanneries, and even liens on real estate—all of which, more than "things" or "assets", represented the fruit of collective labour and supervision and, as such, were subject to temporary uncommoning and eventual recommoning.[83] In the late 16th century, *Ayllu* Angaraes, settled near the Huancavelica mercury mines, leased a communal mine to a widow for 200 pesos, to be spent on behalf of the commons. The community of Huamachuco similarly owned a textile mill, a cattle estate, and its surrounding pastures for 200 years, working them rotationally and collectively for the benefit of the community.[84] In all these cases, cooperation, regimented labour, and communal control mechanisms were the forces articulating collective rights and privative (not private) claims over time. This dialectic also accounts for the moving boundaries between resources held communally and those held particularly but in-*ayllu*. Seen through acts of commoning and uncommoning, they were ultimately one and the same. *Ayllu* holdings included both and thus were not limited to *sapçi* cultivation zones. *Sapçi* holdings, for their part, were not limited to land.

From Chacallongo's vantage point, then, Pelle's decision to communalise a family plot by reinserting it into its commons—only to give the plot back to María and her children in the form of an *yxmauarmi chacran*—seemed like an act of sequestering. Pelle's decision had sown a potential source of social differentiation among commoners' extended families within *ayllus* that fulfilled common obligations and owned land equitably and proportionally. The decision therefore threatened the balance between equity and inequality

81 González Holguín, *Vocabulario de la lengua general de todo el Perú*, 324.

82 Linebaugh, *The Magna Carta Manifesto*, 45.

83 Guaman Poma de Ayala, *El primer nueva corónica*, 247; Puente Luna, "Felipe Guaman Poma de Ayala".

84 Dries, "The *Indios Mineros* of Colonial Huancavelica"; Castro de Trelles, "Quipus coloniales para el conteo de ganado".

found within any commons.[85] In this new scenario, which stemmed from the passing of Diego Caxauarco and the attendant viceregal reassignment of communal lands within the village holdings, Chacallongo probably faulted Pelle as much as it did *Apu* Caxauarco's descendants, who felt entitled to the fields by customary rights established since time immemorial, for breaking an ancient agreement. In other words, communal principles set the limits of hereditary ones, constraining the ways in which "land" could be disposed of within family and household.[86] This clash probably explains why Chacallongo appealed to the Crown for confirmation of its ancestral rights in the first place. Pelle, in Chacallongo's view, was extending a claim over communal plots that it was not going to work collectively but would reassign to one of its individual members. Claims of ancestral possession, while appealing to judges, seemed vacuous from the vantage of *ayllu* norms without the labour obligations that they carried along with the land.

The casting of communal seed over María's holdings thus became a central piece in Chacallongo's insistence on enforcing its collective rights. Other contemporary rulings show that local judges were perfectly aware that seed could belong to a specific household, to be brought to fruition by the labour of its members.[87] But Chacallongo's was *sapçi* seed, of the type mentioned in a 1657 anti-idolatry trial: seed stored in communal granary deposits after the collective harvest. During that trial, villagers in San Juan de Machaca (Cajatambo) were charged with working maize fields whose crops were earmarked for the cult of the group's forebears, original tillers of the plots, and therefore stored as "saucis" [*sapçi*].[88] A similar judicial inquiry from 1667 regarding priestly

85 This also happened in the case of the three widows from Macha cited above. Jurado, "Tierra, estatus y viudez".

86 For a more thorough discussion of this dimension of community land regimes, see Puente Luna, "Customs Apart".

87 In 1611, for instance, a judge in the village of Socos (Huamanga province) gave possession of a series of plots to Leonor Coca Chimbo. According to this ruling, individuals who had planted crops in her fields against her will were entitled to the equivalent in seed ("lo que hubieren sembrado sin su boluntad se le boluera la semilla"). Leonor had to return it and pay for any ploughing as well, but would enjoy the improvements as her own. "Autos seguidos por Doña Catalina", fol. 24r. In 1641, another local judge, this time from the village of Anchucaya (Huarochirí province) gave possession of several plots to Magdalena Llacxa Colqui. His ruling ordered Magdalena to return to her legal rival, María Ticlla Saxa, an amount of seed equivalent to whatever the latter had planted in the former's fields ("no dentren mas en ella sino resiuan sus ssemillas que tienen sembrados sin obedeser la ssentençia"). "María Ticlla Saxa". fol. 14r.

88 Duviols, *Procesos y visitas de idolatrías*, 485, 491. I thank Susan Ramírez for this reference. Maize stored in the common granaries is mentioned in the Huarochirí Manuscript

conduct in the province of Yauyos further clarifies the special status of *sapçi* seed, showing that community, as Karen Spalding once noted regarding neighbouring Huarochirí, extended through time and space to include the dead.[89] Villagers listed maize among the offerings placed on tombstones during the celebration of All Saints' Day (1 November). Individuals and married couples contributed one or two *reales* to pay for mass and eulogies in honour of "the community of the dead of the village", distinguished by *ayllu*. At the donors' discretion, small candles, wine, potatoes, and handfuls of maize were placed atop their graves. Nonetheless, collective contributions complemented particular ones, apparently to guarantee that all those departed received something. Indeed, authorities tendered a customary three pesos and three *reales* of *limosna* (alms) to the priest from the *bienes de comunidad* of each *pueblo*, paid from the sale of produce from collectively farmed *chacras de comunidad*. And, important for understanding Chacallongo's strategy, each *común* contributed half a *fanega*'s worth of "*maiz de la comunidad*", communal maize to be placed on the tombstones.[90]

With his ruling, which ordered María to return the seed (or its equivalent) to Chacallongo, the municipal judge in the 1644 case simultaneously acknowledged that the seed encapsulated the *ayllu's* kinship ties and collective energy while recognising that only labour, María's or Chacallongo's, could bring about a full harvest (thus entitling that person to the produce). From the judge's perspective, if the seed were allowed to germinate and the seedlings to emerge, they would grant Chacallongo an initial claim to the harvest. For María to give the seeds back was a way to counteract their power to collectivise. Scattering them over the fields, conversely, was Chacallongo's plan for redrawing the legal and physical boundaries between the individual and the collective. These actions can be read as a defence of commoning under shifting circumstances and perhaps external, unstated pressures (i.e., an increase in tribute demands).[91] From Chacallongo's viewpoint, the disputed pieces of farmland

(c. 1608) as well: Salomon and Urioste, *The Huarochirí Manuscript*, 103: "yngap çaranta sapçicunamantas". The editors of the manuscript in English translated the phrase in context as "maize belonging to the Inca from the common granaries".

89 Spalding, *Huarochirí*, 61.

90 "Autos que se siguieron por el padre maestro", fols. 570^{r} ("los difuntos del Comun del pueblo"), 576^{r} ("el comun de los difuntos del pueblo"), 741^{r} (maize, potatoes, beans), 764^{v} (candles and maize), 772^{v} ("bienes and chacras de comunidad"), 800^{v}–801^{v}, 815^{r}. ("maiz de la comunidad").

91 More research is needed to determine if, as in the case of Pocoata, a growing imbalance between population and resources, as well as accumulation of individual parcels by local chiefs, contributed to these land conflicts. Serulnikov, "The Politics of Intracommunity

now belonged to a larger holding (a terrace) that, rather than benefiting a specific lineage or household, no matter how prominent or destitute, was meant to aid a certain commons to fulfil its collective obligations. *Sapçi* seed was a powerful signifier, recognised by all the parties involved, that common rights were forged through labour and cooperation, in this case performed during a previous harvest.

Thus, the counter practice of communalising advocated by Chacallongo in 1644, which on paper looks like the reappropriation of the fields by the larger Carania commons, seamlessly makes its way into the legal dossier, transmuted into an act of possession that colonial courts could understand well. By scattering *sapçi* seed over the disputed plot and its boundary markers and by expecting its occupants to work the fields on Chacallongo's behalf, members of this *ayllu* were attempting to "sapçify", or common anew, the fields in question. The harvest would belong not to one but to all its members, thus contributing to the *pueblo*'s tribute quota. The plants and the labour that they demanded to reach full term would gradually accomplish the rest, fully dissolving María's family rights into those of the collective. In one of the entries for *sapçi* in his 1608 Quechua vocabulary, a generally overlooked expression in the first person, González Holguín was likely referring to actions of this sort, of rendering the privative communal: *sapçichani*, or "I communalise".[92] Let us not forget, however, that Carania's municipal judge sided with María, not once but twice, upholding her decision not to let the lands go fallow against *ayllu* and seemingly communal consensus. We now turn to this final aspect of the case.

Land Conflict", 122. The case of the Chupaychu in the mid-16th century presents another possible scenario: too many days spent working the communal parcels destined to fulfil higher tribute quotas meant less time available for the family plots. During the 1562 inspection, at least 60 percent of the households sent one of their members to work in the common fields. Trelles, *The Integration of an Andean Ethnic Group into the Early Encomienda System*, 88–90.

92 González Holguín, *Vocabulario de la lengua general de todo el Perú*, 324. I thank Frank Salomon for his help in translating this phrase, which can also be rendered as "I add to the commons". As Karen Graubart has recently noted, early colonial lords' bequeathing of their patrimonial lands and herds to their communities for the purpose of helping to pay tribute might be another expression of the same collectivising drive, albeit disguised as a generous donation. Graubart, "'*Ynuvaciones malas e rreprouadas*'", 160; Graubart, "Shifting Landscapes", 72–73.

7 (Un)Commoning: Strategy and Practice

Even after a careful reading of the record, it is hard to tease out María's thoughts and motivations. Her two written complaints and the judges' subsequent rulings add up to only a handful of poorly written pages that leave many questions unanswered. From her perspective, the casting of communal seed probably meant the imposition of a male-led majority's will. Moreover, she was likely prompted to go to court by the dire prospect of the lands that her family had tilled for decades being reabsorbed into Pelle's domain (if no heirs were to survive her) or, even worse, shifting to Chacallongo's communal sector. She was, in a way, trying to escape the law of *sapçi*, hoping instead for a kind of exclusive guardianship over her son's patrimonial lands, which would resonate with Iberian practices familiar to Native and Spanish judges alike. As Wesley Chaney argues for village dwellers in Northern China, adjudication of this type "delineated 'ownership'" in ways that made communal parcels under dispute "legible" to the state. As such, litigants might use them "to push adversaries off the commons."[93] Thus, before the municipal judge, María questioned the amount of seed that she was expected to plant or care for on Chacallongo's behalf by reframing her tenure within a different normative logic. Shifting the emphasis from the whole to the part, she declared instead that the boundary lines had always been her property and that the planting of communal seed, especially for Chacallongo, was none of her business. Yet, María could not make her obligations disappear without her claims on the land evaporating as well.

Memorialising her husband's patrilineage and the cross-generational, uninterrupted possession of individual parcels through writing was possibly another of María's aspirations.[94] Like other women in her time, María probably knew that tales of ancestral family possession and female dispossession, translated into legal writing (especially "titles" to land), would resonate with municipal judges (as well as the two Spanish magistrates overseeing her case) familiar with the entanglement of Native and Spanish norms of land and tenure. She was one of the countless Native legal innovators who contributed to Yauyos's

93 Chaney, "Threats to *Gong*", 56.

94 The only surviving page of a municipal ledger from the village of Lambayeque (near the city of Trujillo) registers, in chronological order, the names of individual tillers and their plots between 1586 and 1611. One entry, dated 1609, mentions two women, Catalina Llamo and Ana Pujqui, both of whom claimed, like María in Carania, to have inherited a piece of land from great-grandparents who were alive before the Spanish conquest. Ramírez, "Land and Tenure in Early Colonial Peru", 38; Ramírez, "Despedazando lo común", 298–299.

rich colonial legal culture, always in the making.[95] Similarly, Chacallongo's collective actions show that uncommoning and recommoning were the dialectic behind land management in Carania, a dialectic that could also translate well into legal narratives and genres (i.e., a viceregal decree or a municipal ruling) available to, and perhaps even proliferating because of, individuals and collectives interacting with judges capable of accommodating multiple legal registers within Indigenous jurisdictions.[96] Although rooted in Andean norms, these practices could be turned into strategies catalysed by, and legible to, the Iberian legal processes and expectations with which they constantly intersected.

Nonetheless, although María's decision to file her complaint before the village council could be read as an effort to take advantage of a superior instance of justice to privatise a collective resource by way of colonial law, her strategic appeal was also an attempt to communalise intra- and inter-*ayllu* arrangements—within Pelle and Chacallongo, but also between them—by subjecting these *ayllus'* norms to the oversight and control of the larger Carania commons in its municipal expression. Municipal councils exerted jurisdiction over several *ayllus* and seem to have mainly intervened in disputes *among* them, but they were also more than the sum of their parts. Let us not forget that the Native judge's second, expanded ruling went so far as to contradict the viceregal decree favouring Chacallongo. María's legal strategy was sound because enclosing practices were, of course, intelligible within the Iberian tradition and, in the case of Native communities, upheld by the Crown.[97] However, the strategy came at a cost: María had to recast her defence of the commons in particular terms: as an affair that concerned only herself and not her *ayllu*. Pelle could have stood in María's stead during the trial because, according to the rulings, it had claimed control over this parcel as commonage. Instead, it remained off the record.[98]

On the other hand, Chacallongo's concerted will to overrule the municipal judge's mandate (not once but twice) is a reminder that while *ayllu* governance was included in, and in theory subject to, the municipal council's wider jurisdic-

95 Graubart, "Shifting Landscapes", 63–64; Premo, "Felipa's Braid", 499; Premo and Yannakakis, "A Court of Sticks and Branches", 30.

96 Herzog, "Immemorial (and Native) Customs in Early Modernity", 44–46; Premo and Yannakakis, "A Court of Sticks and Branches", 30–31.

97 Fernández, "The Call to the Commons".

98 The explanation takes us back ten years, to a somewhat confusing chain of events that I can only summarise here: upon Pelle's withdrawal from an earlier intra-*ayllu* pact, Chacallongo welcomed María's husband into its fold, allowing him to use the *rayas* unopposed in exchange for planting two *almudes* of communal seed in them, as dictated by custom since Inca times. Diego's labour obligations to Pelle, however, remained.

tion—as María seems to have known well—*ayllu* norms and practices could and did transcend the *cabildo*. While the record is mostly silent about local politics—it does not even reveal the municipal judge's *ayllu*—it does suggest that the *cabildo's* authority over land status and allocation within the village was not paramount but partial and contested. Carania's *cabildo* seems ill-equipped for dealing with disputes concerning two or more *ayllus*. María's story thus reveals a world of agency at the *ayllu* level and the higher *cabildo* level, but also beyond the latter's control. Indeed, in the years to come Chacallongo remained in the field between Chacasmarca and Chilcasonique despite María's stern opposition and the municipal judge's ruling; the *ayllu* insisted that, like the other seven *tablas* at Cancaurco, it was "for the cultivation and benefit of the community."[99]

Yet ironically, Chacallongo was not totally successful. María's offspring would take their defence to the high court in Lima, placing it partially outside the purview of communal justice, and insist on recognition of their ancestral possession, to little avail. Two generations later, however, another descendant of *Apu* Caxauarco, Don Francisco Domingo de Salazar Caxauarco, would sell the lands originally under dispute to yet another Carania *ayllu*—Tarca—for 50 pesos. With the sale, the fields between Chacasmarca and Chilcasonique joined Tarca's commonage. Don Francisco's actions triggered a new lawsuit, this time between Tarca and *Ayllu* Collana, setting in motion yet again the gruelling cycle of uncommoning and recommoning that animated village life in Carania.

8 Conclusion

The colonial Andean commons is, to a large extent, still a commons of the imaginary. It is mainly through municipal sources and local histories, such as María Jamarca's, that the waxing and waning of these collectives through commoning, as it applied to land, water, and other resources, begin to come to the fore. Yet, as the anthropologists Mario Blaser and De la Cadena suggest, even when the commons is "effectively constituted by commoning [...] the uncommons are right below the surface."[100] *Comunes de indios* held the common and the uncommon together, under a multitiered system of *ayllu* governance and normativity trying to regulate individual and collective energies in flux. It can be argued, borrowing from Judith Farquhar, Lili Lai, and Marshall Kramer's

99 "para que cultibe e benefic[i]e para la dicha comunidad." "Autos que siguen", fol. 11^{v}.

100 Blaser and Cadena, "The Uncommons", 190.

analysis of a southern Chinese village's engagements with state power, that individual and communal elements found at the intra- and inter-*ayllu* levels, perhaps the least theorised and least studied aspect of precontact and colonial Andean commons, existed in a mutual relationship in which they "ar[o]se from each other and [we]re rooted in each other."[101]

While the evidence presented in this essay is hardly sufficient to state categorically that central Andean customs of commoning / uncommoning the land predated the Spanish conquest, it seems to be a reasonable conclusion. Other testimonies describing similar practices and understandings, produced *before* Francisco de Toledo's 1570s massive *reducción general* (general forced resettlement) of the Native population, a momentous undertaking during which—most scholars assume—European modes of land tenure would have been introduced and spread across the Andes, strongly suggest this might have been the case.[102] As I have demonstrated, not all tracts were or became "common to all" through collective labour, normative force and strict communal oversight, as is often assumed. *Sapçi* fields coexisted with farmlands ploughed and possessed by individuals, households, and extended families over variable periods, sometimes several generations. More importantly, lands switched regimes in response to shifting power relations and, in the longer term, state definitions of the indigenous/peasant community, entering and leaving the common-field sector periodically. Even when significant portions of *ayllu* agricultural lands were parcelled out or transferred via sale and inheritance among community members, as had happened in Carania already at the time of María's court case, complex mechanisms of collective oversight governing these parcels, which we can only barely detect in the documents, remained in place and were constantly acknowledged and negotiated. Community was in no way antithetical to particular control and use, as previous ethnohistorical analyses have suggested. Within *ayllu* relationships—what De la Cadena calls being in-*ayllu*—the individual and the collective encroached on one another constantly.

Moreover, these socially constructed relations between persons and things had important but imperfect correlates in the language of Iberian law, custom, and practice; these relations often found partial expression in legal fictions and genres as well as widespread doctrines about individual and collective forms of domain. As such, they became legal strategies as well, successfully deployed by plaintiffs and defendants alike. The legal literacy of this

101 Farquhar, Lai and Kramer, "A Place at the End of a Road", 218.

102 See, for instance, Ondegardo, "Informe del licenciado", 178–180; Ortiz de Zúñiga, *Visita*, 25, 30–31, 42.

story's characters and their familiarity with such forms are beyond question. In Carania and elsewhere, Native subjects constantly exploited these partial correlates or alignments in wills, titles, lawsuits, and *cabildo* records. Similarly, colonial officials registered, selected and even reinvented Native customs, reinscribing them in their own legal traditions.[103] Their control over Native local normativity and the contingencies of a community's reproduction, however, was more of an aspiration than a reality. The important point to remember is that, although cases, such as María's, can be said to reflect heterogenous (and ultimately hegemonic) paradigms about land and tenure, legal fictions and narratives do not fully capture local, historically contingent practices of commoning and uncommoning. They must be reconstructed empirically by examining novel cases and re-examining familiar ones. Indeed, the parties involved in María's timely engagement with the courts can be said to have acted within the bounds of colonial law, but their actions repeatedly exceeded it as well.

Acknowledgments

I extend my gratitude to Tamar Herzog, Manuel Bastias Saavedra, Camilla de Freitas Macedo and the anonymous readers of Brill for their valuable comments on the original essay.

Bibliography

Manuscripts

"Autos originales que se han seguido contra don Martín de Zamudio, don Lorenzo Astocuri y sus herederos por la ocultación de 417 indios." Lima, 1741, Archivo General de Indias, Seville, Lima, 414.

"Autos que siguen don Francisco Aguilar y otros con don Pedro Ximenez y otros sobre el derecho de unas tierras y chacras," Lima, 1634, Lilly Library, Indiana University, Bloomington, Latin American Manuscripts, Peru, box 5, fols. 11^{r}–15^{v}.

"Autos que se siguieron por el padre maestro de la orden visitador que en virtud del real exorto embio el Padre Prouincial contra todos los siete curas de la Provincia de los Yauyos, por las quejas y capitulaciones de los Yndios de dicha provincia," Yauyos, 1667, Archivo de la Provincia Dominica, Lima, Autos, 13, n. 3.

103 Herzog, "Immemorial (and Native) Customs in Early Modernity", 42.

"Autos seguidos por doña Catalina y doña Luisa Cusichimbo, indias del pueblo de Socos en la provincia de Huanta [...], sobre propiedad de unas tierras en el valle de Tomaringa," 1642, Archivo General de la Nación, Lima, Derecho Indígena y Encomiendas, leg. 8, exp. 107.

"Carta del Padre José de Arévalo, misionero de la Compañía de Jesús, al arzobispo de Lima, en la que le informa sobre sus actividades en las misiones de las doctrinas de Carampoma y Laraos." Lima?, 16 May 1760. Archivo Vargas Ugarte, Universidad Antonio Ruiz de Montoya, Lima, Manuscritos., t. 18, doc. 69.

"Juan Agustín Vargas contra Sebastián Rojas", Lima, 1739. Archivo General de Indias, Lima, GO-BI 1, l. 27, d. 138.

"María Ticlla Saxa, india, contra Magdalena Llaxsa Colque, india, sobre tierras." Lima, 1642. Biblioteca National del Perú, Lima, Ms., B749.

"Provission real de los yndios de Hananguanca en rason de su renta," Concepción, 27 June 1669, Archivo Regional de Junín, Huancayo, Protocolos Notariales, fols. 679^{r}–718^{v}.

"Residencia: Diego Dávila Briceño," Lima, 1586, Biblioteca Nacional del Perú, Lima, MS A332/C.

"Residencia: Diego de Escobar," Concepción, 1644, Biblioteca Nacional del Perú, Lima, MS B1482.

"Testamento y almoneda. Francisca Colloc." Cuzco, September 11–30, 1586. Archivo Regional del Cuzco, Protocolos Notariales, 4 (Pedro de la Carrera Ron), fols. 687^{r}–694^{v}.

"Titulación de la comunidad indígena del distrito de Laraos, provincia de Yauyos." Laraos, 1800. Archivo General de Indias, Lima, Títulos de comunidades, leg. 3, cuad. 41c, map 2.

"Venta que hace la comunidad de indios de Lurin Huancas de las tierras de Viñaca y Conoc," Huamanga, 1743, Biblioteca Nacional del Perú, Archivo Astete Concha, Z1010, fols. 140^{r}–141^{v}.

Printed Sources

Libro de visitas de Santo Toribio Mogrovejo, 1593–1605, ed. Benito, José Antonio, Lima 2006.

Duviols, Pierre, *Procesos y visitas de idolatrías: Cajatambo, siglo XVII*, Lima, 2003.

Falcón, Francisco. "Representación hecha por el licenciado Falcón en concilio provincial, sobre los daños y molestias que se hacen á los indios. c. 1567", in *Colección de documentos inéditos, relativos al descubrimiento, conquista y organización de las antiguas posesiones españolas de América y Oceanía* 7, Madrid 1867: Imp. de Frías y Compañía, 451–495.

Garcilaso de la Vega, Inca, *Primera parte de los comentarios reales*, Lisbon 1609: Pedro Crasbeck.

González Holguín, Diego, *Vocabulario de la lengua general de todo el Perú, llamada lengua qquichua o del Inca*. 1608. Reprint, Lima 1989.

Guaman Poma de Ayala, Felipe. *El primer nueva corónica y buen gobierno*, ed. Rolena Adorno, John V. Murra, and Jorge L. Urioste. 3rd ed. Mexico City 1992.

Ondegardo, Polo. "Informe del licenciado Juan [*sic*] Polo Ondegardo al licenciado Briviesca de Muñatones sobre la perpetuidad de las encomiendas en el Peru." 1561, in Lamana Ferrario, Gonzalo (ed.), *Pensamiento colonial critico: Textos y actos de Polo Ondegardo*, 139–204, Lima 2012.

Ondegardo, Polo, "Las razones que movieron a sacar esta relación y notable daño que resulta de no guardar a estos indios sus fueros" 1571, in Lamana Ferrario, Gonzalo (ed.), *Pensamiento colonial critico: Textos y actos de Polo Ondegardo*, Lima 2012, 217–330.

Ortiz de Zúñiga, Iñigo, *Visita de la provincia de León de Huánuco en 1562*, in *Visita de las cuatro waranqa de los chupachu*, vol. 1, ed. Murra, John v., Huánuco, Peru 1967.

Vázquez de Espinosa, Antonio, *Description of the Indies*, Washington 1968.

Literature

Abercrombie, Thomas A., *Pathways of Memory and Power: Ethnography and History among an Andean People*, Madison 1998.

Adams, Richard, *A Community in the Andes. Problems and Progress in Muquiyauyo*, Washington D.C. 1959.

Ågren, Maria, "Making Her Turn Around: The Verb-Oriented Method, the Two-Supporter Model, and the Focus on Practice", in *Early Modern Women* 13: 1 (2018), 144–152.

Albó, Xavier, *La paradoja aymara: Solidaridad y faccionalismo*, La Paz, 1977.

Allen, Catherine J., "Final Commentaries: A Matter of Substance, and the Substance of Matter", in Lozada, María Cecilia and Henry Tantaleán (eds.), *Andean Ontologies: New Archaeological Perspectives*, Gainesville 2019, 332–345.

Amado Gonzales, Donato, "Reparto de tierras indígenas y la primera Visita y Composición General, 1591–1595", in *Histórica* 12:2 (1998), 197–207.

Arguedas, José María, *Las comunidades de España y del Perú*, Lima, 1968.

Bastias Saavedra, Manuel, "The Normativity of Possession: Rethinking Land Relations in Early-Modern Spanish America, ca. 1500–1800", in *Colonial Latin American Review* 29: 2 (2020), 223–238.

Bastien, Joseph W., "Land Litigations in an Andean Ayllu from 1592 until 1972", in *Ethnohistory* 26:2 (1979), 101–131.

Benavides, María, "Apuntes históricos y etnográficos del valle del río Colca (Arequipa, Perú), 1575–1980", in *Boletín de Lima* 50: 9 (1987), 7–20.

Benavides, María, "Grupos de poder en el valle del Colca (Arequipa), siglos XVI–XX", in Matos Mendieta, Ramiro (ed.), *Sociedad andina: Pasado y presente; Contribuciones en homenaje a la memoria de César Fonseca Martel*, Lima 1988, 151–177.

Benavides, María, "Tenencia de tierras agrícolas en el valle del Colca (Caylloma, Arequipa)", in *Revista Peruana de Ciencias Sociales* 2: 1 (1990), 49–76.

Beyersdorff, Margot, "Covering the Earth. Mapping the Walkabout in Andean Pueblos de Indios", in *Latin American Research Review* 42: 3 (2007), 129–160.

Blaser, Mario, and Marisol de la Cadena, "The Uncommons: An Introduction", in *Anthropologica* 59: 2 (2017), 185–193.

Brunschwig, Gilles, "Sistemas de producción de laderas de altura", in *Bulletin de l'Institut Français d'Etudes Andines* 15: 1–2 (1986), 27–52.

Brush, Stephen, and David Guillet, "Small-Scale Agro-Pastoral Production in the Central Andes", in *Mountain Research and Development* 5 (1985), 19–30.

Cadena, Marisol de la, *Economía campesina. Familia y comunidad en Yauyos* (BA thesis), Lima 1980.

Cadena, Marisol de la, "Cooperación y mercado en la organización comunal andina", in *Revista Andina* 4: 1 (1986), 31–58.

Cadena, Marisol de la, *Earth Beings: Ecologies of Practice across Andean Worlds*, Durham 2015.

Campbell, Bruce and Ricardo Godoy, *Commonfield Agriculture: The Andes and Medieval England Compared*, Routledge 2008.

Castro Benavides, Constanza, "The Enclosure of the Ejidos of Bogotá: Imperial Wars and the End of Common Lands in Colonial New Granada", in *Journal of Urban History* 48: 4 (2021), 760–781.

Castro de Trelles, Lucila, "Quipus coloniales para el conteo de ganado: El caso de la hacienda Tulpo del común de los indios de Huamachuco en el siglo XVII", in Curatola Petrocchi, Marco and José Carlos de la Puente Luna (eds.), *El quipu colonial: Estudios y materiales*, 349–377, Lima 2013.

Chaney, Wesley B., "Threats to *Gong*: Environmental Change and Social Transformations in Northwest China", in *Late Imperial China* 41: 2 (2020), 45–94.

Conte, Emanuele, "The Many Legal Faces of the Commons. A Short Historical Survey", in *Quaderni Storici* 3 (2021), 625–640.

Dávila Briceño, Diego, "Descripsion y relacion de la provincia de los Yauyos toda, Anan Yauyos y Lorin Yauyos, hecha por Diego Davila Brizeño, corregidor de Guarocheri" in Jiménez de la Espada, Marcos (ed.), *Relaciones geográficas de Indias*, vol. 1, Madrid 1881, 61–78.

De Dios, Salustiano, Javier Infante, Ricardo Robledo and Eugenia Torijano (coords.), *Historia de la propiedad en España. Bienes comunales, pasado y presente*, Salamanca 2002.

Degregori, Carlos Iván, and Jürgen Golte, *Dependencia y desintegración estructural en la comunidad de Pacaraos*, Lima 1973.

Dries, Mark, "The *Indios Mineros* of Colonial Huancavelica: Collaboration and Resistance in Peru's Most Infamous Mine", Paper presented at the Southwest Seminar on Colonial Latin America, San Diego 2017.

Enríquez Tintaya, Elizabeth, "Resultados preliminares de las investigaciones arqueológicas y puesta en uso social del paisaje cultural Huamanmarca, Carania—Yauyos", in Pieter Van Dalen Luna (ed.), *Arqueología de las Cuencas Alto y Medioandinas del departamento de Lima*, Lima 2014, 83–100.

Farquhar, Judith, Lili Lai, and Marshall Kramer, "A Place at the End of a Road: A Yin-Yang Geography", in *Anthropologica* 59:2 (2017), 216–227.

Federici, Silvia, *Re-enchanting the World: Feminism and the Politics of the Commons*, Oakland 2019.

Fernández, J.W., "The Call to the Commons. Decline and Recommitment in Asturias, Spain", in McCay, Bonnie J. and James M. Acheson (eds.), *The Question of the Commons. The Culture and Ecology of Communal Resources*, Tucson 1987, 266–289.

Gálvez, Modesto, Juan Ansión, and Carlos Iván Degregori, "Lo individual y lo colectivo en la comunidad andina", in *Ideología. Revista de Ciencias Sociales* 7 (1981), 5–16.

Gibson, Charles, *The Aztecs under Spanish Rule. A History of the Indians of the Valley of Mexico, 1519–1810*, Stanford 1964.

Glave, Luis Miguel, "La cuadratura del círculo y las rendijas del encierro: Política de reducción de indios en los Andes en tiempos del virrey Toledo", in Saito, Akira and Claudia Rosas Lauro (eds.), *Reducciones. La concentración forzada de las poblaciones indígenas en el virreinato del Perú*, 103–143, Lima 2017.

Godoy, Ricardo, "The Evolution of Common-Field Agriculture in the Andes. A Hypothesis", in *Comparative Studies in Society and History* 33:2 (1991), 395–414.

Godoy, Ricardo, *Mining and Agriculture in Highland Bolivia. Ecology, History, and Commerce among the Jukumanis*, Tucson 1990.

Godoy, Ricardo A., "The Fiscal Role of the Andean Ayllu", in *Man* 21: 4 (1986), 723–741.

Gonzales Escudero, Damián A., "Una aproximación procesal a la defensa de la tierra indígena en los Andes centrales en el Estado virreinal temprano (1550–1560)", in *Revista de la Maestría en Derecho Procesal* 7: 1 (2017), 71–100.

Graubart, Karen B., "Shifting Landscapes. Heterogeneous Conceptions of Land Use and Tenure in the Lima Valley", in *Colonial Latin American Review* 26: 1 (2017), 62–84.

Graubart, Karen B., "'*Ynuvaciones malas e rreprouadas*': Seeking Justice in the Early Colonial Pueblos de Indios", in Owensby, Brian P. and Richard J. Ross, *Justice in a New World: Negotiating Legal Intelligibility in British, Iberian, and Indigenous America*, New York 2018, 151–180.

Graubart, Karen B., *Republics of Difference. Religious and Racial Self-Governance in the Spanish Atlantic World*, Oxford 2022.

Greer, Allan, *Property and Dispossession. Natives, Empires and Land in Early Modern North America*, Cambridge 2018.

Gluckman, Max, *Politics, Law, and Ritual in Tribal Society*, Chicago 1965.

Guillet, David, "Agrarian Ecology and Peasant Production in the Central Andes", in *Mountain Research and Development* 1:1 (1981), 19–28.

Guillet, David, "Agro-Pastoral Land Use and the Tragedy of the Commons in the Central Andes", in Beaver, Patricia D. and Burton L. Purrington (eds.), *Cultural Adaptations to Mountain Environments*, Athens-Georgia 1984, 12–23.

Guillet, David, "Land Tenure, Ecological Zone, and Agricultural Regime in the Central Andes", in *American Ethnologist* 8: 1 (1981), 139–156.

Guillet, David, *Agrarian Reform and Peasant Economy in Southern Peru*, Columbia 1979.

Harvey, David, "The Future of the Commons", in *Radical History Review* 109 (2011), 101–107.

Hernández Astete, Francisco, "La historiografía andina y la idea de propiedad", in Guerra Martinière, Margarita and Rafael Sánchez-Concha Barrios (eds.), *Homenaje a José Antonio del Busto Duthurburu*, vol. 1, Lima 2012, 273–284.

Herzog, Tamar, "Colonial Law and 'Native Customs': Indigenous Land Rights in Colonial Spanish America", in *The Americas* 69: 3 (2013), 303–321.

Herzog, Tamar, *Frontiers of Possession: Spain and Portugal in Europe and the Americas*, Cambridge 2015.

Herzog, Tamar, "How Did the Commons Become Terra nullius? Contextualising Colonial Debates and Asking About Their Consequences", in *Quaderni storici, Rivista quadrimestrale* 3 (2021), 607–624.

Herzog, Tamar, "Immemorial (and Native) Customs in Early Modernity: Europe and the Americas", in *Comparative Legal History* 9:1 (2021), 3–55.

Itier, César, *Palabras clave de la sociedad y la cultura incas*, Lima 2023.

Izko, Xavier, "Comunidad andina: Persistencia y cambio", in *Revista Andina* 4: 1 (1986), 59–99.

Izquierdo, Jesús, *El rostro de la comunidad. la identidad del campesino en la Castilla del antiguo régimen*, Madrid 2002.

Jurado, María Carolina, "Tierra, estatus y viudez. Variabilidad y tensión en los hogares indígenas rurales; A propósito del repartimiento de Macha (Charcas) en el siglo XVII", in *Andes* 1: 29 (2018), 1–33.

Kosiba, Steve, and R. Alexander Hunter, "Fields of Conflict. A Political Ecology Approach to Land and Social Transformation in the Colonial Andes (Cuzco, Peru)", in *Journal of Archaeological Science* 84 (2017), 40–53.

Linebaugh, Peter, *The Magna Carta Manifesto: Liberties and Commons for All*, Berkeley 2008.

Linebaugh, Peter, *Stop, Thief! The Commons, Enclosures, and Resistance*, Oakland 2014.

Lockhart, James, *The Nahuas after the Conquest. A Social and Cultural History of the Indians of Central Mexico, Sixteenth through Eighteenth Centuries*, Stanford 1992.

Long, Norman, and Bryan R. Roberts, "Introduction", in Long, Norman and Bryan R. Roberts (eds.), *Peasant Cooperation and Capitalist Expansion in Central Peru*, Austin 1978, 3–43.

Matos Mar, José, Teresa Guillén de Boluarte, Julio Cotler, Eduardo Soler, and Francisco Boluarte, *Las actuales comunidades de indígenas. Huarochirí en 1955*, Lima 1958.

Mayer, Enrique, "Los atributos del hogar. Economía doméstica y la encomienda en el Perú colonial", in *Revista Andina* 2:2 (1984), 557–590.

Mayer, Enrique, *The Articulated Peasant: Household Economies in the Andes*, Boulder 2002.

Mayer, Enrique and Marisol de la Cadena, *Cooperación y conflicto en la comunidad andina: Zonas de producción y organización social*, Lima 1989.

Mayer, Enrique and César Fonseca Martel, *Sistemas agrarios en la cuenca del Río Cañete, Departamento de Lima*, Lima 1979.

Medelius, Mónica and José Carlos de la Puente Luna, "Curacas, bienes y quipus en un documento toledano (Jauja, 1570)", in *Histórica* 28: 2 (2004), 35–82.

Mumford, Jeremy Ravi, "Las llamas de Tapacarí: Un documento judicial de un alcalde de indios en la Audiencia de Charcas, 1580", in *Histórica* 40:2 (2016), 171–185.

Murra, John v., *Formaciones políticas y económicas del mundo andino*, Lima 1975.

Murra, John v., "Derechos a tierras en el Tawantinsuyu", in *El mundo andino: Población, medio ambiente y economía*, Lima 2002, 294–307.

Murra, John v., "Una visión indígena del mundo andino", in Felipe Guaman Poma de Ayala *Nueva crónica y buen gobierno*, ed. John V. Murra, Rolena Adorno, and Jorge L. Urioste, Madrid 1987, il–lxiii.

Murra, John v., "Waman Puma, etnógrafo del mundo andino", in Guaman Poma de Ayala, *El primer nueva corónica*, 1980 (fac.), xiii–xix.

Murra, John, *Reciprocity and Redistribution in Andean Civilizations. The 1969 Lewis Henry Morgan Lectures*, Chicago 2017.

Noejovich Chernoff, Héctor, *Los albores de la economía americana*, Lima 1996.

Orlove, Benjamin, and Ricardo Godoy, "Sectoral Fallowing Systems in the Central Andes", in *Journal of Ethnobiology* 6: 1 (1986), 169–204.

Orlove, Benjamin, Ricardo Godoy, and Pierre Morlon, "Sistemas de barbecho sectorial", in Morlon, Pierre (ed.), *Comprender la agricultura campesina en los Andes Centrales. Perú-Bolivia*, Lima 1996, 86–117.

Ossio A., Juan M., "La propiedad en las comunidades andinas", in *Allpanchis* 15: 22 (1983), 35–59.

Pease G. Y, Franklin, "La noción de propiedad entre los Incas: Una aproximación", in Shozo Masuda (ed.), *Etnografía e historia del mundo andino*, Tokyo 1986, 3–33.

Penry, S. Elizabeth, *The People Are King. The Making of an Indigenous Andean Politics*, Oxford 2019.

Premo, Bianca, "From the Pockets of Women. The Gendering of the Mita, Migration, and Tribute in Colonial Chucuito, Peru", in *The Americas* 57: 1 (2000), 63–93.

Premo, Bianca, "Felipa's Braid: Women, Culture, and the Law in Eighteenth-Century Oaxaca", in *Ethnohistory* 61: 3 (2014), 497–523.

Premo, Bianca, and Yanna Yannakakis, "A Court of Sticks and Branches: Indian Jurisdiction in Colonial Mexico and Beyond", in *American Historical Review* 124: 1 (2019), 28–55.

Puente Luna, José Carlos de la, "Felipe Guaman Poma de Ayala, administrador de bienes de comunidad", in *Revista Andina* 47 (2008), 9–52.

Puente Luna, José Carlos de la, "That Which Belongs to All: Khipus, Community, and Indigenous Legal Activism in the Early Colonial Andes", in *The Americas* 72: 1 (2015), 19–54.

Puente Luna, José Carlos de la, and Renzo Honores, "Guardianes de la real justicia. Alcaldes de indios, costumbre y justicia local en Huarochirí colonial", in *Histórica* 40: 2 (2016), 11–47.

Puente Luna, José Carlos de la, "Of Widows, Furrows, and Seed. New Perspectives on Land and the Colonial Andean Commons", in *The Hispanic American Historical Review* 101: 3 (2021), 375–407.

Puente Luna, José Carlos de la, "Customs Apart. Rethinking Inheritance and Competing Land Claims Among Indigenous Commoner Women in Colonial Andean Villages", in *Colonial Latin American Review* 33: 1 (2024), 79–104.

Ramírez, Susan, "El concepto de 'comunidad' en el siglo XVI", in Noejovich Chernoff, Héctor (ed.), *América bajo los Austrias. Economía, cultura y sociedad*, Lima 2001, 181–190.

Ramírez, Susan, "Land and Tenure in Early Colonial Peru. Individualizing the *Sapci*, 'That Which Is Common to All'", in *Medieval Globe* 2: 2 (2016), 33–71.

Ramírez, Susan, "Despedazando lo común. De testimonios orales a títulos escritos", in Ángeles Muñoz, María de los (ed.), *Interpretando huellas. Arqueología, etnohistoria y etnografía de los Andes y sus tierras bajas*, 287–304, Cochabamba 2018.

Rasnake, Roger Neil, *Domination and Cultural Resistance: Authority and Power among an Andean People*, Durham 1988.

Salomon, Frank, "Collca y *sapçi*. Una perspectiva sobre el almacenamiento inka desde la analogía etnográfica", in *Boletín de Arqueología PUCP* 8 (2004), 43–57.

Salomon, Frank, "Guaman Poma's *Sapçi* in Ethnographic Vision", in Adorno, Rolena and Ivan Boserup, *Unlocking the Doors to the Worlds of Guaman Poma and His "Nueva Corónica"*, Copenhagen 2015, 355–396.

Salomon, Frank, "The Long Afterlives of Central-Peruvian Khipu Patrimonies", Paper presented at the *Bard Graduate Center Symposium–Khipus. Writing Histories in and from Knots*, New York 2019.

Salomon, Frank, Carrie J. Brezine, Reymundo Chapa, and Víctor Falcón Huayta, "*Khipu* from Colony to Republic. The Rapaz Patrimony", in Boone, Elizabeth Hill and Gary Urton (eds.), *Their Way of Writing. Scripts, Signs, and Pictographies in Pre-Columbian America*, Washington DC 2011, 353–378.

Salomon, Frank, Carrie J. Brezine, Gino de las Casas, and Víctor Falcón Huayta, "Los khipus de Rapaz en casa. Un complejo administrativo-ceremonial centroperuano", in *Revista Andina* 43 (2006), 59–92.

Salomon, Frank, and Jorge L. Urioste (trans.), *The Huarochirí Manuscript. A Testament of Ancient and Colonial Andean Religion*, Austin 1991.

Schmitt Perea, Rafael, "San Agustín de Guaquis. Evangelización y prácticas curativas en un pueblo colonial de origen prehispánico de Yauyos durante el siglo XVII", in *Yuyarccuni* 4 (2020), 69–89.

Serulnikov, Sergio, "The Politics of Intracommunity Land Conflict in the Late Colonial Andes", in *Ethnohistory* 55:1 (2008), 119–152.

Soler Bustamante, Eduardo, "La agricultura en la comunidad de San Pedro de Huancaire", in *Revista del Museo Nacional* 23 (1954), 90–139.

Spalding, Karen, *Huarochirí. An Andean Society under Inca and Spanish Rule*, Stanford 1984.

Stanley, Amy, "Maidservants' Tales. Narrating Domestic and Global History in Eurasia, 1600–1900", in *American Historical Review* 121: 2 (2016), 437–460.

Stein, William, "La práctica de la antropología económica en los Andes peruanos. Comunidad, unidad doméstica y relaciones de producción", in *Revista Andina* 4: 2 (1986), 549–606.

Stern, Steve J., *Peru's Indian Peoples and the Challenge of Spanish Conquest. Huamanga to 1640*, 2nd ed, Madison 1993.

Tandeter, Enrique, "Teóricamente ausentes, teóricamente solas. Mujeres y hogares en los Andes coloniales (Sacaca y Acasio in 1614)", in *Andes* 8 (1997), 11–25.

Trelles, Efraín, *The Integration of an Andean Ethnic Group into the Early Encomienda System: The Case of the Chupaychu in Huanuco (Peru), 1532–1562* (M.A. Thesis), Austin 1983.

Vassberg, David E., *Land and Society in Golden Age Castile*, Cambridge 1984.

Villella, Peter B., "'For So Long the Memories of Men Cannot Contradict It'. Nahua Patrimonial Restorationism and the Law in Early New Spain", in *Ethnohistory* 63: 4 (2016), 697–720.

Wernke, Steven A., *Negotiated Settlements. Andean Communities and Landscapes under Inka and Spanish Colonialism*, Gainesville 2013.

Woolley, Christopher, "'The Forests Cannot Be Commons'. Spanish Law, Environmental Change, and New Spain's Council on Forests", in *The Americas* 77: 1 (2020), 41–71.

Zagalsky, Paula, "El concepto de 'comunidad' en su dimensión espacial: Una historización de su semántica en el contexto colonial andino (siglos XVI–XVII)", in *Revista Andina* 48 (2009), 57–90.

CHAPTER 5

Ownership and Seigniorial Relationships

Land and Territory in Colonial Tlaxiaco (the Mixteca, Mexico)

Marta Martín Gabaldón

1 Introduction

The territory—understood as the functional and material natural environment over which a specific control is exercised from the political sphere that regulates access to resources based on power relations[1]—is presented to us as a palimpsest. It involves jurisdictional overlaps that are sometimes articulated synchronically and sometimes diachronically. Nevertheless, a proper reading of its scope, through written documents and other (ethno)historical sources, can help us understand the processes involved in the different configurations.

This research focuses on the Mixtec sociohistorical space (present-day state of Oaxaca, Mexico) between the 16th and 18th centuries, particularly the space of the ancient *señorío* (lordship) of Tlaxiaco. Some of the characteristics that modulated the production of territory in this space involved the relatively scarce presence of Spaniards, who were more interested in the control of trade than in the exploitation of the land, and the intensity of the *señorial* (seigniorial) relations that allowed the *cacicazgos*' strong survival until the beginning of the 19th century. The latter led to the survival of distinctly indigenous organisational structures—the *ñuu* and its subdivisions and the *yuhuitayu*—which made the jurisdictional and land tenure system more complex. The articulation of this region in different ecological niches forces us to question ourselves about productive activities and access to different spaces by the social actors interrelated in the Mixteca. The main objective of this work is

1 The definition proposed here is indebted to the perspective on territory developed by Latin American critical geography. For Rogério Haesbaert—without being an a priori, a category of analysis or a prior mental conception—the definition of territory is related to the political and jurisdictional control of space and, therefore, every territory always has a spatial-material basis for its constitution, that is, the land itself and the natural resources housed therein. This definition necessarily integrates the societies that inhabit it and the mechanisms they implement to exercise appropriations, delimitations and modifications on the natural environment. Haesbaert, "Del mito de la desterritorialización a la multiterritorialidad".

DOI:10.1163/9789004722729_006

to reveal investigations into various aspects related to the link between *señorial* relations and land ownership throughout the colonial period, based on what has been observed in the space of the ancient lordship of Tlaxiaco, which occupied different ecological niches. This will allow us to perceive permanence and modifications over time and to detect different strategies deployed by the caciques and the *pueblos* to consolidate their dominion over the land. What I have discerned in this work will allow us to make future comparisons with what happened in other places in the Mixteca Baja, Alta and Costa, to relate the access and control of natural resources with different—and changing—processes of territorialisation.

After providing the study area's political-territorial, social and productive context, I analyse some mechanisms deployed by the caciques during the 16th century to effectively control valuable lands. Next, I reflect on *señorial* relations' 'masked' permanence in the 17th and 18th centuries. Finally, I look at the processes of *composiciones de tierras* (land regularisation) to question the role of the *cacicazgo* and its relationship with the territory in the late colonial period.

The ideas expressed here are, to some extent, based on the contributions made by Arij Ouweneel and Rik Hoekstra, who, in the 1990s, explained the shift from political-territorial and social articulation based on personal association (*Personenverband*) to functioning by territorial association (*Territorialverband*).[2] Likewise, they are tributaries of Bernardo García Martínez's decades of research on the corporative nature of the *pueblos de indios*, which to a large extent retained the characteristics of the old *señoríos*, as can be seen in the presence of lineages, *cacicazgos*, *terrazgueros* (landless renter), tributary systems, and spatial structures, even in colonial times, to varying degrees depending on the territories.[3]

In the Mixteca, the *cacicazgo* is a fundamental institution for analysing ownership regimes. Our knowledge about its functioning in different periods is extensive and has allowed an understanding of the relevant dimensions of its political, social, economic and territorial function. A volume coordinated by Margarita Menegus and Rodolfo Aguirre provided us with one of the most panoramic views.[4] Not surprisingly, Menegus, one of the great scholars of the *cacicazgo*, has contributed very original and precise ideas about its structure and territorial implications in the Mixtec sphere that allow me to articulate the study carried out here.[5] The investigations of Hildeberto Martínez,

2 Ouweneel and Hoekstra, *Las tierras de los pueblos de indios*.
3 García Martínez, "La naturaleza corporativa de los *pueblos de indios*".
4 Menegus and Aguirre, *El cacicazgo en Nueva España y Filipinas*.
5 Menegus, "Balance historiográfico"; *La Mixteca Baja*; "La territorialidad de los cacicazgos y los

Patricia Cruz Pazos, and John Chance allow me to compare what happened regarding *cacicazgo* and ownership in different areas of Puebla. The latter also significantly contributed to the evolution of the Mixtec *cacicazgo* and land tenure in the late colonial period, which must also be considered.[6] For his part, Edgar Mendoza's vision provides knowledge about changes in ownership rights and *señorial* relations in the context of *composiciones de tierras* processes.[7]

These and other investigations offer a rich general analytical framework. However, as Manuel Hermann points out, case studies on the territorial articulation of Mixtec *señoríos* reveal a much more complex picture that prevents us from recognising the validity of a general model.[8] The research presented here follows these lines, focusing on the long duration of a *señorío* in which *señorial* relations, although 'masked', mediated the territorial composition and land tenure until the 18th century.

2 The Mixteca Region and Its Political-Territorial, Social, and Productive Context

The Mixteca, conceived as a socio-historical space, can be considered the heritage territory of the Mixtec ethnolinguistic group, both past and present. It extends through the northwestern portion of the state of Oaxaca—within what the official regionalisation considers the Mixteca itself—through the western part of the Sierra Sur region, through the Coast, through the southern fringe of the state of Puebla—the so-called Mixteca poblana—and the northeastern part of Guerrero—the Montaña region. In addition, the Mixteca was and still is inhabited by other minority ethnic groups, such as the Amuzgos, Triquis, and Chocho-Popolocas, also known as Ngiwas.

Conventionally, three fundamental sub-regions are differentiated to understand the internal articulation of the area: the Mixteca Baja, located in the northwestern sector, also encompassing territories of Puebla and Guerrero; the Mixteca Alta, northeastern and central sector; and the Mixteca de la Costa, to the south, also in a small strip of Guerrero (see Map 5.1). This division was

conflictos con terrazgueros y los pueblos vecinos en el siglo XVIII"; "Cacicazgos y repúblicas de indios en el siglo XVI".

6 Martínez, *Tepeaca en el siglo XVI*; Cruz Pazos, "Del arrendamiento al despojo de tierras"; Chance, "From Lord to Landowner".

7 Mendoza García, "La descomposición de un cacicazgo".

8 Hermann, "Ñuu Yava, Tamazola".

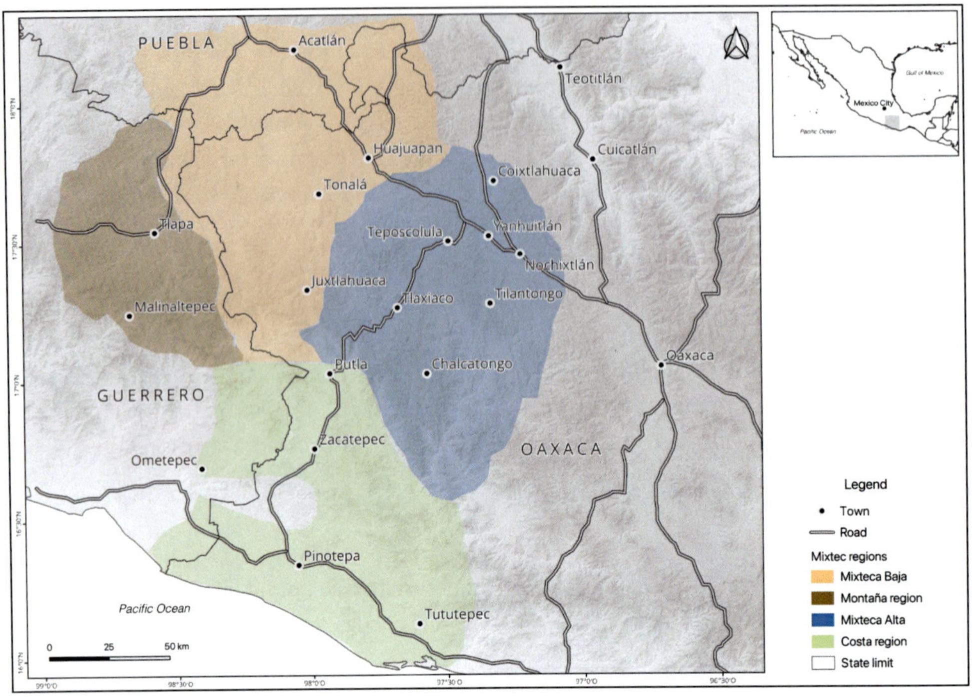

MAP 5.1 Location of the Mixteca and Differentiated Spaces within it
OWN ELABORATION

already conceived in a certain way by the ancient inhabitants of this extensive and heterogeneous territory, as shown by the meanings in the Ñudzahui (Mixtec) language recorded by the friars of the 16th century to refer to each of the parts: for example, *Ñuniñe*, "warm land", referred to the Mixteca Baja, and *Ñundaa*, "flat land", was the plain towards the coast.[9] The division between Alta, Baja, and Costa has a clear geographical correlation, defined by the altitude above sea level of the sierras and small intermontane valleys. However, the complex topography of the Sierra Madre del Sur and the north-south development mean that the broad socio-historical space encompasses multiple climatic units, environments and ecosystems—from low, hot, and arid places to high cold valleys and tropical lowlands. Such diversity is an aspect that significantly affected the historical and cultural development of the region and is central to the questions we ask about the ownership regime that operated during the colonial period.[10]

9 Reyes, Arte en lengua mixteca, I–II.

10 In parallel to the geographical aspect, linguists have perceived that the dialectal grouping

Archaeologists and ethnohistorians have highlighted some features that appear throughout the area, which can give rise to the recognition of a "shared history".[11] Here, I mention only one important constant that concerns political and social organisation: the existence, since the Classic period (400 B.C.–950 A.D.), of *yuhuitayu* (lordships or kingdoms) as the predominant political-territorial model in the three Mixtec areas, whose pre-Hispanic history has been reconstructed thanks to the development of archaeological work, the study of pre-Hispanic codices and colonial documentation.[12]

Let us delve into the indigenous structure of the political-territorial organisation and how it was adapted from the 16th century onwards within the Hispanic juridical order.[13] The primary territorial unit of the Mixtecs was the *ñuu*. The friars of the 16th century noted that *ñuu* was part of the expressions that referred to physical political-territorial entities, such as "hamlet", "village", "town", "territory", and "place by town", although it also had many other translations related to political and social aspects linked to the territory, such as "city", *ñuu canu yucunduta*, or "citizen", *tay ñuu canu*.[14] The *ñuu* was divided into sub-entities that received a different appellative depending on the regional dialectal variant: in the valleys of Teposcolula, Tamazulapan and Tlaxiaco, they used the term *siqui*; in the vicinity of Yanhuitlán, *siña*; and in the Mixteca Baja, the concept was *dzini*. The main Spanish translation was *barrio*. However, they were also mentioned as *colación* or *parroquia*, formed by corporate groups with ethnic and kinship ties, a common origin and shared political and economic relations.[15]

The most complex political-territorial units responded to the concept of *yuhuitayu*. Although there are still many questions regarding its precise functioning and historical development, a fundamental characteristic is that it

of the Ñudzahui language, which belongs to the Otomanguean family, also follows a distribution pattern similar to the geographical one. This circumstance tells us about greater contact intensity between groups within these spaces. See Josserand, *Mixtec dialect history*.

11 In another work, I have extensively reflected on the relevance of conceiving the Mixteca as a socio-historical space. Martín Gabaldón, "La Mixteca o las mixtecas".

12 Other common cultural indicators to consider are religious, calendar and pictographic writing.

13 To learn more about this broad historical process in Hispanic America, starting in the 16th century, see Bastias Saavedra (Chapter 1) in this volume.

14 Alvarado, *Vocabulario en lengua mixteca*, fols. 15^v, 63^v, 105^v, 139^v, 174^v, 195^r, 202^v.

15 It is still being determined whether the differences between the terms are purely lexical or whether they have conceptual implications. The same is true in the Nahua environment with the sub-entities of *altepetl* called *calpolli*, *tlaxilacalli* and *chinamitl*. Terraciano, *Los mixtecos de la Oaxaca colonial*, 165–168.

united two *ñuu* through the marriage of a man (*yya*) and a woman (*yya dzehe*) of the ruling lineage, a position they held hereditarily. Each represented his or her respective *ñuu*, which continued to enjoy autonomy, and his or her stately house, which comprised the palace, lands, relatives, and dependents associated with a lineage. In addition, the *yuhuitayu's* government was associated with the *toniñe*—hereditary authority—and the *tniño*—duty and responsibility towards the human group governed by the lords. Thus, the *yuhuitayu is* presented to us as a political-territorial entity and a political arrangement created by dynastic alliances.[16]

From the 16th century onwards and under the Hispanic normative order, the seats of the *yuhuitayu* became known as *cabeceras* (head towns). However, not infrequently, they were assimilated as *sujetos* (subject towns) according to the status acquired in the territorial reorganisation. Their rights, lands, and other patrimonial elements were assimilated with the concepts of kingdom, lordship, or *cacicazgo*. Some researchers emphasise that Mixtec political-territorial categories were intertwined with social ones, as they were under the powerful influence of kinship.[17]

The *yya tnuhu* or *yya toniñe*, understood as king or lord, was the head of the *yuhuitayu* hierarchy. In addition, a group of nobles or principals, the *tay toho*, accompanied the supreme ruler in his work. These two groups controlled the positions of power and authority, productive plots, natural resources, modes of production, distribution of goods and services, and ceremonial institutions. In addition, they were paid tribute, *daha*, and received personal services from the inhabitants of the *yuhuitayu*, called *tay ñuu* or *tay yucu*, the common people, and the *tay situndayu*, the *terrazgueros*. In return, these people received protection, ceremonial patronage and usufruct rights for their cultivated land.

The institution of the *cacicazgo* was established in the 16th century and recognised the rights of the pre-Hispanic natural chiefs or lords of the different areas of New Spain and other members of the Hispanic monarchy. A very general idea leads us to consider the caciques and *cacicas* as mediating figures between the Spanish administration and the indigenous society in the Indian towns, where they maintained their rights and privileges—land and

16 *Toniñe* can be translated in a broad sense as "government", and Kevin Terraciano makes it analogous with the Nahua *tlatocáyotl*. Terraciano, *Los mixtecos de la Oaxaca colonial*, 162, 248–275.

17 Spores, *Ñuu Ñudzahui la Mixteca de Oaxaca*, 87, 99, 106. Rodolfo Pastor especially emphasised the relevance of kinship and lineage in forming what he conceptualised as kindred, for both the supreme ruler and the principals and the commoners. He considered the sets of families as the fundamental reference units in the politico-social system. Pastor, *Campesinos y reformas*, 28–36.

terrazgo, market rights, tribute, movable and immovable property, and inheritance rights, among others.[18] In this way, the *cacicazgo*—understood as the exercise of a particular jurisdiction—consolidated a power group that had a long place in the colonial political apparatus in the Mixteca and continued to exist, until the first moments of independent Mexico, as a significant landowner.[19]

A principal mechanism of *cacicazgo* integration and maintenance, along with other coercive and voluntary forces, was the creation of alliances between the heads or direct heirs of the various royal lineages sealed by marriage. Also, as Ronald Spores has pointed out, this strategy was essential in the creation of a dense social, political, and economic network that linked numerous towns and political domains, building bridges between different geographical zones, from the tropical lowlands to the valleys in the highlands and cold lands, which contributed to the diversification of natural resources and agricultural products available for consumption within the lordship or for insertion into regional markets.[20] Thus, in the Mixteca, the Mesoamerican tradition of interwoven land control by the lordships is evident to such a degree that, in some specific areas, this control was conceptualised as an "archipelago".[21]

A significant social group linked to the *cacicazgo* was the *tay situndayu* or *terrazgueros*, who paid rent for occupying land, tilled plots, and performed personal services. So, their condition combined economic rent and the *señorial* ties of personal dependence. Thus, using a distinction typical of the *ius commune*, the cacique had *dominio eminente* (the extension of a governmental entity) over the land throughout his *señorío*, which allowed him to exercise his jurisdictional authority over his *terrazgueros*. At the same time, he had

18 We conceive of the *terrazgo* as the rent received by the caciques from the peasants who worked part of their lands for them. Menegus, "Cacicazgos y repúblicas de indios en el siglo XVI".

19 Chance, "From Lord to Landowner" 445–466.

20 Spores, "Marital Alliance in the Political Integration of Mixtec Kingdoms", 297–311. In this sense, it is a possible parallel to the analyses carried out by John Murra in the Andean environment since the 1950s concerning the vertical control of ecological floors. However, the fundamental distinction between the Andean space and Mesoamerica is that the Inca did not demand tribute from his vassals, but labour force. At the same time, the *tlatoani* requested personal services, labour and tribute in kind. Exhaustive research on the functioning of many Mixtec lordships is still needed to articulate a solid theory and empirically understand their possible function in the Mixteca.

21 We owe the spatial notion of *entreveramiento de tierras* to Pedro Carrasco. The imposition on the lordships to deliver certain products as tribute may have interfered with their spatial configuration since it encouraged them to occupy specific lands where they could be obtained. Carrasco, *Estructura político-territorial del imperio tenochca*. For the Mixteca, see Monaghan, "Irrigation and Ecological Complementarity in Mixtec Cacicazgos".

patrimonial lands over which he exercised *dominio directo* as part of his *casa señorial* and ceded *dominio útil* to the *terrazgueros*.[22]

This panorama of indigenous relations and land tenure was forced to adapt, at least nominally, to the traditional European scheme that was intended to be homogeneous throughout the viceroyalty and that distinguished between the settlement lands, community lands (distinguishing between *propios*, those that served to cover common expenses through exploitation or leasing, and *comunales*, those that were subject to common distribution), neighbourhood lands, and particular lands. In many parts of the Mixteca, the *terrazgueros* were exceedingly numerous. However, according to Menegus, the Crown tried to introduce them into the list of regular taxpayers through the creation of Indian republics and the granting of *mercedes de tierras* during the 16th and early 17th centuries. There is evidence of the creation of *pueblos de indios* within the territory of the caciques: apparently, the republic was given only an 'urban' hull for its settlement and its *propios*, omitting those of common distribution, so that for their subsistence they continued to depend on the cacique's lands and the payment of a *terrazgo*, personal service, and obedience.[23]

These characteristics lead me to emphasise the importance of the *cacicazgo* as an administrator of the local economies through the possession of land and the management of the labour force of their *terrazgueros*, which allowed them to build important family patrimonies and to be critical parts of the Oaxacan economic structure.[24] One hypothesis put forward by several authors is that this situation could be maintained for longer in the Mixteca than in other areas of New Spain due to the mediating need of the caciques in a region where the

22 Taylor, *Terratenientes y campesinos en la Oaxaca colonial*, 59; Assadourian, "Agriculture and Land Tenure"; Menegus, *La Mixteca Baja*, 56, 96–97. An interesting discussion of these notions is given in Carrera Quezada, *Sementeras de papel*, 26–33. In the 19th century, *dominio pleno o absoluto* was defined as "el poder que uno tiene en alguna cosa para enajenarla sin dependencia de otro, percibir todos sus frutos, y escluir de su uso a los demás", and the *dominio útil* "el derecho de percibir todos los frutos de una cosa bajo alguna prestación o tributo que se paga al que conserva en ella el dominio directo, tal es el dominio que tiene el vasallo o enfiteuta en la heredad que ha tomado a feudo o enfiteusis". Escriche, *Diccionario razonado de legislación jurisprudencia*, 568. See also Peset and Menegus, "Rey propietario y o rey soberano".

23 Menegus, *La Mixteca Baja*, 50, 56; Menegus, "Cacicazgos y repúblicas de indios en el siglo XVI," 205–220.

24 Margarita Menegus has provided relevant data on the *cacicazgo* of Huajuapan and others in the Mixteca Baja that illustrate this idea, and John Chance shows how the change from lord in charge of local government to landowner, more detached from the affairs of the community, could operate as early as the 18th century. Menegus, *La Mixteca Baja*; Chance, "From Lord to Landowner".

presence of Spaniards was not as intense as in other places.[25] The land, in a rugged orographic environment with hardly any room for valleys of considerable extension, was not a strong attraction for the Spaniards, who preferred to dedicate themselves to commercial activity through the hoarding of specific networks and the management of herds of small livestock that would be inserted, beginning in the 17th century, into the transhumance routes from the Mixteca Baja to the Coast (and back) through the system of *haciendas volantes*.[26]

I established the general characterisation presented in this section based on the work accumulated over decades of research that focused on different areas of the Mixteca. However, I believe that the case studies allow us to understand, in depth, the functioning and dynamics of each *señorío*, *cacicazgo*, *república de indios*, or *cabecera-sujeto* complex (not synonymous, but related categories), in and of themselves and concerning each other. Moreover, work focused on different particular spaces will eventually allow us to detect possible subregional variations in the ownership regimes. Hypothetically, diversifications may be due to circumstances related to the models established in *señorial* relations (different ways of conceiving the *yuhuitayu*), differences in the social management of natural resource exploitation and agricultural activities in different ecological niches, and local responses to the policy of land tenure regularisation under the Hispanic normative order.

In the space of the ancient *señorío* of Tlaxiaco, whose heart is located in the central Mixteca Alta, but which also extends into the environments of the Mixteca Baja, to the north, and from the tropical lands to Costa, to the south, I have detected some particular situations that I contrast below with what happened in other entities in the Mixteca.

3 Mechanisms for Expansion and Control of Space by the *Cacicazgo*

Thanks to the information contained in the visit and demarcation of the jurisdiction of Tlaxiaco carried out in 1599 to implement the *congregación* of its *pueblos*, in addition to other previous information, we know that the early colonial *señorío* of Tlaxiaco extended over a space of approximately 2,000 kilometres squared that unfolds from north to south in a strip of 90 kilometres and from east to west along 65 kilometres, and covered the territ-

25 Spores, Ñuu Ñudzahui la Mixteca de Oaxaca, 82.

26 The *haciendas volantes* consisted of pastures rented to both the caciques and the Indian republics by the Spanish owners of herds and flocks on their annual transhumant journey to the coast. Romero Frizzi, *Economía y vida de los españoles en la Mixteca Alta: 1519–1720*.

ory occupied today by 23 municipalities.[27] Likewise, it extended over 12 subregions—taking a delimiting criterion enunciated by archaeologists[28]—that in pre-Hispanic times housed autonomous settlements of considerable size that could have been linked under the same political-territorial system and where several ethnic groups coexisted and interacted in the political, economic and social spheres: Mixtecs—as the majority—Triquis—as the minority—and Nahuas.

In environmental terms, the predominant meteorological phenomena in the Mixteca—cold air inflows, *alisios* winds, jet streams, and cyclones originating in the Isthmus of Tehuantepec—combined with the enormous topographic complexity and differences in latitude in the space over which Tlaxiaco extended its domain, generate a tremendous climatic diversity. The climates range from steppe in the extreme north and west of the jurisdiction to hot in the extreme south, passing through semi-warm, temperate, and semi-cold; according to humidity levels, there are humid, semi-humid, and semi-dry areas. In the 16th century, this diversity was noted by Spanish visitors as cold, temperate, and warm *temples*. The description recorded by Dominican friar Fray Francisco de Burgoa in the 17th century gives a good account of the ecosystemic diversity of the jurisdiction:

> [...] The kingdom had more than a hundred leagues of traversing, with so many different kinds of climates (*temples*), that leaving the region of snow, one goes down to the region of fire where the vermin are as poisonous as countless flying bugs, biting mosquitoes, worms, spiders, vipers, and ferocious tigers, without other noxious animals at every step, the cliffs are intractable, the cliffs are very high, opaque, and shady, because of the groves of oaks, pines, and leafy cedars that cover them, the rivers are very fast-flowing, they breed very fine trout, and other beautiful fish, because the waters are very thin, and cold, that rush down from the mountains [...]. In the mountains there are peaches, figs, pears, and apples, which are very tasty, and in the lowlands, citrons, oranges, limes, grapefruit, lemons, pineapples, bananas, *mameyes*, and other fruits of great value, and in rare meadows some wheat is sown.[29]

---

27 Comisariado de bienes comunales, "Diligencias para la congregación de Tlaxiaco", 1599. This document was found in the municipal presidency of the *Heroica Ciudad de Tlaxiaco* three decades ago by Ronald Spores and John Monaghan and is currently in the custody of the *Comisariado de Bienes Comunales*.

28 Kowalewski, *Origins of the Ñuu*.

29 Burgoa, *Geográfica descripción*, 305–306. "[...] Tenía más de cien leguas de travesía el reino

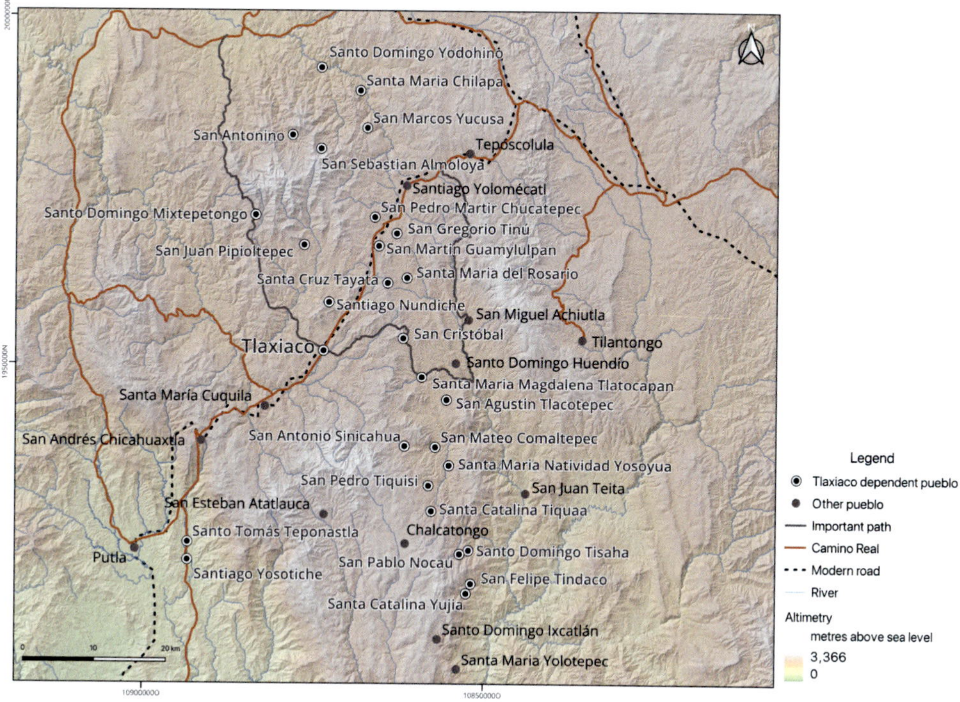

MAP 5.2 *República de indios* of Tlaxiaco in 1599
OWN ELABORATION

This complex ancient *señorío*, turned into a *cabecera-sujeto* complex recognised as *república de indios* by the Spanish authorities, managed to maintain its political and territorial integration until the end of the 17th century, when the first fragmentation occurred with the separation of San Mateo Peñasco in 1687, becoming the new *cabecera* of several surrounding villages (Map 5.2).[30]

de tanta variedad de temples, que saliendo de la región de la nieve, se baja a la del fuego donde son las sabandijas tan ponzoñosas, como innumerables chinches voladoras, mosquitos mordaces, gusanos, arañas, víboras, y tigres ferocísimos, sin otros animales nocivos a cada paso, los riscos son intratables, las sierras altísimas, opacas, y sombrías, por las arboledas de robles, pinos y cedros frondosos, que las cubren, los ríos más caudalosos, crían muy regaladas truchas, y otros pescados donceles, por ser las aguas muy delgadas, y frías, que se precipitan de montes [...]. Danse en los montes duraznos, brevas, peras, y manzanas, de linda sazón, y en las tierras bajas, cidras, naranjas, limas, toronjas, limones, piñas, plátanos mameyes, y otras frutas de mucho vicio, y en raras vegas se siembra algún trigo".

30 AGN, Indios, vol. 29, exp. 297. As was common in New Spain, the rest of the political separations occurred progressively throughout the 18th century. The functioning of this

I must clarify that the territorial extension over which the *república de indios* stretched and, beforehand, which we can think of as the jurisdictional space of the *cacicazgo* of Tlaxiaco, housed, in turn, several minor *cacicazgos* in some of the subject *pueblos*. That is to say, there was an internal game of hierarchies that complicated the understanding of the territorial expressions of the loyalties of the *terrazgueros* with their respective lords. In other words, understanding the juxtaposition of rights over land and the subsequent territorial scope of the jurisdictions—of the *pueblos de indios*, the *cacicazgo* of Tlaxiaco, and the others loyal to it—is still an issue that remains unsolved in this Chapter.[31]

We presume that, in the 15th century, Tlaxiaco had a complex or segmentary *señorial* structure.[32] This implies the existence of five places with their own political-territorial personality—five *ñuu*—that was ultimately led by the same ruler, perhaps in the form of a confederation, as seen in particular on the back of the *Codex Bodley*.[33] The dynamics of interaction with foreign groups since the late 15th century drove the centralisation of power around the Tlaxiaco valley settlement. They may have privileged a particular branch of a lineage over others. The *yuhuitayu* of Tlaxiaco and some other neighbours established a temporary or circumstantial alliance with Culhua-Mexica during the last third of the 15th century. After the military intervention by Motecuhzoma Xocoyotzin, the *ñuu* of the Tlaxiaco valley was established as the tribute collecting centre of a tributary province that encompassed another important neighbouring *yuhuitayu*, that of Achiutla. We believe this event contributed to marking the importance of the *ñuu* settled in the Tlaxiaco valley and boosted both spatial and political hierarchisation. Once the conquest and pacification of this section of the Mixteca Alta had been consummated, the distribution of the *encomienda* took place.

---

complex lordship and its integration mechanisms are the subject of another detailed piece of research. Martín Gabaldón, "Jurisdicción prehispánica y colonial de Tlaxiaco".

31 Bernardo García Martínez understands jurisdiction as a general principle that "se liga con la esencia del principio de asociación que fundamenta toda colectividad organizada políticamente [...]. Quienes la encabezan o representan detentan, en nombre propio o de la colectividad, el derecho a disponer en cierta medida de las personas o los recursos de los dependientes, o de sus servicios y productos, lo cual es el fundamento de conscripciones, levas, tributos, impuestos y otras demandas". García Martínez, "Jurisdicción y propiedad", 48.

32 For some models of segmentary or oligarchic states in Mesoamerica, see Daneels and Gutiérrez Mendoza, *El poder compartido*.

33 The *Codex Bodley is a* pre-Hispanic pictographic document kept in the Bodleian Library of the University of Oxford, whose reverse side narrates the history of the rulers of the Lugar Bulto de Xipe (not yet located with certainty) and, with it, the evolution of the dynasties of Ndisi Nuu-Tlaxiaco. Pohl, "Ancient Books: Mixtec Group Codices. Codex Bodley."

The exercise of jurisdiction over the natives by the first *encomendero*, Martín Vázquez, may have contributed to the territorial delimitation of the colonial *yuhuitayu* and strengthened the political centrality of the valley of Tlaxiaco. In a third instance, the arrival first of the secular clergy—accompanying the *encomendero* and under the auspices of the first bishop of Antequera (present-day Oaxaca de Juárez), Juan López de Zárate—and soon after of the Dominican friars, plus the construction of their conventual house, served to agglutinate the population at the bottom of the valley. This situation happened due to the policy of congregations promoted by Viceroy Don Luis de Velasco, the Elder, in the 1550s.[34] We believe that the inhabitants not only did not put up resistance to the *junta*, but also firmly requested it from the Spanish authorities due to the difficulties in maintaining the previous productive systems—notably, the cultivations in terraces—caused by the drastic demographic drop and the attractiveness of the commercial activities boosted by the passage of the *camino real* (royal road) that connected the Mixteca with the coast. The establishment of Tlaxiaco as the head of the *pueblo de indios* and the subordination of the other *ñuu* that made up the *yuhuitayu* as subject towns must have privileged the ruling lineage in the valley and this gave rise to a powerful colonial *cacicazgo*, represented in the 16th century by Don Felipe de Saavedra and his daughter, María de Saavedra.[35]

Doña María, following the mandates left by her father in his will, married her first cousin, Don Gabriel de Guzmán, then heir to the *cacicazgos* of Yahuitlán—another tremendous political and economic centre—and Achiutla. This union sealed an alliance between two rich *señoríos* and made their caciques, in all probability, the most powerful of their time. Unfortunately, Doña María died without descendants in the mid-1590s. After some years of litigation, the lands belonging to Doña María's *cacicazgo* passed into the hands of the republic of Tlaxiaco. The argument put forward by the *cabildo* was that, although the *cacica* Doña María had not left a will before her death, she had stipulated that her property should fall into the possession of the republic, which the Real Audiencia finally confirmed.[36]

34 AGI, Audiencia de México 538, N. 7, fols. 2^r–10^r. Library of Congress, Kraus MS 140, fols. 411^r–411^v. Newberry Library, Ayer MS 1121, fol. 195^v.

35 Marta Martín Gabaldón, "Jurisdicción prehispánica y colonial de Tlaxiaco".

36 Spores, *Ñuu Ñudzahui la Mixteca de Oaxaca*, 309–311. Unfortunately, after the transfer and unification of files in the current *Archivo Histórico Judicial de Oaxaca* collection, it has not been possible to locate the file that Spores consulted. However, one of the witnesses who came to testify in 1717 in an extensive lawsuit over certain lands of the *cacicazgo* said that he had heard his grandparents say that Doña María left the *cacicazgo* to the community of the *cabecera* of Tlaxiaco. AHJ, Teposcolula Civil, leg. 22, exp. 12, fols. 26^r–26^v.

A lawsuit filed in 1717, precisely because of the occupation of the lands of a livestock *estancia* that had been granted in *merced* to the cacique Don Francisco de Guzmán in the 16th century, allows us to see how the common people and the republic of Tlaxiaco confronted those who pretended to claim possession of lands that were previously associated to the *cacicazgo*, as Doña Manuela Pimentel y Guzmán de Achiutla did.[37] In the 18th century, claims also came from some members of the lineage of the caciques of Copala and Chicahuaxtla (Triqui enclaves), but what we have evidence of is that the governor and principals of Tlaxiaco actively defended the possessions that they considered to belong to the commons and republic and not to any *cacicazgo*.[38] I believe this exciting circumstance shows the survival of old *señorial* relationships that remained 'masked' in the eyes of the Spanish justice system, as I will discuss in the following section.[39]

From what I have explained so far, it can be shown that there was a complex juxtaposition of land rights in the Mixteca, as the Crown, under its jurisdictional superiority, recognised the land rights exercised by both the *repúblicas de indios*—after their formation and recognition in the mid-16th century—and the *cacicazgos*. These rights overlapped in space. In exercising their jurisdiction, we believe the caciques used strategies in the 16th century based on pre-Hispanic times to expand and consolidate their land holdings, which led to conflicts with other *cacicazgos* and Indian republics.

Both the cacique Don Felipe and his daughter, Doña María, sent families of *terrazgueros* to settle and control lands in strategic locations from an environmental point of view. The enclaves were considered *barrios* by the Spanish authorities, even though they were very distant from the *cabecera*. We cannot dwell on the details of the rich information contained in over 600 pages generated by the lawsuits and complaints between the *terrazgueros* and the towns surrounding the places where they settled. However, below I provide a sequence and some relevant data.

The natives of Atoyaquillo, today San Juan Teita, located southeast of Tlaxiaco, accused the cacique and principals of Tlaxiaco of having entered their lands in the places called Yosonuma and Acatlixco. We are still determining

Pastor indicated that, in at least two cases, caciques without direct descendants left their property to their communities, although he does not sufficiently clarify this assertion. Pastor, *Campesinos y reformas*, 79.

37 AHJ, Teposcolula Civil, leg. 22, exp. 12.

38 Documents from the *Comisariado de Bienes Comunales of San Juan Copala* published by García Alcaraz, *Tinujei. Los triquis de Copala*, 217–220. AHMHCT, sección Jefatura política, subsección Gobierno, serie Tierras, subserie Límites, caja 214, exp. 1.

39 For a parallel case, see Jurado's study on Charcas (Chapter 6) in this volume.

the date on which this occupation took place. However, in 1567 Don Felipe and other principals complained against the Indians of Atoyaquillo for having broken the *varas* of justice of three *topiles* (bailiffs) when they accompanied a group of *macehuales* (commoners) who were cleaning the access paths to the lands. This act was a profound symbol of not recognising the authority of Tlaxiaco on the lands they claimed to be theirs.[40]

In 1579, when Doña María was already the *cacica*, the principals of Tlaxiaco accused those of Atoyaquillo and their *sujetos* of having entered their lands, already being tilled, and of having built houses and a church without authorisation. For that reason, they demanded the payment of a tribute to the *cabecera* of Tlaxiaco. Each one of the parties involved presented more than 60 witnesses, and the principals of Tlaxiaco accused Atoyaquillo of having bribed and intoxicated those on their side, so additional testimonies were requested. The first sentence, given on 14 November 1581, favoured Tlaxiaco. The Indians who settled irregularly in the lands of the two places would have to recognise Tlaxiaco as their *cabecera*, or they would have to return to their places of origin. Then, when Atoyaquillo requested that the ruling be revoked, María Girón appeared, who claimed to be an *encomendera* of the town, stating that these lands had belonged to them since time immemorial. After hearing more witnesses, a new sentence in June 1582 finally gave justice to Atoyaquillo. The natives settled in Yosonuma, and Acatlixco had to come with their services and tributes to this *cabecera*. Tlaxiaco, not satisfied with the sentence, requested its revocation and argued that before the same natives of Atoyaquillo had been under the subjection of Tlaxiaco, to whom they paid tribute. The people of Atoyaquillo were accused of rebellion for not answering the accusations.[41]

In 1583, witnesses summoned from Teposcolula were accused of perjury when they testified against Tlaxiaco.[42] A year later, the *cacica* Doña María established a new lawsuit against the cacique of Atoyaquillo, Don Felipe de Santiago, and his republic officers.[43] The fight for these lands was fully justified since they were located in a small canyon in a low and temperate area—at almost 800 metres above sea level less than Tlaxiaco—next to a large river, which allowed the development of irrigation techniques and the production of crops typical of this milieu.

Another front of the conflict took place in Malinaltepec, present-day San Bartolomé Yucuañe, some 25 kilometres east of Tlaxiaco, located on a vital com-

40 AGN, Tierras, vol. 44, exp. 1. AHJ, Teposcolula Criminal, leg. 1, exps. 13 y 44.
41 AGN, Tierras, vol. 44, exp. 1.
42 AHJ, Teposcolula Criminal, leg. 2, exp. 48.
43 AGN, Tierras, vol. 2948, exp. 28.

munication route with the space of what was once the lordship from which the legitimacy of the Mixtec dynasties emanated, Tilantongo. In 1590, the *cacica* Doña María sent ten married couples of *terrazgueros* to found a "barrio" called Ñuuyucu. Thirteen years later, the authorities of Malinaltepec accused four Indians of not following the doctrine nor the call of the communal works in favour of Malinaltepec about five years before, in addition to disturbing other families and trying to convince them to recognise the *cacica* of Tlaxiaco as their legitimate *señora*. In the file, it is openly stated that the lands where the couples settled belonged to the *cacicazgo* of Tlaxiaco. However, the Indians worked for the church and *the común de la república* of Malinaltepec when they were requested to do so.[44]

Finally, I believe that this strategy could have also been implemented long before in the south of the jurisdiction, in the coveted natural tropical environment of the Cañada de Yosotiche,[45] and also in the limits between San Felipe Tindaco, a *pueblo sujeto* to Tlaxiaco, and the neighbouring *señoríos* of Yolotepec and Teozacoalco. In 1545, the *estancia*[46] of San Felipe Tindaco filed a lawsuit against Teozacoalco for the lands of Nixtepetongo or Taxcotepetongo and the *estancia* called Uxitlan (Huixitlán), where five families had been settled.[47]

Unlike what has been observed in other New Spain spaces regarding the distribution of lands to *terrazgueros* associated with *señoríos*, we do not see the operation of the emphyteutic census in the cases presented here.[48] In this case, we consider that this was not a land distribution but an occupation strategy using the traditional link between the *terrazgueros*, the *tay situndayu*, and the lords, the *yya*.

As indicated earlier, the indigenous political-territorial articulation was closely linked to the social. The axis was the recognition of the authority of the *yya*, rulers endowed with sacredness. This circumstance leads some researchers to propose that, although in pre-Hispanic times there must have been a specific

44 AHJ, Teposcolula Criminal, leg. 9, exp. 15.

45 Martín Gabaldón, "New crops, new landscapes and new socio-political relationships".

46 In the colonial records, *estancia* and *sujeto* have the same politic-territorial subordination meaning to the *cabecera*.

47 AHJ, Teposcolula Criminal, leg. 6, exp. 35, fols. 1^r–5^r. This lawsuit was the germ of another series of legal confrontations over land between Yolotepec, San Felipe Tindaco and Tlaxiaco in the last third of the 16th century. AHJ, Teposcolula Civil, leg. 2, exps. 1 y 13.

48 For example, in 1554 in Huejotzingo, the Franciscans urged the lords to distribute part of their patrimonial lands among their *terrazgueros* through the payment of an emphyteutic census. The lords mentioned that "nos den alguna cosa de renta por las tierras que les diéremos". Luis Reyes mentioned in Menegus, *La Mixteca Baja*, 49.

territorial base of the *yuhuitayu*, there were no precise geographical boundaries, and the fundamental binding element of the vassals of a lordship was the tribute.[49] This assertion can be criticised considering what has been said above about the *entreveramiento* of territories. The *señoríos* were aware of the territorial scope of their jurisdiction and their limits, which did not compromise the principle of the personal association of the inhabitants with the lord of the ruling lineage and his *casa señorial*. The conflicts shown here, which arise from the creation of settlements of *terrazgueros* for the occupation of strategic spaces, seem to show us a transitional scenario between traditional Mixtec and Hispanic socio-territorial practices, which were, by the way, also in a moment of reconfiguration of their normative order.

There is an additional analytical element that reinforces the relevance of *señorial* relations. From reviewing the Ñudzahui terms in the colonial documentation, Kevin Terraciano observed that the boundaries between the two kinds of peasants considered commoners were blurred. Thus, the use of the concept *ñandahi*—a commoner, who owned modest plots of land associated with a household, paid tribute, and was subject to rotating work—and *tay situndayu*—*terrazguero*, landless renter, attached to the *aniñe*, or house of the rulers—seems to indicate that, in both cases, their links with the *casas señoriales* constituted a social characteristic of great importance and that it is possible that there was mobility from one status to the other.[50] The study of their dynamics concerning land indeed points to the same thing.

4 Land and 'Masked' *Señorial* Relations

Many of the spatial resettlements inaugurated the legal establishment of *pueblos de indios*. Here, I understand this concept, widely extended in the historiography of the last 30 years, as the Hispanic political-administrative arrangement based on the organisation of the indigenous *señorío* and formed by the Indian political society called the *república de indios*. One of its essential defining characteristics was its corporative character, concretely expressed through a *cabildo* of peninsular inspiration made up of different positions or

49 Jansen and Pérez Jiménez, *Historia, literatura e ideología de Ñuu Dzahui*, 69–70. In contrast, Ronald Spores attributes to the *yuhuitayu* defined and restricted spaces in the demographic-social and geographic aspects, maintaining that they would be constituted by one or two valleys bordering mountains or high hills. Spores, *Ñuu Ñudzahui la Mixteca de Oaxaca*, 103.

50 Terraciano, *Los mixtecos de la Oaxaca colonial*, 220, 226.

offices, which aimed to centralise the political and administrative functions of the towns in the place designated as 'head'. However, the dependencies consigned as *barrios* or *estancias* also had representation, generally through the *alcaldes* or *regidores*.[51] This scene was the ideal projection planned by the Spanish administration. However, it must be said that, in practice, most of the *cabildos* did not conform precisely to the parameters indicated and that, outwardly, they masked practices and forms of operation rooted in the indigenous tradition. That is why it is difficult to provide a generalisable definition.

A royal decree of 9 October 1549 urged the establishment of order in the towns through their inhabitants' congregation and the formation of their republic bodies.[52] Menegus interprets the lists of appraisals for the salaries of *república* officers in the Mixteca to mean that in the last third of the 16th century, *repúblicas de indios* were already established and functioning in most of the important population centres. However, the positions and their functions were established hand in hand with establishing "orden y policía" in the *pueblos*.[53] In particular, the appraisal for Tlaxiaco was made in 1578.[54]

In the Mixteca, unlike many places that were part of the Culhua-Mexica and Purepecha-Tarasco empires, the persistence of elements of traditional native government was much more intense and visible. The hereditary rulers were integrated into the system of government with full functions; the Spaniards soon realised that this delegation to traditional leaders could guarantee the proper functioning of the colonial enterprise due to the extraordinary effectiveness of the local autonomy that prevailed in the region.[55] Thus, during the

51 García Martínez, *Los pueblos de la sierra*, 97–105.

52 "Real cédula a la Audiencia de la Nueva España ordenando sean hechos pueblos de indios, con autoridades municipales elegidas entre el vecindario. Valladolid, October 9, 1549", in Solano, *Cedulario de tierras*, 171.

53 All the valuations preserved for New Spain, related either to the salaries of republic officials or those of the natural lords or caciques, begin in the 1570s, not before. This reflects the fact that from 1550 onwards, Viceroy Velasco made a special effort to optimise the general economic system of New Spain through the implementation of extensive tax reform, which implied more significant observance in the appraisals of the towns. Between 1550 and 1556 numerous tax laws were passed. In addition, a general visitation was authorised, carried out by the *visitador* Jerónimo de Valderrama between 1563 and 1566, who came with the stern mandate of Philip II to increase Indian taxes. Menegus, "Cacicazgos y repúblicas de indios en el siglo XVI", 211.

54 AGN, Indios, vol. 1, exp. 157, fol. 58r.

55 This situation also occurred in the Yucatán Peninsula. The Maya lords (*batabes*), recognised as caciques, continued to rule in the towns after the *repúblicas de indios* were formed, continuing with the dynamics of personal bonds. Quezada, *Maya Lords and Lordships*. In the Mixteca, in addition to the power exercised and managed from within the

first decades of the *cabildo's* functioning, it was common for the caciques to occupy the position of governor.[56] From approximately 1560, once salaries and the annual elective system—with frequent re-election—were regulated, until approximately the 18th century, the principals occupied the most critical positions because effective suffrage was restricted to the highest-ranking males.[57] In other words, the *macehualización*[58] of the indigenous *cabildo* occurred late in the Mixteca. One explanation provided by Rodolfo Pastor is based on the fact that the demographic crises, which worsened at the end of the 16th century, inevitably had an impact on the salaries of the officials of the republic, which decreased and even ceased to be paid on some occasions; then, the economic weight of the positions was only sustainable for the caciques and principals who had already started economic enterprises related, above all, to livestock raising, which allowed them to keep their privileged positions in the *cabildos* for a more extended period.[59] The Mixtec terminology used to refer to the positions also reveals the equating of the rank of a hereditary lord with that of the governor, as shown in a 1681 document in which the nobles of the *siña* of Ayusi referred to the governor of Yanhuitlán as *yya toniñe gobernador* (lord ruler governor).[60]

A strategy used during the 16th century to preserve the noble character of the *cabildo* members was to recruit as candidates for the governorship other caciques or principals who exercised their power in the constituent parts dependent on the *cabecera*, with whom they probably possessed kinship ties.[61] In Tlaxiaco, we can observe that, since the last third of the 16th century, the governorship was already separated from the function of the cacique. However, we can maintain that, at least until the first third of the 17th century, nobles occu-

---

cabildo, the caciques, principals and influential nobles consolidated their power outside the formal system, interceding in the decision-making of the provincial authorities, the *encomenderos* and the clergy through kind of "parapolitical" activities. See Spores, *Ñuu Ñudzahui la Mixteca de Oaxaca*, 233.

56 Since caciques or *cacicas* were often from several *cabeceras*, it was stipulated that he could only serve as governor in the *cabecera* where he lived. Spores, *The Mixtecs in ancient and colonial times*, 167.

57 Spores, *Ñuu Ñudzahui la Mixteca de Oaxaca*, 214–215, 220.

58 The access of *macehuales* (commoners) to the positions of the *cabildo*.

59 Pastor, *Campesinos y reformas*, 90.

60 This document is in the *Archivo Histórico Judicial, Teposcolula Civil* section. Unfortunately, the classification of the documents mentioned by some authors has already been modified, and it is sometimes difficult to trace them today. Terraciano, *Los mixtecos de la Oaxaca colonial*, 282.

61 Terraciano, "The Colonial Mixtec Community", 31, alludes to this and other mechanisms used to guarantee the noble character of the governor's position.

pied it. This was the case when Don Baltasar de Chávez, cacique of San Juan Pipioltepec—currently San Juan Ñumí—one of its subject towns, occupied the position of governor on repeated occasions, starting in 1581; Don Baltasar probably alternated in the position with the husband of the *cacica* Doña María, Don Francisco, cacique of Yanhuitlán, who appears as governor of Tlaxiaco in 1594.[62]

We can observe in this last fact a gender circumstance that separates the functioning of the institutions of the *cacicazgo* and the government of the *pueblos*, depending on whether the Mixtec or Spanish normative order is followed. The Mixtec models of lordship inheritance, which can be traced back to the 11th century in the historical-genealogical records expressed in the *codices*, determined that the transfer of power was carried out by bilateral descent (relatives on the mother's and father's side are on the same plane of importance) and in strict endogamy of royal lineage. Within the *yuhuitayu*, the ruling couple had to possess royal dignity, each in their own right, and thus, in the 16th century, women were recognised as legitimate *cacicas*. The men they married acquired the title of cacique of their places of origin and, with it, the power to defend before the courts the goods and privileges of the *cacicazgo*. If instead they married another cacique, they became recognised as *cacicas* of the lordships of their husbands. However, although the virilocality prevailed after the nuptials, the *cacicas* retained their lordships and the children in common could inherit the titles of both parents. There is no complete consensus today as to whether the male line was privileged in succession; furthermore, the great diversity of Mixtec *cacicazgos* shows us that inheritance did not continuously operate by descent but that it was collaterally accepted (people who have a common ancestor, without being descended from each other), and nor was primogeniture always used.[63] What is clear is that the Hispanic civil and ecclesiastical authorities recognised the dignity, possessions, and prerogatives of Mixtec *cacicas* until the 19th century.

Despite their recognition as indigenous authorities through inheritance, women were excluded from holding public positions in the government structure sanctioned by the Hispanic normative order, that is, in the *cabildo*. However, their son or another male relative could, although without full guarantees of being elected, so the resource used on some occasions was that the *cacicas'* husbands would serve as governors in the *cabeceras* of their wives. This

62 AGN, Mercedes, vol. 13, exp. 19, fol. 14^{r}; AHJ, Teposcolula Civil, leg. 5, exp. 18; leg. 6, exp. 53.

63 Contrast this with what is referred to by Spores, "Mixteca Cacicas"; Menegus, "Balance historiográfico", 221; and Rodríguez Cano, "Apuntes sobre la herencia de los cacicazgos en la Mixteca Baja".

was the case, as just mentioned, when Don Francisco occupied the position in Tlaxiaco when Juan de Guzmán y Velasco became governor of Tataltepec through his marriage to the *cacica* Doña Inés de Zárate, or when Diego de Mendoza, *cacica* Catalina de Peralta's husband, occupied the position in Teposcolula.[64]

Unlike what happened in other significant enclaves of the Mixteca, from the beginning of the 17th century Tlaxiaco did not have figures who held the title of cacique or *cacica* as such, but this did not prevent them from maintaining for a time what we can identify as certain *señorial* relationships woven in the time of the cacique Don Felipe. Doña María died without descendants in the mid-1590s. After some years of litigation, the *república* of Tlaxiaco managed to take over the *cacicazgo's* lands, and they became community lands as *propios*. The *cabildo* argued that, although the *cacica* had not left a will before her death, she stipulated that her goods should pass to the *república*, which the Real Audiencia finally confirmed.[65] Sometime before, in 1581, the *cacica* Doña María had sold or donated some productive lands to the convent of Tlaxiaco.[66] However, among many other events, in 1717, the *cacica* of Santa Catarina (former dependency of Achiutla), Doña Manuela Pimentel y Guzmán and, later, in 1779, Don Martín José de Villagómez, Guzmán y Pimentel de la Cruz—cacique of Acatlán, Petlalcingo, Silacayoapan, Huajuapan, Yanhuitlán, and many other towns—claimed for themselves the *cacicazgo* of Tlaxiaco. Nevertheless, the commoners and the *república* stood firm in defence of the valuable lands that had been transferred to them in the past.[67]

Two arguments incline us to think that the *cuerpo de república* of Tlaxiaco maintained its noble status and managed the lands of the commons, with a strong sense of lordship, for a long time. First, we find that San Juan Ñumí was the seat of a minor *cacicazgo* that extended to neighbouring *pueblos* and recognised, without apparent hostility, the category of *pueblo sujeto* to Tlaxiaco. However, in 1599, it had 300 tributaries, only 62 less than Tlaxiaco, and constituted, by far, the second most populated place in the jurisdiction; besides, it was the *pueblo* that, like its *cabecera*, claimed to enjoy more leagues of land

---

64 AGN, Tierras, vol. 59, exp. 2; Terraciano, "The Colonial Mixtec Community", 31; *Los mixtecos de la Oaxaca colonial*, 283. Note that the father of Doña María, the *cacique* Don Felipe, had no problem with occupying the governorship in Tlaxiaco in 1567. AHJ, Teposcolula Criminal, Leg. 1, exp. 13.

65 Spores, "Mixteca Cacicas," 192–193; *Ñuu Ñudzahui la Mixteca de Oaxaca*, 309–311. See footnote 36.

66 Spores, *Ñuu Ñudzahui la Mixteca de Oaxaca*, 310.

67 AHJ, Teposcolula Civil, leg. 22, exp. 12; García Alcaraz, *Tinujei. Los triquis de Copala*, 217–220.

in contour.[68] The Chávez family held the *cacicazgo* until the 18th century and repeatedly appeared as occupying the governorship and other positions in the *cabildo* of Tlaxiaco.[69] We can hypothesise that they were part of Don Felipe's kin.

The second argument, closely related to the first, has to do with the settlement of another *sujeto* named San Antonio Nduaxico in a place recognised as part of the patrimonial lands of the cacique Don Felipe. Something relevant is that, around 1550, in an even more complex panorama of political-territorial subordinations, Nduaxico was *sujeto* to Ñumí.[70] One of the versions of his will (a transcription in Mixtec and a translation into Spanish made in 1749) was inserted into a lawsuit from 1801 to 1826 about lands between the natives of San Antonio Nduaxico and those of San Juan Ñumí. In this document, originally written in 1573, Don Felipe stated that the lands where San Antón Nduaxico was settled belonged to his *cacicazgo*, and so he left them to Melchor López and Mateo Cocuaa. He confirmed this inheritance in a second part of the will, listing a series of *milpas* and orchards by their Mixtec names and ordering that they not be taken away from those two men.[71]

This critical link that Tlaxiaco had with the northern part of its jurisdiction could have been the background of two *mancomunidad* (association) agreements established at the end of the 16th century and in the middle of the 18th century. In 1594, on the one hand, the governor and principals of Tlaxiaco, on behalf of the natives of their *barrios* and *estancias sujetas* and, on the other hand, Don Francisco, cacique of Yanhuitlán and Tlaxiaco and Achiutla (by marriage), established an agreement that obligated them to pay 206 pesos of gold and three *tomines* to a merchant resident in Yanhuitlán for some goods that the cacique had taken from his store to satisfy the needs of the place where they signed the agreement, the *estancia* of San Pedro Mártir Yucuxaco.[72] This *pueblo*

68 Comisariado de Bienes Comunales, "Diligencias para la congregación de Tlaxiaco", 1599.

69 Baltasar de Chávez was governor in 1581, AGN, Tierras, vol. 400, exp. 1, fol. 55ʳ, mentioned in Romero Frizzi, *Economía y vida de los españoles en la Mixteca Alta*, 98. Juan de Chávez was governor in 1636 and 1642, AHJ, Teposcolula Civil, leg. 10, exp. 42, AGN, Indiferente virreinal, caja 5172, exp. 45. And Pedro Martín de Chávez y Guzmán held the position in 1716 and 1719, AHJ, Teposcolula Civil, leg. 21, exps. 16.069 y 16.158.

70 *Suma de visitas de pueblos*, 387. In the middle of the 16th century, the *cabecera-sujeto* complex into which the old *señorío* of Tlaxiaco was adapted still had a complex structure, with *pueblos sujetos* that, in turn, agglutinated other dependent settlements around them. By the end of the century, this complexity seemed diluted, and all the smaller *pueblos* were considered *sujetos* to Tlaxiaco.

71 AGN, Tierras, vol. 3030, exp. 8, fols. 231ʳ–234ʳ.

72 AHJ, Teposcolula Civil, leg. 05, exp. 18.

was part of the *cacicazgo* that the Chávez family held in San Juan Ñumí and other *pueblos sujetos* until the beginning of the 18th century, as noted before.[73]

In the 18th century, the basis of the old agreements began to fracture, partly concerning the process of *composiciones de tierras*. A lawsuit arose between the *república* of Tlaxiaco and the cacique of Ñumí, Don Pedro de Chávez, after he leased some lands in Santo Domingo Yosoñama to introduce livestock, under the argument that they were part of his *cacicazgo*.[74] This confrontation produced two results: the disregard of the lineage of the caciques of Ñumí and the creation of a contract of a *mancomunidad* agreement. This agreement obliged Tlaxiaco to assume the ascription of the lands of Yosoñama to Ñumí, as long as they evicted the tenant at the end of the fraudulent contract that had subscribed the—now considered—spurious cacique, and that the lands were tilled and used for the maintenance of the community.[75] We can assume, therefore, that the lands were *propios*.

The essence of the two *mancomunidad* agreements is that the parties freely obligated themselves to execute something. In the first case, everyone assumed themselves as principal debtors to pay a debt. In the second, the *mancomunidad* was established under the following formula that appeals to a waiver, which means that each signatory is responsible for the total of the debt or the extent of the commitment: "[…] juntos de man común la voz de uno y cada uno de por sí y por el todo uno solidamente con expresa renunciación de las leyes de duobus reis devendi y la authentica presente hoc ita de fideisoribus y las demás de la mancomunidad […]".[76]

I develop a deeper analysis of the implications of different types of *mancomunidad* agreements (especially those under which land leases were made) in a work currently in progress. However, here I want to highlight what Yanna Yannakakis pertinently observes about them: they reflect legally binding bonds of mutual obligation around a common interest rather than regulating the economic transactions typical of contracts, in which one party performs something in order to receive something else from the other party.[77] In this way,

73 AHJ, Teposcolula Civil, leg. 22, exp. 10; AGEO, Alcaldías Mayores, leg. 54, exp. 5.

74 AHJ, Teposcolula Civil, Leg. 22, exp. 10.

75 AHJ, Teposcolula Civil, leg. 30, exp. 29.18. The type of contract of obligation to which the formula responds has been consolidated in the Hispanic sphere since the 13th century and has been widely developed from the 15th century in notarial records. García Gil, "Los contratos de obligación en Castilla", 294.

76 AHJ, Teposcolula Civil, leg. 30, exp. 29.18, fol. 40^{v}.

77 Yannakakis, *Since Time Immemorial*, 139–170. In this part of the book, Yannakakis analyses in detail the agreements mentioned here, and others, in light of law and native custom.

the *mancomunidad* agreements reproduce, in a certain way, the socio-political relations and intercommunity obligations woven within the ancient *señorío*.

5 Land Acquisitions and Upstart Caciques

Finally, I will look at the process of *composiciones de tierras* in the 18th century to observe how the *cacicazgo* continued to be a source of legitimacy before the Crown to mediate rights over land in the Mixteca.

The first four royal decrees of *composiciones* and *bienes realengos* were issued on 1 November 1591, to regularise possessions after the return of lands considered uncultivated (on which the Crown exercised its royalties) and those that were occupied without authentic deeds.[78] The common lands of the *pueblos de indios*, as well as the lands of the Spanish cities and towns, were left out of this examination.[79] Through these dispositions, the land could be redistributed again or continue in the hands of those who held it in exchange for payment. These *composiciones* had, fundamentally, individual characters. Later, in 1643 and 1674, the collective *composición* was encouraged in highly productive areas with a strong Spanish presence. The lands in question, occupied individually, were not rigorously measured one by one, but deeds were issued after large collective payments had been made.[80]

Beginning in 1692, with the creation of the Superintendencia del Beneficio y Composición de Tierras, under the Cámara y Junta de Guerra del Real Consejo de Indias, the scope of the *composición* process was extended to indigenous areas. This organism was created due to the extensive irregularities detected in the processes, especially between 1660 and 1674. In each Audiencia, one Juzgado Privativo de Tierras y Aguas was appointed, and the ecclesiastical corporations and Indian towns were compelled to *componer* (regularize) their lands.[81] Thus, a long and complex process began in the Mixteca that led the caciques and *pueblos* to request *composición* through the presentation of the *mercedes* granted during the 16th century and by attesting to the legitimacy of the *cacicazgos* and the immemorial possession of the land.[82]

78 Francisco Solano, *Cedulario de tierras*, 43–44, 269–277.

79 Carrera Quezada, *Sementeras de papel*, 139.

80 Solano, *Cedulario de tierras*, 51–59.

81 On the *Juzgado Privativo de Tierras y Aguas*, see Carrera Quezada, "La fundación del Juzgado Privativo" and "La Superintendencia del Beneficio y Composición de Tierras".

82 Mendoza García, "Las composiciones de tierras en la Mixteca la formación del territorio comunal de cabeceras y sujetos"; Menegus, "Del usufructo, de la posesión y de la propiedad".

The royal decrees issued in 1692, 1696, 1707, 1717, 1754, and 1766 set the general pattern for *composiciones* in the Mixteca, which, according to the analyses of Mendoza and Menegus, took three forms: requests from a single *pueblo*, from *pueblos* united with their caciques and from two or more *pueblos* united to *componer* jointly. However, a previous royal decree, dated 4 June 1687, also contributed to the alteration of the Mixtec agrarian structure by distinguishing between the lands belonging to the *cabecera* and those of the *pueblos sujetos* and/or *barrios*, allowing the granting of 600 *varas* for each cardinal direction to previously *pueblos sujetos*.[83] Carrera Quezada perceives in this provision the legal recognition of a minimum territorial basis for the *bienes de comunidad*, which later turned into an argument used by some *sujetos* to promote the separation of their respective *cabeceras* and constitute their own *repúblicas de indios*.[84]

The numerous provisions—both royal decrees issued by the king and his Royal Council and decrees and edicts issued by viceroyalty officials, such as the *juez privativo de tierras y aguas*—gave way to a high degree of casuistry regarding the execution of the *composiciones* based on the diversity of situations in which the *repúblicas* and *cacicazgos* found themselves. In the 18th century, many lawsuits were developed between *cacicazgos* and *pueblos*, between caciques, between *cabeceras* and *sujetos*, and between the *sujetos* themselves. As Menegus emphasises, in many cases, the *composiciones* ended the territorial unity between the lords and the *pueblos*. This led to the disintegration of the *cacicazgo* as a result of the *composiciones* carried out by its *terrazgueros*.[85] As we have seen, the cacique possessed jurisdiction over the land due to the legal endorsement of the condition of the lord by lineage; he was also protected by the recognition, as such, by the indigenous people and ceded in the condition of usufruct certain arable, pasture and grazing lands in exchange for a *terrazgo*,

83 Mendoza García, "Las composiciones de tierras en la Mixteca," 267; Menegus, "Del usufructo, de la posesión y de la propiedad," 196; Menegus, "Las composiciones de tierras en el centro de la Nueva España y en Oaxaca", 369–370. The 600 *varas* arise from the 500 mentioned in the *ordenanza* of the Marqués de Falces of 1567, plus another 100. There is a great deal of historiographical confusion about the nature of this concession, which would lead to the formation of the *tierras por razón de pueblo*, later known as *fundo legal*. Some researchers contributing to the subject are Bernardo García Martínez, Stephanie Wood and Felipe Castro. A synthesis of their positions and a dialogue on the problem can be read in Escobar Ohmstede and Martín Gabaldón, "Una relectura sobre cómo se observa a lo(s) común(es) en México".

84 Carrera Quezada, Sergio, "Las composiciones de tierras en la Mixteca y la formación del territorio comunal de cabeceras y sujetos", 30–31.

85 Menegus, "Del usufructo, de la posesión y de la propiedad".

generally governed by the force of custom. At the time of the *composiciones*, the legal figure wielded by the *pueblos* was that of possession, described as "immemorial" and "peaceful".

Manuel Bastias Saavedra emphasises that the institution of possession is the best way to understand land relations in early Hispanic America.[86] His proposal is based on transcending the anachronism of thinking about the *derecho indiano* based on the power emanating from the monarch and the division between public and private law attributed to Roman law and framing it within the broad normative universe of the *ius commune*. In this broad framework that operated for centuries, the idea of *aequitas* sets the tone for understanding that the functions of justice and the establishment of laws correspond to the natural order of things and the natural power of communities to regulate themselves. Accordingly, he argues that:

> Possession was therefore not the purely factual act of taking hold of a thing; instead, it was a specific legal relationship in which a title was generated through consolidated practices and it was a distinct category—different not only from dominion (*señorío*), but also from other forms of tenure.[87]

Possession, insofar as it implies a legal relationship, made it possible for the *terrazgueros* to go from holding peaceful possession for time immemorial to obtaining a property deed from the *composición* of the land.[88] In this process, the usufruct itself does not occupy a central place in the possession since, in the logic of the latter, the one who occupies on behalf of another does not gain possession over the thing; what is relevant is the very intention of the *terrazgueros* to be owners of the land through their practice consolidated over time.[89]

On the other hand, some caciques, being aware of the possibility of dispossession to which they could be subjected, from the second half of the 17th century, tried to protect their lands. In these cases, the *provisiones reales* as a figure for legal protection were instruments used in later *composiciones*. In other cases, when there were no previous deeds to show before the Spanish authorities, *memorias de linderos* were drawn up, which had to be recognised without contradiction by a series of witnesses, generally from neighbouring places.[90]

86 Bastias Saavedra, "The normativity of possession".

87 Bastias Saavedra, "The normativity of possession", 229.

88 Menegus, "Del usufructo, de la posesión y de la propiedad", 206–207.

89 I thank Manuel Bastias Saavedra for this idea.

90 Menegus, "Del usufructo, de la posesión y de la propiedad", 202; Menegus, "Las composiciones de tierras en el centro de la Nueva España y en Oaxaca", 371.

This is precisely the scenario that we find in some towns around San Mateo Peñasco, an important *pueblo sujeto* to Tlaxiaco until 1687, when it managed to separate and become a *cabecera* in its own right, bringing together the neighbouring settlements.[91] We can observe in this case a circumstance that calls our attention: the *sujetos* were covered by a 'new' *cacicazgo* that mediated their requests.[92]

In April 1858, the *alcalde* of San Agustín Tixihii (Tlacotepec) requested the issuing of a protocolisation and testimony of the *composición* titles made in 1707 due to the significant deterioration of the document and the serious risk of loss. The copy informs us that the *composición* was carried out under the protection of the Royal Decree of 30 October 1692, which coercively imposed the *composición* process and strengthened the control over the lands.[93] The *alcalde mayor* of the Tonalá and Silacayoapan mines was empowered to supervise the *composición* because in many Mixtec demarcations there were royal lands and others that were being possessed in excess, without a deed and with other vices.[94] Under this, Don Pablo de Castro y Morales appeared. He declared to be cacique and Principal of San Agustín Tixihi, Magdalena Peñasco and San Antonio Sinicahua (*sujetos* that claimed to belong to the *cabecera* of Tlaxiaco). He showed a *memoria de linderos* of his *cacicazgo's* lands and he specified that the lands that belonged to San Agustín were being possessed by the natives with his consent because he had ceded to them after his recognition as their cacique. He requested the Juzgado Privativo to obtain a new separate deed for the authorities of San Agustín, offering to serve His Majesty with 40 pesos.[95]

In January 1707, his request was admitted, and testimony was taken from four witnesses, authorities of San Agustín and nearby *pueblos*. They all agreed that Don Pablo enjoyed the *cacicazgo* of San Agustín, Sinicahua and Magdalena Peñasco by a *merced* granted in past times, and the natives recognised this. Therefore, he ceded part of the lands to San Agustín's common, those contained in the *memoria de linderos* presented, without negatively affecting the neighbouring settlements.

---

91 AGN, Indios, vol. 29, exp. 297.

92 I analyse this case in greater depth in Martín Gabaldón, "Configuraciones territoriales 'móviles'".

93 Solano, *Cedulario de tierras*, 377–380.

94 The second superintendent in charge of the compositions, Francisco Camargo Paz, had delegated, in turn, the attorney Baltasar de Tovar, civil prosecutor of the *Real Audiencia*, for the application of the *cédula de composiciones*. AGN, Tierras, vol. 3690, exp. 6, fols. 6^{v}–9^{r}.

95 "Títulos del pueblo de San Agustín Tixihii de la comprensión del partido de Tlajiaco," Donación, March 1927. AGN, Tierras, vol. 3690, exp. 6.

The request was successful, and on 30 June 1707, the writ was issued admitting the *composición* and granting the deeds to San Agustín, following laws XIV to XIX of Título XII, Libro IV, of the *Recopilación de Leyes de los Reynos de las Indias*.[96] In addition, in 1727, before the *alcalde mayor* of the province of Teposcolula, the authorities of San Agustín requested that, in order to defend their territory against possible future introductions from neighbours, they should be given testimony so that neither the cacique nor his descendants could later dispossess them of the lands that were recognised as theirs by *composición*.[97] Although this request does not explicitly state this, it is probable that the 600 *varas* that would constitute the *tierras por razón de pueblo* were officially recognised using this *composición*.

We believe that this last-mentioned request could have been motivated by the Royal Decree of 10 March 1717, which inaugurated a period of great activity in *composiciones* in the Mixteca, as Edgar Mendoza observes.[98]

Magdalena Peñasco and San Antonio Sinicahua likely followed a mechanism similar to that of their neighbour San Agustín to settle their lands. However, the complexity of the process in a territory where the overlapping of jurisdictions was evident, coupled with certain fraudulent practices by the authorities, delayed the resolutions for decades. Mendoza observed that the *juez y subdelegado de ventas y composición de tierras y aguas* in the province of Teposcolula and Yanhuitlán, Mathias Morato, irregularly gave possession of lands to private individuals and was discovered by the natives. Then, he hurriedly fled the jurisdiction in 1749, taking with him the documents (grants and land titles) of several *pueblos*.[99] To solve the problem, in 1764, Don Diego Antonio Neira, the new *alcalde mayor* of Teposcolula, was commissioned as *subdelegado de tierras y aguas*.[100]

In 1767, under this new impulse, Magdalena Peñasco, San Antonio Sinicahua and, again, San Agustín requested the *composición* of their lands because they

---

96 I would like to emphasise, in particular, that Ley XIX of Libro IV, Título XII, described that "Que no sea admitido a composición el que no hubiere poseído las tierras diez años, y los indios sean preferidos". *Recopilación de Leyes*, tomo segundo, 103^{v}–104^{v}.

97 AGN, Tierras, vol. 3690, exp. 6, fols. 19^{v}–22^{v}.

98 Mendoza García, "Apropiación territorial y conflictos". Don Félix Chacón, *alcalde mayor* of Teposcolula, reported in 1717 that only seven *pueblos* had requested *composición* and that 231 were yet to do so in the jurisdictions of Yanhuitlán, Nochixtlán, Tilantongo and Teposcolula. AHJ, Teposcolula Civil, leg. 22, exp. 18.

99 Mendoza García, "Apropiación territorial y conflictos". AGEO, Alcaldías mayores, leg. 54, exp. 12.

100 Mendoza García, "Apropiación territorial y conflictos". AGEO, Alcaldías mayores, leg. 55, exp. 20.

were also included within the boundaries of those granted in 1707 to the cacique Don Pablo. On this occasion, Don Nicolás de Castro y Morales, grandson of Don Pablo, intervened with the *pueblos*. The *cacicazgo* had fallen to him four years earlier after the heirless death of his brother Don Agustín. For that reason, he moved his residence from Puebla to Magdalena Peñasco. His argument for requesting the *composición* was that ten boundaries noted in the 1707 title had been maliciously erased and amended during the long time that the document had been "usurped and lost". Thus, the lands of Magdalena Peñasco and San Antonio Sinicahua, which had not been so previously, could be legitimised. Then, they presented the three *pueblos' memoria de linderos*—all in Ñudzahui language—and witnesses from neighbouring places were summoned to corroborate the information. All recognised Don Nicolás as a cacique in legitimate possession and, as there was no contradiction except in three boundaries on the limits with another *pueblo*, the records were accepted as valid. Then, it was requested that a dispatch be sent to the *juez privativo* to grant the deed.[101]

In the history told here, we find a contradiction for which we have yet to find an explanation. In the 1707 process, the three *pueblos* were said to be *sujetos* to Tlaxiaco, but, as indicated before, we know that they belonged to San Mateo Peñasco from the moment it became a *cabecera* in 1687, agglutinating the settlements that most probably were politically linked to it since pre-Hispanic times. This issue could go unnoticed, but not if we link it to something else that calls our attention and forces us to look at the physical extension of the territory referred to in the *memorias de linderos* and the particular social actors of the 18th century.

As previously stated, the lineage was fundamental in articulating the Mixtec social-political system. However, we find absolutely no genealogical antecedents beyond Don Pablo, who appears for the first time in the historical records in 1707. This fact allows us to formulate the following hypothesis: we can consider him a cacique *advenedizo* (upstart) who entered the scene to satisfy the needs of a symbiotic relationship between his family and the three *pueblos* who sought to legitimise their lands and thus propitiate the separation of their *cabecera*, which they would achieve some years after the *composición*.[102] The fact that in the *composición* proceedings the cacique assumed that they were

101 AGEO, Alcaldías mayores, leg. 56, exp. 12.

102 AGN, Indios, vol. 63, exp. 17. Many types and functions of upstart caciques have been identified throughout colonial America. In other areas, such as in central Mexico, from the 18th century onwards, some lords did not receive legitimate recognition through the Crown but, because they had occupied *cabildo* positions and accumulated social and economic

sujetos to Tlaxiaco and not to San Mateo Peñasco, may be a sign of disaffection towards the latter.

In the petition and granting of titles for San Agustín Tlacotepec in 1707, it was made explicit that the *pueblos* could enjoy the lands where they had settled quietly and peacefully since time immemorial due to the grace of the cacique in exchange for recognising him as their lord.[103] This confronts us with the nature of the relationship between the *repúblicas* and the *cacicazgos* in the 18th century and with their possible conception as a new type of corporation, which assumed dominion over lands that were factually inseparable from the corporation itself.[104]

This also forces us to question the late-colonial seigniorial ties. We can see that, by the 18th century, there were many caciques and *cacicas* who claimed to be from *pueblos* that did not seem to recognise such power in previous centuries.[105] This situation contradicts some of the ideas expressed by Rodolfo Pastor and Marcelo Carmagnani about the loss of the moral bond that united the caciques with the *pueblos*, partly due to leasing *cacicazgo* lands for individual benefit. According to this point of view, the consequence would be the disregard of the caciques by the commoners and the irreparable fracture between the lord and the community.[106] However, what kind of privileges did the three generations of 'new' caciques Castro and Morales in our case study enjoy and what was their real relationship with access to land? Was there a territorial jurisdiction for them (the territory considered personal patrimony linked to their quality of lordship), or did they only fulfil government or administrative functions?[107] Or was their presence merely an artifice deployed by the *pueblos*?

---

privileges, instilled fear and were considered caciques in their towns and set themselves up as interlocutors with the Spaniards. See López Mora, "La aristocracia del pueblo".

103 AGN, Tierras, vol. 3690, exp. 6, fol. 11v. A similar situation can be seen in the argument made in 1802 by a *cacica* of Tlalixtac in the Central Valleys, who argued that her great-grandfather had allowed by his grace some families to settle in the early 18th century in what would later become the *pueblo* of Tomaltepec, in exchange for his recognition as a lord. AGN, Tierras, vol. 1335, exp. 1.

104 Buono, in this book, argues about the link between the corporation and its assets.

105 I have been able to corroborate this situation, for example, from the information gathered by Israel Garrido Esquivel, Head of the Department of the *Archivo General del Consejo de la Judicatura del Poder Judicial de Oaxaca*, about the names of caciques and their respective *pueblos* that appear in the documentation of the old *Juzgado de Teposcolula* from the 16th, 17th and 18th centuries. I thank him for his generosity in sharing these findings with me.

106 Pastor, *Campesinos y reformas*, 166–175; Carmagnani, *El regreso de los dioses*.

107 This question was already raised by Margarita Menegus when she took a close look at

We need to analyse in detail the intervention of the 'new' caciques if we want to make generalisations about their possible role in 18th-century Mixtec society, as well as the relation between *composiciones* and *cacicazgos* from cases like the one reported here.[108]

6 Conclusions

The historical processes presented in these pages clearly show us how, in the Mixtec section analysed, the *señorial* relations between the *yya* (noble rulers, later recognised as caciques) and the *tay yucu* (commoners) and the *tay situndayu* (*terrazgueros*) mediated access to land and natural resources during the entire new-Hispanic period. They also did so to recognise each other's rights under the Hispanic normative system. However, we find these veiled relationships in the space of the ancient *señorío* of Tlaxiaco from the 16th century, when the figure of the cacique disappeared nominally from the scene and the dominion over the land fell to the *república de indios*.

Very often, the processes of (re)territorialisation during the early modern period in Mesoamerica have been explained as both the transformation of the conception of territory based on the personal association of lords with their vassals and as an idea based on a properly territorial association, attributed to the tradition of the centralised European state.[109] According to these conceptions, the former would pose a territory that is challenging to grasp, with imprecise limits. At the same time, the latter would impose a static and well-defined territorial panorama employing laws, edicts and regulations. However, if we can admit that the so-called *Leyes de Indias* rested on the broad normative universe of the *ius commune*, which was structured based on local and personal jurisdictions, often on a micro-scale,[110] we should not be surprised that the deployment of Mixtec territoriality attached to *señorial* relations found ways to thrive, even well into the 18th century. This obliges us to qualify the

the relationship between caciques and their *terrazgueros* in Huajuapan and Tepexi, albeit concerning "traditional" *cacicazgos*. Menegus, "La territorialidad de los cacicazgos", 83.

108 My case study is substantially different from what Edgar Mendoza has analysed for Chalcatongo, where *composiciones* determined the fragmentation of the *cacicazgo*. Likewise, it also shows a situation different from that analysed by Misael Chavoya in the Nochixtlán Valley, where *composiciones* catalysed the existing conflict between two *pueblos sujetos*. Mendoza, "La descomposición de un cacicazgo"; Chavoya, *Pueblos de indios, composiciones de tierras y conflictos por el territorio*.

109 Ouweneel and Hoekstra, *Las tierras de los pueblos de indios*.

110 Bastias Saavedra, "The normativity of possession".

vision that taxatively contrasts indigenous territoriality with a European one imposed through coercive legal mechanisms.

Given this particular panorama, I propose, still hypothetically, that access to natural resources in differentiated environments not only modulated the spaces claimed for themselves by both *cacicazgos* and *repúblicas de indios*—in many cases, coinciding spaces—but could also be related to how they sought to legitimise the lands under the Hispanic normative system. Future research will allow us to compare events in different Mixtec environments to test this idea.

Bibliography

Manuscripts

Archivo General de Indias, Sevilla (AGI), Audiencia de México 538, N. 7.

Archivo General del Estado de Oaxaca, Oaxaca de Juárez (AGEO), Alcaldías Mayores, leg. 54, exp. 5.

AGEO, Alcaldías mayores, leg. 54, exp. 12.

AGEO, Alcaldías mayores, leg. 55, exp. 20.

AGEO, Alcaldías mayores, leg. 56, exp. 12.

Archivo General de la Nación, Mexico (AGN), Indiferente virreinal, caja 5172, exp. 45.

AGN, Indios, vol. 1, exp. 157.

AGN, Indios, vol. 29, exp. 297.

AGN, Indios, vol. 63, exp. 17.

AGN, Mercedes, vol. 13, exp. 19.

AGN, Tierras, vol. 59, exp. 2.

AGN, Tierras, vol. 44, exp. 1.

AGN, Tierras, vol. 59, exp. 2.

AGN, Tierras, vol. 400, exp. 1.

AGN, Tierras, vol. 1335, exp. 1.

AGN, Tierras, vol. 2948, exp. 28.

AGN, Tierras, vol. 3030, exp. 8.

AGN, Tierras, vol. 3690, exp. 6.

Archivo Histórico Judicial, Oaxaca de Juárez (AHJ), Teposcolula Civil, leg. 2, exp. 1.

AHJ, Teposcolula Civil, leg. 2, exp. 13.

AHJ, Teposcolula Civil, leg. 5, exp. 18.

AHJ, Teposcolula Civil, leg. 6, exp. 53.

AHJ, Teposcolula Civil, leg. 10, exp. 42.

AHJ, Teposcolula Civil, leg. 21, exp. 16.069.

AHJ, Teposcolula Civil, leg. 21, exp. 16.158.

AHJ, Teposcolula Civil, Leg. 22, exp. 10.
AHJ, Teposcolula Civil, leg. 22, exp. 12.
AHJ, Teposcolula Civil, leg. 22, exp. 18.
AHJ, Teposcolula Civil, leg. 30, exp. 29.18.
AHJ, Teposcolula Criminal, leg. 1, exp. 13.
AHJ, Teposcolula Criminal, leg. 1, exp. 44.
AHJ, Teposcolula Criminal, leg. 2, exp. 48.
AHJ, Teposcolula Criminal, leg. 6, exp. 35.
AHJ, Teposcolula Criminal, Leg. 9, exp. 15.
Archivo Histórico Municipal de la Heroica Ciudad de Tlaxiaco (AHMHCT), Jefatura política section, Gobierno subsection, Tierras series, Límites subseries, caja 214, exp. 1.
Comisariado de Bienes Comunales, Heroica Ciudad de Tlaxiaco, "Diligencias para la congregación de Tlaxiaco, 1599".
Library of Congress, Kraus MS 140.
Newberry Library, Ayer MS 1121.

Printed Sources

Alvarado, Fray Francisco de, *Vocabulario en lengua mixteca por fray Francisco de Alvarado*, facsimile ed. Jiménez Moreno, Wigberto, México 1962.
Burgoa, Fray Francisco de, Geográfica Descripción de la Parte Septentrional, del Polo Ártico de la América, y Nueva Iglesia de las Indias occidentales, y sitio astronómico de esta Provincia de Predicadores de Antequera, Valle de Oaxaca, t. 1, México 1989.
Recopilación de Leyes de los Reynos de las Indias, facsimile edition of 1680, preliminary study by Manzano Manzano, Juan, 4 vols, Madrid 1973.
Reyes, Fray Antonio de los, Arte en lengua mixteca compuesta por el Padre Fray Antonio de los Reyes de la orden de Predicadores, Vicario de Tepuzculula, ed. Charencey, Count H. of, Alençon 1890.
Suma de visitas de pueblos de la Nueva España, 1548–1550, ed. García Castro, René, Toluca 2013.

Literature

Assadourian, Carlos Sempat, "Agriculture and Land Tenure", in Victor Bulmer-Thomas et al. (eds.), *The Cambridge Economic History of Latin America, Vol. 1, The Colonial Era and the Short Nineteenth Century*, New York 2006, 275–314.
Bastias Saavedra, Manuel, "The normativity of possession. Rethinking land relations in early-modern Spanish America, ca. 1500–1800," in *Colonial Latin American Review* 29:2 (2020), 223–238.
Carmagnani, Marcelo, El regreso de los dioses. El proceso de reconstitución de la identidad étnica en Oaxaca, siglos XVII y XVIII, Mexico 1988.

Carrasco, Pedro, Estructura político-territorial del Imperio Tenochca. La Triple Alianza de Tenochtitlan, Tetzcoco y Tlacopan, México, 1996.

Carrera Quezada, Sergio Eduardo, "Las composiciones de tierras en los pueblos de indios en dos jurisdicciones coloniales de la Huasteca, 1692–1720", in *Estudios de Historia Novohispana* 52 (2015), 29–50.

Carrera Quezada, Sergio Eduardo, Sementeras de papel. La regularización de la propiedad rural en la Huasteca serrana, 1550–1720, Mexico 2018.

Carrera Quezada, Sergio Eduardo, "La fundación del Juzgado Privativo de Tierras y Aguas de la Real Audiencia de México, 1692–1735", in *Revista de Indias* 79:276 (2019), 369–398.

Carrera Quezada, Sergio Eduardo, "La Superintendencia del Beneficio y Composición de Tierras, 1692–1754", in Carrera Quezada, Sergio E. and Juan Manuel Pérez Zevallos (coords.), *En todos los rincones imperiales. Apropiaciones de tierras baldías y composiciones de propiedades agrarias en América y Filipinas (siglos XVI–XIX)*, México 2022, 219–248.

Chance, John, "From Lord to Landowner: The Predicament of the Late Colonial Mixtec Cacique," in *Ethnohistory* 57:3 (2010), 445–466.

Chavoya, Misael, Pueblos de indios, composiciones de tierras y conflictos por el territorio en la Mixteca Alta, Oaxaca, siglos XVII y XVIII (El caso de San Juan Bautista Suchitepeque contra Santiago Amatlán) (Masters Thesis), México 2018.

Cruz Pazos, Patricia, "Del arrendamiento al despojo de tierras: Los caciques Cruz y la hacienda de San Jerónimo (Tepexi de la Seda, Puebla-México, 1728–1805)", in *Memoria Americana* 15 (2007), 41–69.

Daneels, Annick and Gerardo Gutiérrez Mendoza, El poder compartido. Essays on the archaeology of segmentary and oligarchic political organizations, Mexico 2012.

Escobar Ohmstede, Antonio and Marta Martín Gabaldón, "Una relectura sobre cómo se observa a lo(s) común(es) en México. ¿Cambios en la transición del siglo XIX al siglo XX? o ¿una larga continuidad?", in *Documentos de Trabajo del Instituto Universitario de Investigación en Estudios Latinoamericanos* 136 (2020), 4–63.

Escriche, Joaquín, Diccionario razonado de legislación y jurisprudencia, Paris 1851.

García Alcaraz, Agustín, *Tinujei. Los triquis de Copala*, Mexico 1997.

García Gil, Elizabeth, "Los contratos de obligación en Castilla a fines del Antiguo Régimen. Análisis diplomático de los registros notariales de Vélez- Málaga (1775–1806)", in *Tiempos Modernos* 44 (2022), 282–300.

García Martínez, Bernardo, Los pueblos de la sierra. El poder y el espacio entre los indios del norte de Puebla hasta 1700, Mexico 1987.

García Martínez, Bernardo, "Jurisdicción y propiedad: una distinción fundamental en la historia de los pueblos de indios del México colonial", in *European Review of Latin American and Caribbean Studies* 53 (1992), 47–60.

García Martínez, Bernardo, "La naturaleza corporativa de los pueblos de indios", in

Memorias de la Real Academia Mexicana de la Historia correspondiente a la Real de Madrid XLII (1999), 213–236.

Haesbaert, Rogério, "From the myth of deterritorialization to multiterritoriality," in *Culture and Social Representations* 8:15 (2013), 9–42.

Hermann Lejarazu, Manuel, "Ñuu Yava, Tamazola. Historia y territorio en la Mixteca Alta", in Hermann Lejarazu, Manuel (coord.), *Señoríos mixtecos. Su dimensión histórica, geográfica y territorial,* México 2021, 17–76.

Jansen, Maarten and Gabina Aurora Pérez Jiménez, Historia, literatura e ideología de Ñuu Dzahui: el Códice Añute y su contexto histórico-cultural, Oaxaca de Juárez 2007.

Josserand, Judy, Mixtec dialect history (Proto-Mixtec and modern Mixtec text), Tulane 1983.

Kowalewski, Stephen et al., Origins of the Ñuu. Archaeology in the Mixteca Alta, Mexico, Boulder 2009.

López Mora, Rebeca, "La aristocracia del pueblo: caciques advenedizos de Tlalnepantla, México, siglo XVIII", in *Nuevo Mundo Mundos Nuevos* [online], Débats, (January 2011), https://journals.openedition.org/nuevomundo/60656

Martín Gabaldón, Marta, "New crops, new landscapes and new socio-political relationships in the Cañada de Yosotiche (Mixteca region, Oaxaca, Mexico), 16th–18th centuries", in *Historia Agraria, revista de agricultura e historia rural* 75 (2018), 33–68.

Martín Gabaldón, Marta, "Jurisdicción prehispánica y colonial de Tlaxiaco, ¿un territorio integrado? Consideraciones a partir de un estudio transdisciplinar", in Hermann Lejarazu, Manuel A. (coord.), *Señoríos mixtecos. Su dimensión histórica, geográfica y territorial,* Zinacantepec 2021, 77–110.

Martín Gabaldón, Marta, "Configuraciones territoriales 'móviles' en la Mixteca Alta (Oaxaca)", in *Prohistoria. Historia, políticas de la historia* XXVI: 39 (2023), 1–45.

Martín Gabaldón, Marta, "La mixteca o las mixtecas, ¿un espacio sociohistórico marcadamente heterogéneo?", in Hermann Lejarazu, Manuel A. (coord.), *Cartografía mixteca. Estudios interdisciplinarios sobre territorios y comunidades,* Zinacantepec 2023, 19–37.

Martínez, Hildeberto, Tepeaca en el siglo XVI. Tenencia de la tierra y organización de un señorío, México 1984.

Mendoza García, Edgar, "Las composiciones de tierras en la Mixteca y la formación del territorio comunal de cabeceras y sujetos, siglo XVIII", in Hermann Lejarazu, Manuel A. (coord.), *Configuraciones territoriales en la Mixteca. Vol. 1 Estudios de Historia y Antropología,* México 2015, 255–279.

Mendoza García, Edgar, "La descomposición de un cacicazgo: composiciones de tierras y litigios entre don Fernando de Velasco cacique de Chalcatongo y sus pueblos, siglo XVIII", in Hermann Lejarazu, Manuel (coord.), *Señoríos mixtecos. Su dimensión histórica, geográfica y territorial,* México 2021, 213–236.

Mendoza García, Edgar, "Apropiación territorial y conflictos: composiciones de tierras en los pueblos de indios de la Alcaldía Mayor de Teposcolula y Yanhuitlán, 1707–1767", in Carrera Quezada, Sergio Eduardo and Juan Manuel Pérez Zevallos (coords.), *En todos los rincones imperiales. Apropiaciones de tierras baldías y composiciones de propiedades agrarias en América y Filipinas (siglo XVI–XIX)*, México 2022, 395–437.

Menegus, Margarita, "Balance historiográfico. Reflexiones sobre el cacicazgo en la Nueva España", in *Estudios de Historia Novohispana* 27 (2002), 213–230.

Menegus, Margarita, La Mixteca Baja. Entre la Revolución y la Reforma. Cacicazgo, territoralidad y gobierno, siglos XVIII–XIX, Oaxaca de Juárez 2009.

Menegus, Margarita "La territorialidad de los cacicazgos y los conflictos con terrazgueros y los pueblos vecinos en el siglo XVIII", in Roth Seneff, Andrew (ed.), *Caras y máscaras del México étnico. Indigenous Participation in Mexican State Formations*, vol. I, Zamora 2010, 73–94.

Menegus, Margarita, "Cacicazgos y repúblicas de indios en el siglo XVI. La transformación de la propiedad en la Mixteca", in Hermann, Manuel (coord.), *Configuraciones territoriales en la Mixteca. Vol. 1, Estudios de historia y antropología*, Mexico 2015, 205–220.

Menegus, Margarita, "Del usufructo, de la posesión y de la propiedad: las composiciones de tierras en la Mixteca, Oaxaca" in *Itinerarios* 25 (2017), 193–208.

Menegus, Margarita, "Las composiciones de tierras en el centro de la Nueva España y en Oaxaca. La fabricación de nuevos títulos de propiedad indígena", in Carrera Quezada, Sergio Eduardo and Juan Manuel Pérez Zevallos (coords.), *En todos los rincones imperiales. Apropiaciones de tierras baldías y composiciones de propiedades agrarias en América y Filipinas (siglos XVI–XIX)*, México 2022, 367–393.

Menegus, Margarita and Rodolfo Salvador Aguirre (coords.), *El cacicazgo en Nueva España y Filipinas*, México 2005.

Monaghan, John, "Irrigation and Ecological Complementarity in Mixtec Cacicazgos", in Marcus, Joyce and Judith Francis Zeitlin (eds.), Caciques *and their People. A Volume in Honor of Ronald Spores*, Ann Arbor 1994, 143–161.

Ouweneel, Arij and Rik Hoekstra, Las tierras de los pueblos de indios en el altiplano de México, 1560–1920. Una aportación teórica interpretativa, Amsterdam 1998.

Pastor, Rodolfo, Campesinos y reformas: la Mixteca 1700–1856, Mexico 1987.

Peset, Mariano and Margarita Menegus, "Rey propietario y o rey soberano", in *Historia Mexicana* 43:4 (1994), 563–599.

Pohl, John M.D., "Ancient Books: Mixtec Group Codices. Codex Bodley", in *John's Pohl Mesoamerica* [online], FAMSI 2003. http://www.famsi.org/research/pohl/jpcodices/bodley/index.html

Quezada, Sergio, Maya Lords and Lordship: the Formation of Colonial Society in Yucatán, 1350–1600, Norman 2014.

Rodríguez Cano, Laura, "Apuntes sobre la herencia de los cacicazgos en la Mixteca Baja durante el siglo XVI", in Guerrero Galván, Luis René and Alonso Guerrero Galván (eds.), *Construcción histórico-jurídica del derecho prehispánico y su transformación ante el derecho indiano*, México 2019, 69–94.

Romero Frizzi, María de los Ángeles, Economía y vida de los españoles en la Mixteca Alta: 1519–1720, México 1990.

Solano, Francisco, Cedulario de tierras. Compilación de legislación agraria colonial (1497–1820), Mexico 1991.

Spores, Ronald, "Marital Alliance in the Political Integration of Mixtec Kingdoms," in *American Anthropologist* 76:2 (1974), 297–311.

Spores, Ronald, The Mixtecs in ancient and colonial times, Norman 1984.

Spores, Ronald, "Mixteca Cacicas: Status, Wealth, and the Political Accommodation of Native Elite Women in Early Colonial Oaxaca," in Schroeder, Susan, Stephanie Wood and Robert Haskett (eds.), *Indian Women of Early Mexico*, Norman 1997, 185–395.

Spores, Ronald, Ñuu Ñudzahui la Mixteca de Oaxaca: la evolución de la cultura mixteca desde los primeros pueblos preclásicos hasta la Independencia, Oaxaca de Juárez 2007.

Taylor, William B., Terratenientes y campesinos en la Oaxaca colonial, Oaxaca de Juárez 1998.

Terraciano, Kevin, "The Colonial Mixtec Community", in *Hispanic American Historical Review* 80:1 (2000), 1–42.

Terraciano, Kevin, Los mixtecos de la Oaxaca colonial. La historia ñudzahui del siglo XVI al XVIII, Mexico 2013.

Yannakakis, Yanna, Since Time Immemorial. Native Custom & Law in Colonial Mexico, Durham 2023.

CHAPTER 6

Domestic Rights in Indigenous Communal Lands

About the Expression "Menester" *in 16th-Century Charcas, Viceroyalty of Peru*

Carolina Jurado

1 Introduction

This Chapter explores the impact of the *visitas* (inspections) of the *repartimientos de indios*[1] that were implemented at the turn of the 16th century during the processes of *composición* (regularisation) of lands and the sale of *baldíos*[2] concerning the restructuring of indigenous communal lands of the Charcas district in the Viceroyalty of Peru.[3] In particular, it reflects on normative pluralism linked to the delimitation of standardised tenures for particular Indians or their households according to variable criteria, such as the fiscal status of their members, among others. Next, and bearing the diverse implementation in the Charcas context, it proposes an approach to the execution of the 1591 Royal Decrees in the *repartimiento* of Macha (North Potosí), also review-

1 In the Viceroyalty of Peru, at the end of the 16th century, the term *repartimiento* referred to an administrative-labour jurisdiction comprising a certain indigenous population—generally segmented into *parcialidades*, *pachacas*, and/or *ayllus*—around reduction towns, under a hierarchical leadership and in charge of a common territory to guarantee the payment of tribute.

2 The word *baldíos* applied to land is a legal term whose semantics in the Viceroyalty of Peru in the 16th century included references to uncultivated land or land not granted by the King. Also, the process initiated by the Royal Decrees of 1591 was a cornerstone in assimilating vacant or 'unused' indigenous lands to *baldíos*. Finally, after a disputed process, in the 17th century, the jurist Juan de Solórzano Pereyra defined the waters and the *baldíos* as royal domain (*realengos*), stating that "whatever is to be broken and cultivated is and must be of the royal Crown and dominion". See: Jurado, "Baldíos, derechos posesorios y tierra realenga en el primer proceso de composición en el distrito de Charcas". For other meanings of vacant and its relationship with people and things, see Buono (Chapter 2) in this volume.

3 In recent work, Margarita Menegus called attention to how scarcely studied this issue had been in the Mesoamerican historiography for the 17th and 18th centuries, a question also addressed with unequal attention and depth in studies of the Viceroyalty of Peru. See Menegus, "Dos modelos de propiedad", 142.

 DOI:10.1163/9789004722729_007

ing its concrete impact on domestic tenures, quality of life, and the dynamics between domestic and supra-domestic spheres for the manegement of land in the medium-term.

Historical and ethnohistorical research has emphasised the role of *composiciones* of lands and sales of *baldíos* in the 16th century to legitimise the transferral to the Spanish of lands usurped de facto from the Indian *repartimientos* in the Viceroyalty of Peru.[4] With a predominant idea of ownership as perfect and absolute property, it was proposed that the successive *composiciones* of lands had a prominent role in the 'great dispossession' of indigenous societies and in the conversion of their 'ancestral' and collective lands into Spanish property, confirming that those of the late 16th century constituted "the period in which the private property of land was born".[5] Likewise, it was suggested that the expansion of *haciendas* meant for the indigenous people the gradual acceptance of the idea of exclusive rights over land, and that "the visit meant yet another lesson in the idea of exclusive property and a loss of 'unused' land".[6] In particular, in relation to the lands retained by the *repartimientos*, it was argued that, from the Hispanic perspective, the intention was to assign inheritable plots at the domestic and/or individual level, according to Indian fiscal categories and the demography of the *repartimiento*, with the aim of "introducing in this way the notion of property" in the *repartimientos*.[7] This view coincided with historiographical perspectives that emphasised the contrast between Andean and European land tenure systems, particularly as regards the distinction between collective and private, respectively.[8]

On the contrary, recent research has emphasised the complexity of modern European notions of possession and ownership as well as the heterogen-

4 Amado Gonzáles, "Reparto de tierras"; Assadourian, "Agricultura y tenencia"; Glave, "Propiedad de la tierra, agricultura y comercio, 1570–1700"; Jurado, "La composición como concierto"; Palomeque, "Los chichas y las visitas toledanas"; Platt, Bouysse-Cassagne and Harris, *Qaraqara-Charka*; Stavig, "Ambiguous Visions".

5 Glave, "Propiedad de la tierra, agricultura y comercio, 1570–1700", 330. "[…] el periodo de nacimiento de la propiedad privada de la tierra". All translations in this Chapter are by Carolina Jurado and Manuel Bastias Saavedra.

6 Ramírez, "Land and Tenure in Early Colonial Peru", 62; Ramírez, *El mundo al revés*, 156.

7 del Río, *Etnicidad, Territorialidad y Colonialismo*, 134. "[…] introducir de esta forma la noción de propiedad."

8 In addition to the mentioned work of Ramírez (fn 5), see Stern, *Los pueblos indígenas del Perú y el desafío de la conquista española*, 28, 71–72; Pease, "La noción de propiedad entre los Incas", 11; Platt, Bouysse-Cassagne and Harris, *Qaraqara-Charka*, 508. For a critical approach to this cultural dichotomy, see Bastias Saavedra (Chapter 1) in this volume; Puente Luna, "Of Widows, Furrows, and Seed", 375–376.

eous indigenous claims to their lands in a context of intersecting legal traditions and the circulation and reappropriation of European legal knowledge.[9] In this sense, this Chapter suggests moving beyond the private/common and individual/collective dichotomies that have characterised the analysis of the effects of the process of *composición* of lands and its normativity into indigenous lands at the turn of the 16th century with the aim to recover the plurality of protagonists as well as their own categories and practices through different documentary series. In addition, the detailed examination of the Hispanic interference in the *repartimientos'* lands during its *visitas* allows an approach to some aspects of the Andean agrarian dynamics that has attracted the attention of historical research in recent years, such as the management of indigenous communal resources under colonial rule.[10] To this end, I propose an examination of the process of delimitation of inheritable plots at the domestic level within the indigenous communal domains[11] that distinguishes between the

9 Bastias Saavedra, "The normativity of possession"; Greer, *Property and Dispossession*, 12–18; Graubart, "'Ynuvaciones malas e rreprovadas'"; Gonzáles Escudero, "Una aproximación"; Herzog, "Colonial Law and 'Native Customs'"; Pérez Miguel and Honores, "Cacicas, Land, and Litigation in Seventeenth-Century Chincha, Peru"; Puente Luna y Honores, "Guardianes de la real justicia".

10 Graubart, "'Ynuvaciones malas e rreprouadas'"; Jurado, "Doble domicilio"; Jurado, "Tierra, estatus y viudez"; Puente Luna, "Of Widows, Furrows, and Seed"; Puente Luna "That Which Belongs to All"; Zuloaga Rada, "Las haciendas ganaderas de las parroquias indígenas en los Andes norcentrales y del sur en el periodo colonial". Many of them are heirs to the numerous questions raised by a profuse ethnohistorical and ethnographic historiography on Andean communities and their agrarian dynamics from the pre-Hispanic period to the present. See, among others, Abercrombie, *Caminos de la memoria y del poder*; de la Cadena, "Cooperación y mercado en la organización comunal andina"; del Río, "Estrategias andinas de supervivencia"; Glave and Remy, *Estructura agraria y vida rural en una región andina*; Golte, *La racionalidad de la organización andina*; Masuda, Shimada and Morris, *Andean Ecology and Civilization*; Mayer, *Casa, chacra y dinero*; Morlon, *Comprender la Agricultura Campesina en los Andes Centrales*; Murra, *Formaciones económicas y políticas del mundo andino*; Penry, *The People Are King*; Rasnake, *Autoridad y poder en los Andes*; Sendón, *Ayllus del Ausangate*.

11 In this Chapter, we use the term domestic units or households to refer to units that may include co-residents who, whether or not they have kinship ties, share a common living space. For a discussion of the category and its relation to family, see Jurado, "Tierra, estatus y viudez", 1 fn. 4; Jurado, "Doble domicilio"). Furthermore, the use of the term communal to designate those lands or resources under the corporate domain of the *repartimiento de indios* of the 16th century does not imply assigning to their members pre-Hispanic immanences, nor attributes linked to the Castilian communities of the Medieval and Modern period as well as those instituted in the American territories during the Republican period. For an ethnohistorical and ethnographic reflection on the relationship between the Andean *ayllus* (as socio-political groupings governed by kinship) and the concept of

different perspectives contained in the plurality of normative orders and jurisdictional powers that coexisted in the Charcas district in the late 16th century. Likewise, considering that the same dispositions could be executed in a variety of forms and degrees, given the executive centrality acquired by officials and the diverse responses of the social structures in the local contexts, the normative precepts are contrasted with the concrete forms in which they were socially appropriated in the *repartimiento* of Macha, in order to see the specific social relations that were generated around the land.[12] In this sense, the *repartimiento* of Macha (North Potosí, Charcas) constitutes a nodal empirical case, because it lets us evidence the disputed normative dispositions around the land extensions adjudicated to households and/or particular Indians and the concrete and diverse domestic and supra-domestic practices and rights of management of communal resources inside the *repartimiento* in the medium-term.

2 "Enough for Their Labour, Crops, and Herds":[13] Some Antecedents of Spanish Interest in Indigenous "Needs"

After a disorderly process of granting land—either by means of prerogatives contained in *capitulaciones*; by royal decrees of grace or mercy, and general and/or particular *provisiones* (provisions), or by means of the *Ordenanzas de descubrimiento y nueva población* [1573]—by the late 16th century, the Castilian monarchy began a series of processes aimed at regularising the Spanish agrarian possessions in the American viceroyalties.[14] Beginning with the Royal Decrees of El Pardo on 1 November 1591, the Crown upheld the legitimacy of its superior claims over lands, with the exception of those under indigenous

community, see Mossbrucker, *La economía campesina y el concepto de "comunidad"*; Sendón, *Ayllus del Ausangate*, 25–35; Zagalsky, "El concepto de 'comunidad' en su dimensión espacial".

12 Recent perspectives have emphasised the importance of analysing the concrete social and power relations around land by adding a focus on the strategies and negotiation of the social actors themselves. See Congost, "¿Una nueva historia social del mundo rural?"; Congost, Gelman and Santos, *Property Rights in Land*, 196–199; Lanteri, Barcos, and Jiménez, "Pluralismo de derechos de propiedad y privatización de tierras del común en las épocas moderna y contemporánea", 126.

13 The Royal Decree of 1591 stated: "(…) y rrepartiendo a los yndios lo que buenamente [h]uvieren menester para que tengan en que labrar y hacer sus sementeras y crianzas". AGI, Indiferente, 433, L. 2, f. 48^v.

14 Ots Capdequi, *España en América*.

rule, because "I have succeeded entirely to the dominion that the lords who were of the Indies had, and the dominion of the uncultivated soil and land of the Indies that was not granted by the lords my predecessors or by me, is of my royal Crown and patrimony".[15] This argumentation was the cornerstone for the inspection of the juridical instruments that were the basis for the control of land in Spanish hands, the restitution of irregularly occupied lands or their *composición*—that is, the payment to the Royal Treasury of an agreed amount in exchange for an appropriate juridical instrument—promoting sales of *baldíos* and the restructuring of urban spaces in the overseas possessions of the American continent. Likewise, the territoriality of the Indian *repartimientos* was to be inspected with the aim of guaranteeing the 'necessary' lands for their contemporary and future needs, enough for their labour, crops and herds, granting the royal benefit to all those lands considered 'surplus' by the judges.

In previous years, the Crown had issued dispositions regarding indigenous lands in order to protect their integrity and to prevent the rearing activities of Spanish cattle from damaging the lands of the Indian *repartimientos*.[16] In addition, formally, each distribution or grant of land was to be made without prejudice to the natives, and the local judges were charged with ascertaining whether the Indians were harmed by the cession.[17] In spite of this, the defence of indigenous territories against Spanish incursions and those of other ethnic groups demanded their constant litigation in the forums of justice.[18] During 1572–1575, while implementing guidelines elaborated by the Junta Magna, the Viceroyalty of Peru saw the reformulation of settlement patterns and the indigenous territoriality through their forced concentration in *pueblos de indios*. The transfer of the dispersed indigenous population to new towns was accompanied by a broader fiscal and evangelisation project, which also introduced

15 AGI, Indiferente, 433, L. 2, f. 48r. "[…] haber yo sucedido enteramente en el señorío que tubieron en las Indias los señores que fueron dellas es de mi patrimonio y Corona real el señorio de los baldíos suelo y tierra dellas que no estuviere concedido por los señores rreies mis predecesores o por mi".

16 Of the provisions gathered in the Recopilación de Leyes de Indias, the Crown's early concern that *encomenderos* could not have succession to lands vacated by the death of the Indians in their *encomiendas* in 1546 (Book VI, Title I, Law 30) stands out, alongside the prohibition of the Spaniards to raise pigs in towns of their *encomiendas* or in "términos donde los indios tuvieren sus labranzas" in 1549 (Book VI, Title IX, Law 19) and the order that the *estancias* of the Spaniards should be "lejos de los pueblos de indios y sus sementeras" in 1550 (Book IV, Title 12, Law 12).

17 Mariluz Urquijo, *El régimen de la tierra en el Derecho Indiano*, 24–26.

18 Stern, *Los pueblos indígenas del Perú y el desafío de la conquista española*, 185–211.

new political institutions that reduced the jurisdiction of their leaders, classified the indigenous people according to their fiscal category (*caciques* or indigenous leaders, tributaries, widows, and orphans) and linked their lands to the demographic volume of the *repartimiento*.[19]

In relation to indigenous territoriality, it was proposed that the lands of the *repartimientos* be divided into three parts: domestic lands, granted in usufruct to the families, in the broad sense, *ejido* (common-use lands usually for the *pueblo's* cattle), and lands under collective work and whose product was destined for the *caja de comunidad* (communal chest).[20] The *Instrucción General* [1569–1570], drawn up by Viceroy Francisco de Toledo, ordered inspectors to gather information on the existence of common goods and their uses. Furthermore, he added an interest in knowing about the lands occupied by settlers or *mitimaes*[21] and about the predisposition of the Indians to cultivate community crops, ordering that the Indians' "*chacaras* and lands held in the villages that they abandon not be taken from them, as long as they are within one league of the villages where they are resettled."[22]

Viceroy Toledo was also interested in obtaining information about indigenous access to plots of communal lands, ordering inspectors to inquire about

19 del Rio, *Etnicidad, Territorialidad y Colonialismo*, 124–132; Gade, "Reflexiones sobre el asentamiento andino desde la época toledana hasta el presente"; Málaga Medina, "Las reducciones toledanas en el Perú"; Saito and Rosas Lauro, *Reducciones*.

20 Málaga Medina, "Las reducciones toledanas en el Perú", 293; Pease, "La noción de propiedad entre los Incas", 15–16.

21 Sarabia Viejo, *Francisco de* Toledo, I, 22–35. The presence of Indians belonging to other *repartimientos* or *mitimaes* (settlers) was presented in the *Instrucción General* [1569–1570] as an eminently fiscal problem, establishing that those *mitimaes* present in the *repartimiento* for more than ten years should be settled so that they would pay tribute and serve like *originarios* (native Indians). In relation to their lands, the Viceroy ordered the inspectors to find out the lands granted to the *mitimaes* by the Incas and their restitution when necessary. Sarabia Viejo, *Francisco de Toledo*, I, 23.

22 Sarabia Viejo, *Francisco de Toledo*, I, 35. "[…] no se les tomen ni quiten las chacaras y tierras que tenian en los pueblos que despoblaren como esten dentro de una legua de los pueblos donde se redujeren". Years later, in his *Apuntamientos Aclaratorios de la Instrucción General*, carried out in Potosí in March 1573, Viceroy Toledo qualified his initial instruction, warning the inspectors that they should only remove lands beyond one *legua* to compensate persons harmed by the creation of the *pueblo de reducción*, "porque por otro ningun caso se les ha de quitar sus tierras por lejos que las tengan" (Sarabia Viejo, *Francisco de Toledo*, I, 265). The above, surely a product of the negotiations and lawsuits filed by the indigenous communities, was more in keeping with the spirit of the Royal Decree of 19 February 1560, by which Philip II understood that the Indians would be reduced to towns "si no se les quitan las tierras y granjerias que tuvieren en los sitios que dejaren", ordering that the lands they had had up to the time of the reduction be kept for them. However, the Royal Decree issued by Philip II in December 1573, and used to create Law 8,

how the lands tilled under Inca rule were distributed and "whether they were given in perpetuity or for a period of time [...] and whether the children of the Indians inherited the lands that their fathers tilled and whether they are inheriting them now and whether the Incas and caciques provided for them".[23] A few years earlier, in 1567, the same concern had motivated the inspector Garci Diez de San Miguel to interrogate the Chucuito Aymara leaders (in Charcas) about "whether the Indians of this province each have lands designated as their own or whether all the lands are held in common and are distributed each year among the Indians by their caciques".[24] The testimonies collected by Diez de San Miguel reiterated the generational continuity of land rights in the hands of the households, underestimating—according to John Murra—the role of the indigenous leaders and their ethnic groups as collectivities, in order to defend a threatened resource.[25] Despite this, the response of Cacique Don Martín Cusi made the picture more complex, as it indicated his centrality at the time of confirmation of the transmission of rights of use to descendants and/or when exercising the right to determine who benefited from its access and how it was transferred. According to his testimony:

> [...] the Indians have their lands and *chacaras* divided among them and that he is in charge of visiting them every year so that no one enters the land of another and that when an Indian dies who leaves no children and leaves a wife, he declares that he gives part of the lands to the wife and the rest is distributed among the Indians who need them of the *ayllu* where the Indian who died belonged to, and if the said deceased does not leave an heir, all the lands are distributed among his *ayllu*.[26]

Title 3, Book 6 of the Recopilación de Leyes de Indias, took up the sense of the initial Vice-regal Instruction for Peru, determining that "los sitios en que se han de fundar pueblos y reducciones tengan (...) un exido de una legua de largo donde los indios puedan tener sus ganados".

23 Sarabia Viejo, *Francisco de Toledo*, I, 23. "[...] si se daban perpetuas o por tiempo (...) y si los hijos de los indios sucedían en las tierras que sus padres labraban y si suceden agora y si los proveían los Ingas y caciques".

24 Diez de San Miguel, *Visita*, 35. "[...] si los indios de esta provincia tiene cada uno tierras señaladas por suyas o si todas las tierras son de común y se reparten en cada un año entre los indios por sus caciques."

25 Murra, *El mundo andino*, 300–301.

26 Diez de San Miguel, *Visita*, 35. "[...] los indios tienen sus tierras y chácaras señaladas y que él tiene a cargo cada año visitarlas para que ninguno se entre en la tierra del otro y que cuando acaece morir algun indio que no deja hijos y deja mujer da éste que declara parte de las tierras a su mujer y las demas reparte entre los yndios del ayllo donde era el indio que fallecio entre los que los han menester y si el dicho difunto no deja heredero se

Just a few years later, Viceroy Toledo ordered an interrogation of the indigenous leaders of the viceregal space about the domestic delimitation of the plots within the *repartimientos*, in the intertwining of versions that affirmed the existence of annual land distributions[27] and the legal literature that linked the indigenous idleness and the tyranny of the Inca and caciques with the absence of "their own thing" at the minimum level. The latter was the case for, for example, magistrate Juan de Matienzo [1567], who maintained that the Indians had not had "something of their own, but all in common" and suggested that the inspectors should demarcate the lands of caciques and *principales*, then the lands of the common and, finally, "to the Indians, to each one in particular, so many *topos* (or measures) that they know and understand that they are theirs and no one should be able to take them away or take them from them".[28] Lastly, Viceroy Toledo himself commanded that the inspectors "divide the land among the natives (*naturales*) in such a way that each one would know what was his own", in order to avoid—as Viceroy Toledo said—the payment that many caciques had been demanding, until then, from their indigenous people to assign them fertile lands.[29]

In this sense, numerous studies have pointed out that Viceroy Toledo promoted the redistribution of 'private property' or individual lands to the Indians as a priority objective of the demographic concentrations (*reducciones*), in addition to communal lands. In fact, Viceroy Toledo pointed out to the Indian *corregidores* (local Spanish official) that they could not sell lands located far from the new indigenous villages without his permission, if they were communal lands, or permission from the Real Audiencia (Royal Court) if they were

reparten todas las tierras entre su ayllo". In a similar sense, the indigenous chronicler Guamán Poma de Ayala described, in 1615, that, annually, during the month of July, the plots and farms were inspected and distributed and "amojonan cada uno lo que es suyo desde su antepasado y de sus padres". Guamán Poma de Ayala, *Nueva crónica y buen gobierno*, 240.

27 Thus, for example, in 1571 the official Polo de Ondegardo recalled having witnessed the distribution of lands in Collao and Chucuito, stating that "estas tierras dividían en cada un año y dividen hoy dia en la mayor parte del reino (…) y que tampoco dividían los herederos ni podían disponer de ella en ninguna manera". Ondegardo, "Notables daños de no guardar a los indios sus fueros", 59–60.

28 Matienzo, *Gobierno del Perú*, 15. "[…] hasta aquí cosa propia sino todo en común […] a los indios, a cada uno en particular tantos topos (o medidas) que sepa y entienda que son suyas y nadie se las ha de poder quitar ni tomar."

29 ABNB, Expedientes Coloniales, 1764.131, f. 93^{r}. I thank Ana Presta for giving me this documentary source. "[…] dividiesen las tierras entre los naturales de manera que cada uno conociese lo que era suyo."

lands "of particular Indians".[30] However, it should be noted that, within the framework of the adaptations and concessions of the project to the local reality, Viceroy Toledo had to give up the idea of external assignment of lands within the *repartimientos*, settling for supervision by the *corregidores* of its annual distribution made by the caciques.[31] Thus, a few years later, Viceroy Toledo admitted in his *Instrucción y Ordenanzas de los corregidores de naturales* that:

> [...] the said division cannot be carried out in most parts of the kingdom, especially in the cold lands because they sow the potato fields seven years at a time and divide them a year before so that they can work and benefit from them [...] and so for now the said division cannot be carried out without great difficulty.[32]

Based on the above, Viceroy Toledo ordered respect for the officials' assignment in those *repartimientos* where it had already been implemented, while in the places where its execution was difficult, the *corregidor* was present so that "each one receives the amount that may benefit him according to the people and family that he has".[33]

Two decades later, once again, the Andean *repartimientos* of the Viceroyalty of Peru had to face the generalised inspection and demarcation of their collective lands, providing versions of inter-group boundaries that would become the starting point for legal instruments of territorial defence. The land visitas promoted by the Royal Decrees of 1591 became a field of tension and negotiation, intended to strengthen the Toledan social order that linked the indigenous demography with its territorial scope with the aim to regulate domestic territorial access by favouring the intergenerational inheritance of plots of land.[34]

30 ABNB, Expedientes Coloniales, 1764.131, f. 91^{r}.

31 Zuloaga, "Las reducciones", 325 fn 15.

32 ABNB, Expedientes coloniales, 1764.31, ff. 93^{r}–93^{v}. "[...] la dicha divicion no se puede hazer en los más lugares del reyno expecialmente en las tierras frías porque siembran los pagos de papas de siete en siete años y los dividen un año antes para que los labren y beneficien [...] y así la dicha divicion no se puede hacer sin mucha dificultad por ahora." John Murra drew attention to the distinct agricultures of maize and Andean tubers, proposing that even the access to and inheritance of the respective *chacras* must have differed markedly. Murra, *El mundo andino*, 298; Murra, *Formaciones*, 45–57.

33 Sarabia Viejo, *Francisco de Toledo*, II, 417. "[...] a cada uno le quede la parte que pudiere beneficiar conforme a la gente y familia que tubiere".

34 del Río, *Etnicidad, Territorialidad y Colonialismo*, 124–134.

3 Pluralistic View and Jurisdictional Culture: Royal Decrees, Viceregal Instructions, and Other Norms at the Local Level

In order to understand the impact of the land visitas at the Indian *repartimientos* during the processes of *composición* and the sales of *baldíos* in the late 16th century for the delimitation of standardised tenures for the indigenous households, it is necessary to recover the plurality of jurisdictional and normative powers of the *ius commune* and the corporate and hierarchical framework of the *ancien régime*, into which the execution of the Royal Decrees of 1591 was inserted. In this sense, far from being part of a rigid set of strictly enforced laws, the royal dispositions were integrated with precepts of different origins and scopes, including those of divine origin, others derived from nature, or from powers, such as the Church, and others born of communal government and precepts established by custom.[35] Carlos Garriga has labelled 'jurisdictional culture' as the characteristic by which whoever was vested with the political power—that is, the capacity to state the law (*derecho*)—also possessed the power to declare what the law was, establishing rules or administering justice, to the degree and in the scope that corresponded to his jurisdiction.[36]

In this sense, the Royal Decrees of 1591 were unavoidable; through them, it was determined that "the *Indios* receive whatever they may need (*menester*) so that they can cultivate and grow their crops and raise their livestock, confirming what they have at present and giving them anew whatever they may need."[37] The determination of a potential quantity of 'necessary' lands for the Indians—and their counterpart, the surplus lands—found antecedents in the royal normative order. Thus, the Royal Decree of 14 May 1546 related the term *menester* to the demand for tribute, stating that the inhabited lands, due to the death of the Indians, were to be granted to neighbouring towns "up to the amount they may need for the payment and settlement of the tributes levied on them, and some more".[38] Viceroy Toledo had also used the term, relating it to indigenous subsistence—when he accused the paramount leaders of the

---

35 Tau Anzoátegui, "Órdenes normativos y prácticas socio-jurídicas"; Vallejo, "El cáliz de plata"; Clavero, "La Monarquía, el Derecho y la Justicia". Also, see Bastias Saavedra (Chapter 1) in this volume.

36 Agüero, "Las categorías básicas de la cultura jurisdiccional"; Garriga, "Las Audiencias".

37 AGI, Indiferente, 433, L. 2, f. 48^{v}. "[…] a los yndios lo que buenamente [h]uvieren menester para que tengan en que labrar y hacer sus sementeras y crianzas confirmandoles en lo que tienen de presente y dandoles de nuevo lo que les fuere necesario".

38 Recopilación de Leyes de Indias, Libro VI, Título 1, Ley 30. "[…] hasta en la cantidad que buenamente hubieren menester para paga y alivio de los tributos que les fueren tasados y algunas mas".

repartimiento of granting their Indians "less [lands] than necessary [*que habían menester*] for their subsistence"[39]—and also relating it to the demographic diversity of the household—as it was mentioned before-. On the contrary, the dispositions of 1591 used the term *menester* in connection with the land where the natives should sow and carry out their work, without adding further determinations, perhaps to allow it to adapt to the diversity, peculiarities, and circumstances that surrounded each local context.[40]

It was Viceroy Don García Hurtado de Mendoza's duty to select the procedures for the local examination, to name commissioned judges, to determine the jurisdictions, and to write their Commissions and Instructions. Viceroy Hurtado de Mendoza appointed the Augustinian Friar and Doctor in Holy Theology, Luis López, Bishop of Quito, as the first commissioned judge for the district of Charcas on 16 August 1592, "while the order for the best execution of the said Royal Decree was being considered and resolved [in Lima]".[41] This initial period, from the arrival of the Royal Decrees of 1591 to the Viceroyalty of Peru until the end of 1593, constituted a hinge period, characterised by disputed, provisional, fluid, and dialogued interpretations of the Royal documents both in the viceregal and local environments, creating spaces for individual and conflicting initiatives, in particular, around the ways they were executed in the indigenous territories.[42]

The Viceregal Commissions given to the judges—Friar López in August 1592 and, a year later, Alonso Maldonado de Torres in September 1593—did not mention the reordering of the indigenous territoriality, instead focusing on their roles as judges of Spanish *composiciones* of lands. It was possibly the initial Instructions that accompanied them—of which there is no record yet—that gave more details to both judges in relation to their simultaneous roles as land inspectors of the *repartimientos de indios*. In that sense, in documentation dated August 1593, Friar López called himself "judge to give and distribute

39 Sarabia Viejo, *Francisco de Toledo*, II, 417. "[…] menos [tierras] de las que habían menester para su sustentación."

40 With the same semantic breadth, Tamar Herzog recorded its repeated presence in the *composiciones* of land of the 18th district of Quito, in which 'need' and the argument that certain indigenous communities had received "too much land in relation to their needs" were used as powerful instruments for indigenous dispossession. Herzog, "Colonial Law and 'Native Customs'", 315.

41 "Comisión a don Pedro Osores de Ulloa". In Jurado "'(…) muy mañoso para esto'", 12. "[…] en el entretanto que se trataba e resolvia [en Lima] la orden que se prodria tener para la mejor execucion de la dicha Real Cedula."

42 Jurado, "Diálogos transatlánticos e interpretaciones locales de las Reales Cédulas de 1591", 134–139.

lands to the natives of the province of Charcas" and mentioned surface measures instructed by Viceroy Hurtado de Mendoza.[43] In relation to this task, in January of the same year, Friar López described his actions in each *repartimiento*, which included the gathering of oral testimonies, the written reception of the list of communal lands and the granting of the juridical instruments. In his words:

> [...] the first thing I tell them is that they should not speak to me in writing or ask me for anything but that they should represent their needs to me orally and that the Indian scribe of their council make a record of the lands, [...] the titles that they are to be given for their lands I order they pay them from their community [...] and in general when I am detained in one town it is for four days and in others no more than two.[44]

Friar López argued that the execution of the Royal decree provided the opportunity to repopulate the *pueblos de indios* because, through the sale of the lands of the *repartimientos*, the return of the indigenous people who had fled would be achieved. This was accompanied by the expulsion of the *forasteros*—indigenous people living outside their original *repartimientos*—even if they acquired the land through sale and purchase.[45] Like Viceroy Toledo before, Friar López mentioned the problem of *forasteros*' presence when he dealt with the reorganisation of indigenous corporative land. This could reveal different uses of and access to a diverse range of social actors concerning communal resources, which will be considered in the last section of this Chapter.

With only a few days assigned to each *repartimiento*, it was not Friar López who demarcated the collective tenancies, as he considered that "after having [I] distributed and assigned lands to the *Indios*, the *corregidores* of the place will then enter and demarcate [the lands] for the *Indios* to avoid quarrels and secure what each keeps".[46] In spite of the many differences among the commis-

43 AGN-A, XIII, leg. 886, fol. 983r. "[...] juez para dar e repartir tierras a los naturales indios de la provincia de los Charcas".

44 "De lo que escrivio a Su Señoria el maestro don fray Luis Lopez, obispo electo de Quito, en razón de las compusiciones de tierras como juez comisario dellas, 31 de enero de 1593". AGI, Lima, 273, fol. 76v. "[...] lo primero que les digo es que no me hablen por escrito ni me pidan cosa alguna sino que de palabra me representen su neçesidad y el escrivano yndio de su cavildo haga la memoria de las tierras, [...] los títulos que se les [h]a de dar de sus tierras mando que los paguen de su comunidad [...] y en general quando mucho me detengan en un pueblo es quatro días y en otros no mas de dos."

45 "De lo que escrivio a Su Señoria ...". AGI, Lima, 273, fols. 77r–79r.

46 "De lo que escrivio a Su Señoria ...". AGI, Lima, 273, fol. 76r. "[...] después de aver [yo]

sioned judges in the execution of the 1591 Royal Decrees, the official Maldonado de Torres also entrusted the task of distributing the *repartimiento* land to the Indian *corregidores*. He explained this in his correspondence of October 1593, when he described that he left it to the *corregidores* that "they distribute and give the Indians enough land for their work, pasture, and crops [because] a century would not be enough, if I were to go to each valley to distribute and give them land and to see and measure the remaining land".[47] This concurred with the spirit of the *Ordenanzas para corregidores* of Viceroy Toledo [1580], which reserved to these officials the supervision of the distributions of *repartimiento* made by the caciques. Likewise, it is possible that this similarity in the procedure for the demarcation referred to Viceregal Instructions that guided the actions of two such disparate commissioned judges in different jurisdictions in a similar execution, appealing to the *corregidores* of the districts visited for the internal distributions after the judges had granted the list of lands confirmed as the communal domain of each *repartimiento*.

Despite the above, after nine months in office, Friar López began to appoint Spanish boundary setters (*amojonadores*) for the inspected *repartimientos*. If service constituted the paradigm of the political relationship of the subjects of the Castilian monarchy in the 16th and 17th centuries, conceived as a relationship based on loyalty and on mutual obligations and bilateral rights, for a royal official, service was an obligation in itself, with practical manifestations in different areas of activity and in the different political spaces in which he carried out his office.[48] As Sebastián de Covarrubias Orozco [1611] summarised, service was "the act that is done by serving"[49] (*la obra que se haze sirviendo*) and it is in these terms that we propose to understand the initiative of Friar López in commissioning Spanish *amojonadores* with the judicial power to carry out what, until then, had been entrusted to the Indian *corregidores*.

Friar López elaborated precise orders, that denoted the knowledge of the dynamics of the Aymara *repartimientos* of the Charcas region, to reorganize the domestic rights of lands of collective domain. The analysed issue was mentioned not only in his Instructions, given to Captain Gonzalo Martín (neigh-

---

repartido y señalado tierras a los yndios, los corregidores del partido entren luego amojonando a los yndios para quitarles de pleytos y dejarles seguro lo que les queda".

47 "Copia de lo que escrivio a Su Señoria el licenciado Alonso Maldonado de Torres, oydor desta Real Audiencia en razón de las compusiciones de tierras como juez comisario dellas. 8-10-1593". AGI, Lima, 273, fol. 84^{v}. "[…] que ellos repartan y den a los yndios tierras suficientes para sus labores pastos y obranças [porque] si yo hubiese de yr a cada valle a repartirles y darles tierras y a ver y medir las que quedan no bastaría un siglo".

48 Esteban Estríngana, "El servicio".

49 Covarrubias Orozco, *Tesoro de la lengua Castellana*, f. 27^{v}.

bour of the town of Oropesa) on 12 August 1593, to delimit the lands that Friar López had awarded to the *repartimientos* of Capinota and Sicaya and to the Uros Indians of Charamoto—summarised by Mercedes del Río[50]—but also in his Commission, given two days before. This was the result of the officer's reflection on his experience, his theological training, and his deep knowledge of the indigenous society.[51]

From its comparative reading, what stands out is the precept of taking away from the *ayllus*—the basic indigenous supra-domestic unit of most *repartimientos*—the control over variable portions of the corporate territoriality, granting, to the households, farms that came from the variety of lands assigned to the whole *repartimiento*.[52] Friar López affirmed that "by ancient custom they usually have them divided by *ayllus*", lawsuits, abuses, and inequalities in the land distribution arose, given that "often some *ayllus* of a hundred Indians have more land than others of two hundred".[53] This supports the assertion that Indian land claims were interwoven with a hierarchy of overlapping rights of different kinship groups ranging from households, *ayllus*, *pachacas*, and *parcialidades* (moieties) to more global units, thus intertwined with the social-political and ceremonial structure of the Andean world.[54]

On the other hand, Friar López determined that the Indian domestic use rights would no longer be referred to supra-domestic organisational spheres—such as the *ayllus*—which exercised control over specific lands according to symbolic, historical, parental and/or other dimensions unrelated to demography. In addition, according to him, the particular tenures would be recorded in "a white book in which all *Indios* will be registered with a record of the lands that each is given and their heirs to serve as titles *ad perpetuam rei memoriam*".[55] Finally, Friar López confirmed that these lands were part of the

50 del Río, *Etnicidad, Territorialidad y Colonialismo*, 134.

51 Thirty years earlier, Friar López had founded the convent of Challacollo in the highlands of Oruro, knew the Uru language and had evangelised the Soras of Capinota in Cochabamba. See del Rio, *Etnicidad, Territorialidad y Colonialismo*, 133.

52 According to the Instructions of Friar López, "y anssi el horden que se a de thener de aquí adelante que aquellas tierras queden adjudicadas para un pueblo an de ser común para todos los yndios". AGN-A, XIII, leg. 886, fols. 985ᵛ–986ʳ.

53 AGN-A, XIII, leg. 886, fol. 983ᵛ. In Spanish: "[…] por la antigua costumbre de que las suelen tener repartidas por ayllus"; "[…] suele acaezer que unos ayllos de cient indios tienen mas tierras que otros de ducientos".

54 Murra, *El mundo andino*, 294–307; Murra, *La organización económica*, 62–81; Platt, Bouysse-Cassagne and Harris, *Qaraqara-Charka*, 508.

55 AGN-A, XIII, leg. 886, fol. 986ʳ. In Spanish: "[…] un libro vlanco en el qual se enpadronaran todos los yndios con la memoria de las tierras que se dan a cada uno y sus herederos que servian de titulos *ad perpetuam rey memoria*".

collective or common territoriality of the *repartimientos* in such a way that "the other [lands] that are left over shall not be sold or leased, but shall always remain to be distributed to any Indians who have returned".[56] Given the testimonies that affirmed the generational continuity of the plots at the household level—for example, the one mentioned above for Chucuito—Friar López's provision possibly sought to erode the right to determine who benefitted from the use and how it was transferred; a right exercised until then by the indigenous leaders and the supra-domestic instances they represented, and that the judge now intended to transfer to the households.

In the same sense, Friar López provided that the domestic access rights were inheritable, generation after generation, "so that the said Indians and their heirs and successors may forever hold and possess the said lands as theirs and have them known to belong to each one in particular".[57] Possibly, seen from the indigenous leadership hierarchies and the domestic units, the instruction would stress the need for land rotation according to demographic, ecological, and/or agrarian fluctuations, elements that, 20 years earlier, had altered the determinations of Viceroy Toledo.[58] In fact, different investigations have pointed out that Andean land measures—such as the *topu*—were not specific, universal measures, but rather the representation of the notion of measurement, whose extension varied according to the ecological conditions of the land and which translated into a right of use over lands that produced a certain amount of products necessary for the reproduction of those who worked them.[59]

This had been contemplated by Friar López in the plots to be assigned to the *indios del común* (commoners), stating that "as far as the particular *Indios* are concerned, prudence is needed [*menester*] to distribute them according to

56 AGN-A, XIII, leg. 886, fol. 986r. "[...] las demas [tierras] que sobraren no se [h]an de poder vender ni arrendar sino que [e]sten siempre en pie para yr rrepartiendo a los yndios que de nuevo entraron".

57 AGN-A, XIII, leg. 886, fol. 983v. "[...] para que los dichos indios e sus herederos e suscessores para siempre xamas tengan e posean las dichas tierras por suyas conocidas cada uno en particular".

58 The difficulties and regulatory uncertainties regarding the scope of the inheritance of particular tenancies in a corporate domain led the Real Audiencia of Lima in 1629 to request specific provisions from the Consejo de Indias, because, according to its magistrates, "por no haber dejado claro el tema de las sucesiones, de tal forma que a la muerte de los indios, los curas se encargan de persuadirlos o simplemente fraguar cesiones para formar capellanías que terminan disfrutando." Glave, "Propiedad de la tierra, agricultura y comercio, 1570–1700", 390.

59 Murra, *Formaciones económicas y políticas del mundo andino*, 14; Pease, "La noción de propiedad entre los Incas", 17–18.

their needs [*necesidad*], as some will have more and others less".[60] It meant a need that could be related to the demographic composition of the household, the fiscal status of its members, and/or the quality of the allotted lands. However, when referring to the members of the leadership hierarchies, the document linked the term need or *menester* to the order designed in the *Visita General*. Thus, the same judge indicated that *amojonadores*:

> [...] they will indicate *chacaras* for the caciques, taking into account the ordinance of Don Francisco de Toledo, who stated in the General Visita of the land that the Indians were to benefit the main cacique [*principal*] with what I believe was one fanega of maize and to the lower-ranking caciques less, and also potato crops, for which he will execute the *visita* and the ordinances.[61]

Finally, the lands 'needed' for the Indian *repartimientos* had to exclude *forasteros* and, therefore, they were not counted in the rate of the host jurisdiction. Many of them were *mitimaes* who guaranteed the political-ecological control of different production zones, determining interdigitated territorialities that were pointed out, by and since the key studies of Murra, as a long-term pattern of settlement of diverse Andean societies.[62] If, in the General Inspection under the government of Viceroy Toledo, the *mitimaes* who had been living there for ten years were incorporated into the tributary lists of the *repartimiento*, 20 years later the instructions of Friar López proposed their physical expulsion, subtracting them from the lands that the *repartimiento* had 'needed'. The expulsion of the *forasteros* was the firm opinion of Friar López who, in previous correspondence, had suggested Viceroy Hurtado de Mendoza remove the *cacicazgo* from any indigenous leader who accepted them in the *repartimiento's*

60 AGN-A, XIII, leg. 886, fol. 985v. "[...] en lo que toca a los yndios particulares [h]a menester prudencia para repartirles conforme a su necesidad que unos tendran mas y otros menos".

61 AGN-A, XIII, leg. 886, fol. 985v. "[...] señalaran chacaras para los caciques advirtiendo la hordenanza del señor don Francisco de Toledo que dexo en la Visita General de la tierra que [h]avian venefficiar los yndios al cacique principal que creo fue una fanega de maíz y a los prinzipales segundas perssonas al rrespeto menos y tanvien sementera de papas para lo qual mandara ver la Vissita de los yndios y hordenancas." For a comparative analysis of the measures pointed out to the leadership hierarchies of the Charcas region according to the summaries of the General Inspection of Viceroy Toledo, see Jurado, "It is not fair that he is treated as indio particular", 305–312.

62 Murra, *Formaciones económicas y políticas del mundo andino*; del Río, "Estrategias andinas de supervivencia"; Platt, Bouysse-Cassagne, and Harris, *Qaraqara-Charka*, among others.

lands and who then found a way to establish himself as an instruction on the area under his jurisdiction.[63]

Although we have not found the early Instructions given by Viceroy Hurtado de Mendoza to the officials appointed in the years 1592–1593, there is a record of his *Instrucciones a los visitadores* of October 1594.[64] Their analysis allows us to contrast another perspective on how to interpret the execution of what in the Royal Decrees of 1591 was understood as the lands that the Indians could need (*buenamente hubieren menester*). Although more general and in contradiction with some of the indications provided by Friar López, the Viceregal Instructions addressed the issue by stating that:

1. The Indians' or caciques' "own" lands (*tierras o heredades suyas propias*), inherited or obtained in Toledo's General Inspection and/or purchased from those who had possessed them with legitimate juridical instruments, were not to be taken away and confirmed.[65]
2. To confirm and give lands "anew up to the amount they may need [*huvieren menester*]" to those Indians or caciques who had them "in such modest amount that they do not reach what they need [*han menester*]".[66]
3. To declare as vacant and ill-gotten (*mal habidas*) those lands that, in the verbal inquiry, were found to have been usurped by caciques or Indians without cause or juridical instrument, "leaving them those which legitimately belong to them and which they should need [*hovieren menester*]", in accordance with what had been done with the other Indians and caciques.[67]
4. Those lands declared to be vacant (*vacas*) were to be granted to Indians or caciques, by auction, with the "instruction that the said Indians may not sell or transfer them except to another Indian or Indians".[68]
5. The dismembered lands of the *repartimientos* were to be exchanged.
6. Those caciques or Indians who could farm more land than others were to be given "in more quantity than the others who have less possiblity".[69]

63 "De lo que escrivio a Su Señoria ...". AGI, Lima, 273, fol. 77v.
64 "Instrucción que dio el virrey don García de Mendoza a los comisarios de tierras". Lima, 8 octubre 1594. Escalona Agüero, *Gazofilacio Real*, fols. 207–209.
65 "Instrucción". Escalona Agüero, *Gazofilacio Real*, fol. 208.
66 "Instrucción". Escalona Agüero, *Gazofilacio Real*, fol. 208. "[...] de nuevo hasta en la cantidad que huvieren menester"; "[...] tan moderadas que no lleguen a las que han menester".
67 "Instrucción". Escalona Agüero, *Gazofilacio Real*, fol. 208. "[...] dexandoles las que legitimamente les pertenecieren i [h]ovieren menester".
68 "Instrucción". Escalona Agüero, *Gazofilacio Real*, fol. 208. "[...] gravamen y aditamento que los dichos indios no las puedan vender ni traspasar sino fuere a otro indio o indios".
69 "Instrucción". Escalona Agüero, *Gazofilacio Real*, fol. 209. "[...] en mas cantidad que a los otros que tienen menos posible".

As can be seen, Viceroy Hurtado de Mendoza did not mention supra-domestic spheres, such as *ayllus*, from which to take away interference in the management of corporate territoriality, but rather, in his Instructions, he identified Indians and caciques as the main social actors. Likewise, the Viceregal Instructions ordered the granting and confirmation of particularised land allocations, differentiated by the productive capacity of the domestic units, within the framework of communal lands that could not be alienated by sale—with the exception of those made to other Indians and/or to the indigenous political units. In this sense, it is important to point out that the creation and/or strengthening of the rights of access and management of domestic plots was framed in the royal recognition of the indigenous rights over their lands as inalienable communal domain. Thus, only as an exception and by means of judicial proceedings was the alienation of part of the corporate lands of the *repartimiento* allowed, when the Indians themselves requested it and it was proven that, given their demographic composition, the 'needs' of the community were always covered.[70] Finally, in his Instructions, Viceroy Hurtado de Mendoza encouraged the cohesion of the indigenous domain through the geographic concentration of lands and the exchange of lands in pursuit of less intermingled Andean territorialities. Despite this objective, nothing was said about the tenancies held by the *forasteros*, unlike what was established by Friar López in Charcas.

To summarise, we can point out that the different jurisdictional powers that coexisted in the land visitas of the Indian *repartimientos* enabled the officials to interfere in inquiries about the temporal depth of possession, the modes of access to land, and its hereditary transfer by the indigenous households, making visible and ordering, according to European perspectives, the internal rules and agreements that governed the management of the indigenous corporate domain that, until then, had only been evident to its members.

4 Domestic Tenancies in Indigenous Communal Territories, Before the Charcas Judge: The *Repartimiento* of Macha in Context

Friar López visited the Potosí area at the beginning of 1593, a period in which he entrusted the Indian *corregidores* with the demarcation of lands within the *repartimientos*.[71] According to the paramount leaders of the *repartimiento* of

70 Ots Capdequi, *España en América*, 85.

71 Platt, Bouysse Cassagne, and Harris, *Qaraqara-Charka*, 597. "[…] por haberse cometido por

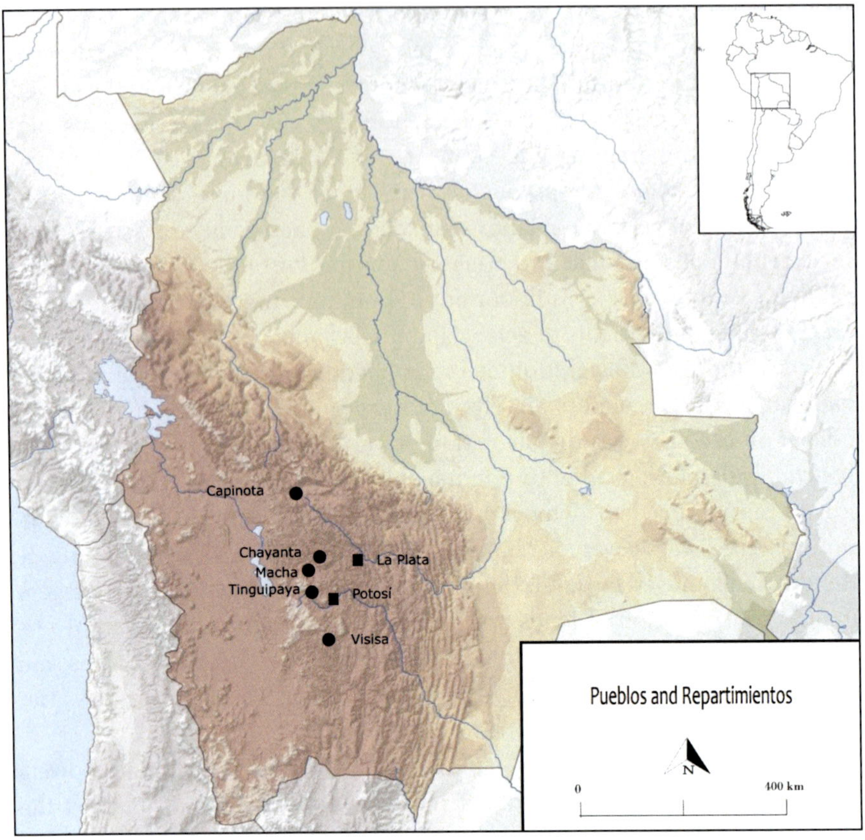

MAP 6.1. Map of *pueblos* and *repartimientos* mentioned in the text
OWN ELABORATION FROM GOOGLE EARTH SATELLITE IMAGE

Visisa (South of Potosí), he had confirmed their lands but "because the Bishop of Quito has given these demarcations of the Indians to the corregidores, they have never been made, due to the many occupations they have".[72]

As for the nearby *repartimiento* of Tinguipaya, there is a record that Friar López strengthened the material base of the leaders of the Hurin *parcialidad* by selling them not only the lands of Pina Pina, disputed with the *repartimiento* of Moromoro, but also Colcabamba lands, which had belonged to Moromoro.[73]

el señor obispo de Quito a los corregidores, estos amojonamientos de los indios nunca se han hecho, por las muchas ocupaciones que tienen".

72 Platt, Bouysse Cassagne, and Harris, *Qaraqara-Charka*, 597.

73 Nicolas, *Los ayllus de Tinguipaya*, 95–105.

On the other hand, according to 18th-century documentation, in Tinguipaya's highlands, the judge recognised a list of boundary markers linked to the lands of the *parcialidades*. According to Vincent Nicolas' analysis, the *mojones* (boundary marks) indicate an incomplete territorial demarcation (intentional or not) between the *parcialidades* of Tinguipaya, which maintained their autonomy from each other even until the 18th century, when they presented their separate *Memorias de tierras* (land records). However, the inspection focused on the boundaries of the *repartimiento* from the outside, creating "a territorial space closed on itself and centered around the village", which implied a redefinition of intergroup relations.[74]

The above situation differs from what was done at the end of 1593 in the *pueblo de reducción* San Pablo de Capinota (*repartimiento* of Paria). Based on an exceptional documental corpus which recorded particular allotment according to the indigenous fiscal categories, Mercedes del Río proposed that the *amojonador* appointed by Friar López divided into plots the bands of land controlled, up to that time, by the *ayllus* of the *repartimiento*. Through a standardised order of demarcation and distribution, the Indian tributaries and *reservados* (tax-exempted) received plots of half a *fanegada*,[75] while the widows and single women obtained a quarter of a *fanegada*. On the other hand, the cacical elite consolidated their possessions, maintaining plots in each productive zone, whose measurements far exceeded those determined by the instructions of Viceroy Toledo. Finally, in this new order dictated by the *amojonador*, del Río drew attention to the high degree of mixing of plots and its strong impact on the strengthening of decision-making at the household level.[76] However, it is important to point out that, although this historical record allows an extraordinary approximation of the formal order established by the official, the concrete use of the lands by the *repartimiento* may have caused notable transformations according to their changing reproductive needs, reassembling and transforming in everyday life what was divided in the official's instruction.

A final example of the diverse judicial praxis of the officials who executed the Royal Decrees 1591 comes from the neighbouring jurisdiction of Cusco at the beginning of 1595, the period of incidence of the Instructions of Viceroy

74 Nicolas, *Los ayllus de Tinguipaya*, 99–100. "[…] un espacio territorial cerrado sobre sí mismo y centrípeto alrededor del pueblo […]".

75 According to del Río's calculations, the tributaries had access to plots equivalent to 1.9 hectares while the widows had 1 hectare. del Río, *Etnicidad, Territorialidad y Colonialismo*, 141, fn. 37.

76 del Río, *Etnicidad, Territorialidad y Colonialismo*, 132–163.

Hurtado de Mendoza. Occupied by the *composiciones*, the Judge Maldonado de Torres commissioned the scribe Juan López de Arrieta to inspect the indigenous lands in the valley of Chinchaypucyo. As analysed by Donato Amado Gonzáles in the *Reparto de tierras del pueblo de Sumaro*, the scribe, as well as the *amojonador* Gregorio Otazú, found that the lands of the *ayllus* were not separated nor delimited, and therefore they assigned four *topus* of maize lands and a quarter *topus* of potato-producing lands to each tributary, and two *topus* of lands to the widows, the elderly and the sick of each *ayllu*. Thus, the lands assigned according to the fiscal status were mentioned by *ayllu*s, with the warning that:

> [...] said Indians nor their successors in [the lands] cannot sell or alienate [...] and in the absence of [descendants] they are to remain for the other Indians that there may be [...] because they are not given any ownership [*propiedad*] of them but are only usufructuaries.[77]

They also confirmed to the paramount leader 14 *topus*, assigned six *topus* of land "to the *cacicazgo*", and gave two *topus* of land for worship, under the care of the caciques and *alcaldes* (municipal judges).[78] Finally, the distribution of plots was recorded in the *Libro de reparto de tierras* in order to serve as title (*le sirva de título*), as it was in fact used by the members of the Sumaro town, even in the Republican period.[79]

Into this heterogeneous context, the empirical case of the *repartimiento* of Macha can be inserted. As in the case of other northern Potosí *repartimientos*, the actions of Friar López at the beginning of 1593 had to be reconstructed from later mentions, as contemporary records have not yet been found.[80] The territory of the *repartimiento* of Macha formed the core region of the province

77 Amado Gonzáles, "Reparto de tierras", 203. "[...] los dichos yndios ninguno de ellos ni sus sucesores en ellas no puedan vender ni enajenar [...] y a falta de ellos han de quedar y quedan para los demas yndios que adelante hubiere [...] porque no se les da propiedad alguna de ellas, sino solamente el ser usufructuario".

78 Depending on the quality of the land, the measurement varied, since in the town of Sumaro the *topu* was 50 *varas* wide and 100 *varas* long, while in the town of Chinchaypucyo it was 40 *varas* wide and 80 *varas* long. Amado Gonzáles, "Reparto de tierras", 199.

79 Amado Gonzáles, "Reparto de tierras indígenas y la primera visita y composición general, 1591–1595", 205.

80 Thus, for example, some later records show that in the nearby *repartimiento* of Sacaca, Friar López left to its paramount leaders "el titulo original de las tierras" and a count of the demographics of the *repartimiento* classified into: total, married, single, elderly, young, and children. Platt, Bouysse Cassagne, and Harris, *Qaraqara-Charka*, 643.

of Chayanta, with its main *pueblo de reducción* (San Pedro de Macha) located 30 *leguas*, or approximately 167 kilometres, from Potosí. Within its province, Macha was one of the most densely populated districts and its lands included the high land bordered by the Azanaques Cordillera and extended, SW–NE, towards the warm valleys around the Río Grande. The combination of different altitudinal ecologies allowed them to combine the grazing of camelids, cattle, and sheep with the cultivation of tubers, maize, wheat, grapes, and even products from warmer areas, such as *ají* (chilli peppers). Three months before the beginning of the process of inspection and *composición* of lands, the president of the Real Audiencia of Charcas, Juan López de Cepeda, and the town council of the city of La Plata granted many of the *repartimiento's* lands to their relatives. When Friar López arrived, their holders revalidated their legal instruments by means of a *composición* payment, despite the fact that the Macha indigenous leaders contested the action through an extensive litigation before the Audiencia, which, for decades, regarded them as common lands.

In this context of deep dispossession of the communal domain by relevant members of the Charcas institutions, territorial scarcity, and the active indigenous litigation had an impact on the delimitation of domestic tenures within the *repartimiento*. Far from responding to standardised measures that related to the quality of the land, the fiscal status, and/or the demographics of the households and/or quantities prefixed in normative instructions, in the *repartimiento* of Macha, the Spanish dimensions of indigenous domestic plots seem to have followed the fluctuations generated in the interplay of the demography of the *repartimiento*, the territorial dispossession, the changing opinion of different officials, and the constant litigiousness of the indigenous leaders.

In his correspondence of 1608, the Fiscal (prosecutor) of the Audiencia of Charcas, Don Francisco de Alfaro explained to the Consejo de Indias that "the bishop of Quito, who was the commissioner of the instruction he gave to the *corregidor* to distribute the lands, ordered the Indians to be given the amount of three cargas de sembradura of maize to each one".[81] The measure of land, calculated as the amount of maize to be sown, differed from the measures of extension (*fanegada*) granted in Capinota in 1593; it was not even equivalent to the amount obtained by its tributaries, but tripled it.[82] The measure used

81 Gandia, *Francisco de Alfaro*, 387. "[...] el obispo de Quito, que fue el comisario de la instrucción que dio al corregidor para repartir las tierras, mando diesen a los yndios raçon de tres cargas de sembradura de maiz a cada uno".

82 According to the Fiscal Don Francisco de Alfaro, based on calculations made with the

also differed from that which was implemented in Cusco, where *topus*—whose extension varied according to the quality of the land—were granted. However, the measure chosen in Macha seemed to respond to an accepted calculation in the Viceroyalty of Peru, given that, one of the main detractors of the actions of Friar López, the Spaniard Martín de Goicoechea Martiartu stated that "in accordance with the order practised and kept in this Kingdom, each tributary Indian was to be given three cargas de sembradura of maize".[83]

In 1602, Magistrate Ruiz Bejarano set out to finish one of the judicial disputes that Macha had with the different Spaniards who had obtained lands from the *repartimiento*. In order to do so, the court then sent the Spaniard Lazarte de Molina who ordered three *cargas de sembradura* to be given per tributary, which was appealed by the parties.[84] Therefore, in 1605 the Audiencia sent the Magistrate Don Manuel de Castro y Padilla to measure the lands and guarantee that each Indian had enough to sustain himself.[85] According to Martiartu's complaint,

> [...] the magistrate Don Manuel de Castro y Padilla, judge of this Real Audiencia, who went to the said lands [...] did not want to give them more than one carga so as not to dispossess the said powerful people who, as I say, have established large estates in the said lands.[86]

In this opportunity, it was evident that the measures of land that each tributary 'needed' were adjusted in a variable way, to avoid the dispossession of the Spanish neighbours of the region. Historical records produced in the inspection (*revisita*) of the *repartimiento* of Macha in 1619 contained greater precision. During the *revisita*, its paramount leaders stated that Magistrate Castro y Padilla had indicated "to the tributaries one [carga de sembradura of maize],

information gathered in the *repartimiento* of Macha, three *cargas de sembradura* of maize were equivalent to 1.5 *fanegas*. BN-A, CGGV, Doc. 3947.

83 AGI, Charcas, 48, s/f. "[...] conforme a horden praticada y guardada en este Reyno se le avia de dar a cada yndio tributario tres cargas de tierra de senbradura de maíz".

84 "Carta de la Real Audiencia de Charcas al Virrey. La Plata, 1 de febrero de 1611". ABNB, Correspondencia de la Audiencia de Charcas, 670, s/f.; Gandia, *Francisco de Alfaro y la condición social de los indios*, 387.

85 "Copia de la carta de la Audiencia de La Plata al Virrey del Perú. La Plata, 4 de septiembre de 1605". ABNB, Correspondencia de la Audiencia de Charcas, 510, fol. 1r.

86 AGI, Charcas, 48, s/f. "[...] [e]l licenciado don Manuel de Castro y Padilla, oydor de esta Real Audiencia, el qual fue a las dichas tierras [...] no les quiso dar mas de una carga por no desposeer a las dichas personas poderossas que, como digo, tienen fundadas grandes haziendas en las dichas tierras".

to the *reservados* at half and to the old men at two almudes, and the same to the old women and widows".[87]

The magistrate had not only calculated land extensions that, in general terms, conformed to the power relations of the region, but had, in effect, assigned domestic or individual land holdings to accommodate Indians according to their fiscal category and to avoid the restitution of alienated lands. Thus, for example, according to the paramount leader of Macha in 1619, Castro y Padilla had assigned one *carga* and three *almudes* to the lands that the Sulcahavi *ayllu* owned in the Charichari valley for the sustenance of Magdalena Yucrama and Isabel Payco, defined as "old and principal Indians". Likewise, he had assigned to another Sulcahavi widow, María Chuquema, one *carga* in the same valley.[88] The land measures—raised for the fiscal category to which the three women belonged—possibly responded to their status as "*principales*", rather than to their fiscal character, protecting the estamental and symbolic precedences within the group.

The execution of magistrate Castro y Padilla was again appealed by the litigants. Using the argument that related the Indian fiscal character and the demography of the *repartimiento*, the leaders of Macha insisted judicially on the granting of three *cargas de sembradura* per tributary. In their words, after the distribution of Castro y Padilla,

> [...] we are not given enough lands, not even half of which is enough so that 500 tributary Indians can be sustained on them, among whom—as the said register shows—there are Indians who have from six to 11 children and from six downwards everyone else, without many unmarried women in the *repartimiento*, in addition to old men [who do not tribute], old women, orphans, and widows.[89]

The argument found strength in the correspondence of Fiscal Alfaro, who related the land measurements to the social reproduction of each indigenous household. According to his findings, he maintained that:

---

87 AGN-A, Sala XIII, Leg. 914, s/f. "[...] a los tributarios a una [*carga de sembradura de maíz*], a los reserbados a media y a los viejos a dos almudes y lo mismo a las viejas y biudas."

88 AGN-A, Sala XIII, Leg. 914, fol. 381v.

89 "Petición de Macha", in Platt, Bouysse-Cassagne, and Harris, *Qaraqara-Charka*, 620. "[...] no se nos dan tierras ni aun con las dos partes menos para que en ellas se puedan sustentar 500 indios tributarios, entre las cuales—como por el dicho padron consta—hay indios que tienen de seis hasta 11 hijos y de seis abajo todos los mas, sin muchas mujeres solteras de que tiene el repartimiento se aumente viejos reservados, viejas, huerfanas y viudas".

> [...] the lands need [*an menester*] a year and a half, so that to harvest one carga they need [*an menester*] three, and even if they do not have one they do not sow almudes and when each one harvests four *hanegas*, which is almost fifty, I beg Your Majesty to warn that one house of a tributary Indian is four people [...] so that if in each house we put three people, each one needs at least one and a half *hanega* every month, so that the harvest does not give more than two months to eat.[90]

Fiscal Alfaro's words referred to a strict calculation linked to productivity, yield, and consumption of a central good for the Andean populations, such as maize, without resorting to other related criteria such as, for example, the presence of *forasteros* in the lands of the *repartimiento*, nor the *legua* of land around the *pueblo de reducción*, present in royal decrees, viceregal instructions, and forensic practice.[91]

Thus, in a context of deep territorial dispossession legitimised by the praxis of the land inspector, the introduction of domestic tenures in the Macha *repartimiento* adjusted to the power relations of the surrounding agrarian space and left, according to the cacical litigation, numerous non-tributary domestic units without material reference. As will be discussed in the following section, far from undermining the jurisdiction of supra-domestic spheres, such as *ayllus* and *parcialidades*, the above reinforced them, enhancing their coordinating roles in the rotation and adjustment of plots in relation to the quality, quantity, and ecological distribution of the population. Also, the process transformed the relationships between the members of the *repartimiento* in terms of access to land, with a notable worsening of their quality of life—as pointed out by Fiscal Alfaro—and of internal tensions. As will also be discussed below, the *repartimiento* of Macha is a key empirical case because it provides subsequent records that allow us to glimpse the social effects of the process analysed in the medium-term.

---

90 Gandia, *Francisco de Alfaro y la condición social de los indios*, 387. "[...] las tierras an menester año y vez, de suerte que para senbrar 1 carga an menester 3 y que teniendo, aun, no una no senbraran almudes y quando cada uno dé de cosecha 4 hanegas que sale casi a cinquenta suplico a Vuestra Magestad advierta que una casa de un yndio tributario uno con otro son cuatro personas [...] por suerte que en cada casa pongamos tres personas cada uno a menester por lo menos hanega y media cada mes de suerte que no tienen cosecha para comer dos meses".

91 The procedural argumentation that appealed to the royal and viceregal dispositions regarding the lands that, located within a *legua* of distance from the *pueblo de reducción*, belonged to the *repartimiento* is reiterated in numerous judicial processes that settled the dominion and possession of particular lands. For an analysis of its judicial use in the 18th century, see, among others, Herzog, "Colonial Law and 'Native Customs'", and Dueñas, "The Virgin and the land surveyor".

5 Domestic Land and Collective Dynamics in the Macha *Repartimiento* at the Beginning of the 17th Century

Despite the decreasing demographic curve, at the beginning of the 17th century, the leaders of the *repartimiento* of Macha continued complaining about the lack of fertile land for all its members. As mentioned above, since the end of the previous century, the *repartimiento* had lost access to plots in the nearby valleys, such as the Guaranga ravine and portions of the Carasibamba valley. A snapshot of the internal rearrangement of the *repartimiento*, after the passage of the inspectors and the later officials in charge of recomposing its territoriality, can be observed through the analysis of the *Padrón por el que pagan su tasa* (c. 1612–1619).[92] This record is a hierarchical enumeration, by Hanan or Hurin parcialidades and *ayllus*, of the Indian group of the *repartimiento* as per their fiscal category, accompanied by a mention of the assigned valley plots and the amount of livestock owned by each unit, if applicable. The analysis of this record provides an approximate, formal, and static view of the distribution of use rights within the *repartimiento*, given that the population may have reassembled the allocations with other criteria, depending on the changing needs of social reproduction; the political, parental, and symbolic status of the population; and the ecological requirements of the lands themselves. However, considering what has been discussed so far, as well as the scarcity of intracommunal records in Andean archives, the analysis of these kinds of records may yield further information to consider. From a demographic perspective, it can be noted that the *parcialidades* were unequal in population numbers, with Hanansaya having recorded 98 more tributaries than Hurinsaya. On the other hand, in relation to the valley lands recorded, as Table 6.1 indicates, the total *cargas de sembradura* of maize would indicate that Hanansaya controlled greater total amounts of land, while the Hurinsaya did not have access to sufficient land to grant one *carga de sembradura* of maize to each of its tributaries.

If one looks at the qualitative information on the household holdings, the *Padrón* did not record the agricultural or livestock possessions of the highest members of the leadership hierarchy of the *repartimiento*, such as the paramount leader or the *segundas personas* (lower-ranking leaders). If the Instructions of Viceroy Hurtado de Mendoza [1594]—by which the grant given by Viceroy Toledo was to be respected—were applied, the leaders of *parcialidad* could have continued to have access to two *fanegas de sembradura* of maize (or four *cargas*), while the *segundas personas* could make full use of one *fanega de*

92 AGN-A, XIII, leg. 914, s/f.

TABLE 6.1 Total of Indian tributaries and land measurements by *ayllus* and *parcialidades* of the *Repartimiento* of Macha, 1612–1619

Parcialidad/Ayllu	Maize(in *cargas de sembradura*)	Number of Tributaries
Ha/Alacollana	60,5	56
Ha/Sulcahavi	99,5	107
Ha/Guaracoata	94	107
Ha/Tapunata	73,5	70
Ha/Alapicha	90,5	75
Total Hanansaya	418	415
Hu/Mahacollana	84,5	116
Hu/Sulcahata	37	32
Hu/Guacoata	48,5	80
Hu/Condoata	53	50
Hu/Mahapicha	58	72
Total Hurinsaya	281	350

"PADRÓN POR EL QUE PAGAN SU TASA", AGN-A XIII, LEG. 914 S/F

sembradura of maize (or two *cargas*). In relation to the *ayllu* leaders, according to the *Padrón*, each of them had access to two *cargas de sembradura* of maize, even though Viceroy Toledo had granted them only one.[93]

On the other hand, the situation of the census units—or units delimitated in the document by the official—headed by tributary Indians differed according to the *parcialidad* to which they belonged. While in Hanansaya the vast majority of tributaries recorded one *carga de sembradura* of maize, in Hurinsaya the situation was more heterogeneous, due to the scarcity of land. Thus, for example, in the Mahacollana *ayllu*, there were married tributaries with numerous children with one or half a *carga de sembradura* of maize, married couples without children with one *carga* and other couples with one to three *almudes* "for lack of lands" (*por no aver tierras*),[94] while other single tributaries registered one *carga*. The Guacoata *ayllu* of the same *parcialidad* presented a similar situation, with married tributaries without children with plots of one *carga* and married tributaries with numerous children with half a *carga*, married tributaries that "do not have a plot in any part of the valleys" and single

93 AHCNM, Caja Real, 18, s/f.

94 AGN-A, XIII, leg. 914, fol. 436v.

tributaries without plots. The disparity of situations between both *parcialidades*, the absence of standardisation in land measurements among Hurinsaya tributaries, the lack of correlation between the demography of the census unit and the extension of the plot within the same *ayllu*, as well as Hurinsaya tributaries without land allocation, could all indicate the interference of supra-domestic spheres as still being in charge of the allocation of plots, their rotation and/or exclusion according to parental, socio-political, demographic, ecological, or other criteria not evident to those who were not part of the community. In other words, the aforementioned variation in the relationship between census units and communal land plots could suggest that the effort of officials to create or reinforce internal land assignments and domestic inheritance did not succeed in eliminating the roles played by supra-domestic units and their leaders in the periodical land distributions. Finally, it should be noted that, even for those tributaries with maize-producing plots, these did not exceed the one *carga de sembradura*, so that, bearing in mind the calculations of Fiscal Alfaro, those who gained access to plots with one *carga de sembradura* could only sow two *almudes* of maize, which barely guaranteed the consumption of the household for two months.

Other fiscal statuses showed the same heterogeneity in relation to the extension of their maize cultivation fields: while in Hanansaya the census units headed by old men and women had half a *carga de sembradura* of maize, in Hurinsaya the situation was again more heterogeneous. Thus, in addition to census units with the above measures, the Mahacollana *ayllu* had, for example, census units headed by old men without a plot, widows with children with two *almudes*, old women without *chacras*, and orphans with a half a *carga* and/or without a plot. In addition, many old women and disabled Indians from both *parcialidades* had an *almud de sembradura* of maize but without precise indication of the valley in which it was located, which suggests that the enumeration lacked any real material reference. Finally, approximately one percent of the total census units of the *Padrón* did not record measurements of maize-producing lands at all.

As reflected in the above, the tenancies of fiscal statuses, such as old, widowed, and *impedidos* (disabled), were not standardised according to the *Padrón* of Macha, demonstrating that the daily agrarian reality of the *repartimiento* had demanded the management of supra-domestic spheres that adjusted the scarcity of land according to the internal demands of a population hierarchised not only by fiscal criteria, but also by morally sanctioned parental, symbolic, and socio-political norms. Likewise, the dispossession of land, generated within the framework of the *composiciones*, had concrete effects not only on human's relations with the land but, above all, on the social relations internal to the *repartimiento*, generating census units that, at the time of the inspection, did not register any access to valley's lands. This was also accompanied by a generalised worsening of the population's quality of life, with domestic land extensions that did not guarantee the basic annual needs of maize production, making it difficult to generate an agricultural surplus capable of being commercialised for social reproduction.

If the viceregal and local guidelines emphasised the indigenous domestic unit as the basic unit of production and consumption, ideally satisfying in a regular way most of their subsistence needs through the control of inheritable land within a corporate territoriality, the lack of sufficient land for Macha *repartimiento* conspired against its consolidation as a productive unit, demanding the presence of collective management spheres that would achieve the social reproduction of the group as a whole. This was also reflected in the *Memoria de chácaras y anejos* which, by *parcialidades*, was presented by its leaders in 1619 and which listed the lands of the *repartimiento* of Macha by *parcialidad* and *ayllu*. According to it, the *parcialidades* did not control a concentrated area of land but rather the plots separated from each other, in an interdigitation that overlapped lands of both segments, especially in the valley. The strength of the supra-domestic spheres can be tested, even up to the middle of the 17th century, when the list of *mojones* granted by Joseph de la Vega Alvarado, the judge in a new process of *composiciones*, provided a demarcation of lands according to *ayllu*.[95] Its persistence reveals a set of norms, practices, and rules that governed the relationship between people and land within the corporate and parental structures of the Andean *repartimientos* that are difficult to find in the records.

Although *forasteros* were not registered in the *Padrón* because they were not considered part of the Macha *repartimiento*, other documentary sources confirmed the presence of more than 400 *forasteros* near its two *pueblos de reducción*.[96] Their analysis would exceed the scope of this Chapter, but it should be noted that their repeated mentions in different documentary series warn us of the importance of incorporating a perspective that considers, as proposed by Angelo Torre, the set of social actors that could have had access to communal resources beyond the members of the administrative units.[97]

Finally, the importance of supra-domestic spheres at the beginning of the 17th century could also be delineated through a deepening into the evolution of the generational inheritance of individual and/or domestic tenancies, a notion

95 Platt, *Estado boliviano y ayllu andino*, 173–181; Nicolas, *Los ayllus de Tinguipaya*, 99.

96 Jurado, "Doble domicilio", 622.

97 Torre, "Introduction", 600–604.

that had animated part of the juridical literature and local instructions since the end of the previous century. As mentioned above, for the *repartimiento* of Macha we have a record that the Magistrate Castro y Padilla assigned plots to Indians according to their fiscal categories; however, according to Don Pedro Soto, *cacique gobernador* in 1619, the royal official had only granted the lands for life. Thus, after the death of three widows to whom the magistrate had assigned plots in specific valleys—and perhaps motivated by the desire of their descendants to have access to the same lands or in order to keep them under his own personal influence—the paramount leader claimed that Castro y Padilla had determined that "after their death, [the lands] should be returned to the said *ayllu* [Sulcahavi] so that they own them and be succeeded by the remaining *indios* and *principales*".[98] Thus, the leader requested the *corregidor* of Chayanta, Antonio Salgado, to return the lands to the supra-domestic spheres "so they can be enjoyed be the *indios* and *indias* of said *ayllu* as their own".[99] This plasticity in the implementation and definition of rights of use and access on the one hand and rights of management and transference on the other, in a local and intergenerational dimension, allows us to give diachronic depth to the ethnographic analyses of the indigenous communities of the region, by suggesting that different historical conjunctures have been able to influence, shape, and contribute to the strengthening of the roles played by Andean households in the management of common use resources at present.[100]

The *corregidor* Salgado resolved the process in favour of the paramount leader's petition, interpreting not only the decisions made more than a decade earlier by the Charcas magistrate, but also the internal corporate rules, far from the intergenerational family inheritance that had been promoted since the late 16th century. The erosion of supra-domestic land management was possibly underway, but it was by no means homogeneously established among officials.

98 AGN-A, XIII, Leg. 914, fol. 381^{v}. "[…] despues de muertas, [las tierras] bolbiesen y quedasen para el dicho ayllo [Sulcahavi] para que fuesen suyas y sucedan en ellas los demas yndios e yndias principales de [e]l". For an exhaustive analysis of the litigation, see Jurado, "Tierra, estatus, viudez". For an analysis of a similar dynamic in the *pueblo* of Santiago de Catania (Huarochirí, present-day Peru) in the mid-17th century based on the concepts of commoning, uncommoning and recommoning, see Puente Luna, "Of Widows".

99 AGN-A, XIII, Leg. 914, fols. 381^{v}–381^{r}. "[…] para que las gozen los yndios e yndias del dicho ayllo como cosa suya".

100 Harris, "El parentesco y la economía vertical en el Ayllu Laymi (Norte de Potosí)", 59; Mayer, *Casa, chacra y dinero*, 62–69; Platt, "Espejos y maíz".

6 Final Considerations

For different areas within the Viceroyalty of Peru, the delimitation of domestic and inheritable plots, generation after generation within the Andean *repartimientos* was an objective of different magistrates and officials since at least the 1570s. However, the inspections carried out during the first process of *composición* of lands and sales of *baldíos* stand as a central juncture when weighing their practical execution. Ordered by the Royal Decrees of 1591, the regularisation of Spanish possessions through the payment of *composición*, sales of *baldíos*, and the structuring of urban spaces was accompanied by the inspection of the collective territoriality of the indigenous communities in order to guarantee the lands 'necessary' for their contemporary and future social reproduction. The royal order to guarantee to Indians enough lands linked in an imprecise way the indigenous 'needs' (*menester*) with their own agricultural-livestock capacity, and disposed of all those lands of indigenous domain, considered 'surplus' by the inspectors, for the royal benefit.

Its execution by the commission judges appointed by the Viceroy, Hurtado de Mendoza included a plurality of instructions and jurisdictional powers that made the existence of a supposedly homogeneous Hispanic perspective on the restructuring of Andean communal lands more complex. Some of the nuances that differentiated the dispositions executed in different jurisdictions of the Viceroyalty of Peru were to demarcate and grant plots to the Indians, taking management away, or not, from the *ayllus*, to standardise them according to the tributary categories or to grant variability according to the demography and/or productive capacity of the households, to expel *forasteros*, or not, from the lands of the *repartimiento*. For the district of Charcas in particular, there are fragmentary records that uncover the diverse impact of Friar López' actions in the delimitation of rights of use and management of the communal lands of the *repartimientos*. Moreover, the execution of the Royal Decrees of 1591 carried out by the second commissioned judge, Don Pedro Osores de Ulloa, between the years 1594 and 1597, has been overshadowed. But even during Friar López' period there was a diversity of actions, taking into account the fact that in some regions Friar López appointed Spanish *amojonadores* to delimit domestic and particular tenancies, while in others he entrusted the task to the local *corregidores* who, according to some complaints, postponed its execution.

This was the case for the *repartimiento* of Macha (North Potosí), for which Friar López instructed the *corregidor* of Chayanta to distribute three *cargas de sembradura* of maize to each tributary, a task that seems never to have been carried out. A lengthy litigation brought by its indigenous leaders allowed an approximation of the way in which the power relations of the agrarian environment shaped the delimitation of the 'necessary' extensions for each census unit, independently of the concrete yields calculated by the *Fiscal* of the Audiencia. One of the objectives of this Chapter has been to approach the social relations generated around the use and control of the land in the *repartimiento* of Macha after the passage of the inspectors linked to the committees of *composición* and the successive officials in charge of recomposing its diminished territoriality. For this purpose, and moving away from the dichotomies private/common and individual/collective, we proposed an interweaving of qualitative and quantitative information that would enable us to understand the domestic allocations and their attributions of use and exploitation of natural resources and the attributions of control and management of the supra-domestic spheres as a whole, regulated and morally sanctioned by the group contained in the *repartimiento*. Thus, 20 years after the land inspections developed within the framework of the first *composición* of lands and sales of *baldíos*, the *repartimiento* of Macha recorded in the *Padrón por el que pagan su tasa* (c. 1612–1619) census units with allocations of maize lands and manifested its particular distribution by the magistrate Castro y Padilla in a context of deep dispossession that, apparently, especially affected the Hurinsaya. In the case of Macha, the supra-domestic spheres, such as the *ayllus* and *parcialidades*, demonstrated their involvement in land management at least until the middle of the 17th century, even if the intrusions of officials in making communal rules evident to outsiders and regulating them according to their criteria left their mark.

Bibliography

Manuscripts

Archivo General de Indias, Sevilla (AGI)
Charcas 48
Indiferente 433, L. 2
Lima 273

Archivo General de la Nación-Argentina, Buenos Aires (AGNA-A)
XIII, legajo 886
XIII, legajo 914

Archivo Histórico de la Casa Nacional de la Moneda, Potosí (AHCNM)
Caja Real 18

Archivo y Biblioteca Nacional de Bolivia, Sucre (ABNB)
Correspondencia de la Audiencia de Charcas 510
Correspondencia de la Audiencia de Charcas 670
Expedientes Coloniales 1764.131

Biblioteca Nacional-Argentina, Buenos Aires (BNA)
Colección Gaspar García Viñas (GGV), Documento 3947

Printed Sources

Covarrubias Orozco, Sebastián de, *Tesoro de la lengua Castellana, o Española* [1611], Barcelona 1943.

Escalona Agüero, Gaspar de, *Gazofilacio Real del Reyno del Perú* [1645], La Paz 2018.

Guamán Poma de Ayala, Felipe, *Nueva crónica y buen gobierno* [1615], Murra, John, Rolena Adorno and Jorge Urioste (eds.), Crónicas de América 29, Madrid 1987.

Matienzo, Juan de, *Gobierno del Perú* [1567], Travaux de l'Institut FranÇais d'Etudes Andines XI, París-Lima 1967.

Ondegardo, Polo de, "Notables daños de no guardar a los indios sus fueros [1571]", in González, Laura and Alicia Alonso (eds.), *El mundo de los Incas*, Madrid 1990.

Recopilación de Leyes de Indias. Recovered from: https://www.memoriachilena.gob.cl/602/w3-article-93485.html

Literature

Abercrombie, Thomas, *Caminos de la memoria y del poder. Etnografía e historia de una comunidad andina*, La Paz 2006.

Agüero, Alejandro, "Las categorías básicas de la cultura jurisdiccional", in Lorente Sariñena, Marta (coord.), *De justicia de jueces a justicia de leyes: hacia la España de 1870*, Madrid 2006, 21–58.

Amado Gonzáles, Donato, "Reparto de tierras indígenas y la primera visita y composición general, 1591–1595", in *Histórica* XXII: 2 (1998), 197–207.

Assadourian, Carlos, "Agricultura y tenencia de la tierra antes y después de la Conquista", in *Población y Sociedad* 12/13 (2005/6), 3–56.

Bastias Saavedra, Manuel, "The normativity of possession. Rethinking land relations in early-modern Spanish America, ca. 1500–1800", in *Colonial Latin American Review* 29: 2 (2020), 223–238.

Clavero, Bartolomé, "La Monarquía, el Derecho y la Justicia", in Martínez Ruíz, Enrique and Magdalena de Pazzi Pi (coords.), *Instituciones de la España Moderna 1. Las Jurisdicciones*, Madrid 1996, 15–36.

Congost, Rosa, "¿Una nueva historia social del mundo rural?", in *Boletín del Instituto de Historia Argentina y Americana Dr. Emilio Ravignani* (Nº especial) (2022), 86–103.

Congost, Rosa, Jorge Gelman and Rui Santos, *Property Rights in Land. Issues in social, economic and global history*, London-New York 2017.

de la Cadena, Marisol, "Cooperación y mercado en la organización comunal andina", in *Revista Andina* 4:1 (1986), 31–58.

del Río, Mercedes, *Etnicidad, Territorialidad y Colonialismo. Tradición y Cambio entre los Soras del siglo XVI y XVII (Bolivia)*, La Paz 2005.

del Río, Mercedes, "Estrategias andinas de supervivencia. El control de recursos en Chaqui (siglos XVI–XVIII)", in *Anuario del IEHS* IV (1989), 53–84.

Diez de San Miguel, Garci, *Visita hecha a la provincia de Chucuito* [1567], Lima 1964.

Dueñas, Alcira, "The Virgin and the land surveyor: Andean pueblo boundary making in the Highlands of late colonial Ecuador", in *Colonial Latin American Review* 31:3 (2022), 304–326.

Esteban Estríngana, Alicia, "El servicio: paradigma de relación política en los siglos XVI y XVII", in Esteban Estríngana, Alicia (ed.), *Servir al rey en la Monarquía de los Austrias. Medios, fines y logros del servicio al soberano en los siglos XVI y XVII*, Madrid 2012, 11–45.

Gade, Daniel, "Reflexiones sobre el asentamiento andino desde la época toledana hasta el presente", in Segundo Moreno and Frank Salomon (comps.), *Reproducción y Transformación de las Sociedades Andinas. Siglos XVI–XX*, Quito 1991, 69–90.

Gandia, Enrique de, *Francisco de Alfaro y la condición social de los indios: Río de la Plata, Paraguay, Tucumán y Perú, siglos XVI y XVII*, Buenos Aires 1939.

Garriga, Carlos, "Las Audiencias: justicia y gobierno de las Indias", in Barrios, Feliciano (coord.), *El gobierno de un mundo. Virreinatos y Audiencias en la América Hispánica*, Cuenca 2004, 711–794.

Glave, Luis, "Propiedad de la tierra, agricultura y comercio, 1570–1700: el gran despojo", in Contreras, Carlos (ed.), *Compendio de historia económica del Perú*, Lima 2009, 291–423.

Glave, Luis Miguel and María Isabel Remy, *Estructura agraria y vida rural en una región andina: Ollantaytambo entre los siglos XVI–XIX*, Cusco 1983.

Golte, Jürgen, *La racionalidad de la organización andina*, Lima 1980.

Gonzáles Escudero, Damián, "Una aproximación procesal a la defensa de la tierra indígena en los Andes centrales en el Estado virreinal temprano (1550–1560)", in *Revista de la Maestría en Derecho Procesal* 7:1 (2017), 71–100.

Graubart, Karen, "'Ynuvaciones malas e rreprouadas': Seeking Justice in the Early Colonial Pueblos de Indios", in Owensby, Brian and Richard Ross (ed.), *Justice in a New World: Negotiating Legal Intelligibility in British, Iberian, and Indigenous America*, New York 2018, 151–180.

Greer, Allan, *Property and Dispossession: Natives, Empires and Land in Early Modern North America*, Cambridge 2018.

Harris, Olivia, "El parentesco y la economía vertical en el Ayllu Laymi (Norte de Potosí)", in *Avances* 1 (1978), 51–64.

Herzog, Tamar, "Colonial Law and 'Native Customs': Indigenous Rights in Colonial Spanish America", in *The Americas* 69:3 (2013), 303–321.

Jurado, María Carolina, "Diálogos transatlánticos e interpretaciones locales de las Reales Cédulas de 1591: comunicación política y oficiales reales en torno a las composiciones de tierras y venta de baldíos en el virreinato del Perú", in *Revista Complutense de Historia de América* 50:1 (2024): 127–150.

Jurado, María Carolina, "Baldíos, derechos posesorios y tierra realenga en el primer proceso de composición en el distrito de Charcas. Virreinato del Perú, 1591–1597", in *América Latina en la Historia Económica* 29: 1 (2022), 1–24.

Jurado, María Carolina, "La composición como concierto. Prácticas judiciales en espacios rurales durante el primer proceso de visita y composición de tierras y de extranjeros en Charcas. Virreinato del Perú, 1591–1597", in *Prohistoria* XXI: 29 (2018), 19–42.

Jurado, María Carolina, "Tierra, estatus y viudez: variabilidad y tensión en los hogares indígenas rurales. A propósito del repartimiento de Macha (Charcas) en el siglo XVII", in *Andes* 29:1 (2018), 1–33.

Jurado, María Carolina, "'it is not fair that he is treated as indio particular': The Indian Elite in the Repartimiento of Macha under Colonial Rule. Viceroyalty of Peru, 1540–1619", in *Colonial Latin American Review* 25: 3 (2016), 300–324.

Jurado, María Carolina, "'(...) muy mañoso para esto'. Comisiones para don Pedro Osores de Ulloa, segundo juez de composición de tierras de Charcas, 1594–1596", in *Corpus* 4:2 (2014), 1–24.

Jurado, María Carolina, "Doble domicilio: relaciones sociales y complementariedad ecológica en el norte de Potosí (Bolivia) del temprano siglo XVII", in *Chungara. Revista de Antropología Chilena* 45: 4 (2013), 613–630.

Lanteri, Sol, María Fernanda Barcos and Serrano Jiménez, "Pluralismo de derechos de propiedad y privatización de tierras del común en las épocas moderna y contemporánea. América y España en perspectiva comparada", in *Anuario IEHS* 35: 1 (2020), 123–134.

Málaga Medina, Alejandro, "Las reducciones toledanas en el Perú", in Gutiérrez, Ramón (coord.), *Pueblos de indios. Otro urbanismo en la región andina*, Quito 1993, 263–316.

Mariluz Urquijo, José, *El régimen de la tierra en el Derecho Indiano*, Buenos Aires 1978.

Masuda, Shozo, Izumi Shimada and Craig Morris (eds.), *Andean Ecology and Civilization. An Interdisciplinary Perspective on Andean Ecological Complementarity*, Tokyo 1986.

Mayer, Enrique, *Casa, chacra y dinero. Economías domésticas y ecología en los Andes*, Lima 2004.

Menegus, Margarita, "Dos modelos de propiedad indígena en la transición. De la época colonial al siglo XIX", in Álvarez, Salvador, Margarita Menegus and Alejandro Tortolero, (comps.), *Derechos de propiedad y crecimiento económico en la historia agraria: contribuciones para una perspectiva comparada en América y Europa*, Bogotá 2018, 137–152.

Morlon, Pierre (ed.), *Comprender la Agricultura Campesina en los Andes Centrales*, Lima-Cusco 1996.

Mossbrucker, Harald, *La economía campesina y el concepto de "comunidad". Un enfoque crítico*, Lima 1990.

Murra, John, *El mundo andino. Población, medio ambiente y economía*, Lima 2002.

Murra, John, *La organización económica del Estado Inca*, México 1999.

Murra, John, *Formaciones económicas y políticas del mundo andino*, Lima 1975.

Nicolas, Vincent, *Los ayllus de Tinguipaya. Ensayos de historia a varias voces*, La Paz 2015.

Ots Capdequi, José, *España en América. El régimen de tierras en la época colonial*, México 1959.

Palomeque, Silvia, "Los chichas y las visitas toledanas. Las tierras de los chichas de Talina (1573–1595)", in *Surandino Monográfico* 1: 2 (2010), 1–71.

Pease, Franklin, "La noción de propiedad entre los Incas: Una aproximación", in Masuda, Shozo (ed.), *Etnografía e historia del mundo andino: Continuidad y cambio*, Tokio 1986, 3–33.

Penry, Elizabeth, *The People Are King. The Making of an Indigenous Andean Politics*, New York 2019.

Pérez Miguel, Liliana and Renzo Honores, "Cacicas, Land, and Litigation in Seventeenth-Century Chincha, Peru", in Ochoa, Margarita and Sara Vicuña Guengerich (ed.), *Cacicas. The Indigenous Women Leaders of Spanish America, 1492–1825*, Norman 2021, 189–214.

Platt, Tristan, *Estado boliviano y ayllu andino. Tierra y tributo en el norte de Potosí*, Lima 1982.

Platt, Tristan, "Espejos y maíz: el concepto de yanantin entre los Macha de Bolivia", in Mayer, Enrique and Ralph Bolton (eds.), *Parentesco y matrimonio en los Andes*, Lima 1980, 139–182.

Platt, Tristan, Therese Bouysse-Cassagne and Olivia Harris, *Qaraqara-Charka. Mallku, Inka y Rey en la provincia de Charcas (siglos XV–XVII). Historia antropológica de una confederación aymara*, La Paz 2006.

Puente Luna, José de la, "Of Widows, Furrows, and Seed: New Perspectives on Land and the Colonial Andean Commons", in *Hispanic American Historical Review* 101:3 (2021), 375–407.

Puente Luna, José Carlos de la, "That Which Belongs to All: Khipus, Community, and Indigenous Legal Activism in the Early Colonial Andes", in *The Americas* 72: 1 (2015), 19–54.

Puente Luna, José Carlos de la and Renzo Honores, "Guardianes de la real justicia:

Alcaldes de indios, costumbre y justicia local en Huarochirí colonial", in *Histórica* 40: 2 (2016), 11–47.

Ramírez, Susan, *El mundo al revés. Contactos y conflictos transculturales en el Perú del siglo XVI*, Lima 2002.

Ramírez, Susan, "Land and Tenure in Early Colonial Peru: Individualizing the *Sapci*, 'that which is common to all'", in *The Medieval Globe* 2: 2 (2016), 33–70.

Rasnake, Roger, *Autoridad y poder en los Andes. Los kuraqkuna de Yura*, La Paz 1989.

Saito, Akira and Claudia Rosas Lauro (eds.), *Reducciones. La concentración forzada de las poblaciones indigenas en el virreinato del Perú*, Lima 2017.

Sarabia Viejo, María Justina, *Francisco de Toledo. Disposiciones gubernativas para el Virreinato del Perú, 1569–1574*, Sevilla 1986.

Sendón, Pablo, *Ayllus del Ausangate. Parentesco y organización social en los Andes del sur peruano*, Lima 2016.

Stavig, Ward, "Ambiguous Visions: Nature, Law, and Culture in Indigenous-Spanish Land Relations in Colonial Peru", in *Hispanic American Historical Review* 80: 1 (2000), 77–111.

Stern, Steve, *Los pueblos indígenas del Perú y el desafío de la conquista española. Huamanga hasta 1640*, Madrid 1982.

Tau Anzoátegui, Victor, "Órdenes normativos y prácticas socio-jurídicas. La justicia", in *Academia Nacional de la Historia*, Buenos Aires 1999, II, 283–316.

Torre, Angelo, "Introduction", in Special Issue "Ethnography of the Commons", in *Quaderni Storici* 3 (2021): 593–606.

Vallejo, Jesús, "El cáliz de plata. Articulación de órdenes jurídicos en la jurisprudencia del Ius Commune", in *Revista de Historia del Derecho* 38 (2009), 1–13.

Zagalsky, Paula, "El concepto de "comunidad" en su dimensión espacial. Una historización de su semántica en el contexto colonial andino (siglos XVI–XVII)", in *Revista Andina* 48 (2009): 57–90.

Zuloaga Rada, Marina, "Las haciendas ganaderas de las parroquias indígenas en los Andes norcentrales y del sur en el periodo colonial", in *XI Congreso Internacional de la AEB*, Sucre, 2023.

Zuloaga Rada, Marina, "Las reducciones: el proyecto, su aplicación y su evolución en Huaylas, Perú (siglos XVI y XVII)", in Saito, Akira and Claudia Rosas Lauro (eds.), *Reducciones. La concentración forzada de las poblaciones indigenas en el virreinato del Perú*, Lima 2017, 307–346.

CHAPTER 7

Concordias, Sentencias Arbitrales and *Vistas*

Ownership and Possession of Grassland in the Valleys of Ansó and Hecho (17th–19th Centuries)

Íñigo Ena Sanjuán

1 Introduction

On 25 October 1881, the representatives of the Aragonese town councils of Ansó and Hecho met at the borderline between the valleys, in the area called la Escarroneta. The purpose of the meeting was to maintain good relationships between the two and to solve any issues that may have arisen regarding grazing on the pastures between both valleys. The municipal corporations agreed that the relationships between them would continue to be regulated according to an agreement called *concordia*. The minutes of the meeting state:

> And second, and considering the *concordia* as a document that settles the regime and procedures that the town councils of Ansó and Hecho must follow, [it has been decided] that it [the agreement must] be considered as being in force both in practice and in court for all the situations stipulated and defined in the *concordia*, and if it was suspected that its clauses could be violated by any law or authority, both municipalities may appeal to higher echelons requesting that all its covenants have force and vigour.[1]

In short, the town councils agreed that the compromise would be respected even if any authority or law contradicted its covenants. They would defend the pact in court and would share the costs. Interestingly, the agreement had been signed almost three centuries earlier, in 1604, and was one among many other

1 "Y segundo, que considerandose dicha Concordia como un documento que establece el regimen y marcha en que se han de producir los referidos Ayuntamientos de Ansó y Hecho, que se conceptue con fuerza y valor lo mismo particularmente que en juicio para todos los actos estipulados y definidos en la misma, y como de que por la sospecha que sus disposiciones puedan ser contrariadas por alguna ley ó autoridad, se recurra en alzada á la superioridad ambos Municipios suplicando tenga fuerza y valor en todos los artículos contenidos en la misma"; in AMA, 228/4.

 | DOI:10.1163/9789004722729_008

pacts and agreements between the valleys of Ansó and Hecho. The 1604 pact was a *concordia*, a compromise between the valley councils to regulate the possession and use of common pastures. These pacts lasted decades, sometimes centuries, and were constantly redefined by conflicts and negotiations between the signing parties and were revived through meetings of the corporations at the boundaries of both valleys.

This Chapter intends to explain how the ownership, possession, and use of grassland were regulated in the Aragonese Pyrenees between the late medieval period and the 19th century. Even though the text focuses on the valleys of Ansó and Hecho, the actors, negotiations, procedures, and legal formulae used in this region were very similar to those of the rest of the mountain range, both on the Northern and Southern slopes. The Chapter aims to examine the production, form, interpretation, and implementation of norms regarding the property and possession of pastures which were commons of both valleys. Historiography has emphasised that the notion of ownership prior to the 19th century was different from the regimes which took shape and were consolidated after the rise of the modern, liberal states.[2] Property was the result of practices, that is, of regular human actions, defined by and defining the context in which they are performed.[3] Due to their normative character, practices usually gave rise to conflicts which had to be solved through negotiations. This is to say that ownership, possession, and use were constantly negotiated.[4]

The legal instruments used by the actors, corporations, and communities varied and were interpreted differently throughout the medieval, early modern, and modern periods. However, the formulae were widespread in the Iberian world—and beyond—and present many similarities. It is therefore surprising that they have received so little historiographical attention. The instruments must be contextualised in the wider framework of the *convenientiae* or compromise contracts which were shaped by uses and customs but offered considerable margin for negotiation between the parties involved.[5] The so-called *pacerías* or *passeries* are the best-known example of these formulae. These agreements, whose name probably derives from the Latin word "pax" (peace), were signed by French and Spanish valleys to settle disputes and to ensure good relationships among them in certain areas, such as trade, the transit of people,

2 Grossi, *Un altro modo di possedere*; Congost, "La 'gran obra' de la propiedad".

3 Bastias Saavedra, "The Normativity of Possession", 229. A wider theoretical framework can be found in Duve, "What Is Global Legal History?". For the notion of practice, see Stern, "The Practical Turn".

4 Lana Berasain and Laborda Pemán, "El anidamiento institucional".

5 Grossi, El orden jurídico medieval, 116–118.

and the use of natural resources, especially pastures.[6] Some of the instruments examined in this Chapter are identical to these *pacerías*, but they have received far less historiographical attention.[7] The predominance both in qualitative and quantitative terms of compromise contracts, such as the *sentencias arbitrales* (arbitration agreement) and *concordias* (compromise agreements) over judicial sentences, is a clear demonstration of the preference of locals for negotiation and pact over litigation in court. As argued below, this can be explained by the lower cost, faster resolution and higher effectiveness and flexibility of the agreements in comparison with the verdict of judges.

Leaving aside the idealisation of the pacts by some older studies, more recent works are rather descriptive and make assumptions regarding the existence and capacity of the state prior to the 19th century. For some authors, it is clear that the state, whatever or whoever it was, tended to curtail local autonomy and to intervene in local affairs, especially from the 18th century onwards. They also assert that the state played a key role in the decline of the agreements.[8] This Chapter intends to observe those pacts from a different perspective. The starting premise here is that the modern state did not exist prior to the mid-18th century. The polities to which the valleys of Ansó and Hecho belonged—the Crown of Aragon first and the Hispanic monarchy later—were polycentric, plural, and jurisdictional political entities.[9] In practical terms, this means that, even though the Aragonese monarchs had granted the valleys the possession and use of pastures through privileges and charters in the medieval period, thereafter the valley councils discussed the validity of the privileges and regulated how, when, and by whom grassland was owned and exploited. Although the monarch continued to be the supreme arbiter, access

6 The best-known example of *pacería* is the Tribute of the Three Cows, the oldest transboundary agreement in Europe still in force, signed by the Navarrese Valle de Roncal and the Bearnese Vallée de Barétous in 1375. A seminal article is Cavaillès, "Une fédération pyrénéenne sous l'ancien régime". It was compiled together with works by other authors in Cavaillès, *Lies et passeries dans les Pyrénées*. For the Tributo de las Tres Vacas, see Idoate, *La comunidad del Valle de Roncal*, 144–145.

7 Le Nail, "Présentation", vii–viii. In fact, some of the agreements between valleys from different sides of the borderline were also called *concordias*, such as the pact signed by the valleys of Ansó and Aspe in 1608, located in AMA, 216/18.

8 Cavaillès, *Lies et passeries dans les Pyrénées*; Soulet, *Les Pyrénées au XIXe siècle*; Razquín Lizarraga et al., "Las facerías internacionales en el Pirineo". This is also visible in works from other disciplines, such as geography or ethnography; see Gorría Ipas, *El Pirineo como espacio frontera*; Pallaruelo Campo, *Pastores del Pirineo*.

9 Hespanha, As vésperas do Leviathan; Cardim et al., Polycentric Monarchies; Benton and Ross, Legal pluralism and empires.

to land was decided by those corporations in a largely autonomous way.[10] Thus, this Chapter explores how the valley councillors, officers, shepherds, and inhabitants of Ansó and Hecho produced and put into practice norms regarding the possession, ownership, and use of the *términos, montes, puertos,* and *partidas*—the different terms used to name grassland—between the 17th and 19th centuries.

To do so, sources from local and regional archives have been examined. There are no documents of the conflicts between the valleys in the archives of the monarchy, as those issues were solved in Saragossa, the Aragonese capital, and, above all, in the local arenas. The funds of the court of the Justicia de Aragón and the Real Audiencia, which are preserved in the Archivo Histórico Provincial de Zaragoza, contain some lawsuits between both valley councils. The interest of the records of the trials lies in the arguments used by the actors to ascertain their rights over grassland: they invoked immemorial possession, uninterrupted use or the leasing of pastures, just to cite a few. Yet the lawsuits are not as important as the sources of the local archives. As the medieval and early modern documents of the municipal archives of Hecho were lost during the Peninsular War (1808–1814), the backbone of this Chapter are the documents of Ansó's municipal archives. The use of municipal sources is rather uncommon, as well as one of the main strengths of this Chapter. There are studies focused on remote villages and valleys, but they mainly rely on royal laws and ordinances kept in regional archives. The funds of municipal archives, usually poorly classified and organised, allow historians to explore the daily practice of the pacts between Pyrenean valleys through different types of sources, ranging from the minutes of the valley councils to the agreements between valleys.[11] The pre-eminence of local sources in this Chapter is an eloquent demonstration of the highly local character of the regulation of the possession and use of land before the modern era.

To analyse these instruments and the practices associated with them in detail, and for the sake of clarity, the diverse types of documents are examined in separate sections. The following section briefly introduces the institutional structure and legal status of the valleys of Ansó and Hecho, together with the pastures that were under dispute and the medieval and early modern precedents of the conflicts between both valleys. The third section examines the

10 This is very similar to what it is described in Herzog, *Frontiers of possession*.

11 In the inventories, these pacts are catalogued under simple categories, such as *concordias, sentencias arbitrales, vistas* or *mojonaciones*, among others. This classification, however, does not help to understand how the norms regarding pastures worked, as these sources were normally hybrid and included references to other texts.

abovementioned *concordia* from 1604 and other agreements and *sentencias arbitrales* of the 17th century. The fourth section explores the performance of those pacts through the meetings of the representatives of the valley councils, the imposition of fines, and the examination of milestones between the 17th and 19th centuries.

2 The Valley Councils and Their Privileges over Grassland

Towns and villages on both slopes of the Pyrenees were organised into valleys. Even though every locality had its own council, the villages of the same valley met in a general assembly.[12] This was the case for Ansó and Hecho. While the former consisted of two localities, namely the town of Ansó and the village of Fago, Hecho had a varying composition throughout the medieval and the early modern period. The main town was Hecho, and the villages of Urdués and Siresa were also part of the valley for some periods. Normally the head towns of the valley had more representatives, power, and influence at the meetings of the valley council. Both the towns and the valleys were corporations, that is, their assemblies, magistrates, and officers exerted jurisdiction over all of their respective territories.[13] The life of the communities was regulated by the ordinances they formed that the king approved through his officers. The ordinances regulated the functioning of the offices and institutions and determined how, when and by whom pastures and forests could be exploited, the fines and punishments in case of infringement, the supervising officers, etcetera.[14]

Grassland was central in the Pyrenean economies, which were based on cattle breeding. According to the availability of grass, pastures were divided into carefully regulated categories. Every piece of grassland was reserved for certain animal species and opened and closed at different times of the year. Mountain pastures, for instance, were exploited from approximately May to September, when sheep moved to the lowland in the phenomenon known as transhumance. As in almost every Pyrenean valley, the economies of Ansó and Hecho were mainly based on sheep breeding. The inhabitants of the valleys

12 Geography was not deterministic, though. With Ansó, for instance, some villages of the valley of the Veral river did not belong to the valley of Ansó (for example, Biniés), while the village of Fago, which is not located in the Veral valley, depended on the town of Ansó.

13 Agüero, "Las categorías básicas de la cultura jurisdiccional".

14 Tomás Faci and Laliena López, *Ansó*, 73 and ff.; Calvo Eito, *Valle de Hecho*, 50–54. The successive ordinations of Ansó can be found in AMA, 223/5 and 223/6.

also raised cattle, goats, and oxen, as well as horses and pigs, but the bulk of the animals were—and in some cases still are—sheep.[15]

To feed their flocks, Hecho and Ansó enjoyed wide areas of grassland. Pastures had been granted to the valleys by the medieval monarchs as a reward for their loyalty and their defence of the frontiers against the French and the Navarrese. In the case of Hecho, the privileges that endowed the valley with land date from 1122, from the reign of Alfonso I of Aragon, and were ratified by his successors in Aragon and the Hispanic monarchy until 1758, when Fernando VI ratified them for the last time.[16] As for Ansó, in 1234 Jaime I of Aragon promulgated a privilege by which he granted the valley the *partidas* and *términos* (areas of grassland), which still belong to Ansó and Fago (see Figure 7.1). The privilege was ratified by other kings, such as Pedro IV of Aragon, Carlos I, and Fernando el Católico.[17] Although the privilege was ratified for the last time in 1626 by King Felipe IV, royal confirmation was neither the only nor the main or most frequent form of proving possession.[18] Ownership and possession over the pastures were ratified through trials and judicial sentences, especially through the lawsuit called "firma" or "jurisfirma", by which the Justicia de Aragón, during the *foral* period, and the Real Audiencia, after 1711, inhibited any judge from disturbing the possessor of an asset or right in his/her possession. The claimant had to argue why those assets or rights belonged to or were possessed by him/her. The valleys of Hecho and Ansó resorted to this legal formula to ensure the possession of some pastures.[19] Similarly, when the valley councillors or the proxies of the valley councils signed agreements, they accepted the parties' ownership, possession, and/or rights of use over land. The acceptance was later invoked as a recognition of ownership and/or possession.

The pastures which were under dispute are located between the two valleys, near the headwaters of the river Aragón Subordán. Today, this area is called Guarrinza and belongs to Ansó and Hecho jointly, but in the medieval and early modern period it was known as Soasqui. By virtue of Jaime I's privilege

15 Fillat Estaqué et al., *Pastos del Pirineo*; Pallaruelo Campo, *Pastores del Pirineo*; Fernández Otal, *La Casa de Ganaderos de Zaragoza*; Gómez de Valenzuela, *Documentos sobre ganadería*; Pascua Echegaray, *Señores del paisaje*; Vaccaro and Beltran, *Social and ecological history of the Pyrenees*.

16 Calvo Eito, *Valle de Hecho*, 55–57.

17 Tomás Faci and Laliena López, *Ansó*, 148–153. The privileges and successive confirmations can be found in AMA, 205, 219, 223, 256.

18 This is the last confirmation that could be located in the archives of Ansó; in AMA, 223/4.

19 An example of this is the *firma* gained by the valley council of Hecho in 1691 and quoted again below; in AHPZ, J/766/20. For the legal formula, see La Ripa y Marraco, *Ilustración*, 185–279.

FIGURE 7.1
Eighteenth-century sketch of the Ansó Valley. The pastures which were under dispute were on the right side of the picture, around number 23, the item called Guarrinza.
ARCHIVO HISTÓRICO PROVINCIAL DE ZARAGOZA, C/MPGD/120.

from 1234, Soasqui and other pastures close to it (Segarra, Allarat, Reclusa, Estibiella, Tortiella) came to be the property of the Ansó Valley. As in almost every Pyrenean valley, many lands that belonged to Hecho and Ansó were commons, i.e., they could be freely used by the *vecinos* (literally, neighbours; inhabitants of the valleys).[20] This does not mean that they could be used at whim. As mentioned above, commons were thoroughly regulated by the valley councils. They established periods for the use of grassland, limits on the number of heads of livestock that could graze in every pasture, officers to supervise and impose

20 Other pastures were the *propios*, that is, they belonged to the valley, but could not be exploited by the *vecinos* freely, but it was the valley council which decided who could use them. Those pastures were often leased under certain conditions to foreign sheep breeders, called *herbajantes* (from "hierba", meaning grass); in Gómez de Valenzuela, *Documentos sobre ganadería*, 18–26.

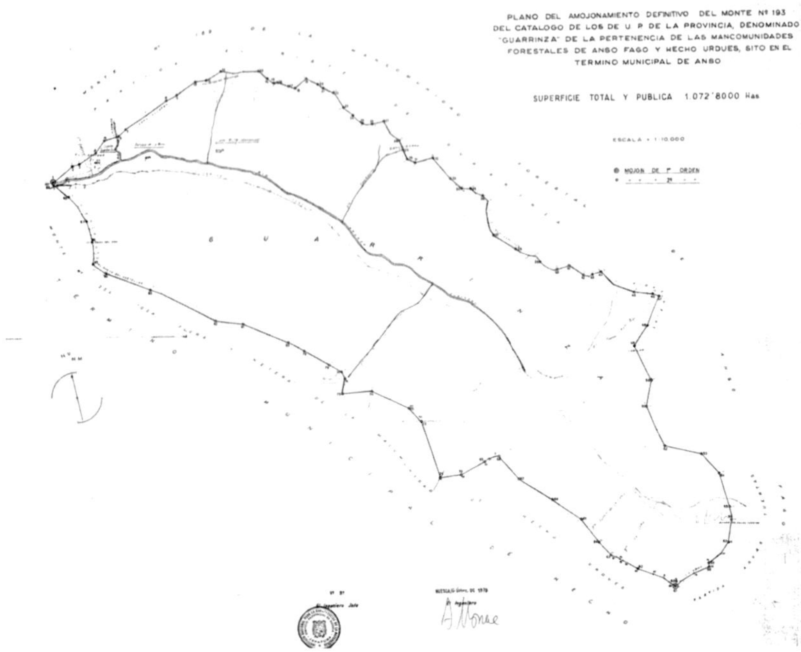

FIGURE 7.2 Modern map of the *partida* called Guarrinza (previously Soasqui). CATALOG OF MONTES DE UTILIDAD PÚBLICA OF ARAGON; HTTPS://APLICACIONES.ARAGON.ES/INAMUP/ (LAST CONSULTATION ON 15-III-2023).

fines on those who contravened the norms, among others: a series of rules, in short, to ensure the sustainable exploitation of the commons.[21]

From the very moment of the concession of the privilege by Jaime I to Ansó in 1234, conflicts between the two valleys arose. The sheep breeders of Hecho wanted to keep using the pastures that had been granted to Ansó. The monarch ordered that, although the pastures belonged to Ansó, the *vecinos* of both valleys would be allowed to use the grassland. But disputes persisted and, in the early 14th century, one of King Jaime II of Aragon's officers tried to settle them by issuing a sentence. There was a period of 100 years of relative peace but, from the early 15th century, conflicts between Ansó and Hecho reappeared. The council of Hecho argued that the ecclesiastical Chapter of San Pedro de Siresa had been granted the pastures that belonged to Ansó centuries before the promulgation of the privilege of Jaime I (1234). The monastery was an inde-

21 Ostrom, *Governing the commons*; De Moor et al., "Ruling the Commons"; Lana Berasain and Laborda Pemán, "El anidamiento institucional".

pendent ecclesiastical corporation, but it was located in the Hecho Valley and was closely related to it. Seven people from Hecho and eight from Ansó died in fights between them, and the attempts of the king and his officers to settle the disputes were in vain.[22]

The conflict came to an end thanks to a *sentencia arbitral* promulgated in 1431. This instrument was a verdict given by one or more arbiters, generally appointed by the involved parties who were incapable of reaching an agreement by themselves. In some cases, the arbiters were not appointed by the parties, but by a third party, for instance, a king or a bishop; this normally happened when the conflict was acrimonious. Arbiters were usually noblemen, local authorities, magistrates, and/or clergymen. Sometimes, as in one of the cases mentioned below, the arbiters were locals, people who knew the terrain and the history of the opposing parties firsthand.[23] In other cases, for example, in the abovementioned Tribute of the Three Cows, the parties resorted to non-locals to give a *sentencia arbitral*. In that case, the valleys of Roncal and Barétous appointed some officers and *vecinos* from Ansó as arbiters.[24] When new conflicts arose, the arbiters acted as mediators and impartial interpreters of the *sentencia*, whose clauses were binding and could not be contested. Therefore, the parties gave up the possibility of appealing to higher authorities. In theory, nothing but a later agreement between the parties could derogate the clauses of a *sentencia arbitral*, but, in practice, conflicts arose as a consequence of opposed interpretations of the pacts by the parties. In any case, the advantages of this formula vis-à-vis judicial sentences include lower costs, swifter resolutions, and better adaptations of the verdict to the local circumstances, as arbiters knew, sometimes first-hand, the reality of the parties and/or the issue under dispute.

In 1431, the arbiter was a nobleman named Ximeno de Urrea. He listened to the representatives of both Ansó and Hecho, who presented their privileges and tried to prove their rights over the pastures in dispute, and eventually gave a verdict. The arbiter decided that Soasqui, Segarra, Allarat, and Reclusa belonged to Ansó; however, he also established that the *vecinos* of Hecho could use Soasqui freely and the rest of the pastures with some restrictions. The

22 Tomás Faci and Laliena López, *Ansó*, 173–178.

23 For further references and examples, see Baró Pazos, "Los límites territoriales", 430–432. I thank Camilla de Freitas Macedo for this reference.

24 In turn, the Frenchmen mediated between Roncal and Ansó when they could not solve their conflicts autonomously. This arbitration formula was known as "tercera tierra"; in Gorría Ipas, *Las relaciones transfronterizas*, 101–103.

agreement was to last 101 years.[25] Tomás Faci and Laliena López point out that the *sentencia arbitral* of 1431 represented a milestone in the relationships and agreements between Ansó and Hecho, as it laid down the guidelines for the possession and exploitation of the pastures between both valleys. Nevertheless, they also explain that the *sentencia* did not put an end to the disputes and they enumerate and briefly describe other pacts signed between both valleys to define the limits of the valleys and to regulate the use of grassland.[26] Here the most relevant early modern precedents of the 17th-century agreements are succinctly described.

In 1516, the representatives of Ansó, Hecho and the Chapter of San Pedro de Siresa inspected the milestones that marked the limits of the valleys. These examinations, called "*vista*", "*visura*" or "*mojonación*", consisted in inspecting the signs with the shape of a cross carved in rocks ("mugas", "buegas", "mojones")—which were in the borderline between the valleys—and renewing those that were no longer visible.[27] In the case of the *mojonación* of 1516, it is worth noting that the ecclesiastical Chapter of Siresa was very present, as the valley council of Hecho had used the privileges of the ancient monastery to claim rights over the pastures that belonged to Ansó. In any case, the parties constantly alluded to the "spirit of iniquity" that had existed between them and insisted that they had to preserve the harmonious relationship they had built. The representatives of the valleys and the chapter of Siresa examined the milestones of Landarrera, Reclusa, Allarat, Estibiella, Tortiella, Sayestico, Laliena, Lajerito and Maquerán, that is, of the *partidas* that surrounded Soasqui.[28]

Three years later, in 1519, the valleys of Hecho and Ansó resorted again to the mediation of arbiters to solve their differences regarding the passes that gave access to the pastures they both exploited. Unlike the previous *sentencia arbitral*, which was dictated by a mediator who was not from the valleys, in 1519 the arbiters were local authorities—*alcaldes* and *jurados* of Ansó and Hecho, and *vecinos* of both towns—together with people from other localities, such as a notary from the town of Sos del Rey Católico. The *sentencia arbitral* included a *mojonación*. For instance, the first pass (*paso* in the sources) whose use was discussed was the so-called "estrecho de Bubalo". The local authorities of Hecho "have pretended and still pretend from immemorial time until today that they have the right, use and possession of passing with their livestock" without per-

25 AMA, 219/6.

26 Tomás Faci and Laliena López, *Ansó*, 179–182.

27 This procedure is further explained below, in the fourth section.

28 AMA, 223bis/36. Some of the names of the *partidas* are different today (for example, Lajerito—Acherito).

mission from the town council of Ansó.[29] The arbiters first examined the limits of the pass by inspecting and renewing the milestones. Then, they decided that the *vecinos* of the Valley of Hecho could use the pass whenever they wished, both up and down the mountain. They also determined that the guards of the pastures appointed by the town council of Ansó could not prevent them from going through the pass. The same process was repeated with other passes, such as Celia, Navasal, and el Achar de la Forca. One of the parties claimed its right to use the pass, the milestones were inspected and the right to use it was granted by the arbiters.[30]

Another *sentencia arbitral* was issued by the Archbishop of Saragossa, Hernando de Aragón, in 1570. It regarded the *partidas* of Allarat and Segarra. The clergyman decided that, if there were more than 1,200 heads of Ansó's livestock in those pastures, the herds of Hecho could not enter.[31] In the 1590s, conflicts over the use of Soasqui arose again. The parties did not manage to reach a pact regarding the limits of the common pastures. In 1593, the Real Audiencia of Aragon issued a judicial sentence which confirmed that the *término* of Soasqui and the land granted by King Jaime I to Ansó legitimately belonged to that valley. The court ruling is particularly interesting because it contains the arguments and evidence provided by the attorney of Ansó. He invoked the use and possession of land since time immemorial, the imposition of fines and the leasing of pastures to foreign herders as a demonstration that all those *partidas* were owned by Ansó.[32] In 1596 a new revision of the boundaries between the valleys took place. It was ordered by the king himself through the Real Audiencia and executed by the Justicia de Jaca (a judicial officer of the main city of the Aragonese Pyrenees), hence its name, "*mojonación real*". The disputes would not be settled until 1600 and 1604, when another *sentencia arbitral* and a *concordia* were signed.[33]

The wide areas of grassland located on the borderline between Ansó and Hecho were under dispute for centuries. Even though the land had been granted to the valley councils by the Aragonese monarchs through privileges, the possession and use of land were controversial and had to be continually negotiated. Both corporations, together with the ecclesiastical Chapter of Siresa,

29 "[…] han pretendido y pretenden de tiempo immemorial aca estar en drcho uso y possession de passar liberamente con sus ganados".

30 AMA, 223bis/19. For some passes, the arbiters established limits on the dates and seasons they could use them.

31 AMA, 256/9.

32 AMA, 223/13. As in the case of the *sentencia arbitral*, this judicial sentence also contained a *mojonación*.

33 For the *mojonación real*, see AMA, 223bis/20.

claimed rights over grassland and several mountain passes. Solutions did not come from above, from the monarchs or the royal courts, but generally from below, from the local actors and corporations. After bloody conflicts, they devised formulae to regulate the possession and use of land, recognising Ansó's jurisdiction over the *partidas* and *términos* but granting rights of use to the *vecinos* of Hecho. The pacts had to be periodically renewed, as conflicts did not cease to arise.

3 The End of the Disputes: The 17th-Century *Sentencias* and *Concordia*

In the 17th and 18th centuries, the local authorities, *vecinos* and sheep breeders of Hecho continued to contest the exclusive possession of grassland by Ansó through their practices: they drove their flocks to graze into Ansó's pastures, they built a bridge to facilitate the access of their cattle into the grassland, and they chopped wood in the *partidas*. The local authorities and guards of Ansó considered that these practices threatened or directly violated the *sentencias arbitrales* that had been signed in the Middle Ages, and conflicts arose again. However, in the 17th century the valleys signed a series of agreements that settled their differences and laid the foundations for a more stable and peaceful relationship. In addition to the verdicts of the Aragonese Real Audiencia and Justicia, the valleys of Ansó and Hecho signed several *sentencias arbitrales* and, for the first time, a *concordia*. Those would be the norms that served as the basis for the management of the common pastures and passes between the late 17th and early 20th centuries.

The first of those agreements was the *sentencia arbitral* approved in Saragossa in 1600. Ansó and Hecho had several lawsuits, "both civil and criminal", over the possession of the pastures.[34] Both valley councils decided to give up litigation and settle their differences by appointing arbiters who issued a sentence to solve the disputes over the broad area of Soasqui and other *términos* close to it, such as Estibiella, Allarat, and Segarra. The passage of the flocks had to be regulated too. The arbiters of the *sentencia* were the Viceroy and the Gobernador General of the Kingdom of Aragon. As in any other *sentencia arbitral*, they ordered the parties to accept their verdict and to cease all conflicts and lawsuits against each other. If one of the parties accused the other of breaching the agreement, its accusation would be immediately accepted, without having

34 "assi cibiles como criminales"; in AMA, 223bis/41.

to present any proof. The councils of Ansó and Hecho, as well as the clergymen of Siresa, secured their oath with all their assets and rights. In the event of a violation of the *sentencia*, the offended party could resort to whichever judicial authority it wished. Furthermore, the representatives of the valleys gave up their right to appeal to their own judges, as well as the advantages and rights that the Aragonese *fueros* offered. If there was any doubt regarding the contents and application of the *sentencia*, the valley councils should ask the arbiters or their successors in their offices.

The first issue addressed by the *sentencia* was the possession and use of Soasqui. Many sentences and pacts had been issued to solve the disputes over that big *término*, but conflicts persisted. The arbiters ratified that Soasqui belonged to Ansó, so the valley council would exert jurisdiction over it. The *vecinos* and *herbajantes* of Hecho could nevertheless lead their herds to Soasqui, so they could graze there, as they had done since time immemorial.[35] Livestock could enter Soasqui from 15 June. Fines for those who contravened the order were defined. Both valley councils would appoint guards of the pastures on the second day of Easter. In case of doubts about the use of Soasqui, they would resort to the abovementioned Justicia de Jaca y sus Montañas.

The possession and use of other *partidas* were regulated too. Reclusa remained untouched. Regarding Allarat and Segarra, the arbiters ratified previous *sentencias arbitrales*, namely those promulgated by Ximeno de Urrea in 1431 and by Archbishop Hernando de Aragón in 1560. The *partidas* belonged to Ansó, but the *vecinos* of Hecho could use them if there were less than 1,200 heads of Ansó's livestock on them. Moreover, the Viceroy and the Gobernador General of Aragon established that the herds of the Hecho Valley could enter Allarat and Segarra if the herds of *vecinos* or *herbajantes* from Ansó had left them for longer than one day and one night. As for the *partida* of Estibiella, the arbiters recognised that debates over its limits were still heated. The "*mojonación real*" mentioned above had not settled the differences between Ansó and Hecho, so they put forward another *mojonación*—although, as shown below, it did not work. Finally, the arbiters established fines for those whose livestock grazed where or when it should not. Nevertheless, the herds of the valleys could use the *partidas* in common and the passes of the other party.[36]

35 The *vecinos* and *herbajantes* of Hecho would not have to ask the ecclesiastical chapter of San Pedro de Siresa for permission to use the pastures. Given that the valley council of Hecho had invoked the privileges of the church of Siresa to prove that pastures did not belong to Ansó, this clause reveals that the *vecinos* of Hecho were not subordinated to the clergymen of Siresa.

36 AMA, 223bis/41.

Even though it represented a milestone in the normalisation of the relationships between Hecho and Ansó, the *sentencia arbitral* of 1600 did not settle the disputes completely, apparently. Four years later, in June 1604, the valley councils signed a new pact.[37] On that occasion, there was no arbiter, hence the agreement was not a *sentencia arbitral*, but a *concordia*. The main difference between both types of pacts is that while the terms of the *sentencia arbitral* are decided by one or more arbiters appointed by the parties, in the *concordia* the local authorities or their representatives negotiated the clauses of the pact themselves. The aims of both the *sentencias* and the *concordias* were identical, namely, to restore the peace between both communities, and both were neither according to law nor against it; however, while the *sentencia arbitral* was a sort of external decision, the *concordia* was an endogenous compromise. Just like *sentencias arbitrales*, *concordias* were widespread in the Spanish world.[38] In fact, any compromise, no matter the parties involved, was called *concordia*. Thus, the fiscal pacts between the king and the ecclesiastical estate were *concordias*, and so were the debt-restructuring agreements negotiated by the town councils and their creditors in the Crown of Aragon. Even the pacts to share out an inheritance or fiscal burdens were *concordias* too. Any kind of compromise or agreement which was not determined by law and did not contradict it could be called *concordia*.[39] The advantages of this mechanism vis-à-vis litigation are obvious: they were less expensive and time consuming, and solutions were more satisfactory for all parties than a trial would offer, hence the greater stability of the agreements; besides, the pacts left room for renegotiation of the resulting regime.

37 The ecclesiastical Chapter of San Pedro de Siresa also signed the *concordia*.

38 See, for instance, the *concordias* between Spanish and Portuguese towns in the peninsular borderline; in Herzog, *Frontiers of possession*, Chapter 3. A similar formula with a different name, the so-called *convenios*, can be found in colonial Mexico; see, for instance, Yannakakis, *Since time immemorial*, 209–210.

39 I studied the *concordias* in the Crown of Aragon in my doctoral thesis, but as fiscal and, above all, as financial instruments. However, the term *concordia*, just like the word *censo*, was an umbrella term that encompassed several kinds of contracts. Arguably, the *concordia* was the epitome of the pre-modern political world, both in the Crown of Aragon and in the Spanish monarchy: it embodied the autonomy of every corporation to define its own rules through negotiation, the wide diversity of contracts and norms and the judicial/non-administrative character of pre-modern societies, hence the polycentrism, pluralism, and jurisdictionalism of the medieval and early modern political world. Put differently, *concordias* were at the core of the political culture of the Crown of Aragon and, somehow, of the Spanish monarchy; see Ena Sanjuán, "The Vertebrae of the Leviathan", esp. 163–208.

The *concordia* of 1604 was a 24-covenant agreement that regulated the use of pastures and passes, the fines in case of infringement depending on the type of livestock and on the place where the violation took place, the examination of milestones, and determining the people who were entitled to seize livestock. It therefore was a long text with many clauses to ensure that all the parties complied with it. The councils of the two valleys and the Chapter of Siresa committed themselves, all their assets and those of the *vecinos* of the villages and towns of the valleys to fulfil the pact. If any party breached the pact, the offended party could request any judge, either ecclesiastical or secular, to foreclose the assets until satisfied. They gave up the jurisdiction of their own judges. Moreover, they ratified the *sentencia arbitral* of 1600 except in those clauses in which the *concordia* contradicted it; for these, the covenants of the newest agreement would prevail. They agreed that every lawsuit between them would cease within two months.

As in the case of the *sentencia arbitral* approved four years earlier, the first article of the *concordia* was devoted to Soasqui, more specifically to the *partida* of Aznar Malo. The parties defined the limits of the *partida* through a *mojonación* and decided that both could use it. Regarding grazing in Soasqui, the *concordia* established that the herds of the *vecinos* of the valleys and their *herbajantes* could enter the *término* from 1 June of every year, notwithstanding previous agreements. The pact also established fines and defined the procedures for seizing livestock. It contained a general *mojonación* of Soasqui too. The parties explicitly recognised that the *partidas* of Lajerito and Sabucar were not part of Soasqui, but the herders and *herbajantes* of Hecho and Siresa were allowed to use their pastures. Several articles of the *concordia* revolved around the seizing of livestock. Fines varied according to the type of livestock—they were higher for bigger animals—and the place where they were captured. The jurisdiction of these fines corresponded to the judges and town councils of Ansó and Hecho, and there was no possibility of appealing to other judicial authorities. The passage of herds was carefully regulated too. The fees for trespassing the other's *partidas* were specified and the limits of those pastures were also clearly defined, together with the direction of the herds when they went through them.[40] Finally, the *concordia* established that the parties would be obliged to revise the milestones that marked the limits of every *término* and *partida* every three years, starting on 1 July and not stopping until the examination concluded, "to avoid litigations and differences between the parties, so

40 The passes that were regulated were Braslavilla, Laliena, Garatoverza, Peñamelera, Pueyarraso, Forcala and la loma de Celia.

they live with peace and quietness that God Our Lord desires".[41] Nevertheless, it seems that this clause was not fulfilled.

The *concordia* of 1604 rectified some aspects of the *sentencia arbitral* of 1600 and ratified many others. For the parties, the pact represented an instrument with which they could solve the conflicts over the possession and use of the *término* of Soasqui and the passes for the herds of Ansó and Hecho. Broadly speaking, the authorities of Hecho and Siresa assumed the privileges of Jaime I that granted Ansó all the pastures which were in the limits between both valleys and, in turn, the council of Ansó had to accept that the *vecinos* and *herbajantes* of the neighbouring valley could exploit those pastures under the same conditions that they did. Though obvious, it is worth emphasising that the ownership, possession, and use of land were regulated by the corporations themselves in a rather autonomous way. They appointed arbiters to solve their differences, discussed the limits of every *partida* or simply negotiated among themselves to avoid expensive, endless, and often futile litigation. Monitoring, fines, seizing of livestock and the appointment of officers and judges depended, in short, on the valley councils.

Nevertheless, the *concordia* had to be modified in 1651, as some norms did not work as the valley councils had expected. The formula they used was called "*adición*", which could be translated into English as "addendum". Just like the *concordia*, the *adición* was negotiated by representatives of both valleys. The agreement did not derogate the original pact, but clarified some clauses and added some norms. Thus, the seizing of cattle was regulated again, establishing different procedures and fines, prohibiting the slaughter of livestock in the common pastures again, establishing severe punishments for those who contravened the norm, and settling new fines for those whose flocks entered into specific pastures and fields. The parties agreed that, instead of inspecting the milestones in the borderline between the valleys every three years, as the *concordia* of 1604 said, they would revise the milestones every six years, starting in 1652. Furthermore, the representatives of the valley councils decided that they would meet every year on the abovementioned *partida* of la Escarroneta, on the feast of Saint Luke (18 October), to solve the disputes that may have arisen throughout the previous year. The authorities should be at the frontier at 10 in the morning or they would have to pay 200 *sueldos* to the other party.[42] As explained in the following section, the representatives of the valley met regularly at la Escarroneta until the 1920s.

41 "[…] á fin, y efecto de que asi se eviten pleytos, y diferencias entre dichas partes y se viva con la paz, y quietud de qe Dios Ntro Sor mas se sirve"; AMA, 256/8.

42 AMA, protocolos notariales 67, fols. 103r–109r.

Leaving aside Soasqui, the limits, ownership, possession, and use of other areas of grassland continued to be sources of conflict for some decades. The *partida* called Estibiella was one of the burning issues. After the signing of the *concordia*, the town councillors of Ansó consulted a jurist about the legal status of the *partida*. Its limits had been defined in the *mojonación real* of 1596, redefined in 1600 through the *sentencia arbitral*, and again some years later by the same officer who had carried out the *mojonación real*. The town councillors of Ansó asked the lawyer whether the last definition of the limits was final and binding. The jurist answered that the last *mojonación* should prevail. The local authorities of Ansó also asked him about the seizing of livestock made by some *vecinos* of Hecho in Estibiella. They wanted to know whether they should be accused and before whom. The lawyer recommended them to file a lawsuit before the local justice of Ansó, since the Justicia de Aragón had no jurisdiction over that kind of affair. The source also reveals that the *concordia* of 1604 was not being fulfilled, as the councillors of Ansó asked the lawyer about the possibility of claiming the fines established in the agreement in the event of a breach, as the valley councillors of Hecho had breached the clause of examining the milestones of the pastures every three years. The lawyer confirmed that they could accuse them of breaching the pact. Finally, the authorities of Ansó asked if they should ask a judicial authority to seize ("aprehender") a *partida*, the Faja de la Rueba. The lawyer answered that the best court to refer this to was the Real Audiencia.[43]

A few years later, in 1623, the councillors of Ansó resorted to the Justicia de Aragón to ask for protection for the *puertos* of Estibiella and Tortiella. To gain a *firma* (legal protection) from the judge, the attorney of Ansó had to justify the possession of the land by the valley council of Ansó. First, he defined the valley of Ansó as the town of Ansó and the village of Fago and recalled its limits, which were publicly known since time immemorial. Second, he recalled the limits of Estibiella and Tortiella, which had been recognised by Hecho and Siresa in the *mojonaciones*. Third, and more importantly, he argued that the valley council and *vecinos* of Ansó were the "true lords and owners" ("verdaderos señores y poseedores") of Estibiella and Tortiella, as their flocks had grazed there for centuries, they had cut wood, they had appointed guards to watch the pastures and seize livestock and they had leased grassland to foreign herders continuously since time immemorial. The Justicia accepted the arguments of the attorney of Ansó and executed the *firma* of the two *puertos*.[44]

---

43 AMA, 205/9. This *consulta* could not be dated. It has been described here because there is a date *post quem* (1615) and apparently there had not yet been an *aprehensión* of Estibiella and Tortiella.

44 AMA, 223/16 and 205/22.

The conflict over Estibiella would be solved through another *sentencia arbitral*, approved in 1664 and ratified in 1665. In this case, the process preceding the promulgation of the *sentencia* is known thanks to the notarial archives of Ansó. A presbyter of the ecclesiastical Chapter of Siresa, a representative of the valley of Hecho and another of the valley of Ansó met and appointed four arbiters and four clergymen, two from Hecho and two from Ansó.[45] They were asked to dictate a sentence within four months. The parties committed all their assets and revenues to respect and observe the decision of the arbiters.[46] In fact, the *sentencia arbitral* was a new *mojonación* of some *partidas* whose limits had been discussed until then. Together with surveyors from Ansó and Hecho, the arbiters examined the crosses that marked the limits of every *partida* and renewed or carved new crosses on the surfaces of the milestones. The limits of Estibiella were examined both in its lower and upper parts. The arbiters established that the herds of the *vecinos* and *herbajantes* of Ansó could not trespass the limits of Estibiella and Sayestico, while the herds of Hecho could move through Estibiella to their own land without permission from Ansó. The milestones of another *partida*, Aznar Malo, were also revised and redefined. As in the other *sentencias arbitrales*, the parties committed themselves to obey the pact. They would also give up any privilege, charter, judge, lawsuit, etcetera. The *mojonaciones* which did not contradict this *sentencia arbitral* remained in force. Clauses to ensure compliance with the pact, together with fines, were established. If there were doubts or discord, the councils of Ansó and Hecho would resort to the arbiters while they were alive. Once they died, each valley could appoint an arbiter to mediate between them.[47]

In the 1690s, several events altered the peace that reigned among the relationships between the valleys. Further research will have to clarify whether or not the conflicts that emerged in the last decade of the 17th century were provoked by the high levels of municipal indebtedness of the valley of Ansó.[48] In 1690, the valley council of Hecho, together with the ecclesiastical Chapter of Siresa, gained a *firma* against the valley council of Ansó regarding the *partida*

45 They were a priest of the church of Ansó, a friar of the Convent of San Francisco of Jaca, and two monks of the *Real Monasterio de San Juan de la Peña*, one of them being Domingo La Ripa, a famous historian from Hecho.

46 AMA, protocolos notariales 84, fols. 51^{v}–54^{r}.

47 AMA, 219/16. Curiously, the councillors of Hecho and Ansó rewarded the arbiters with bearskins.

48 This would be a key issue in the decline and collapse of the Crown of Aragon and the Spanish monarchy and the emergence of the Spanish modern state. Both Ansó and Hecho signed *concordias* with their respective creditors in the 18th century to reschedule their debts; they can be found in AHPZ, J/2088 and J/2089.

of Soasqui. The verdict of the Justicia de Aragón included the *sentencia arbitral* of 1600 and the *concordia* of 1604 as proof that the *vecinos* and *herbajantes* from Hecho could freely use Soasqui. As in other legal documents, their rights were proved through immemorial and continuous use, the appointment of guards, the imposition of fines… Through the *firma*, any judicial authority was inhibited from intervening in any affair related to the pastures and forests of Soasqui, allowing the *vecinos* and *herbajantes* of Hecho to continue using it.[49]

It is likely that the valley of Ansó, at the behest of its creditors, had hindered the entry of flocks from Hecho in the *partida*. Like in the Middle Ages, the valley council was going through financial trouble and tried to maximise revenue by exploiting the pastures as much as they could. The creditors of Ansó—more specifically the priests of its parochial church—were owed four annual payments in arrears, so they resorted to the Real Audiencia of Aragon, from which they gained an *aprehensión* in 1691. The *aprehensión* was an Aragonese *foral* trial by which a judicial authority took an asset or right under its protection until who it belonged to was decided. It was very frequently used in cases of default.[50] Sometimes, the asset was entrusted to a third party. In this case, the Audiencia gave temporary control of Soasqui to the town of Berdún, as the priests did not trust any other town or valley council. The verdict of the Audiencia forbade the *vecinos* and *herbajantes* of Hecho to cut green wood in Soasqui.[51]

It is not clear how long the *partida* remained under the control of the creditors but, in 1692, the town councillors of Ansó sent some questions to a lawyer in Saragossa. They were considering the possibility of altering the terms of the *sentencia arbitral*, approved almost a century earlier in 1600, as they thought that the council and *vecinos* of Hecho pretended to have the same rights over Soasqui as they had. A councillor and some herders from Hecho had cut wood to build a bridge over a creek so their livestock could enter the *partida*. The town councillors of Ansó asked the jurist whether it would be convenient to negotiate with the valley councillors of Hecho or whether it would be more effective to file a lawsuit against them. The lawyer answered that it would be better to negotiate within the framework of the *sentencia arbitral*, saying that "solving the differences among neighbouring communities through a *sentencia arbitral* is always a more accurate means, as it is faster than lawsuits that cause delay".[52] Even non-local actors preferred compromise over trials, as they knew

49 AHPZ, J/11177/1.

50 La Ripa y Marraco, *Ilustración*, 1–184.

51 AHPZ, J/766/20.

52 "[…] y siempre es medio mas proporcionado el terminar las diferencias entre Lugares cir-

that *concordias* and *sentencias arbitrales* meant lower expenses and consumed less time than endless legal processes.[53]

Apparently, the authorities of Ansó never acted against their *vecinos* of Hecho, since both valley councils were acting jointly by the turn of the century, as shown in the next section. The conflicts that had afflicted the valleys of Ansó and Hecho for centuries were finally settled through negotiations and the signing of agreements in the 17th century. Both corporations—as well as the ecclesiastical Chapter of Siresa—agreed that the pastures of the borderline between both valleys belonged to Ansó and that they could be exploited by both parties under certain conditions. Therefore, the property, possession and use of land were not determined by royal privileges, courts and officers—even if local actors periodically invoked them and resorted to their authority and legitimacy—but by the people and corporations who claimed rights to them.[54]

4 Reinterpreting the Agreements through Performance

The pacts between the valleys laid the foundations for a more stable and harmonious coexistence and use of the pastures. Even though no new agreement was signed after 1665, the *sentencias arbitrales* and *concordias* were periodically renewed and reinterpreted through the inspection of the milestones that marked the boundaries of the valleys and the *partida* of Soasqui, as well as the meetings between the two corporations to judge the fines imposed by the guards and the seizing of livestock. As explained above, sources are not simply *concordias* or *mojonaciones*, but normally combine the regulation of the management of the pastures by the authorities that exert jurisdiction over them with the definition of the limits of every *puerto*, *partida*, and *paso*. Rather than the mechanical application of the clauses, the *vistas* and *mojonaciones* were a sort of ritual through which the representatives of both valleys performed the pacts, usually readapting the norms to new situations and conflicts.

The inspection of the milestones (in the sources called "*visura*", "*vista*", "*mojonación*") was very similar to what municipalities all over the Spanish

cunvezinos por sentencia arbitral que se concluie con mas brebedad, que los procesos que traen consigo la dilacion que experimentamos en todas las causas".

53 AMA, 223/11.

54 This follows the lines proposed in Herzog, *Frontiers of possession*.

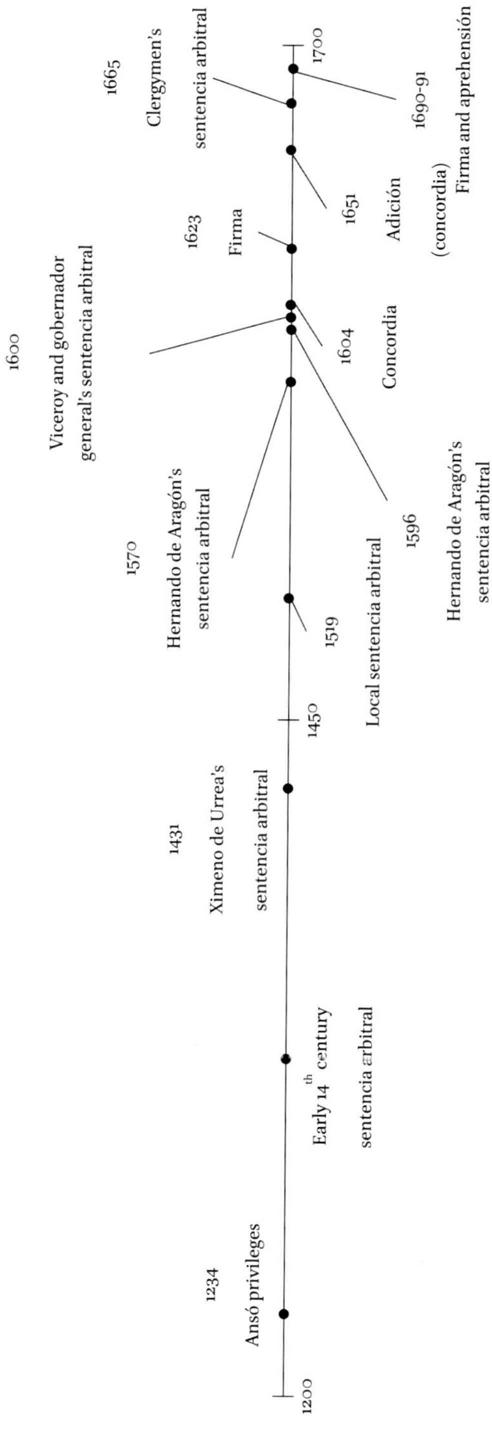

FIGURE 7.3 Timeline of the *sentenciae arbitrales* and *concordias* signed by the valley councils
OWN ELABORATION BASED ON THE SOURCES CITED IN THE TEXT

monarchy (and beyond) did since the Middle Ages.[55] The examination of the successive inspections reveals that the procedure was always the same.[56] The representatives of both valley councils arranged a meeting at some point on the frontier. The meeting could be either stipulated by a pact between the parties or at the behest of one of them. Normally the highest authorities of every valley attended the meeting (*justicia* and *jurados* in the pre-Bourbon period, *alcalde*, *regidores*, and/or *síndico procurador* after 1707), together with witnesses from both parties and two notaries, one from each town, to witness the meeting. They all started walking up and down the mountains, checking that the crosses on the milestones were in a good state and visible; if they were not, they were carved again. This could take several days, as the frontier between the valleys was long and the terrain was usually steep.

After the *mojonación real* of 1596, the *buegas*, *mugas*, or *mojones* (milestones) were examined in 1619, 1640, and 1652, at least. Although it was a *sentencia arbitral*, the agreement of 1665 included a *mojonación*, as the arbiters revised and redefined the limits of several *partidas*. In theory, the milestones had to be examined every six years, according to the addendum to the *concordia* (*adición*) approved in 1651, but in practice the inspection took place less often. Even though they followed the guidelines of the *sentencia* of 1665, in 1699 the valley authorities made some new crosses to redefine the extension of some *partidas*. For instance, the limits of Estibiella and el Pueyo de Agua had not been clearly defined in the *mojonación real* or in the last *sentencia arbitral*, so they carved new crosses to establish their limits. The valley council of Hecho and the Chapter of Siresa thought that the arbiters of the *sentencia arbitral* should have been consulted, as the agreement said, but still they were not. The commission examined every *partida* between both valleys, from Segarra to Lajerito. Interestingly, the parties clashed over the participation of the representatives of the Chapter of Siresa in the *vista*. The authorities of Hecho considered that the clergymen should not participate. This is important, as the valley council of Hecho had traditionally used the alleged privileges of the ecclesiastical Chapter to claim rights over the grassland that belonged to Ansó. The representative of the clergymen complained about the petition of

55 Baró Pazos, "Los límites territoriales". The author makes a clear difference between the revision of the milestones that marked the jurisdictional boundaries of every municipality and the demarcation of pastures. In the case of Ansó and Hecho, the *mojonaciones* were mixed, as the limits of some pastures were the limits of the jurisdiction of the valley councils too.

56 A historiographical synthesis on the issue of demarcations can be found in André, "Introducción". Again, I must thank de Freitas Macedo for the reference.

Hecho, and so did the representatives of Ansó, who considered that the priests were entitled to participate in the examination.[57]

As explained above, the differences between *vecinos* and herders were settled by the valley authorities every year on 18 October, in the meetings called "vistas de la Escarroneta". *Vistas* were meetings in which the representatives of the valleys solved the conflicts between them according to the *concordias* and *sentencias arbitrales* they signed.[58] In 1653, two years after the approval of the *adición* that established the meetings, the representatives of the valleys should have met, but the councillors from Hecho did not attend the meeting, so the representatives of Ansó demanded of them the fine settled in the *adición* (200 *sueldos jaqueses*). In several *vistas* in the 1680s there was no grievance, so the judges limited themselves to ratifying that the pacts between the valleys were in force. In 1700, both corporations fined some herders, but they did not revise the milestones. Half a century later, in 1751, they met in the same place and reaffirmed the validity of the *concordia*, *adición*, and *sentencias*, derogating any norm that contradicted them. They also confirmed the decisions made in 1747 regarding a *puerto* and set a deadline for the guards of the pastures to report on the confiscations they made or the fines they imposed. In 1752, the milestones of the borderline between the valleys were examined by members of both corporations. One year later, in 1753, the judges appointed by virtue of the *concordia*—one from Ansó and the other from Hecho—agreed on the fines that the herders whose livestock had damaged pastures or fields should pay. Remarkably, no representative of the Chapter of Siresa participated in any of these *vistas*. According to the *concordia*, only the local authorities of Hecho and Ansó were judges who could decide the validity and amount of the fines.[59] The same event that in the 17th century provoked an intense conflict between the valleys, namely the building of a bridge over the river of Soasqui by *vecinos* of Hecho, was politely resolved in 1746 through a petition of the valley council of Hecho to Ansó to send people to collaborate in the construction of a bridge. Ansó sent some *vecinos* and partially paid for the works.[60] This demonstrates that the relationships between the valleys were good in the 18th century.

---

57 AMA, 223bis/21.

58 Suman, *Apuntes para el diccionario geográfico*, 172, 278. Similar *vistas* were celebrated with the neighbouring valley of Roncal in Navarre. The representatives of both valley councils met regularly in the chapel of Puyeta, at the borderline between the valleys, and settled their differences.

59 AMA, protocolos notariales, 70, fols. 56^{v}–57^{v}; 115, fols. 75^{r}–76^{r}, 110, fols. 142^{v}–143^{v}; 121, fols. 71^{v}–72^{v}; 124, fols. 15, 59; 125, fols. 59^{r}–65^{v}, fol. 57; 126, fol. 14^{v}.

60 AMA, 136, municipal records, 15–V-1746 session.

But the peaceful coexistence between the valleys achieved through the *concordia* and *sentencias* was interrupted in the 1750s. In 1754, a proxy from Hecho presented a claim before the Real Audiencia.[61] He accused the *vecinos* and guards from Ansó of violating two clauses of the *sentencia arbitral* of 1600 and the *concordia* of 1604, two articles regarding the seizing of cattle. The proxy asked the Real Audiencia to ratify the *firma* gained by Hecho in 1690, thus inhibiting the *vecinos* and authorities from Ansó from disturbing the herders from Hecho. The Audiencia ordered an inquiry, collecting testimonies from inhabitants and herders from the neighbouring town of Aragüés del Puerto. On the basis of those testimonies, the judges accepted the petition of Hecho. But the sentence did not settle the differences as, three years later, in 1757, the valley council of Hecho again resorted to the Real Audiencia, asking the judges to order the valley councillors of Ansó to meet them in Soasqui to renew or settle the limits of the *partida*, as some of them were formed by trees that had been destroyed by wind and floods. The proxy of Ansó tried to dissuade the judges from ordering a new *mojonación*, but the *oidores* of the Audiencia sent a *receptor* (a court officer) to conduct an inquiry and collect the testimonies of inhabitants of neighbouring valleys.[62] It is not clear whether the *mojonación* performed in 1765 and described below was the consequence of this trial, but Ansó and Hecho did not resort to third parties to solve their differences again. In any case, litigation became more intense in the mid-18th century. Demographic and economic expansion, political changes and/or more local and regional factors may have caused this change, which can be observed in the funds of the Real Audiencia. The lawsuits between herders and farmers in Northern Aragon or between the *vecinos* of Ansó to determine the use of the land of the valley are just two examples of the increasing litigation.[63]

Yet the valley councils of Ansó and Hecho managed to recompose their good relationships. In 1765, the representatives of both corporations met again in

---

61 The attorney was Francisco Javier La Ripa, a descendant of one of the monks who acted as an arbiter in the *sentencia arbitral* of 1665. He became a judge of the *Audiencia* himself almost two decades later and wrote the book on the *foral* trials of Aragon cited in this chapter. It is not clear why the actors involved could not solve their differences without having to resort to an external court.

62 AHPZ, J/11177/1.

63 AHPZ, J/10808/1 and J/2020. Hypothetically, there would have been a generalised collapse of the medieval-born instruments and practices in the mid-18th century, which would have been resolved through new practices that constituted the embryo of the modern state. It is also possible that the increasing litigation is a biased perception due to the partial destruction of the funds of the *foral Real Audiencia* in the Sieges of Saragossa, during the Peninsular War.

la Escarroneta and agreed that they would preserve their rights and keep the pacts between them intact. The inspection and renewal of the milestones started on 2 September in Bubalo, one of the common mountain passes. As night fell, they stopped in Landarrera. The next morning, they continued to examine the crosses and to renew those which were not visible. In total, the milestones and crosses examined amounted to 152: 57 of the *término* of Soasqui and 95 of other *partidas*. They sometimes cited the pacts in which the milestones were established. Some crosses could not be found, so they had to carve a new one or simply report its disappearance. The minutes of the *mojonación* include an episode that took place once the examination of the milestones had concluded: two presbyters from San Pedro de Siresa appeared and argued that the Chapter should have been asked to participate in the *mojonación*, as they were legally entitled to do it. The authorities of Hecho replied that the priests had no proxy from the Chapter, so they were acting as private individuals, and recalled that, according to a judicial sentence, only the valley council of Hecho had the right to intervene in the delimitation of the *términos* between Ansó and Hecho.

The clauses of the *concordia* and *sentencias* continued to be interpreted and performed in the following decades and throughout the 19th century. It seems there was a break in the *vistas* during the Peninsular War but, after this, the agreements between Ansó and Hecho were publicly renewed again. Periodically, the representatives of the two valleys met in la Escarroneta. They read the *concordia* and reaffirmed its validity, solved doubts regarding the interpretation of the pact and decided the fines that herders should pay, the authorities that could judge a dispute, or the pertinence of livestock confiscations. In short, they continued reviving the regime of the pacts which had been approved more than two centuries earlier.[64]

The *mojonaciones* and *vistas* were the ways in which the 17th-century agreements were brought into practice. The use of grassland was regulated by judges of both corporations by virtue of the *sentencias arbitrales* and the *concordia*. The disputes between the valley councils and the herders of Ansó and Hecho could be solved amicably, without resorting to external authorities and costly trials. Furthermore, the possession, limits and use of the *partidas*, *montes* and *términos* between both valleys were constantly renewed in a sort of public ceremony. The dominion of Ansó over grassland, as well as the right of the *vecinos* and *herbajantes* of Hecho to exploit those pastures, was publicly recognised in the meetings between the corporations.

---

64 AMA, 228/4.

5 Conclusions: Negotiated Ownership and Possession

The valleys of Ansó and Hecho—just like the rest of the Pyrenean valleys—were heavily reliant on livestock breeding and, by extension, on grassland. Pastures were the cornerstone of their societies and economies, so their councils carefully regulated their ownership, possession, and use. On the one hand, local historiography knows the actors involved and instruments used to define ownership well, but it usually contextualises them inaccurately; on the other, general historiography has convincingly challenged narratives and paradigms regarding the medieval and early modern societies, but many works still offer inexact views of how property worked, due in part to their dependence on archival sources that do not fully reflect the actual practices around the pastures.

Medieval and early modern formulae for holding land had little to do with current forms of ownership. The norms that regulated the possession and use of land were socially and historically embedded. This is to say that holding a piece of land implied negotiation with others, generally through corporations, historical legitimacy, and social recognition of possessing and using land. In the case of the pastures between Ansó and Hecho, both valley councils invoked privileges granted by the Aragonese monarchs in the Middle Ages. Even though those privileges were the original source of legitimacy to exert dominion over grassland, possession and use were performed on a daily basis. Property rights were defined by the practices of herders who led their flocks to graze in the *partidas* and *términos* between both valleys, the guards who seized livestock, and the judges who imposed fines. Sometimes those practices led to conflicts which were usually solved through agreements, such as *concordias* or *sentencias arbitrales*, rather than through expensive, long trials in far-off courts. By using those instruments, the parties, their representatives and/or the arbiters appointed by the valley councils defined the limits of each *partida*, *monte*, *término*, *paso* and *puerto*, and regulated when, how, and who could use each pasture and pass. They also established sanctions for those who contravened the norms, as well as mechanisms to enforce those penalties, such as guards of the pastures and judicial authorities from both valleys to judge each case.

The 17th-century *sentencias arbitrales* and, above all, the *concordia* of 1604 constituted a solid, stable, and flexible framework to jointly hold and exploit the pastures between both valleys. They were periodically renewed and performed through *vistas* and *mojonaciones*. These events had something of a public ceremony, as the representatives of both valleys read the agreements aloud, thus recognising that grassland belonged to Ansó but could be used by the *vecinos* and *herbajantes* of Hecho. In the *vistas* and *mojonaciones* they inspected and renewed the crosses on the surface of the milestones. The valley authorities also interpreted the clauses of the pacts to judge every case and revised the confiscations and fines imposed throughout the year.

It is likely that the continuous performance and reinterpretation of the pacts was the cause of their long survival. The *concordia* of 1604 and the *sentencias arbitrales* were mentioned in every meeting until 1878 and regularly thereafter. For instance, the minutes of the meeting of 1906 narrate how the councils of Ansó and Hecho met in la Escarroneta and their secretaries read the "*concordias*".[65] Of course, the original aims of the *concordia* probably had little to do with the modern readings of the text. 19th- and 20th-century actors spoke about *concordias* in the plural and barely mentioned the *sentencias arbitrales*, which had been the most common type of agreement. Nonetheless, more than three centuries after the signing of the *concordia* of 1604, the councils and *vecinos* of Ansó and Hecho continued to regulate the use and possession of grassland by recreating ancient norms and practices. Both local and more general historiographies have taken for granted that the emergence of the modern state provoked either the disappearance or the denaturation of the pacts. Yet, in fact, locals continued to adapt the norms to new contexts as they had done for centuries. Why most of those pacts eventually disappeared is something that only further research can clarify.

Glossary

adición addendum, in this article, to a *concordia*.

amojonamiento/*mojonación* definition of the limits of a piece of real estate, generally a field or pasture, by setting milestones all around the perimeter.

aprensión/*aprehensión* type of litigation of the Aragonese law by which a judicial authority took an asset or right under its protection until it was decided to whom it belonged.

buega/*muga*/*mojón* milestone. They normally had crosses carved on their surface.

concordia compromise, pact between two or more parties. It can solve a dispute on a wide range of issues (the sharing-out of an inheritance or of fiscal burdens, rescheduling the payment of debt). It is ideated by the parties involved, not by a third party.

---

65 "[…] con objeto de avistarse en cumplimiento de lo estipulado en sus respectivas concordias dándose en el acto lectura de las mismas por sus respectivos secretarios"; in AMA, 228/4.

firma type of litigation of the Aragonese law by which the *Justicia de Aragón* during the *foral* period and the *Real Audiencia* after 1711 inhibited any judge from disturbing the possessor of an asset or right in his/her possession.

herbajante leaseholder of the pastures of a valley or town.

monte mountain or hill; grassland.

pacería agreement between a French and a Spanish valley which was intended to regulate the relationships between both, keep peace between them and/or to regulate the ownership, possession and use of natural resources such as pastures or water.

partida area within a *término*.

paso mountain pass.

puerto mountain pastures where sheep and cattle graze during the summer.

sentencia arbitral pact between two or more parties to settle a dispute between them. It was a verdict dictated by a third party (arbiter/s) who had been appointed by those involved in the dispute.

término wide area of grassland.

vecino inhabitant of a village, town, valley or city. He (women were usually excluded) had political rights, such as participating in the municipal assemblies, holding offices or driving his cattle to the pastures of the community.

vistas/***visura*** meetings of two or more valleys to examine the milestones in the borderline between them and/or to solve the conflicts that had arisen according to the *concordias* and *sentencias* they had signed.

Bibliography

Manuscripts

Archivo Histórico Provincial de Zaragoza (AHPZ)

C/MPGD/120.

J/766/20.

J/2088.

J/2089.

J/10808/1.

J/2020.

J/11177/1.

Archivo Municipal de Ansó (AMA)

136, municipal records, 15–V-1746 session.

205,

/9.

/22.

216,
 /16.
219,
 /6.
 /16.
223,
 /4.
 /5.
 /6.
 /11.
 /13.
 /16.
223bis,
 /19.
 /20.
 /21.
 /36.
 /41.
228,
 /4.
256,
 /8.
 /9.
protocolos notariales,
 67, fols. 103^{r}–109^{r}.
 70, fols. 56^{v}–57^{v}.
 84, fols. 51^{v}–54^{r}.
 110, fols. 142^{v}–143^{v}.
 115, fols. 75^{r}–76^{r}.
 121, fols. 71^{v}–72^{v}.
 124, fols. 15, 59.
 125, fols. 59^{r}–65^{v}, f. 57.
 126, fol. 14^{v}.

Printed Sources

La Ripa y Marraco, Francisco Xavier. *Ilustración a los quatro Processos Forales de Aragón*. Zaragoza 1764, Imprenta de Francisco Moreno.

Suman, Mateo. *Apuntes para el Diccionario geográfico del Reino de Aragón: Partido de Cinco Villas: según el Ms. 9–5723 de la RAH* ed. Salvo Salanova, Josefina and Álvaro Capalvo, Zaragoza 1802.

Literature

Agüero, Alejandro, "Las categorías básicas de la cultura jurisdiccional", in Llorente Sariñena, Marta (ed.), *De justicia de jueces a justicia de leyes. Hacia la España de 1870*, 2007, 21–58.

André, Sylvain, "Introducción. Breve balance historiográfico sobre apeos y amojonamientos: entre Edad Media y Época Moderna", in *Magallanica. Revista de historia moderna* 8, 16 (2022), 242–254.

Baró Pazos, Juan, "Los límites territoriales en el derecho histórico. Su fijación en la legislación y en la jurisprudencia", in *Anuario de Historia del Derecho Español* 75 (2005), 413–444.

Bastias Saavedra, Manuel, "The Normativity of Possession. Rethinking Land Relations in Early-Modern Spanish America, ca. 1500–1800", in *Colonial Latin American Review* 29, 2 (2020), 223–238.

Benton, Lauren A., and Richard Jeffrey Ross (eds.), *Legal pluralism and empires, 1500–1850*. New York 2013.

Calvo Eito, Constancio (ed.), *Valle de Hecho. Estudio antropológico y etnológico: etapas, desde 1755, el clero en el valle, desde 1842, censo de población, desde 1861, censo ganadero, desde 1870, censo escolar. Historia, costumbres, tradiciones y desarrollo de la vida diaria, vivida y contada por sus propios vecinos*, Zaragoza 2016.

Cardim, Pedro, Tamar Herzog, José Javier Ruiz Ibáñez, and Gaetano Sabatini (eds.), *Polycentric Monarchies. How Did Early Modern Spain and Portugal Achieve and Maintain a Global Hegemony?*, Eastbourne 2012.

Cavaillès, Henri, "Une fédération pyrénéenne sous l'ancien régime", in *Revue Historique* 105 (1910), 1–34.

Congost, Rosa, "La "gran obra" de la propiedad. Los motivos de un debate", in Congost, Rosa and José Miguel Lana Berasain (eds.), *Campos cerrados, debates abiertos. Análisis histórico y propiedad de la tierra en Europa (siglos XVI–XIX)*, Pamplona 2007, 21–52.

De Moor, Tine, Miguel Laborda Pemán, José Miguel Lana Berasain, René Van Weeren, and Angus Winchester, "Ruling the Commons. Introducing a new methodology for the analysis of historical commons", in *International Journal of the Commons* 10, 2 (2016), 529–588.

Duve, Thomas, "What Is Global Legal History?", in *Comparative Legal History* 8: 2 (2020): 73–115.

Ena Sanjuán, Íñigo, *The Vertebrae of the Leviathan. Municipal Debt and State Formation in the Eighteenth-Century Crown of Aragon* (PhD thesis), Florence 2022.

Fernández Otal, José Antonio, *La Casa de Ganaderos de Zaragoza. Derecho y trashumancia a fines del siglo XV*, Zaragoza 1993.

Fillat Estaqué, Federico, Ricardo García González, Daniel Gómez, and Ramón Reiné (eds.), *Pastos del Pirineo*, Madrid 2008.

Gómez de Valenzuela, Manuel, *Documentos sobre ganadería altoaragonesa y pirenaica (siglos XV y XVI)*, Zaragoza 2007.

Gorría Ipas, Antonio Jesús, *El Pirineo como espacio frontera*, Zaragoza 1995.

Gorría Ipas, Antonio Jesús, *Las relaciones transfronterizas en los Pirineos. una aproximación a su historia*, Zaragoza 2023.

Grossi, Paolo, *El orden jurídico medieval*, Madrid 1996.

Grossi, Paolo, *Un altro modo di possedere: l'emersione di forme alternative di proprietà alle coscienza giuridica postunitaria*, Milano 1977.

Herzog, Tamar, *Frontiers of possession. Spain and Portugal in Europe and the Americas*, Cambridge, Massachusetts 2015.

Hespanha, António Manuel, *As vésperas do Leviathan. Instituçoes e poder político. Portugal. Séc. XVII*, Rio de Mouro 1986.

Idoate, Florencio, *La comunidad del Valle de Roncal*, Pamplona 1977.

Lana Berasain, José Miguel, and Miguel Laborda Pemán, "El anidamiento institucional y su dinámica histórica en comunidades rurales complejas: dos estudios de caso (Navarra, siglos XIV–XX)", in Dubert, Isidro y Hortensio Sobrado (eds.), *Os traballos da vida. Estudos sobre o mundo rural, séculos XVI–XIX*, Santiago de Compostela 2022, 151–175.

Le Nail, Jean-François, "Présentation", in Le Nail, Jean-François, Henry Cavaillès, Bernard Druène, Christian Desplat, Alfredo Floristán Samanes, Antonio Jesús Gorría Ipas, Annie Brives, François Baby, and Michel Papy (eds.), *Lies et passeries dans les Pyrénées*, Tarbes 1986, iii–ix.

Ostrom, Elinor, *Governing the commons. the evolution of institutions for collective action*, Cambridge, New York 1990.

Pallaruelo Campo, Severino, *Pastores del Pirineo*, Madrid 1988.

Pascua Echegaray, Esther, *Señores del paisaje. ganadería y recursos naturales en Aragón, siglos XIII–XVII*, Valencia 2012.

Razquín Lizarraga, Martín María, Eduardo Aranguren Ibáñez, Marc Taull Taull, José Antonio Fernández Otal, Vicente Ferrer Lorés, P. Gascouat, and Rosa María Canals Tresserras, "Las facerías internacionales en el Pirineo. Historia, actualidad y futuro", in Canals Tresserras, Rosa María, and Leticia San Emeterio (eds.), *Nuevos retos de la ganadería extensiva. Un agente de conservación en peligro de extinción*, Pamplona 2012, 3–28.

Soulet, Jean-François, *Les Pyrénées au XIXe siècle. L'éveil d'une société civile*, Bordeaux 2004.

Stern, David G., "The Practical Turn", in Turner, Stephen P. and Paul Andrew Roth (eds.), *The Blackwell guide to the philosophy of the social sciences*, Malden 2003, 185–206.

Tomás Faci, Guillermo, and Jorge Laliena López, *Ansó. historia de un valle pirenaico*, Huesca 2016.

Vaccaro, Ismael, and Oriol Beltran (eds.), *Social and ecological history of the Pyrenees. State, market, and landscape*, Walnut Creek 2010.

Yannakakis, Yanna, *Since time immemorial. Native custom and law in colonial Mexico*, Durham 2023.

CHAPTER 8

Amparos and *Mapas*

Communal Land Possession and Dispossession in the Late Colonial Andes

Alcira Dueñas

1 Introduction

Alan Greer's idea that ownership regimes developed by Europeans and Amerindians involved diverse and simultaneous practices of land acquisition and loss is an appropriate departure point that invites further granular and singular iterations of land ownership regimes. Intertwining a local-global perspective, such approaches could capture ownership's unfixed, processual quality and its own historicity. The multiplicity of historical relationships between people, land, and various forms of government that took place in the colonial Andean landscape came to generate complex orders of ownership. Rather than a clear-cut structured and regulated system, ownership remained a work in progress well into the sunset of the colonial regime and beyond.[1] From within this formative framework, questioning the stability of the foundational notion of possession and its probatory means in the courts of justice offers a productive angle for discerning Andean land and judicial authority relations, including ownership.

Calling attention to long-term processes and local legal procedures, this Chapter suggests that, in its long trajectory, the colonial administration of justice effectively undermined its own practices for legitimising the possession of indigenous commons' lands, which were well-established processes from the 16th century. In the process, it destabilised the very notion and protection of possession for Andeans. In the late 18th century, *amparos de posesión* (writ of protection of possession) lost probatory power as possession protective orders, while new empirical media, such as landscape cartography, emerged in the Tarma province. Maps proved to be more expeditious in supporting Spanish land claims, accelerating the dissolution of the communal space in the Andes. As representations of ownership, land maps found more receptivity in the

1 Even in Europe, the institution of property was still in its formative stages at the time it travelled to America with the early Spanish immigrants. Greer, *Property and Dispossession*.

courtrooms towards the 18th century, in line with contemporary changes both in the probatory means of possession and space representational techniques in Lima. But these were also times when a steady decline in the long-term protection of possession occurred more frequently in some Andean settings of colonial Peru and Ecuador. What seems an inconsistency, however, was in fact integral to the colonial formation of a territorial regime of *haciendas* and *estancias* tied to a landed aristocracy, which was consolidated out of the dispossession of the lands held in common by the *pueblos de indios* (indigenous villages). At their inception, the *pueblos de indios* had obtained land grants in the form of *ejidos*, or communal lands, allocated in common usufruct to the *pueblo*, such as grasslands, hunting grounds, woodlands, corrals, watering holes, and foraging areas, along with *solares*, or land plots, allocated to families for their usufruct. To be sure, not all indigenous lands in the *pueblos* were *tierras de repartimiento* (royal land allocations) given in usufruct at the inception of the *pueblo*. There were also lands individually owned by Indians, mostly newcomers, who eventually purchased lands in the *pueblo*. It was only the communal lands of Vico and Pasco, given to them in *repartimiento*, with which this chapter is concerned.

In this Chapter, special attention is given to the late colonial practices tied to land ownership, including legal rituals, cartographic evidence, and procedures inscribed in the land. The actions of *jueces comisionados* (Audiencia-appointed judges) in Tarma pointed to the emergence of new representations of ownership based on cartographic texts and landscape paintings, which eventually rendered ineffective the *amparos de posesión* that protected the possession of the *pueblos*' communal lands.[2] Although possession and ownership were closely related, possession specifically alluded to the holder's (or holders') effective use of the land ("real" and "corporal") even if the possessor did

2 In this Chapter, I understand "titles" as solemn juridical documents that constituted either possession, ownership, or usufruct rights over a piece of land. Even though civil law theory maintains that facts engender rights, a long history of colonial forensic practice in the Andes shows that documents in themselves were the source of or generated rights. It is well known that the lack of legal titles or documents, to be submitted in court, frequently complicated the protection and enforcement of indigenous rights. Even though *amparos de posesión* or *mandamientos de posesión* were not technically land titles, Andean authorities consistently petitioned for and deployed them in court in the face of dispossession. This was the case because this written document (and its associated public ceremonies) gave possession its legal force and the holder the right to land. See Guevara Gil, *Propiedad agraria y derecho colonial*, 211–212. Most pueblos de Indios did not receive written land titles at the time of their foundation but instead *titulos de amparo* or *mandamientos de amparo*. Landowners consistently demanded *titulos de repartimiento* be shown, generally to counter native land claims, but this has rarely been documented.

not have other instruments to prove ownership.[3] This Chapter also examines how Andeans themselves intervened locally and in the Audiencia (Royal Court) of Lima itself to modulate the notion of possession related to communal lands, by both manipulating the social memory of the town through *amparos de posesión* and destabilising the rationale of the procedures of the *juez comisionado* through the intervention of the indigenous *procurador general de naturales* (attorney general for natives).[4]

I closely read the 1776–1778 conflictive encounters of the caciques (Andean ethnic lords or *kurakas*) and Indian *cabildos* (municipal councils) from Vico and Pasco in the Tarma province with the powerful Lima aristocrats in the region over the possession of valuable communal pastures and *majadas* (corrals) or *canchas* in Quechua. These *pueblos* had long been dispossessed by the Conde de las Lagunas' *mayorazgo* (entailed lands) located in the surrounding area.[5] I use this instructive case as a three-fold analytical device to discern, first, how land maps became evidence of ownership in the court. Second, I demonstrate how colonial legal rituals and protocols, originally implemented to investigate and sanction land possession, turned into de facto mechanisms of dispossession. That is, the *vistas de ojos* (visual land inspections) and the *deslindes* (boundary demarcations) intended to substantiate the veracity of land claims, along with a combination of Bourbon-era land maps and instru-

3 Scholarly discussions of possession are varied. The symbolic means of vast territorial possession by conquest were the focus of Patricia Seed's *Ceremonies of Possession*. For the legal mediation and translation of indigenous land rights, see Herzog, "Colonial Law and 'Native Customs'". Bastias Saavedra, in "The Normativity of possession", 223–238, cautions about the tendency to project contemporary notions of property onto the early modern past, neglecting its normative context of possession protection and its precedence in the rights to land over the modern concept of property. For a juridical and historical analysis of possession in the Cuzco region, see Guevara Gil, *Propiedad agraria y derecho colonial*; Hostnig, Palomino, and Decoster, in *Proceso de composición y titulación de tierras*, offered a rich compilation of land dispossession records from Andean Peru. For the possession/dispossession dynamics in colonial Colombia, see Lopera Mesa, "Creando posesión vía desposesión", 120–156. For a detailed analysis of possession and *amparos* in New Spain, see Owensby, *Empire of Law*.

4 Starting in 1763, the Procurador General de Naturales was an indigenous legal representative of the Indians at the *Real Audiencia*, or high court. By 1772, he was designated as "Fiscal Procurador".

5 The *mayorazgo* was basically a strategy used by landowners to perpetuate territorial ownership within a specific family lineage. This ownership was inalienable and constituted exclusively in the name of an older son, with specifications of the intended line of inheritance, assets to be protected by it, etc. Interestingly, among the various kinds of *mayorazgos* defined in Spanish law, there was also the *mayorazgo de femineidad* that gave daughters, extending to an exclusively female lineage, the right to the entailed land. Cornejo, *Diccionario histórico*, 420–442.

ments of ownership of lands obtained in *composición*, served to formalise the transfer of *pueblo* communal lands to the domain of Spaniards and other non-Indians in late colonial Peru.[6] Although caciques and *alcaldes* (municipality judges) of Vico appear together as witnesses of the *vistas de ojos* and eventually as individual declarants in the proceedings of the case, it is difficult to distinguish other specific roles they played in the defence of the *pueblo* lands.

Andean historiography on land relations has made significant strides in the last half a century, moving from the socio-economic and political histories of large agrarian structures[7] to more nuanced localised studies that incorporate transdisciplinary approaches.[8] Numerous ethnohistorical studies have illuminated colonial indigenous groups' internal dynamics related to lands and the associated cultural, social, and intellectual practices, while studies in legal history have also contributed to cross-cultural understandings of land tenure and ownership relations as well.[9] In studying the role of law in shaping ownership regarding indigenous commons, however, the instructive potential of looking at local procedural praxis and protocols associated with land conflicts has been little explored.[10] This approach invites meticulous archival digging and critical

6 *Composiciones de tierras* were a process of legitimising de facto Spanish occupations of land qualified as "vacant"; for a fee, the Crown would graciously grant proof of ownership. The years 1590–1596, 1615–1622, 1665 and 1722–1725 yielded the majority of *composiciones de tierras* in the Andes. Stavig, "Ambiguous Visions", 92. By law, the *composiciones* were contingent on respecting indigenous commons and causing no damage to neighbouring properties. *Composiciones* could, therefore, be challenged in court and Andeans brought numerous lawsuits to reverse them. See *Recopilación de Leyes*, Libro IV, Título XII, Leyes XV–XXI. For an emblematic example from the Sucusuma valley (Charcas), see Jurado, "Títulos de la tierra", 49–64. Andeans themselves eventually also obtained *composiciones de tierras*. Jurado, "Baldíos, derechos posesorios y tierra realenga" 1–24, discusses the polysemic nature of the term *baldíos* (vacant lands), arguing that *composiciones* reasserted royal power over vacant and *realengos* (royal lands). It is important to mention that, although the *composición* was not in itself a title but a juridical act leading to a title, the expression *titulos de composición* is used in the litigation papers several times in reference to the ownership instruments given to Lagunas and his wife as beneficiaries of several *composiciones de tierras*. See also Jurado (Chapter 6) in this volume.

7 For the sake of space, only a short sample of the large historiography is offered here: Larson, *Colonialism and Agrarian Transformation*; Keith, *Conquest and Agrarian Change*; Burga, *De la encomienda a la hacienda capitalista*.

8 Ramirez, Provincial Patriarchs; Spalding, Huarochiri; Stern, Peru's Indian Peoples.

9 Murra, *Formaciones económicas y políticas*; Penry, *The People Are King*; Rappaport, *The Politics of Memory*; Graubart, "Shifting Landscapes"; Bastien, "Land Litigations", 101–131; Vieira-Powers, *Andean Journeys*; Puente Luna, "Of Widows, Furrows and Seed".

10 A recent exception examines the various interpretations of "baldios" (vacant lands) and the right to possession as expressed in the practices of *jueces de comisión* during the implementation of the first *composiciones de tierras* in 1600 Charcas, where they rendered

close reading to 'extract' the saliency of the fine technicalities of the law applied on-site and subject it to an interpretation of larger transformations in Andean land relations.

I build the argument of this Chapter in sections thus: I first introduce the environment and social settings of the dispute (Vico, Pasco, and Llacsahuanca) to provide some context for the case. In the subsequent section, I intertwine the contours of the litigation with a detailed critical analysis of the legal procedures used to investigate the conflict, showing how they constructed the dissolution of the commons through a selection of probatory evidence and the questionnaire application. Next, I demonstrate that the cartographic mechanism's visual and textual rhetoric along with the judge's approach to the *vista de ojos* and *mensuras* (measurements) served to instrumentalise dispossession. These two sections lead to a synthesised examination of the power contest between *amparos* and maps in the Bourbon provincial courts. Before concluding, a view of contending perceptions of commoning by Lagunas and the Andeans offers a wider perspective on this protracted litigation as an iteration of the continuous formation and destruction of ownership regimes in the Andes.

2 Vico, Pasco, and Llacsahuanca

The general resettlement programme that the Habsburg undertook in Peru produced the colonial towns of Vico and Pasco.[11] Vico lay to the south of and a league away from Pasco, on a central and narrow inter-Andean valley, at 4104 metres and 4184 metres of altitude respectively.[12] As of 1772, the Quechua-speaking Yaros Yanamates, along with *mitmaqs* from Yanacache, appeared resettled in Pasco.[13] Restricted agriculture of high-altitude crops, such as bar-

indigenous lands as *baldias* and available for sale. Jurado, "Baldios, derechos posesorios y tierra realenga", 1–24; Jurado, "Titulos de la tierra, y nociones posesorias y de dominio", 49–64.

11 The programme relocated Andean communities into *reducciones*, as they were spaces more suitable for their conversion to Christianity, tribute-payers and Spanish law-abiding "Indian" subjects. See discussions on the nature of this process and its historical iterations in Mumford, *Vertical Empire* and Penry, *The People are King*, and the various works compiled in Saito and Rosas' *Reducciones*.

12 The larger area had been the homeland of the Yauros until the mid-17th century, who presumably corresponded to the Wankuy *ayllus* in the 18th century. As a *pueblo de Indios*, Pasco appears interchangeably designated as "Villa de Pasco" and "Pasco" in the litigation documents. In 1776, ten years before the creation of the system of *Intendencias* in the area, Vico and Pasco belonged to the colonial jurisdiction of the Tarma province.

13 Archivo General de la Nación, Perú (AGN), Causas Civiles, leg. 179 cuad. 1512, 1772, fol. 2r.

ley, maca, and potatoes, alternated with sheep herding to the north of the long Mantaro River, 22 kilometres south of Vico from the Chinchaycocha Lake. In the 18th century, Pasco and Vico residents may have worked temporarily in the silver mines located in Cerro de Pasco 19.3 kilometres north of Pasco. Also drawn by the prospect of silver mines, Spaniards moved in, thereby intensifying demand for land as expanding *estancias* and *haciendas* increasingly absorbed communal lands, while the indigenous population rapidly declined.[14] Mining shaped the history of the Villa de Pasco, particularly in the 18th century. Along with the Spanish landowners, miners of different backgrounds came to work in the mills, or *obrajes*, established in the mining district of Cerro de Pasco for grinding silver metal.[15] According to the Tarma Contador in 1772, the ethnic groups that resettled in Vico were the Yaros Yanayacos and those in Pasco were the Yaros Yanamates along with *mitmaqs* from Yanacache.[16]

Llacsahuanca itself had a long history before it became an *estancia* and later landed in Lagunas' estate. Royal economies of grace and patronage galvanised empire building through gifting lands to meritorious imperial subjects. In addition to strategic marriage alliances, these land grants helped the lineage of the Vasquez de Velasco and its 1696 matrimonial alliance with the Casa Tello through Doña Ana Maria to amass large land holdings and other valuable assets in the Tarma region and in Lima and passed them down through inheritance to Lagunas and his descendants in the late colonial years. The family managed territorial wealth mostly through renting out rather than directly undertaking productive activities in the land. The *estancia* Llacsahuanca was apparently formed in the late 16th century through a *composición* to the conqueror ancestors of Lagunas. Along with the Paucartambo *obraje*, Llacsahuanca became the largest portion of a *mayorazgo* constituted in 1725 by Lagunas' grandmother,

---

This information was reported by the accountant of the province. The *mitmaqs* were groups of Andeans resettled by the Inca.

14 For the Tarma province in general, the local indigenous population not only declined vis-à-vis the non-Indians (roughly by 54%) by the last decade of the 18th century, but also the *originarios* represented only 13% of the already decreased native population at large. Concurrently, from the early decades of the century, the province's population of non-Indians steadily increased. Arellano Hoffmann, *Notas sobre el indígena*, 29–30.

15 Biblioteca Nacional del Perú (BNP), Impresos Varios (IV), Mariano Carrillo. Abril 3, 1782, p. 15. The year of Pasco's foundation is uncertain. Lagunas maintained that it was after the foundation of his *mayorazgo* in 1725, which would obviously support his point that Pasco encroached upon his Llacsahuanca lands. The Andean authorities contested this claim as will be seen later.

16 AGNP Causas Civiles, leg. 179, cuad. 1512, fol. 2r. 1772. The *mitmaqs* were groups of Andeans resettled by the Inca whose colonial identity was grounded both in their labour status under the Inca and in their own traditions and social practices of origin.

Doña Ana María Tello de la Cueva, acting as the executor and holder of her deceased husband's assets. Before his death, the spouses had agreed to create a "*título y vínculo de mayorazgo*" in the name of their son Joseph Ventura Vasquez de Velasco, Lagunas' father, worth a third and a fifth of the total assets belonging to the Paucartambo *obraje* and the *estancia* Llacsahuanca.[17] The family managed landed wealth mostly through renting out rather than directly undertaking productive activities in the land. Residing permanently in Lima, Lagunas was one of many absentee landowners, living off the rent of his vast landed assets in the Tarma province and his real estate in Lima. His legal affairs were attended to remotely by various attorneys and a network of high-ranking officials in the Lima Audiencia and the Tarma provincial *corregimiento* (district).[18]

3 Dispossession Through Litigation

The consolidation of Lagunas' *mayorazgo* in 1725 conjured up old tensions with Vico, since the inception of Llacsahuanca when Juan Tello, its first owner, challenged the grasslands commons of Vico in 1576, three years after the Indian town's foundation. Vico's *cabildo* successfully defeated his pretensions with newly issued *amparos de posesión*.[19] On 8 October 1776, Pasco and Vico's lawsuit came as a response to Lagunas' legal challenge (1771–1772), suing the Royal Treasury for the alleged destruction of his Paucartambo *obraje* in 1746 during the construction of a fort to counter Juan Santos Atahualpa's insurrection in the frontier, and also demanding monetary restitution from the Royal Treasury.[20] The lawsuit involved Pasco because Lagunas denied its commons, claiming that it was not even a *pueblo de Indios* but a recent and illegal foundation

17 AGNP, Real Audiencia, Causas Civiles, leg. 53, doc. 359. Lima, 1725, fols. 1^{r}, 10^{v}. From 1725, they rented out both the *obraje* and the *estancia*, which included 41,000 sheep, to various renters.

18 AGNP, Real Audiencia. Causas Civiles. leg. 326, cuad. 2975. 1794, fols. 1^{r}–19^{v}.

19 The Lima Audiencia ruled in favour of Vico and ordered Tello to move his cattle a league away from the town's lands and onto the other side of the San Juan River. BNP, Impresos Varios, Mariano Carrillo. 3 April 1782, p. 16. The 1776 lawsuit by the Indians suggests that the Lima *Audiencia* mandate had lingered unenforced for more than two hundred years, which unleashed more successive lawsuits.

20 Lagunas' lawyer in Lima, Melgarejo, and a powerful Audiencia ally and lawyer, Mariano Carrillo, rendered the destruction of the Paucartambo *obraje* and the land disputes by Vico and Pasco as threatening the economic stability of the *mayorazgo* and Lagunas' very noble status. In fact, his noble title was about to expire due to overdue taxes (Lanzas y Medias Anatas), for which he had pleaded for a waiver since 1769 and again in 1782. AGNP,

situated next to his Paucartambo *obraje* and inside Llacsahuanca. All in all, Lagunas' lawsuit included specific claims against parts of Vico's common grasslands, including "canchas y majadas",[21] and questioned the presence of Pasco on his land altogether. While the *cabildos* from Vico and Pasco filed their lawsuits in the local jurisdiction of the Spanish provincial magistrate, or *corregidor*, Lagunas had started his own litigation from above, filing an initial complaint before the king himself in 1771 and then formalising a lawsuit in the Audiencia de Lima where he had connections to lawyers and judges.[22]

As is common procedure in land disputes, the Lima Real Audiencia ordered the land judge and *corregidor* of Tarma, Don Francisco Javier de Arcona, to conduct the reconnaissance and visual inspections of the location of Pasco, Vico, and the Paucartambo fort, "drawing a map with the corresponding dimensions in the clearest and most specific way you can."[23] Prior to the *vista de ojos*, Don Juan Jose Melgarejo, a lawyer for Lagunas, asked the Lima court that, for the inspection and the drawing of the map draft, the judge should be delivered "the titles and maps" Lagunas furnished so that the judge could "proceed to do the inspection of the lands with them."[24] Most of the witnesses invited to the stand by Lagunas' lawyer were Spanish "*vecinos* [neighbors] and *hacendados*, mine owners and *azogueros*", and members of the colonial frontier militias, or a combination of the two. According to Corregidor Arcona, the interim *protector de naturales* (protector of the Indians) legally representing the Indians presented 60 witnesses to the interrogatory in his office, including "caciques, *alcaldes, regidores*, ministers, and other members of the *comun* [community] from Vico and Pasco." Except for Cacique Don Joseph Chavin Palpa, unfortunately there is no reference whatsoever to these indigenous witnesses' names or their declarations in the proceedings.[25] The questions fielded to the witnesses were only

---

Real Audiencia. Causas Civiles, leg. 169, doc. 1431. 1769. BNP, Impresos Varios, Mariano Carrillo. 3 April 1782, pp. 13–15. Carrillo claimed that the Villa de Pasco and more than 60 mills for crushing metal were illegally situated in the lands of Lagunas' *estancia*.

21 Gonzáles Holguín defined the Quechua term "canchas" as both corrals and herds. González Holguín, *Arte y Diccionario Quechua*, 50. He also translated the Spanish term "majadas" into Quechua as "llama canchas". González Holguín, *Vocabulario en la lengua general del Perú*, 301. Notably, Puente Luna describes *canchas* as a form of Andean commons (*sapçi*) since they were "built and maintained by community members". Puente Luna, "Of Widows, Furrows, and Seed".

22 BNP, Impresos Varios, Mariano Carrillo. 3 April 1782, pp. 2–3.

23 "levantándose un mapa con las dimensiones correspondientes en la forma más clara y específica que podais." AGNP, Lima, Tierras de comunidades, leg. 11, cuad. 92, fol. 7^{v}.

24 "proceder con ellos a hacer la inspección del as tierras." AGNP. Lima, Tierras de comunidades, leg. 11, cuad. 92, fols. 48^{r}.

25 AGNP, Lima, Tierras de comunidades, leg. 11, cuad. 92, fols. 42^{r}, 47^{v}–48^{r}. Cacique Don

geared to verifying the existence of the two *pueblos de indios* vis-à-vis the foundation of the *mayorazgo* in 1725. All the Spanish witnesses asserted that Vico was very old, and that Pasco was definitely founded after the *mayorazgo*. But they overlooked the possibility that the *pueblos* existed prior to 1725 and perhaps with a different name. None of them acknowledged that Pasco was given *tierras de repartimiento* and called it "Villa de Pasco", which suggested that Pasco was not even a *pueblo de indios*. As discussed below, Cacique Don Joseph Chavin Palpa's declarations made clear the underlying incorrect assumption in this question and declared that Pasco had indeed existed as a *pueblo de indios* since at least 1603.[26]

Lagunas' second lawyer, Sebastián Arias y Araujo from Pasco, insisted that the judge conduct the ocular inspection closely following the single *linderos* (boundaries) listed in the Lagunas' "títulos de Llacsahuanca" and the map, which the Audiencia heeded. Arias demanded simultaneously that the indigenous litigants "would present their titles." There is no indication that the *corregidor* asked the Indians to furnish their own maps, and the citation to Caciques Don Joseph Chavin Palpa (Pasco) and Don Joseph Pio de la Barrera (Vico) only required them to furnish "their titles", thus only accepting unproblematically the maps of Lagunas, before the reconnaissance, on 3 February 1778.[27]

The *corregidor's* report of the visual inspection and the verification of distances in the map he attached (see Map 8.1) are a rendition of the various stops that were to be made at every single boundary recorded in Lagunas' "instrumentos" (documents of proof), including his map. Vico's *cabildo* disputed at least four of those boundaries, the first one being Cotocoto, the first stop recorded in the report. Arcona conveyed that, according to the native litigants, Cotocoto was the original head town before they were resettled by Visitador Juan de Fuentes and re-Christened on 23 April 1573, as Nuestra Señora de la Concepción de Vico. Arcona added that "today there is no trace left of it" (*hoy no le ha quedado vestigio alguno*).[28] There, the Vico Indians exhibited some royal

Joseph Chavin Palpa was the last witness to be questioned. He was introduced as "Gobernador y cacique principal …, minero y azoguero de Su Majestad, dueño de ingenios y Sargento Mayor del Batallón de los Naturales." Corregidor Arcona designated Juan Antonio Racines as substitute Protector de Naturales, because the protector of record, Christobal Zabala, was absent from the region. The fact that no interpreter, or *lengua*, was listed as present in the interrogatory suggests that no indigenous depositions were made by local Quechua speakers or native speakers of languages other than Spanish.

26 AGNP, Lima, Tierras de comunidades, leg. 11, cuad. 92, fol. 42^{r}.

27 AGNP, Lima, Tierras de comunidades, leg. 11, cuad. 92, fol. 47^{r}.

28 AGNP, Tierras de comunidades, leg. 11, cuad. 92, fol. 48^{v}. "Y habiendo llegado al sitio y

provisions and *títulos de amparo* to substantiate their boundary claim.[29] Since Lagunas also claimed Cotocoto as part of Llacsahuanca, Arcona decided to settle the dispute by measuring the statutory one league's distance from Vico's square outward to verify the extension of the town's lands. He concluded that Vico had exceeded the original size of the *repartimiento* lands (1573) and proceeded to render his findings in a map he attached to the report, showing the distances from the town's plaza out to each of the *linderos* listed in Lagunas' documents and map. In practice, he rendered these lands "in excess" as open to royal disposition and out of the domain of the *pueblo* community, thus evoking older interpretations of these lands "in excess" as vacant.[30]

From 1576, Vico Indians deployed their *títulos de amparo* as a weapon to defend their communal lands in the absence of other proof of ownership. They were the treasure trove documents of their town's foundation issued in 1573 by the judge visitor. For the most part, in the 18th century, *pueblo* communities were unable to furnish proof of the lands assigned to them at the time of the original *repartimiento*, since they either got lost over the years or they were simply not issued in a written manner at the time of the town's foundation. Even ownership titles of individual Andeans and communities were rare.[31] It is then remarkable that, after about 200 years, the Vico authorities had still conserved these *amparos* from the time they were resettled on 6 April 1573. In that year, on behalf of the king, the Royal Visitador Fuentes granted *repartimiento* lands to the *ayllus* (the basic indigenous political unit) resettled in the

lindero que llaman Cotocoto, pueblo que dicen haber sido en la antigua cabeza de los indios de Vico y hoy no le ha quedado vestigio alguno, me presentaron los indios de dicho pueblo unos títulos de amparo con varias reales provisiones con ellos sujetándose en todas al auto de visita de Juan de Fuentes de 23 de abril de 1573 en que los reduce a la mansión en que hoy se hallan en el pueblo de Nuestra Señora de la Concepción de Vico, señalándoles un lengua en contorno para su estabilidad."

29 These are the surviving records of the creation of Vico by Inspector-General (Visitador) Fuentes, which apparently established one league as *repartimiento* lands around the town's plaza. The Vico *cabildo* officers countered that the *amparos* included Cotocoto, which Lagunas claimed as part of Llacsahuanca according to the documents Arias submitted on behalf of Lagunas.

30 Analysing the interpretations and actions of *jueces comisionados* in Charcas (1600) during the first *composiciones de tierras*, Jurado, in "Baldios, derechos posesorios y tierra realenga", 19–21, argues that not only did they come to assume they could, on the king's name, dispose of indigenous communal lands held "in excess" of their subsistence needs, but they also tended to exclude what "baldios" meant for native colonial actors themselves. See also, Jurado (Chapter 6) in this volume. In Vico, Juez Comisionado Arcona dismissed the meaning of places like Cotocoto to the detriment of Andeans' spatial referents of collective identity in the past and present.

31 Owensby, *Empire of Law*, 129.

town of Vico. Even though *títulos de amparo* were not ownership titles, Vico had long used them to protect the original *repartimiento* lands. They exhibited *amparos* in litigation, a few times successfully, as valid instruments to defend their communal right to land usufruct in the face of several previous challenges by Lagunas and his predecessors. Some judicial officials, such as Protector General de Naturales Don Diego de León Pinelo, supported the granting of *amparos de posesión* in 1656 to Cacique Don Francisco Chavin Palpa "so that it serves him as a better title to the lands."[32]

What the Vico *cabildo* argued about Cotocoto reveals the Indians' effort to adapt to the Spanish culture of possession the best they could to beat the power of the *instrumentos* and maps exhibited by their counterpart. In the *pueblo* social memory, the 1573 colonial resettlement must have been a time of significant historical change. The previous head town, or *cabecera*, in Cotocoto remained in the *pueblo*'s memory as part of their colonial homeland, a symbolic centre, a rather cultural and social argument with little or no validity in a colonial court in the Bourbon era. The *cabildo* officers and the caciques in 1778 remembered Cotocoto as a landmark of colonial chronology for their commons, after they were relocated to Vico. In his report, the *corregidor* disavowed the importance of this cultural and legal significance for the Indians, noting that there was no remnant of the town, no traceable mark of *pueblo* commons attributable to the Vico Indians, although this was a significant part of what the Indians claimed to be theirs. In fact, when Cacique Don Joseph Chavin Palpa answered the judge's questions about the status of Vico and Pasco as *pueblos de indios* ("with church and designated lands and commons") and their age with respect to the creation of Lagunas' *mayorazgo*, he referred to the same historical moment of the town's foundation and pointed to the *amparos*, as well as to the "títulos del repartimiento". These social and community memories held in common and in lived spaces constituted part of the genealogy of the pueblos that Andeans wanted to associate with their possession.[33]

32 "para que le sirva de mejor título de las tierras." AGNP, Causas Civiles. leg. 179, cuad. 1512, fol. 96r. Cacique Don Francisco was the great-great grandfather of Pasco's Cacique in 1778, Don Joseph Chavin Palpa. Even the "libros de reparto" served as a community land title elsewhere in the Andes. These land registries were drawn up upon the first *composiciones de tierras* when *visitadores* distributed "royal lands" to the *ayllus* of the town. In Sumaro (Cuzco) in 1595, this alternative function of the "libros de reparto" was clearly stipulated in the title: "Se le dara a entender para que le sirva de título". Amado Gonzalez, "Reparto de tierras", 205.

33 Bastias Saavedra ("The lived Space", 17) explains that ownership was also tied to lived spaces and marked by the shared local memories of community members. In Vico, the memories of landmarks like Cotocoto played a similar role.

Cacique Don Joseph Chavin Palpa found among the *cacicazgo's* titles an indication of possession that verified the existence of Pasco as a *pueblo de indios* as early as 1601, prior to the foundation of Lagunas' *mayorazgo*. This was the appointment year of his third grandfather, Cacique Don Francisco Chavin Palpa, as Cacique Principal and Gobernador of the Repartimiento de Yaros Yanamates. The title specified that the Yaros Yanamates resided in Pasco, *pueblo de indios*, in 1601.[34] In the 1650s Cacique Don Francisco Chavin Palpa had petitioned for subsequent *mandamientos de amparo* to defend six endangered sites of Pasco's commons. Viceroy Conde de Alba de Aliste approved the *mandamientos*, which also confirmed the residence of the protected Indians in Pasco, *pueblo de indios*. They also proved that the possession of Pasco's commons was confirmed several times with *mandamientos*.[35] The recurrence of these *mandamientos de amparo* reveal the continuous challenges posed to Pasco's commons despite the legal function of these instruments, which eventually came to exemplify the prevalence of "precarious possession" over the right to hold the land. Indeed, and despite the *mandamientos*, Lagunas denied the existence of these commons and referred to the residents of Pasco as "intruders".[36]

4 Mapping for Dispossession

Arcona's cartographic interpretation and inspection method deserve more pondering. Measuring one league from Vico's plaza outward, he excluded de facto the possibility that Llacsahuanca both exceeded its original granted ex-

---

34 AGNP, Tierras de comunidades, leg. 11, cuad. 92, fol. 42^r. "Vico es más antiguo que la Villa de Pasco y las tierras que se le señalaron constan en sus títulos." Cacique Don Joseph Chavin Palpa had previously stated that Pasco was indeed a *pueblo de indios*: "ahora ciento setenta y cinco años era pueblo con iglesia y consta la posesión de los indios de Pasco en los titulos de cacicazgo de mis antepasados los que en caso necesario manifestará." He conserved those titles in 1772 and added them to the file later. AGNP, Real Audiencia, Causas Civiles, leg. 179, cuad. 1512. 1772, fol. 89^r.

35 The *mandamientos de amparo* were issued on 26 June 1654; 28 December 1655; 5 April 1656 and 28 November 1656. AGNP. Causas Civiles, leg. 179, cuad. 1512, fols. 94^r–94^v; 96^r; 100^v. The commons from Quinuacatay; Cau Cay; Atoc; Enquiguasin, Manyanquin and Yacallumay, located in the Repartimiento de Yaros, received protection. The witnesses of the ceremonies of possession were the native *alcaldes ordinarios* (municipal council judges) and *regidores* (aldermen) of the Pueblo de Pasco.

36 Owensby, *Empire of Laws*, 129. AGNP, Causas Civiles, leg. 179, cuad. 1512, ff. 105^v–106^r. Lagunas accused Don Joseph of illegally granting the Indians lands on his own.

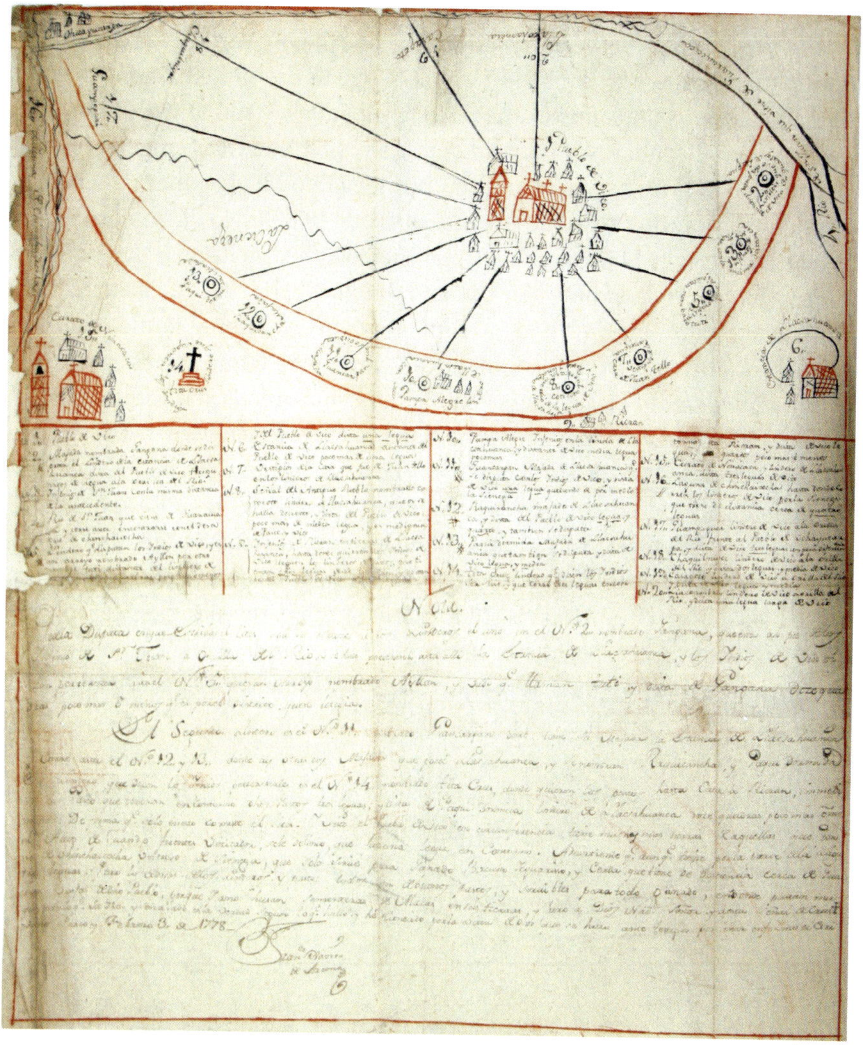

MAP 8.1 Map of the *pueblo de indios* of Pasco
AGNP, MAPAS Y PLANOS, PLANO NO. 043

tension (even if not as far as one league away from Vico's plaza) and that it was too close to the *pueblo* lands.[37]

Thus, Cotocoto appeared unproblematically registered in 1778 as part of the *estancia* and was claimed by Lagunas as his own in the instruments and the map he furnished to prove his land possession.

37 By law, *estancias* must be situated at least two miles away from the Indian land commons. Recopilación. Law 20, Title 3, Book 6.

On the other hand, and according to the Protector de Naturales Alberto Chosop, who drew from the *Recopilación*, Arcona did not verify if Llacsahuanca lands conformed to Law 20, Title 3, Book 6, which prohibited *estancias* from being too close to the lands of the *pueblos de indios*.[38] Along with Cotocoto, however, Vico disputed two other *linderos*. The first one was Gangana (*mojón* No. 2 in Map 8.1) next to the San Juan River, claimed by Lagunas, and which Vico denied, pointing to a site known as "Tuti" (*mojón* No. 5 in Map 8.1) as the actual *lindero* of Llacsahuanca. Thus, Vico claimed as its own twelve more *cuadras* (blocks) of land between Tuti and Gangana. The second disputed land was "Guancarpan" (*mojón* No. 11 in Map 8.1) where, according to the map, the *majadas*, or corrals, of the Llacsahuanca's cattle stood, and which ran up to two other *majadas* of Llacsahuanca known as Raquicancha and Paquidormida (*mojón* Nos. 12 and 13 in Map 8.1). Vico claimed these *linderos* as theirs, adding that they extended to the site known as "Titacruz" (*mojón* No. 14 in Map 8.1). The *cabildo* considered these their own grasslands, including those running all the way to Rieran, measuring around three leagues (*mojón* No. 9 in Map 8.1).[39]

Looking closely at the representation of boundaries and verified distances on the map, however, some facts stand out as striking, revealing aspects of the use of land maps as legal evidence in Tarma. If the standard one league around the town were to be applied as the yardstick to decide which party expanded beyond the legal mark, it would in fact be Llacsahuanca that encroached several times upon Vico's lands. At least five out of the 20 boundaries inspected, including two of the disputed ones (Gangana and Cotocoto), fell inside the one-league circumference of lands belonging to the *pueblo*, meaning that the *estancia* encroached upon them, thus contradicting Arcona's concluding statements against Vico's claims.[40] What emerges here more clearly is the corroboration of

38 See fn. 53, below.

39 AGNP, plano no. 043. *Majadas* were important corrals where Andeans collected fertilising manure. In fact, the toponym "Raquicancha" denotes the existence of an Andean corral, or "cancha", for llamas. The Andean commons in this case included, all in all, a series of *majadas* (Raquicancha and Paquidormida), llama *canchas*, highland pastures (from Raquicancha and Paquidormida to Titacruz), and farming land (Gangana and the lands between Tuti and Gangana), as well as woodcutting grounds elsewhere.

40 In fact, two of the other boundaries claimed by Lagunas as part of his lands were not even disputed by Vico, but, when applying to the map the respective distances glossed in its legend this corroborates that Llacsahuanca had encroached upon the *pueblo* lands in at least the four boundaries named Gangana (No. 2, which lay three-quarters of a league away from the town's plaza), Ingenios de San Juan (No. 3, same distance), Cotocoto (No. 8, half a league from the town's plaza) and Pampa Alegre (No. 10, half a league away from the town's plaza). In two other boundaries, the distance to the town's plaza was barely one league (Tuti and Guancarpan). AGNP, Mapas y Planos, plano no. 043. Although the carto-

the bias in measuring, mapping, and reporting by Arcona. At a time where, elsewhere in the Americas, measurements were not yet given a status of exactitude, the single distances he reported in the map's legend, packed with a substantial amount of text in a rather fine print (numbered 1–20 in Map 8.1), in fact, contradict his own conclusion in the report of the *vista de ojos*. The legend lists the various distances measured from the boundaries inward to the town's plaza, as opposed to the outward approach Arcona chose to measure the townlands when settling the Cotocoto dispute in the report. Therefore, Llacsahuanca's uneven encroachment is unveiled in the map legend but not acknowledged as a major statement in the conclusion of the visual inspection report that Arcona submitted to the Audiencia. With respect to Pasco, Arcona included no inspection report, although he glossed a map with 38 *mojones* (boundary markers) without reporting any distances to the town. In the "Notes" section of the map legend, he concluded that, because no one from the *pueblo* submitted titles, he had to go by Llacsahuanca's titles, submitted by Lagunas' lawyer. And "from them, I know that [Pasco] is erected in the lands of the said *estancia* and that its inhabitants have received no common grasslands."[41]

graphic technique in Map 8.1 seems incipient, it is important to remember that the use of landscape paintings in the court was but a moment in the long history of the modern legal practice of land surveying. Modern maps began to display substantial written text, descriptions, and measurements that were estimates rather than exact measures. As with modern land surveying itself, these landscape maps were but discrete points in a long and dissimilar process, rather "gradual and uneven". On the other hand, the purpose of land surveying in the colonial Americas seems to have been "to remake the property landscape rather than to record and preserve existing arrangements." Greer, *Property and Dispossession*, 312.

41 AGNP, Tierras de comunidades, leg. 11, cuad. 92, fol. 49r. The "Notes" section of the Pasco map legend also asserted that the whole *pueblo* compound of church, royal treasury, and other buildings were situated in the grasslands and corrals of Llacsahuanca. In addition, it specifies that neither the Cacique, nor the Alcalde or any other minister from Pasco submitted documents of any kind to Arcona. AGNP, plano no. 024. Indeed, the file bears no reference to either summoning native witnesses nor their declarations. It did copiously record, however, details of the only witness declaration rendered. In it, Lagunas' wife wholeheartedly supported her husband's claims and described the residents of Pasco with notorious stereotypes. AGNP, Causas Civiles, leg. 179, cuad. 1512, fol. 2r. 1772. The map also renders glosses for the 38 boundaries noting geographical features, roads, economic activities, and resources, and religious buildings. Arcona reported on the inspection of the Paucartambo fort, detailing the building structure, size, materials and objects found. The emphasis is placed on the source of the materials (from the Llacsahuanca's grounds), the bounty of local food and other resources used for the building of the fort and the support of the sentinels working there. The report supports Lagunas' claims about the destruction of his *obraje* and his demand for restoration from the *Real Hacienda*. AGNP. Plano No. 024a.

When asked the question about his knowledge of the existence of Pasco as a *pueblo de indios*, its cacique, Don Joseph Chavin Palpa, responded that the town had existed since at least 1601 as a "town with a church" and that the possession of Pasco's lands could be verified in his ancestor's *cacicazgo* titles.[42] Whether Arcona was aware of them or not, the *mandamientos de amparo* that the Lima Audiencia issued on 28 November 1656 to Cacique Don Francisco Chavin Palpa appeared attached to the 1771–1772 lawsuit file that Procurador Fiscal Don Alberto Chosop helped put together to advance the case in Lima on behalf of the Pasco Indians. In April 1697, the Audiencia extended a new *amparo* to Cacique Don Francisco Chavin Palpa confirming possession of Pasco's lands. In August 1772, Chosop asked the Audiencia to send the provision that approved Pasco's *mandamientos de amparo* and the *amparos* themselves to the *corregidor* and commissioned judge, before conducting the *vista de ojos* and *deslinde*.[43] Although the Audiencia approved the request, the fate of the visual inspections of 1772 remain unknown and went unreported in the file. It seems incomprehensible why, in the new lawsuit of 1776–1778, the Audiencia and Arcona chose not to look at or at least acknowledge the *mandamientos de amparo* that protected Pasco's right of possession of its commons, not to mention the request for the *cacicazgo* titles that Don Joseph Chavin Palpa mentioned and offered to furnish during the 1778 interrogatory.

What could explain the oversights discussed above in this legal case? And what does that tell us about the protection of the communal lands managed by the native *cabildo* in the Bourbon period? What can be said about the role of legal cartography in land tenure change, and, overall, in the administration of justice in a late colonial and relatively remote setting? Concerning the apparent discrepancies in the map legend vis-à-vis the land judge's report, the truth is that even in the "Notes" (a conclusion section under the map legend and before his oath and signature), Arcona reiterated the outcome of the inspection of Vico. That is, that the totality of the *pueblo* encompassed substantially more lands than the one league officially distributed at the town's foundation by Visitador Jose Fuentes in 1573.[44] That statement is clearly what the *corregidor* intended the Audiencia to focus on. The map legend in these 18th-century land

42 AGNP, Tierras de comunidades. L11 C92, fol. 42^{r}. 1778. See Note No. 32 above.

43 AGNP, Real Audiencia, Causas Civiles, leg. 179, cuad. 1512., fols. 94^{r}–96^{v}. 1772. The documents Chosop requested were significant because they contained pertinent Audiencia mandates, describing the specific "canchas, pastos, las dichas tierras en cuestión y la dispossesión perpetrada contra mis partes." (fols. 101^{r}–101^{v}). Lagunas' lawyer rejected this request asking for the procedure to continue without waiting for the documentation.

44 AGNP, plano no. 43.

maps was a rather convoluted narrative with details on some *mojones* indicated in the map. It may well be that this section was included as pure formality, and that the reader would expect the judge to have verified it beforehand. It may also be that the mapmakers and the surveyors, of whom the file gives no information, took the 20 measurements independently from that of the Cotocoto *mojón*, which seems to be the only one the *corregidor* reported to have personally inspected.[45]

Regardless of the technical issues of the visual inspection, there was a stark contrast between the legal resources at the disposal of both parties and how the judges handled their respective stakes. The Indians from Vico were represented by a substitute fiscal protector that Arcona chose for them among local *vecinos* and who, in turn, chose mostly anonymous declarants on behalf of the Indians for the interrogatory and as witnesses of the visual inspection. Perhaps this explains why the *amparos* from 1656 and the *cacicazgo* titles from 1603 never reached the hands of the judge before the *vista de ojos*.

Lagunas, instead, enjoyed representation by two lawyers, one in Lima and one in Pasco. Significantly, this aristocrat enjoyed the protection of an influential network of upper-ranking members of the Lima Audiencia, who enabled his land claims against Vico and Pasco with potent resources that the indigenous *cabildos* could not possibly have accessed. A powerful lawyer of the Audiencia, Don Mariano Carrillo, who had also been a lawyer of the Lima *cabildo*, produced a meticulous *alegación en derecho* (juridical argumentation) defending the Lagunas' claims over Llacsahuanca and supporting his demands on the Real Hacienda. The *alegación en derecho* was a strategy lawyers had used since the 16th century.[46] They sought to create a public forum about a case, usually to defend the vested interests and honour of the elites, geared toward forming a legal clientele (a kind of public opinion) that would exert persuasive pressure over the judges. *Alegaciones en derecho* were costly and required a publication license by the Audiencia and the oversight of its *Escribanos de Cámara* before

45 AGNP, Tierras de comunidades, leg. 11, cuad. 92, fol. 49^{r}. The Audiencia of Lima ordered the *vista de ojos* in 1777, asking that the measurements were to be verified by the judge. It is also possible that the inspection was conducted that day without the presence of an *escribano* (scribe), as Arcona noted before his signature. It also appears that the *corregidor* ordered others to make the copy of the map (admitting that he would simply annotate it) and perhaps others conducted the measurements of the 20 boundaries, which required arduous walking in the rugged Andean terrain of Vico.

46 The legal aspects of 18th-century *alegaciones en derecho* are discussed in Camallonga, "El derecho en las alegaciones jurídicas del siglo XVIII", 277–317. Jordà Fernández, in "Alegaciones jurídicas del siglo XVII en Cataluña", 56–58, offers a more juridical typology and definition of *alegaciones en derecho*.

they were printed and circulated. The 16th-century *alegaciones* were lengthy discussions of the jurisprudence that supported the case, glossed with long references to Roman Law and jurists and appeals to Christian moral values. The *alegaciones* of the 18th century, like Carrillo's, superseded the former in expediency, precision of juridical doctrine and argumentation, an example of the rationalistic spirit of the Bourbon times and the long-term changes in colonial legal culture. *Alegaciones* were certainly a privilege of the Spanish elites, often used to defend in court the entitlements that the "economy of grace" bestowed upon them. As the final report with the judgement of the *juez comisionado* dismissed the claims of Vico and Pasco, it is clear that the *alegación en derecho* empowered Lagunas' defence of the various prerogatives historically concretised in the *estancia* Llacsahuanca and his own noble title as "Conde".

Even though *alegaciones en derecho* lay far away from the universe of possibilities for the Indian *cabildos* and the caciques *gobernadores* from Vico and Pasco, they did live to see, at least in 1772, how the changes the indigenous *letrados* introduced in the Procuraduría de Naturales allowed the first indigenous Procurador Fiscal to temper the ownership ascriptions of Lagunas and legally deconstruct the power of his *mayorazgo* titles over the Indians' *amparos de possession*. Don Alberto Chosop was the first indigenous protector and Procurador de naturales that the Lima Audiencia appointed, after decades of pressure by an El Cercado native *cabildo*, and he acted as the "Fiscal Procurador" of the case in question in the Audiencia.[47] His discussions and requests countered both Lagunas' arguments in court and the procedures of the *juez comisionado* with meticulously devised ideas in support of the two *pueblos*' possession of their commons. Chosop refused upfront Lagunas' allegations against Vico and his casting of doubts about the existence of Pasco as a *pueblo de indios* with entitlements to common lands. In plain language, he demanded that the Audiencia deny Lagunas the right to "posesión y propiedad" and the restitution of possession for the *indios del común* from Vico and Pasco through various arguments.[48]

First, Chosop disputed the power of the *mayorazgo* titles as the basis of Lagunas' "posesión y propiedad" of the disputed lands, and their assumption that because the king authorised the *mayorazgo* and because they paid for the *composición*, the *amparos* the Indians exhibited were less authoritative ["no estan tan autorizados"].[49] The titles of the *mayorazgo*, in Chosop's words, stated

47 For the long history of such advocacy and intervention in legal change, see Dueñas, "Indian Colonial Actors", 51–73 AGNP, Causas Civiles, leg. 179, cuad. 1512, fol. 48^{v}.

48 AGNP, Causas Civiles, leg. 179, cuad. 1512, fol. 48^{v}.

49 AGNP, Causas Civiles, leg. 179, cuad. 1512, fol. 91^{r}.

clearly that it would be established "sin perjuicio de las tierras de Pasco." Therefore, these titles were useless, and they simply did not support the current aspirations of Lagunas, which amounted to both depriving Pasco of its lands altogether, even taking over the "fundo urbano" where the *pueblo* rests and expecting the Indians to pay rent for it. In support of his claim, Chosop cited the "Leyes de Toro" about foundations, which state that all existing buildings in *mayorazgo* lands remain in the hands of their holders or possessors. Also, none of the previous owners had dared to claim dominium over Pasco, even more so as the *mayorazgo* was founded just 46 years before and the town had been so for more than 200 years. Therefore, the right of the *pueblo* to their lands would prevail over Lagunas' entitlement to his *mayorazgo*, since the law established that sales and *composiciones* had to be done "without harming the Indios" and that they had to replace their lands and *pueblo* sites with plenty of lands and "mountains for their tillage and an ejido of a league long where they can have their cattle without mixing with those of the Spaniards according to law 8 title 3 book 6 of the Recopilación."[50]

Second, in order to establish the foundation year of Pasco, Chosop required the court to conduct an archival excavation of the 1573 *visitas* reports to locate the specific information about the foundation of Pasco and the *repartimiento de tierras* they received by the grace of the king.[51] This request was an effort to reconstruct the history of the spaces in dispute, looking for signals of possession in the records that carried part of the towns' social memory in *visitas* reports. The community memory was also recorded in writing in past *amparos de posesión* and *cacicazgo* titles that Chosop enlisted to advance the defence of the towns' right to the lands through possession.[52] Since 1771, Chosop had also argued that, even if Lagunas' allegation that Pasco was situated inside

50 "sin perjuicio de los indios" "montes para sus labranzas y un ejido de una legua de largo donde puedan tener sus ganados sin que se mezclen con los de los españoles según la ley 8 titulo 3 libro 6 de la Recopilación." AGNP, Causas Civiles, leg. 179, cuad. 1512, fols. 91ᵛ–92ʳ.

51 AGNP. Causas Civiles, leg. 179, cuad. 1512, fols. 77ʳ–77ᵛ. The accountant in charge of the search found no record of Pasco from 1573, arguing that earthquakes had disturbed the archive. He found records from 1659 and 1683, however, that referred to the *pueblo de Indios* of Pasco whose inhabitants were recorded as "nativos" (potentially children of *forasteros*) but, based on locals' depositions, he estimated that Pasco's foundation occurred at least before the 17th century.

52 In 1772, Fiscal Protector Chosop connected possession to the social memory of the towns' foundations and brought to bear legal documents protecting possession to demonstrate the nexus. Bastias Saavedra, in "The Lived Space", 3–21, also established a link between social memory and possession in land demarcation practices in late colonial Valdivia.

Llacsahuanca were true, the Laws of the Indies on *reducciones*, or Indian resettlements (Law 14, Title 3, Book 6), established that, if the lands, pastures, waters and woodlands the *pueblos* needed fell into lands of Spanish owners, they should receive equivalent compensation somewhere else, and they had no right to dispossess the Indians. Further, the Andean Fiscal Protector emphasised that Law 20, Title 3, Book 6 established that the *pueblos* should receive at least three leagues for large cattle raising and at least one for small livestock, in addition to the lands for planting.[53] Therefore, Chosop requested restitution for Vico and Pasco of their possession of the lands in dispute. Chosop's arguments would have invalidated the 1777 *vista de ojos*, since the distances in the maps should all have conformed to the established distances from *estancias* to indigenous commons, as opposed to just marking the one league that the judge upheld in 1777. Vico and Pasco would then be the legitimate possessors of the disputed lands.[54] But that was not the case. Apparently, the *estancia* continued the *despojo*, or encroachment of the *pueblos*' commons, after 1772, since the *cabildos* had to go back to court in 1776 for a new attempt to recover the full possession of their commons.

In the end, however, in 1776–1778 the two parties were unequally enabled to furnish and choose the type of evidence to show in court. At the request of Lagunas' lawyers, Melgarejo and Arias, the court allowed them to provide the judge, before the inspection, with the maps representing their stakes in the case and asking specifically that they should be used in it. They also furnished the titles of Llacsahuanca and demanded that the Vico and Pasco *cabildos* bring their respective titles, not maps, to the inspection. When Arcona summoned the Indians, he prompted them to bring their titles but made no suggestion that they could or should draft and submit their own land maps. This is important because at that time land maps were already being allowed in court and furnished by indigenous *cabildos* elsewhere in the Andes.[55]

53 These laws in fact determined the minimum distance between *estancias* of livestock raising and the *pueblo* lands. Other laws, such as Law 12, Title 12, Book 4, explicitly prohibited the *estancias* from having livestock anywhere near the *pueblos de Indios*. It even allowed Indians to sacrifice, without penalty, all livestock from *estancias* that were found roaming in *pueblo* lands.

54 AGNP, Causas Civiles, leg. 179, cuad. 1512, fol. 76r. 1772. He added that if affected Spaniards wanted to appeal these rulings, they should do so directly to the Council of the Indies and no other tribunal, according to that law.

55 In Cariamanga (Loja), for example, the native *cabildo* submitted land maps of their own when litigating to defend their commons. See ANE, caja. 9, exp. 15, fol. 174r.

5 *Amparos* and *Mapas*

The use of land maps in litigation certainly predated the 18th century and existed both in the Americas and Europe prior to the Spanish conquest. As is well known, pre-colonial and colonial Mesoamericans produced scores of multipurpose maps. Their use of land maps as evidence to settle intercommunity land disputes and entitlements in Montezuma's *tecalli* or *teccalcu* courts, for example, has been documented.[56] In late 15th-century Europe, a time when maps appeared to play purely illustrative and informational purposes in Castilian courts, landscape maps also became probatory and/or disproving tools in disputes over land and water rights.[57] In Spanish America, maps were linked to the process of land tenure change and their use as evidence in court signalled the inception of the land dispossession process.[58] In the colonial Andes, landscape maps became more visibly used as legal evidence in the 18th century as appropriations of indigenous lands by Spanish land grabbers intensified. In the Cerro de Pasco region, a few miles away from Pasco and Vico, silver mining had taken momentum, attracting an influx of Spanish *forasteros* that strained the land market and endangered the stability of indigenous communal lands.

At least in the 18th century, technically speaking, the ability to furnish maps to the judge was apparently open to all parties in the land dispute. In colonial Ecuador, for example, indigenous communities furnished maps in court during that period. Interestingly, however, such maps appeared as evidence in land disputes between native communities only. In Vico and Pasco, and, as opposed to the legal cartography tradition of Mesoamerica, in most litigations confronting Spanish landowners with *pueblos de indios*, maps by indigenous communities were rendered non-existent.[59] The Spanish law may not have precluded the

56 Interpreting early accounts by Europeans Alonso de Zurita and Fray Bernardino de Sahagun, Ana Pulido Rull argues that land disputes were common in pre-Columbian New Spain, where land maps were also used as evidence in courts. The author argues that the Second Audiencia (1531–1535) had been accepting Amerindian maps and manuscripts as evidence since the early land disputes and had given the pressure of Indian litigants (Pulido Rull, *Mapping Indigenous Lands*, 2–3; Ruiz Medrano, *Mexico's indigenous communities*, 284). These legal changes, in turn, established the genre of indigenous map painting in the colonial era.

57 Vassberg, *Tierra y sociedad en Castilla*.

58 Harley, *La nueva naturaleza de los mapas*.

59 In similar cases from late colonial Ecuador, however, the indigenous litigants claimed to have submitted maps to the court, but they "mysteriously" disappeared before the *vista de ojos* took place. Archivo Nacional del Ecuador, Quito (ANEQ). Serie Indígenas (SI), "4 Cuaderno." Quito, 10 December 1768; ANEQ, Serie Indígenas, caj. 88, exp. 19.

ability of indigenous *pueblos* to represent their communal land claims in a self-produced map. But the late colonial legal culture and procedure management often defined an asymmetrical field, not to mention the unequal access of the parties to legal capital (technical and costly resources).

Occupation and contestation in the case of concern here transpired in a spatial continuum of landscape and courtroom, and maps bridged the two. It seems that, during the 18th century, innovation in legal evidence favoured the use of maps as synthesising visual evidence, supported with lengthy text and numbered glosses. They appeared to care more for exact measurements of lands, natural resources with ubiquitous captions and descriptive assessments of wealth, productive practices and landmarks of economic potential.[60] Although this kind of cartography often neglected the actual topography and relief of the Andes, maps' mimetic appearance endowed them with an almost mystical power of persuasion, meaning that the coloured image of the landscape and the official report of the inspection often obscured the inconsistency of the measurements. Geographers, art historians and some historians of law, among other scholars, have extensively demonstrated that maps are fundamentally social constructs of reality that represent discrete understandings of space shaped by ideologies that undergird vested interests. Alain Pottage poses that "a view of the land is inevitably a view from somewhere."[61] Jordana Dym and Karla Offen's take on maps and the transformation of land tenure is particularly pertinent to the colonial Andes. Maps, they argue, are crucial instructive devices for explaining how, by way of either occupation or contestation, among other factors, spaces undergo redefinition and resignification for people over time.[62] As representations of spatial reality, maps also had the power to create and recreate ascriptions of ownership in such a contested continuum.

60 In 1787, for example, as part of a general survey of communal lands ordered in Lima for the Partido (province) El Cercado to assess the existing *pueblo* lands "in excess", later to be sold in *composición*, a *deslinde* took place in Surco on 26 September. The ensuing report on the procedural measurements detailed meticulous land measures taken from "ángulos y triángulos por el orden de planimetría que cada uno de ellos contiene … con que queda medida geométricamente deslindada y amojonada dicha primera suerte de tierras con el nombre de Ygueretа." The procedure preceded the drawing of the land plan with the participation of architect surveyors and *jueces comisionados*. AGNP, Fondo Campesinado, Tierras y Haciendas, leg. 9, doc. 52, "Medida de chacra de ygueretа," 1787, p. 17, in Andazabal and Rojas, *Indios, tierras y caciques*, 8–29. Elsewhere in Lima, the curriculum of lawyer's education also changed significantly in the late 18th century, turning toward scientism and exact sciences and giving more emphasis to land surveying.

61 Pottage, "The Measure of Land".

62 Dym and Offen, "Maps and the Teaching of Latin American History", 3.

The *amparos de posesión*, by contrast, contained elements that made them vulnerable vis-à-vis titles obtained through *composición*, something that became more evident in the late colonial period. First, even if the courts upheld possession as a more decisive basis for land entitlement than ownership by land title, and even if they were mandates issued by the viceroy as president of the Audiencia or by its judges from the 16th century on, the *mandamientos de amparo* were not proof of ownership. Rather than validating property rights, the *mandamiento de amparo* fundamentally endorsed the possession of the land and granted recipients legal protection against any real or impending infringement of their rights by others in cases of de facto *despojo*, or potential usurpation. More specifically, the *mandamiento de amparo* granted the recipient the right to defend their lands in a legal forum or court to continue to enjoy possession.[63]

Second, even as early as the 16th century, the "amparo" had been in jeopardy in the Andes as abusive *corregidores* and other local functionaries made a personal business out of first demanding that caciques and other Indian litigants furnish *amparos*, and then issuing these documents to them for a fee. As a result, Viceroy Toledo himself altogether prohibited *corregidores* from issuing *mandamientos de amparo* and made them the exclusive prerogative of the Viceroy and Audiencia judges on his behalf.[64] In advancing the resettlement programme in 1570 Jauja, Toledo conducted inquiries on legal costs and found out that caciques and communities paid outrageous amounts of money to *corregidores*, *escribanos* and *letrados* for the much needed *mandamientos de amparo*, legal advice and other necessary documents.[65] Over time, the clash between the local powers and the indigenous communities rendered the *amparos* ineffective, even though the Audiencia often leaned towards protecting native land possession through *amparos*. However, the reiteration of community's complaints for *desalojo*, petitions for *amparo* and their recurrent lawsuits over the same land disputes reflected the gradual loss of *amparos*' juridical force and the institutional disregard for the enforcement of laws.

Towards the mid-18th century, as the courts shifted towards accepting a narrower set of titles as evidence of land ownership, the vulnerabilities of the

63 See a detailed exposé of the institution of *amparo's* formative process in Lira, *El Amparo Colonial*, 24.

64 Levillier, "Ordenanzas", 42–43.

65 To simplify litigation paperwork and avoid mediation in the processing of Indian petitions for protection, Toledo conducted mass burnings of documents he deemed obstructive and empty of legal value. According to Toledo's accountant (Salazar), the legal costs of Andeans in 1570 Jauja amounted to more than $200,000 pesos. Torres de Mendoza, *Colección de Documentos inéditos*, 246–247; Levillier, "Ordenanzas", 257–259.

amparos reached a critical point. Generally speaking, the text of the *amparos* tended to be generic and responded to a standard template basically indicating the name of the aggravated party, the grievance and the petition, as well as the decision of the judge mandating the pertinent protection of possession through either restitution or removal of the usurper from the encroached land. Since it was an executive order of the Audiencia that carried the power of a mandate (*mandamiento de amparo*), eventually the judges referred to them as "titulos de amparo", just like Arcona did when the Vico Indians showed him the 1573 *amparos* in Cotocoto. But the document of *amparo* itself usually lacked specificity about land location, quantity, distances and other precise identification deemed important as part of the Bourbon interest to centralise and rationalise the administration of the government. Eventually, the *amparos* issued to protect the common lands of the indigenous *pueblo* communities could no longer match the power of *estancieros* (*estancia* owners) and their titles of *composición*, whose authenticity and truthfulness were authenticated by royal notaries, as well as the detailed location, boundaries, distances, owners and origin of the *amparo*.

Lagunas supported his claims for the grasslands of Vico and Pasco with the titles obtained through *composición* from his predecessors which listed the *estancia's mojones*. The territorial ownership of Llacsahuanca during its colonial lifetime came about as a compound of subsequent *composiciones de tierra, mercedes de mita* and *encomiendas* that granted land and native labour for the *estancia's* growth (starting in 1573).[66] In 1696, before the *mayorazgo* was consti-

66 BNP, Impresos Varios, Mariano Carrillo. 3 April 1782, pp. 16–17. According to Lagunas' legal advisor and lawyer of the Lima Audiencia, the first beneficiary of the *composición* of Llacsahuanca was Juan Tello (titles confirmed in 1576), who also received several *mercedes de mita*. Viceroy Toledo granted Juan Tello 30 *mitayos* and an *encomienda* of 30 Indian tributaries in 1576. In 1595, upon Tello's death, Cristobal del Villar bought Llacsahuanca and obtained titles through *composición*. Llacsahuanca returned to the Tello family in 1597 when Fernando Tello purchased it. His son, Juan Tello Jr., obtained another *mita de obraje* in 1601 worth 130 *Indios*. In 1696, Doña Ana Maria Tello bought in auction an additional land and, in 1700, she received ownership confirmation for the *obraje* of Paucartambo. Altogether, the "fundo", or piece of property, was finally "composed" in 1713 in favour of Don Gonzalo Ramirez de Baquedano and, finally, again in 1724, in favour of Doña Ana Maria Tello for $600 pesos. By then, Llacsahuanca's titles listed all the *mojones* and lands disputed later in 1772 and 1776. This relation ends by asserting that Doña Ana Maria Tello took possession of Llacsahuanca "sin contradicción ninguna", after a *vista de ojos* and *deslinde* took place, for which the Indians from Vico, Pasco, Uchumayo and Catgusmayo were allegedly summoned. The *mita* was a forced labour obligation for Indians and *mercedes* were royal rewards for service. For a discussion of the *estancias* in the Andes, see also Ramírez, *The World Upside Down*.

tuted in 1725, Lagunas' grandfather also acquired lands (Paucartambo *obraje*) through marriage. The *corregidor* accepted his *instrumentos* without objection, even though the Indians from Vico had previously defeated Lagunas with the same *amparos* in 1576, when the Audiencia ordered him to move his livestock away from Vico's commons and to the opposite bank of the San Juan River.[67] Although still incipient in 1778, landscape cartography played its own part in adding a sense of visual evidence of the Lagunas' land boundaries vis-à-vis Vico and Pasco, and imbued the findings of the *vista de ojos* and *deslindes* with an almost undisputable power of persuasion. Over the years, Lagunas' landed properties effectively consolidated and expanded by land transfers from the *pueblos*' commons. Cotocoto itself was 'reduced' to a *mojón* and eventually absorbed by Llacsaguanca. The *corregidor* uncritically assumed Cotocoto belonged to Lagunas' *estancia*, even though the *estancia* was formed after the foundation of Vico in 1573. Arcona could not contemplate the different perceptions of the native commons by Vico residents who seem to have identified Cotocoto, their original head town, and its surrounding lands as part of their commons, the commons of both *pueblo* memory and *pueblo* land.

The fact remained, however, that the "titulos de amparo" from 1573, a powerful protection tool of the Toledan era, almost as old as the first *títulos de composition* given to Llacasahuanca's first grantees, bore little or no probatory value of collective possession in the eyes of the late colonial officials, who focused primarily on the map and the titles Lagunas submitted to the Audiencia. After the *vista de ojos* took place, Arcona himself acknowledged that "para la mayor inteligencia hice copiar el mapa que por V.A. se me remite, anotándolo con la mayor claridad con sus nombres y números para la mayor especificidad."[68] The *corregidor* basically used Lagunas' map to endorse the visual representation of communal dispossession that Lagunas intended and apparently accomplished. After Lagunas' death, Vico and Pasco continued to fight in court for their communal lands, as his son Don Joseph Vasquez de Velasco, the second Conde de las Lagunas, continued to deny the encroachment of Llacsahuanca into the commons claimed by the towns of Vico and Pasco and turned the accusation back on the Indian towns in 1786 and 1789, when he finally received official recognition of his possession over the lands occupied by Pasco.[69]

---

67 AGNP, Tierras de comunidades, leg. 1, cuad. 92, fol. 6[r].

68 AGNP, Tierras de comunidades, leg. 11, cuad. 92, fols. 49, 50–50[v].

69 AGNP, Causas Civiles, leg. 257, cuad. 2261. 1786. AGNP, Causas Civiles, leg. 283, cuad. 2509, fol. 1[v]. 1789. The Audiencia adjudicated the case in 1784, ordering the Tarma lieutenant assistant to mark (*señalar*) the one league of land to Vico according to the 1573 text by Visitador Juan de Fuentes, and: "[…] consiguiente a él se ejecutó la posesión que corresponde

The fact that the judge's report method of 'copying-and-pasting' Lagunas' own map to render in writing and image the visual inspection was unapologetically acknowledged no less than three times in both the written and visual report, and previously requested by the Audiencia, raises questions about the meaning of "legal evidence" in the Andean late colonial courts. Neither the Audiencia nor the judge seemed to see any bias in authorising Lagunas' map as the sole guiding script of the visual inspection, not to mention that the measurements were in fact wrongly interpreted against the common interests of Vico, as demonstrated above. Perhaps the powerful aristocrat benefitted from higher credibility in court given his noble status.[70] It is also possible that the judge proceeded one-sidedly with this guide only out of trust and pragmatism in approaching a difficult terrain.

Even if only incipiently, the use of maps in this manner is indicative of a new trend in legal procedure of land disputes that already existed in other Andean locales, such as Machachi and Imantad in the northern Andean Audiencia of Quito. Altogether, nevertheless, it appears that the use of land maps, which unilaterally strengthened the interests of landowners, appeared to be in themselves acceptable evidence of territorial ownership. Impartiality seems not necessarily to be an attribute of justice and appeared to be a peculiar quality in the settlement of late colonial land disputes, particularly when they confronted Andean communities with Spanish or Creole landowners. In any case, the interpretation of evidence and the modulation of procedure by the *juez comisionado* in this land dispute is a telling example of *casuismo* (casuistry) in Spanish early modern legal practice. That is, rather than following the letter of regulations, the law was a process of constant construction, attending

al Lagunas en las partes de su estancia de Llacsahuanca que circunvalan aquel terreno las que fueron manifestadas tanto por efecto o consecuencia de aquellas obligaciones como *por el resultivo de sus peculiares títulos* que se tuvieron presentes: comprendiéndose en dicha posesión *todo el considerable terreno que ocupan la Villa de Pasco* y los molinos de moler metales que varios particulares rodean su circunferencia con conocimiento del dominio que en todo aquel sitio pertenece al referido Conde … Bartolomé de Bedoya. (Relator de la Audiencia de Lima)". Emphasis added.

70 Social status was of tremendous importance in colonial legal culture. Don Pablo Vasquez de Velasco, Lagunas, not only held the noble title which he acquired by marriage to the actual Countess of Lagunas, Doña Nicolasa de Ontañón y Valverde, who in turn inherited it from her parents and direct descendants of the conquistadors; Don Pablo himself also descended from a powerful lineage of Spanish nobles and high-ranking members of legal and religious institutions. His great-grandfather was president of the Audiencias of Quito and La Plata. His grandfather was a knight of the Orden de Santiago and *oidor*, or judge, of the Lima Real Audiencia. His father Joseph Vasquez de Velasco was a knight of the Order of Calatrava. AGNP, Causas Civiles, leg. 326, cuad. 975. 1794.

to the unique circumstances of each case and with the concurrence of various legal views, which altogether explains the variation of juridical pondering over time.[71]

This procedural practice, on the other hand, was by no means unique to the Tarma regional jurisdiction. In the 1760s–1790s similar patterns appeared in land disputes of *pueblos de indios* ascribed to the Audiencia of Quito, where *amparos* confronted the new autonomy of maps as evidence that eventually formalised communal dispossession.[72] Such practices simultaneously reveal that the late colonial state had substantially moderated or even forgotten its 16th-century preoccupation with settling and securing Indian subjects of the king in manageable social economic and religious spaces for imperial control. The defence of indigenous common lands—upholding their possession with *amparos* the Audiencia issued on behalf of the king—seemed to have waned as the official expectation of yielding new income to the royal treasury prompted growing land transfers to the non-Indian domain. These lands had been both given in *composición* and retained within elite families through *mayorazgos* that came to challenge the survival of even colonial forms of communal lands.

6 Misunderstanding Andean Commoning

It is possible to interpret the land conflicts under discussion from the alternative perspective of the Andean culture of commoning within the colonial situation that underlay land tenure changes. Greer discussed the notion of commons as tied to practices of commoning in both pre-Columbian and colonial New Spain, New England, and New France.[73] The commons was a collective practice of land use specific to each group, and access to it depended on local custom and rules. For colonial Andeans, the practice of commoning was embedded in local knowledge and practices that obeyed group rules that may or may not have been colonial in origin, although they did change according to

71 Anzoátegui, *Casuismo y sistema.*

72 ANEQ, Serie Indígenas, "4 Cuaderno." Quito, 10 December 1768. For a full discussion of this case, see Dueñas, "The Virgin and the Land Surveyor." See also, similar cases in ANEQ, Serie Indígenas, caj. 88, exp. 19; ANEQ, Serie Indígenas, caj. 96, exp. 1775–1776: ANEQ, Serie Indígenas, caj. 99, exp. 15. Cariamanga (Loja) 1777–1797. In the 1768 case, it was clear that the community of Machachi's *cacicas* had faced the loss of *pueblo* lands for the last century as powerful Spanish landowners and the local *corregidores* basically ignored their *amparos* in recurrent lawsuits where the maps and the challengers' instruments prevailed.

73 Greer, *Property and Dispossession*, 253.

the rhythm of colonial relations.[74] The practices of Andean commoning in Vico and Pasco were varied and, as in Carantia, they defied colonial juridical definitions of communal space. These villages' commoning practices superseded the rigidity and oversimplification of imaginary lines between *mojones* arbitrarily placed on a map. They challenged restrictive land sizes that were stipulated generically in Toledo's resettlement programme and other mandates for the *pueblos*.

Commoning for these two locales related to collective activities and relations involved in their use of territory, which also varied during the year. Andeans attached to region's local and collective memories of recent and distant pasts, which shaped their understanding of what the commons meant even in colonial times. Their customs and arrangements for land access superseded the letter of titles given by *composición* and the abstractions of predefined maps. The *mojones* in Lagunas' map were placed in an orderly, imaginary circular landscape around the town, where the imposing presence of nearby mountains, for example, is rendered invisible. The long-transited grazing trails and journeys to watering holes that supported Andean sheep raising were often movable, cyclical and hard to represent on a piece of paper or to perceive in a single *vista de ojos*. Their woodcutting grounds were more dispersed, irregular and shifting than a one-league rule of unspecified terrain can ordain. Their commons and commoning, in sum, obeyed an Andean ecological specificity and social and cultural dynamics irreducible to the simplified representation of territorial cartography.[75]

Herding sheep regularly, or during land fallow periods, and perhaps woodcutting together and by turns around the disputed boundary of Cotocoto, for example, were forms of commoning, and were established and changed by long-established custom. Cacique Don Joseph Chavin Palpa and the Vico authorities remembered Cotocoto as the original place of resettlement and Pasco as a "pueblo con iglesia", or a town with a chapel. Pasco was the town where his ancestor, Cacique Don Francisco Chavin Palpa, was displaced to exercise the *cacicazgo* of the Yaro Yanamate *ayllu* in the early 1700s, and perhaps also earlier. Such memories evoked local Andeans' coming together to Cotocoto

---

74 Analysing the internal aspects of land tenure in the central Andean village of Carantia, in 1644, Puente Luna's "Of Widows, Furrows and Seeds", 376–407, proposes that commoning, or collective practices of land use, and uncommoning, or "in-ayllu" family holdings, in fact, happened concurrently within the *ayllu*, defining a coexistence of communal and single-family rights. They obeyed a shifting dynamic of labour and local control of production, land holdings, cyclical practices, planting options, etc.

75 On the problems of local settlement practices in the accuracy of maps in 18th century Angola, see Alfagali (Chapter 9) in this volume.

and the surrounding lands to graze their sheep and perhaps llamas, sharing stories and engaging in a common sacred landscape. For them, Cotocoto was then a common by local rule and group customs, just as were the Pasco lands and other resources and spaces they used in common since the foundation of the town in 1573. Thinking strictly from the colonial perspective of the *pueblo* communal lands, Lagunas and the *juez comisionado* viewed Cotocoto as part of the lands of Llacsahuanca, simply because it lay out the one-league rule for Vico's commons and, therefore, readily assumed it lay inside the *estancia* grounds completely.

Lagunas' and Arcona's assumptions, on the other hand, may have responded to a mental framework rooted in older colonial practices of land tenure. The original meaning of the term *estancia* may help to discern the dispute from another angle. *Estancias* were originally understood as spaces devoted to cattle raising in a transitory fashion though not solely for that purpose. In the early years of Spanish America, cattle raising was rather transhumant and relied mostly on pastures from the city's *ejidos*, or commons, *pueblos de indios*' commons, and even on lands that were not held in common. Towards the 1570s, the Viceroy and some cities offered *mercedes* (grants) to ranchers, sanctioning their ownership rights of *estancias* (an established corral and additional infrastructure for stock raising), which generally lacked clearly specified boundaries, although the grant specified site and size. Over time, some *estancias* came to control vast amounts of land, often as *mayorazgos*, although they were not originally meant to have full and exclusive rights to ownership.[76]

This old practice of grazing cattle in the *pueblos*' commons might explain the origin and evolution of both Llacsahuanca and the litigation under discussion. As discussed above, Lagunas' *estancia* started as a grant to Juan Tello somewhere around 1576, not too long after the foundation of Vico and Pasco, and it expanded rapidly thereafter through royal grants. It is likely that the colonial practice of ranchers accessing the *pueblos*' pastures continued for centuries in Llacsahuanca and that, towards the late 18th century, Lagunas came to assume Cotocoto and other pastures, including the *canchas* and *majadas* from Vico and Pasco, as his own entitlement to exclusive rights to the land.[77] If we are to

76 Greer, *Property and Dispossession*, 254–255. By law, the grants only gave *estancias* limited right to pastures, waters and other grazing resources with the expectation that *estancias* would not infringe upon the rights of other rangers or the *pueblo* commons, whose control Indians were supposed to retain. In 1541, Charles v opened all pastureland in Peru to common use; however, stock-grazers managed to secure ownership rights, particularly in the Peruvian Andes. Keith, *Conquest and Agrarian Change*, 61.

77 This was perhaps what Lagunas meant as he asserted, according to Chosop, that he had

accept that the early *estancias* evolved from itinerant practices of stock raising that relied on *pueblo* commons, the disputed lands in question may well have been part of a formerly integrated commons that included llama *canchas* or sheep *canchas* kept by the Vico and Pasco communities. The whole commons may have been severed by the colonial intervention in 1573, and came to be understood as two different domains: the *pueblo* commons (of Vico and Pasco) and the *estancia* (belonging to Lagunas).[78] The protracting lawsuits over ownership and possession in Llacsahanca and the two *pueblos* may thus be viewed as episodes in a long history of the formation and disintegration of the Andean commons, with the 1777–1778 litigation exposing perhaps a form of *uncommoning* from without, in which the pressure of *estancia* owners obtained the support of the justice authorities.

7 Concluding Remarks

Andean *pueblos*' commons were simultaneously constituted by benevolent royal *repartimiento* and threatened by the king's magnanimity to Lagunas' lineage. This was the case even though Vico's commons had been protected by Lima's Audiencia in 1576 and Pasco had received a series of *amparos* in the 1650s. By the late colonial period, land judges in some areas of the Andes began to disregard the protection of Andean commons' possession, giving preponderance to ownership ascriptions embedded in the letter of ownership documents that, in turn, dictated the autonomous force of maps' visual discourse. In Vico and Pasco this was the case even though *amparos* were still used elsewhere. The judge's ignoring of the *mandamientos de amparo* in 1772 and then in 1778 for these towns, however, signalled the vanishing economy of grace for the Indian republic, rendering a dislocation of the reciprocal bonds it was meant to generate between the monarch and his Indian subjects, as their possession was not ultimately upheld by the courts. Also, the procedural culture of the judge reveals how a strictly Spanish legal definition of the commons (one league of common lands from the town centre) came to prevail at the expense of its social and cultural definition by Andean memories and social practices.

---

the dominion of the lands from Pasco, which he acquired in *composición*, as purchased from the king, "cuando eran tierras sueltas." AGNP, Real Audiencia, Causas Civiles, leg. 179, cuad. 1512, fol. 88^{v}. 1772.

78 The sources for this case do not allow me to reconstruct the pre-1573 history of the lands that came to constitute Llacsahuanca as an *estancia*, nor those that eventually were distributed to the *ayllus* that came to be resettled in Vico and Pasco.

Along with understanding ownership as a changing process of formation, this Chapter has demonstrated that changes in both the practices of land judges and probatory means of possession influenced ownership normativity, instrumentalising the shrinking of *pueblo* communal lands. The land conflict in Tarma is one telling example of how the consolidation of territorial ownership and a landed aristocracy introduced protracting volatility to a time-honoured right to indigenous lands that supported communal possession over other claims. These confrontations between the ways in which possession and ownership are defined in the Andean late colonial courts were, in the end, articulated by colonial actors occupying asymmetrical positions in the distribution of royal grace.

Finally, looking closely at micro-level iterations of changes in ownership regimes affords scholars a concurrent opportunity to reflect on the politics of colonial archival formation. The silences of the record-makers in this case speak loudly. Aside from the Cacique Don Joseph Chavin, the choices of *escribanos* and the land judges when reporting on the trial render the native residents of Vico and Pasco nameless and voiceless. Even the presence or absence of an interpreter in the courtroom went unrecorded. In contrast, it is worth noticing the intervention of the native *fiscal protector*, even if only recorded in the 1771–1772 lawsuit. Don Alberto Chosop empowered his defence of the two *pueblos*' rights of possession by digging deep into the genealogy of the *pueblos*, demanding state records on the *visitas* and *revisitas* of the *pueblos* from the 16th and 17th centuries. He wrote pointed *memoriales* (memoranda) re-centring the discussion on possession, rather than on land titles and maps, reminding both the land judge and Lagunas of the *pueblos*' rights of possession of their commons. Chosop put together a full dossier that, alongside his *memoriales*, included a series of old *mandamientos de amparo*, as well as *cacicazgo* titles and Indians' powers of attorney. He created a legal narrative that recentred the discussion toward *pueblo* memory and the local knowledge of Vico's and Pasco's caciques. These archival interventions shaped the design of ownership regimes in different ways as efforts to control Andean commons emerged from myriad actions documented with various emphases and omissions. The archival strategies considered here, overall, expose the glaring erasure of Andeans' presence and interventions in the colonial archive of land tenure, which stood in stark contrast to the pervasive voices empowering the vested interests of powerful landowners in the official record.

Acknowledgements

This chapter owes much to the intellectual generosity of Renzo Honores and Herman Barreto, and the productive conversations during the Max Planck Institute workshop on "Ownership Regimes" in Frankfurt. I am particularly grateful to Alessandro Buono for his insightful suggestions. The reviewers of this publication helped me improve the content in various important ways.

Bibliography

Manuscripts

Biblioteca Nacional del Perú (BNP), Impresos Varios, Mariano Carrillo, págs. 1–15.

AGNP. Real Audiencia, Causas Civiles, leg. 53 cuad.359. Lima, 1725, fols. 1^{r}, 10^{v}.

AGNP. Real Audiencia. Causas Civiles, leg. 326 cuad. 2975. 1794, fols. 1^{r}–19^{v}.

AGNP. Real Audiencia. Causas Civiles, leg. 169, doc. 1431. 1769.

AGNP. Real Audiencia. Causas Civiles, leg. 257, cuad. 2261. 1786.

AGNP. Real Audiencia. Causas Civiles, leg. 283, cuad. 2509, fol. 1^{v}.

AGNP. Real Audiencia. Causas Civiles, leg. 1772. Fol. 88^{v}.

ANEQ, Serie Indígenas, caj. 96, exp. 12. 1775–1776.

ANEQ, Serie Indígenas, caj. 99, exp. 15. Loja, 1777–1797.

Archivo General de la Nación, Perú (AGNP), Causas Civiles, leg. 179 cuad.1512, fols. 2^{r}–106^{r}.

Archivo Nacional del Ecuador, Quito (ANEQ), Serie Indígenas, caj. 88, exp. 19. cuad. 4. 1768.

Printed Sources

Cornejo, Andres D., *Diccionario Histórico y Forense del Derecho Real de España*, Madrid 1779.

Gonzáles Holguín, Diego, *Arte y Diccionario Quechua—Español*, Lima [1608] 1901. https://www.google.com/books/edition/Arte_y_Diccionario_qquechua_esp%C3%A3nol/oKpkAAAAMAAJ?hl=en&gbpv=1

Gonzáles Holguín, Diego, *Vocabulario en la lengua general del Perú llamada Quichua y en la lengua española*, Madrid 1586: Antonio Ricardo.

[Anon.], "Recopilación de Leyes de los Reynos de las Indias", Madrid 1680: Iulian de Paredes. http://bdh-rd.bne.es/viewer.vm?id=0000013942&page=1

Levillier, Roberto, "Ordenanzas dictadas por el Virrey Don Francisco de Toledo para la Ciudad del Cuzco y sus términos" in Levillier, Roberto (ed.), *Gobernantes del Perú. Cartas y papeles, siglo XVI*, Madrid 1925.

Torres de Mendoza, Luis, *Colección de Documentos inéditos relativos al descubrimiento, conquista y organización de las antiguas posesiones españolas de América y Oceanía*, Tomo VIII, Madrid 1867: M. Bernaldo de Quirós.

Literature

Amado Gonzales, Donato, "Reparto de tierras indígenas y la primera visita y composición general 1591–1595," in *Histórica*, 22:2 (1988), 197–207.

Andazabal, Rosaura and Omar Rojas, *Indios, Tierras y Caiques del Perú. Ss. XVIII–XIX*, Lima 2015.

Anzoátegui, Táu, *Casuismo y Sistema. Indagación histórica sobre el espíritu del Derecho indiano*, Buenos Aires 1992

Arellano Hoffmann, Carmen, *Notas sobre el indígena en la intendencia de Tarma*, Bonn 1984.

Bastias Saavedra, Manuel, "The Normativity of Possession. Rethinking Land Relations in early-modern Spanish America, ca. 1500–1800", in *Colonial Latin American Review* 29:2 (2020), 223–238.

Bastias Saavedra, Manuel, "The Lived Space. Possession, Ownership, and Land Sales on the Chilean Frontier. Valdivia, 1790–1830", in *Historia Crítica* 67 (2018), 3–21.

Bastien, Joseph W., "Land Litigations in an Andean Ayllu from 1592 until 1972", in *Ethnohistory* 26:2 (1979), 101–131.

Burga, Manuel, *De la encomienda a la hacienda capitalista, el valle de Jetequepeque del siglo XVI al XX*, Lima 1976.

Camallonga, Carlos Tormo, "El derecho en las alegaciones jurídicas del siglo XVIII", in *Saitabi* 60: 50 (2000), 277–317.

Dueñas, Alcira, "Indian Colonial Actors in the Lawmaking of the Spanish Empire in Peru", in *Ethnohistory* 65:1 (2018), 51–73.

Dueñas, Alcira, "The Virgin and the Land Surveyor. Andean Pueblo Boundary Making in the Highlands of Late Colonial Ecuador", in *Colonial Latin American Review* 31:3 (2022), 304–326.

Dym, Jordana and Karl Offen, "Maps and the Teaching of Latin American History", in *Hispanic American Historical Review* 92:2 (2012), 213–244.

Greer, Alan, *Property and Dispossession. Native Empires and Land in Early Modern North America*, Cambridge-New York 2018.

Guevara Gil, Jorge Armando, *Propiedad agraria y derecho colonial: Los documentos de la hacienda Santotis, Cuzco (1543–1822)*, Lima 1993.

Graubart, Karen B., "Shifting landscapes. Heterogeneous Conceptions of Land Use and Tenure in the Lima Valley", in *Colonial Latin American Review* 26:1 (2017), 62–84.

Harley, John Brian, *La nueva naturaleza de los mapas. Ensayos sobre la historia de la cartografía*, México 2005.

Herzog, Tamar, "Colonial Law and 'Native Customs'. Indigenous Land Rights in Colonial Spanish America", in *The Americas*, 69:3 (2013), 303–321.

Hostnig, Rainer, Palomino, Ciro Dongo and Jean-Jacques Decoster (eds.), *Proceso de composición y titulación de tierras en Apurímac-Perú, Siglos XVI–XX*, vol. 1, Cusco 2007.

Jordà Fernández, Antoni, "Alegaciones jurídicas del siglo XVII en Cataluña. La obra de Josep Ramon", in *Ius Fugit. Revista interdisciplinar de estudios histórico-jurídicos* 17 (2011–2014), 55–104.

Jacobsen, Nils, *Mirages of Transition. The Peruvian Altiplano, 1780–1930*, Berkeley, Los Angeles, London 1993.

Jurado, Carolina, "Baldíos, derechos posesorios y tierra realenga en el primer proceso de composición en el distrito de Charcas, Virreinato del Perú, 1591–1597", in *América Latina en la Historia Económica* 29:1 (2021a), 1–24.

Jurado, Carolina, "Títulos de la tierra y nociones posesorias y de dominio en Charcas a fines del siglo XVI. La composición del Valle de Sucusuma. Virreinato del Perú, 1592–1600", in *Diálogo Andino* 65 (2021 b), 49–64.

Keith, Robert G, *Conquest and Agrarian Change. The Emergence of the Hacienda System on the Peruvian Coast*, Cambridge 1976.

Larson, Brooke, *Colonialism and Agrarian Transformation in Bolivia. Cochabamba 1550–1900*, Princeton 1988.

Lira González, Andrés, *El amparo colonial y el juicio de amparo mexicano. (antecedentes novohispanos del juicio de amparo)*, México 1972.

Lopera Mesa, Gloria Patricia, "Creando posesión vía desposesión. Visitas a la tierra y conformación de resguardos indígenas en la Vega de Supía, 1559–1759", in *Fronteras de la historia* 25:2 (2020), 120–156.

Murra, John v., *Formaciones económicas y políticas del mundo andino*, Lima 1975.

Owensby, Brian, *Empire of Law and Indian Justice in Colonial Mexico*, Stanford 2008.

Penry, S. Elizabeth, *The People Are King. The Making of an Indigenous Andean Politics*, New York 2019.

Pottage, Alain, "The Measure of Land", in *The Modern Law Review* 57:3 (1994), 361–384.

Puente Luna, José Carlos de la, "Of Widows, Furrows, and Seed. New Perspectives on Land and the Colonial Andean Commons", in *Hispanic American Historical Review* 101:3 (2021), 376–407.

Pulido Rull, Ana, *Mapping Indigenous Lands. Land Grants in Colonial New Spain*, Norman 2020.

Ramírez, Susan, *Provincial Patriarchs. Land Tenure and the Economics of Power in Colonial Peru*, Albuquerque 1986.

Ramírez, Susan, *The World Upside Down: Cross-Cultural Contact and Conflict in Sixteenth-Century Peru*, Stanford 1998.

Rappaport, Joanne, *The Politics of Memory. Native Historical Interpretation in the Colombian Andes*, Durham 1998.

Ruiz Medrano, Ethelia, *Mexico's indigenous Communities. Their Lands and Histories, 1500–2010*, Boulder 2010.

Saito, Akira and Claudia Rosas (eds.), *Reducciones. La Concentración forzada de las poblaciones indígenas en el Virreinato del Perú*, Lima 2017.

Seed, Patricia, *Ceremonies of Possession in Europe's Conquest of the New World*, Cambridge 1995.

Stavig, Ward, "Ambiguous Visions. Nature, Law and Culture in Indigenous-Spanish Land relations in Colonial Peru", in Hispanic American Historical Review 80:1 (2000), 77–111.

Stern, Steven J., *Peru's Indian Peoples and the Challenge of Spanish Conquest. Huamanga to 1640*, Madison 1993.

Spalding, Karen, *Huarochiri. An Andean Society Under Inca and Spanish Rule*, Stanford 1984.

Vassberg, David, *Tierra y Sociedad en Castilla. Señores, poderosos y campesinos en la España del siglo XVI*, Barcelona 1986.

Vieira-Powers, Karen, Andean Journeys. Migration, Ethnogenesis, and the State in Colonial Quito, Albuquerque 1995.

CHAPTER 9

Sobas, *Ilamba*, and Residents

On the Diverse Meanings of Land in Angola's Hinterland in the 18th Century

Crislayne Alfagali

1 Introduction

Throughout the 17th century, as the bulk of Portugal's overseas interests shifted from the Indian Ocean to the Atlantic, the territorialisation of the Portuguese Empire became an essential issue for its overseas political communications. The control of maritime spaces, as well as political and trade networks based on alliances with local populations, had become, by then, unsatisfactory. The non-contiguous empire once described by Luís Felipe Thomaz was giving way to a new territorial paradigm. Land occupation and the delimitation of territories were becoming crucial elements of Portuguese colonisation.[1]

The area under Portuguese influence in part of the lands of the ancient Ndongo Kingdom, known then as the Kingdom of Angola, was not an exception to this process. In the 16th and 17th centuries, military campaigns and missionary incursions, as well as colonial and private agents acting as traders or country dwellers, made it possible to learn more about the countryside of Luanda.[2] But it was above all in the second half of the 18th century that this colony's territory was reassessed under the reformist plans of the Marquis of Pombal. The population and the construction of new villages aimed at structuring and controlling its spaces under a reforms programme to expand royal authority in the Portuguese colonies by harnessing "to the maximum extent the potentialities of hitherto unexplored" as well as poorly explored territories.[3]

A general attempt was made at unifying the spaces in terms of asserting Portuguese sovereignty by means of a political occupation that also set out

1 Thomaz, *De Ceuta a Timor*, 207–243; Hespanha and Santos, "Os poderes num império oceânico", 395–413.

2 Montecúccolo, *Descrição histórica dos três reinos do Congo, Matamba e Angola.*

3 Delson, *Novas Vilas para o Brasil colônia*, 140. Another way of approaching this topic is by analysing cartographic documents. Since the early decades of the 18th century, European diplomats strove to legitimise the political appropriation of oversea territories. See Kantor, "Cartografia e diplomacia".

 | DOI:10.1163/9789004722729_010

to disseminate the (assumedly superior) European values among the Crown's subjects—the 'natives of the land' (*naturais da terra*). In the hinterland of the Kingdom of Angola, Pombaline policies sought to reorganise space, for example, by creating towns and civil settlements. The construction of the Royal Iron Foundry of Nova Oeiras is another example of the enterprise to create manufacturers and rethink the organisation of the hinterland. These efforts to dominate countryside areas and populations were countered by many forms of resistance. In the Kingdom of Angola, likewise, the Portuguese programmes to restructure the region had to face the previous local logics of territorial occupation. As this case study will show, lineage land-tenure relations underwent fundamental changes in the 18th century through the Portuguese effort to strengthen their presence in Angola, and through the exploitation of local natural resources.

From the initial contacts intermediated by the Kingdom of Kongo, the supplying of ships for transatlantic slave trade, as well as the very permanence of foreigners on lands of the ancient Ndongo Kingdom, hinged on alliances with the Mbundu leaders and on the labour of their subjects. The Portuguese presence in the Kingdom of Angola in the 17th and 18th centuries was either based on vassalage agreements with *sobas* defeated in war or alliances with other local rulers interested in trade deals. Among the local leaders, the *sobas* became the principal negotiators for the Portuguese, since they determined who could travel across their territories, thereby establishing trade agreements and deciding on allocations of free and slave workers. They acted as essential intermediaries among the local powers.[4]

The *sobas* were local rulers under the rule of either African kings or the king of Portugal, upon becoming vassals of the Portuguese Crown. According to Jan Vansina, they occupied leadership positions in monocephalic chiefdoms—which are known, in Portuguese, as *sobados*.[5] In the Portuguese sources, additional Mbundu authorities appear subordinated to the *sobas*: the councillor, the *kota* (plural *makota*) and the *sobeta* (a subordinate leader under the jurisdiction of a powerful *soba*), as well as the *tandala*, *ngolambole* and *kimbanda*—authorities with spiritual, combatant, and/or political functions. Another figure that appears is the *kilamba*, described by Virgílio Coelho as a sorcerer "in charge of placating the fury of nature's geniuses";[6] however, the meaning of this title underwent changes over time as a result of Portuguese influence and the *kilamba* was later known for having strong ties with the colonisers.

4 See Heintze, *Angola nos séculos XVI e XVII*; Carvalho, *Sobas e homens do rei*.

5 Vansina, *How societies are born*, 196.

6 Coelho, *Em busca de Kàbàsà*, 161.

Though the correlation of forces among Africans and the Portuguese changed noticeably—because of changes in the colonial interests, Portuguese occupation and the wars of the 17th century, which led to the conquest of Ndongo—the maintenance of alliances with local rulers remained a constant practice. While some chiefdoms survived and new ones emerged, many others succumbed to the violence of military conquest and the demands of the slave trade. The continuance of the Portuguese presence in the Kingdom of Angola was only made possible by the subjugation of African sovereign rulers.

The power of *sobas*, in turn, was based on the number of subjects within their dominions. The more subjects they had, the larger their plantation fields (known as *arimos*) and the quantity of food they could produce—hence, the more promptly they would begin to amass wealth and incorporate new subjects. Such chiefdoms exercised control over lands and natural resources, as well as over the labour force used to exploit them. The colonial exploitation that followed the Portuguese conquest, thus, did not fully annihilate the autonomy of local leaders. Despite an assumed asymmetric reciprocity, the subjection of the *sobas* to the king of Portugal gave them some leeway for acting, since it was actually based on an idea of interdependence. According to the scholars who have studied this topic, the history of political and economic relations of the *sobados* with their conquerors encompasses a complex mesh of relations that shifted from "collaboration to resistance" and from "adaptation to rejection".[7]

The relations of the Mbundu people with their territory were linked to "complex supernatural bonds [that] united each kinship group to its lands and integrated the people and territory into a single collectivity".[8] However, it is necessary to problematise the idea of a 'single collectivity'. As Mariana Candido has demonstrated, in West Central Africa people accumulated wealth not only in people, but also in land. Rulers, elites and commoners not only "claim[ed] and register[ed] land [from as early as] the 17th and 18th centuries", but also entered into a series of disputes over property in the 19th century with Portuguese colonial settlers: "different local actors have clashed over who has the right to use land and have claimed rights over occupancy".[9] West Central Africans valued landownership and there were local landownership rights and regimes.

The rearrangement of the *sobados* in consonance with supernatural guidelines and/or in search of better croplands did not observe the fixed layout of

7 Dias, "O Kabuku Kambilu (c. 1850–1900)", 15.

8 For instance, it was believed that the spirits of a lineage's ancestors would only find rest if the bodies of the dead were buried in lands belonging to that lineage. Miller, *Poder político e parentesco*, 239.

9 Candido, *Wealth, land, and property in Angola*, 1, 35.

the Portuguese cartography. For this reason, in 1797, Governor Miguel Antonio de Melo pointed out a number of flaws in a map used in his period:

> Since the *banzas* or African villages are built with straw houses and move almost daily from previous sites to new ones—which are never close to those left behind—every time they either wish to, or are led to do so by their omens and superstitions, what one observes to be peopled on a map today will be found deserted tomorrow, full of thicket and inhabited by beasts.[10]

Armed resistance against the conquerors and the spoliation of the African territory was a relevant strategy, but it was not the only one. Based on their own political culture and on the accumulated experience with Portuguese colonisation, the local rulers submitted pleas and informed opinions and sent letters and signed agreements to ensure the maintenance of their lineage powers, as well as to avoid the disaggregation of their people and the loss of their lands, wealth, and privileges.[11]

A similar process can be seen in the history of appropriations of indigenous lands in Portuguese America. The conquest of its territory was characterised by violent combats with the indigenous peoples. Further, the colonial encampments became mechanisms for controlling the local populations, their natural resources and access to the labour force. The establishment of fixed settlements with a permanent territorial delimitation went against the features of the social and cultural structure of many indigenous societies. Among the Mbundu in Angola, as well as among the indigenous populations on the other shore of the Atlantic Ocean, village displacements were frequent and occurred in response to certain situations, such as the depletion of natural resources and conflicts among political rulers.

This Chapter studies the landownership conflicts that resulted from the installation of an iron foundry in the region of Ilamba, in the Angolan hinterland, in the second half of the 18th century. The expropriation of African lands in West Central Africa in the pre-19th-century periods is a subject rarely addressed in historiography. This case study contributes to reflecting on the

---

10 Arquivo Histórico Ultramarino (therefore AHU) AHU_CU_001, Cx. 86, D. 66.

11 According to Silvia Lara, one may speak of the political experience that accumulated in the regions occupied by the Portuguese. Such experience was based on European and, in this case, Central African parameters that set up a distinctive "political syntax", in other words, a political culture that determined the way in which local leaders dealt with the Portuguese and other Europeans. Lara, *Palmares & Cucaú*, 232.

issue, since it examines the colonial mechanisms of spoliation of lands and natural resources from the local African chiefdoms. Furthermore, the analysis also considers the local rulers' strategies for maintaining their political power over time.

2 *Sobas*, the Portuguese, and the Possession of the Lands of Ilamba

Ilamba province is cited in written sources dating as far back as 1586. It was the first to be conquered by the Portuguese, who used to refer to it as 'our Ilamba'. The boundaries of the lower Ilamba lands were set by the Ndande River (in the north of the Kwanza River), as well as by the Luinha and Lukala Rivers to the east; they extended for nearly 40 kilometres to the west, up to the eastern side of Luanda and the Kilunda Lake, on the left shore of the Mbengu River, that is, almost to the Atlantic Coast. Its most prominent ruler was Mubanga, a member of the Ndongo lineage.[12]

The region of Ilamba had valuable resources for West Central African societies. The chiefdoms of Ilamba had been mining iron ore since long before the first Portuguese initiatives to exploit the mineral locally. It was not a coincidence that Ilamba became the spot of the foundries of Nova Oeiras and Novo Belém in the mid-1760s.[13] Access to iron ore, as well as to the local salt pans appreciated the value of those lands, which were an object of dispute among the *sobas* themselves, as well as between the *sobas* and the subjects of the Portuguese Crown.[14]

When the Governor of Luanda decided to establish iron ore foundries in the region, conflict initially emerged through quarrels over landownership. It is evident that the Governor of Luanda needed to use some of the mines, which were then controlled by the local rulers. In addition to the mines, the governor planned that a portion of the lands of the settlement of Nova Oeiras be used as vegetable gardens to provide sustenance for the workers of the foundry and its supporting services.[15]

12 Heintze, *Angola nos séculos XVI e XVII. Estudos sobre Fontes, Métodos e História*, 192–193; Freudenthal and Pantoja (eds.), *Livro dos Baculamentos*, 47; Montecúccolo, *Descrição histórica dos três reinos do Congo, Matamba e Angola*, Vol. I, 33; Ito, *Uma 'tão pesada cruz'*, 81.

13 The history of these iron foundries can be found in: Alfagali, *Blacksmiths of Ilamba*.

14 Miller, *Poder político e parentesco*, 267.

15 The then governor said, regarding the lands of the region: "Since I am told that from the Luinha River—where Nova Oeiras is to be established—to the Zundo Fair, one finds admirable lands, encampments and seedbeds shall be built all along them, provided that they are vacant". AHU_CU_001, Cx. 52, D. 73.

MAP 9.1 Ilamba (Detail)
FURTADO, LUIS CANDIDO CORDEIRO PINHEIRO. MAP OF WEST CENTRAL AFRICA COAST, 1791. BIBLIOTECA PÚBLICA MUNICIPAL DO PORTO—BPMP_C-M&A-PASTA 24 (16) 01.

The historical documents allow the identification of the lands of some *sobas* located more closely to the site selected for the foundries: Nguengue a Kimbemba, owner of iron mines—"a *soba* who shares boundaries with another one", namely, Kyambata kya Ngoto. "And as one continues in a compass of only 10 or 12 leagues [nearly 50 kilometres], the following *sobas* are also found": Itombe ya KaNdongo, Nzambi a Keta, Ngola a Kiato, Ngolome, Kabuku Kambilu, Kisala kya Kabuku, Nzamba Nsungui, Kabuto and Kilamba Pedro Ambaxi. This list was produced by Captain Joaquim de Sousa Lobo during a 1768 expedition commissioned by Governor Francisco de Sousa Coutinho.[16]

Captain Lobo's depiction shows that he perceived the boundaries between the lands of the African *sobados*. Governor Sousa Coutinho even affirmed this in his governmental letters of January 1767, in which he stated that the foundry built in Luinha was located on the "grounds" of Soba Nguengue a Kimbemba. The foundry of Novo Belém, located at the heart of Ilamba's low areas, was placed on the "grounds" of Kilamba Ngongue a Kamukala.[17] In other words, the Portuguese built the two foundries in areas that belonged, in political and economic terms, to these *sobas* and to *ilamba* (*kilamba* in singular form, *ilamba* in plural form).[18]

16 Instituto de Estudos Brasileiros (IEB)/ USP, Coleção Alberto Lamego, AL-083-099.
17 AHU_CU_001, Cx. 52, Doc. 73.
18 In Bantu languages, the plural form is mostly constructed by removing a prefix (for instance, *kilamba*, whose plural is *ilamba*).

A historical record dating back to February 1767—two years after the building of both foundries began—informs us that the ownership of lands in the region was claimed by *sobas* who lived close to the fortified village of Muxima. In that year, the village's *sargento-mor*[19] wrote about the conflicts between Muxima's residents and *sobas* for the "possession of the lands where the foundry is established".[20] The residents claimed to have bought those areas from the *sobas*, who, in turn, accused the residents of having stolen them. The governor ordered the iron foundry's general intendant to disregard those quarrels and only listen to individuals capable of presenting documents that evinced their ownership. He required the documents of the sale, because he was not certain whether "the *sobas* could or could not sell the lands of their State".[21] This is the first reference, amid the context of the foundry's construction, to the idea that Mbundu lands could not be sold. This episode reveals that there were also other, local rules—which were well-known to the Portuguese—which governed the relations of West Central African peoples with their territory.

The issue was not settled on this occasion. In April 1767, the foundry's intendant wrote to the governor suggesting that the settlement of Nova Oeiras should be built along the *banza* of Soba Muxixi, located along the banks of the Lukala River. The reply was that such a step would not be productive, and the intendant's idea was dismissed.[22] It is no surprise that one year after their exchange of letters, Soba Muxixi claimed the "lands of Luinha".[23] In all likelihood, the intendant pressed on with the occupation up to Muxixi's lands, even though he did not count on the government's approval in Luanda. Beyond the land issue, this episode also illustrates some tensions that pervaded the history of the Kingdom of Angola in the form of disputes between the government of Luanda and the colonial agents in the countryside.

Other *sobas* from the region participated in this conflict. As also happened in Muxima, disagreement erupted in the village of Massangano between *sobas* and residents over the lands of the foundry. Once again, the governor doubted the residents by pondering that no *soba* could have undertaken such a negotiation: "the *sobas* commonly cannot sell their lands, as they are a kind of *morgado* [entailed estate] [*uma espécie de morgado*]". The Luanda order was

19 *Sargento-mor* is a military rank.

20 "Pertenção (*sic*) das terras aonde se assenta a fábrica".

21 "Os *sobas* pod[iam] ou não vender as terras do seu estado". Biblioteca Nacional de Portugal (BNP), C 8742, F6364, fl. 148.

22 BNP, C 8742, F 6364, fl. 167.

23 IEB/USP, AL-083-003.

that lands considered "vacant" should be occupied until their alleged owners presented their "title deeds" proving either a "good or bad sale", that is, the legitimacy of their dealings.[24] If a vacant plot had a previous owner, he would be obliged to cultivate it under "penalty of having it expropriated for not promptly doing so".[25] Thus, the foundry's intendant was not authorised to occupy productive lands.

And the *sobas* did claim the possession of lands—not only in the context of the iron ore foundry in Ilamba. In 1759, when the Jesuits were expelled from the Kingdom of Angola, their properties were confiscated by the Royal Treasury.[26] The large diversity of Jesuit possessions at that time included houses, farmlands, *arimos*, and estates that were among the properties with the largest food production both in Luanda and in its hinterland. The possession of those areas was claimed by the inhabitants of Luanda and of its country, as well as by the *sobas*. The governor stated that those claims were leading to unsettled, "eternal suits" and affirmed: "some *sobas* want to be entitled to a large part of [those lands], since they have always claimed that [the Jesuits] held them in bad possession after usurping them from their ancestors with the subtleness and industriousness that was natural to them".[27]

> Regarding the Jesuits and the jurisdiction over those lands, he also expressed:
>
> In addition to the *sobas*, we also have some residents with eternal suits, who contended with [the Jesuits] for this very reason. The same suits concern the *Misericórdia* charity institution of this city: for over 50 years, a bitter litigation has dragged on through them on the enforcement of an inheritance to this charity, left by a man to whom they were heirs and will executors. The man died 137 years ago, leaving an inheritance of 400,000 Cruzados, which they imbibed into themselves and never conceded, even

24 IEB/USP, AL-083-003.

25 AHU_CU_001, Cx. 52, Doc. 73.

26 Regarding the Jesuits in the Kingdom of Angola, for Catarina Madeira Santos, "the missionary assistance of the Society of Jesus in the Angolan country in the 18th century was rather inexpressive. Since the restoration of 1648, the Jesuits had been leaving the countryside missions to dedicate themselves first and foremost to the school of Luanda (whose construction began in 1607) and to the *arimos* (agricultural estates or properties) they owned in various locations—above all, in the Bengo River region". Santos, *Um governo 'polido' para Angola*, 129.

27 "Há alguns sobas que querem ter direito a muita parte delas porque sempre clamaram que [os jesuítas] as retinham em má posse e as usurparam a seus antepassados com as sutilezas e as indústrias que lhes eram naturais", AHU_CU_001, Cx. 46, D. 4261.

> after the *Misericórdia* charity obtained favourable rulings by the Court of Appeals against them [the residents].[28]

Beyond the legal dimension, it must be pointed out that these disputes were taking place between the residents of areas under Portuguese administration—predominantly, members of the Portuguese and African elites—the *Misericórdia* charity and the *sobas*, that is, all vassals of the Crown who were independently in charge of their own populations.

Many remarks can be made about this document regarding quarrels for land possession. The reference to "they have always claimed" underscores that the local rulers had claimed the possession of those territories long before. As vassals of the Portuguese Crown, West Central African elites knew that the king of Portugal and his administrative staff owed them protection, respect, and the assurance of their "instances, privileges, honours, and statutes", as was recorded on their allegiance treaties.[29] However, they were not always listened to, even amid so many tensions, and so they found ways of legitimising their conquests and rights by ratifying their lineages. It is important to note that many vassals were enslaved by the Portuguese and had their lands seized.

One of the key issues for the Governor of Luanda at that time was the need to foster agriculture as a means to fight food scarcity and the poor distribution of water. In a 1768 *bando* (ordinance), the governor ordered the mapping of all deserted *arimos* along the Nzenza, Ndande, and Kwanza rivers. This docu-

28 "Além dos sobas há também alguns moradores que com causas eternas contendiam com eles [os jesuítas] sobre o mesmo; e igualmente a Misericórdia desta cidade, que há mais de cinquenta anos traz com eles um renhido pleito sobre a satisfação de um legado que deixou [à] dita Casa um homem de quem foram herdeiros e testamenteiros, que faleceu há cento e trinta e sete anos, importando a herança quatrocentos mil cruzados, que todos [ensoparam?] em si; e nunca satisfizeram o legado ainda depois de alcançar a Misericórdia sentenças da Relação contra eles", AHU_CU_001, Cx. 46, D. 4261.

29 Vassalage treaties have been constantly revisited by historiography. Beatrix Heintze has been a pioneer who exhaustively studied this reality and the documents it produced. For Heintze, the term 'vassal' was introduced by the Portuguese overseas as a power instrument, by which lineage chiefs became "vassals of the king of Portugal under a legal, documented and recognised procedure set up in the presence of witnesses", thus becoming a "type of inter-state dependency". The defeated party promised to comply with all imposed conditions and swore an oath of loyalty and obedience. The victors, in turn, made a "pledge of protection and investiture". Heintze also distinguishes between "voluntary vassalage"—when local chiefs, either for political or economic reasons, sought on their own initiative to join the Portuguese—and vassalage imposed by force, but points out that the former type was less frequent. As a rule, the vassal status was imposed on local leaders in such a way that the Portuguese dictated the terms of the treaties. Heintze, *Angola nos séculos XVI e XVII*, 395.

ment shows how the actions of colonial agents themselves served to instigate conflicts over the land. In it, the governor vows to transfer deserted properties to those who denounce their unproductive status and commit to cultivating them. Now, if, in order to obtain access to a land it sufficed to denounce its poor use, then one may have expected a large number of denouncement cases. The document also informs us that the Kingdom of Angola's lands either had the status of *sesmarias* or of "improper purchases from the *sobas*".[30] This citation further indicates that the *sobas* were not wont to sell their lands, and, therefore, any purchase of their areas would probably be illegal. Portuguese colonisation was based on local rule, and that implied also recognising land claims from local rulers and recognising the ways of understanding their ownership.

The governors' regulations ordered a survey of "all allotted lands, who bestowed them, what powers they had to do so, and who possesses them today",[31] since news was circulating that some lands granted by *sesmaria* were not being cultivated. In such cases, areas without an owner would be granted to those who committed themselves to cultivating them within five years. If, by the end of this period, their occupants had not fulfilled their commitment, these lands could be reassigned to new ones.[32] This provision draws on the 1375 *Sesmarias* Law, which was compiled in the Ordinances of Kings Afonso, Manuel, and Phillip, with some modifications in the records of these three sets.[33]

3 Negotiating Access to Land: *Sobas* and Residents

Defining residents, or dwellers, as a social category in Angola is a rather challenging task. The available documents describe them either as free or freed individuals of diverse origin—African, Portuguese, or Portuguese African—who lived in the vicinity of Portuguese strongholds, estates, villas, and fortified villages. The historiography of the region indicates that, over time, an elite consisting of Portuguese African families established itself primarily in Luanda.

---

30 IEB/ USP, AL-083-92.

31 "De todas as terras que são dadas, quem as deu, e que poder tinha para isso, e quem as possui".

32 AHU, Códice 544, fl. 8v.

33 The *sesmarias* regime first came into existence in the reign of Ferdinand I, to counter the decrease in the Portuguese rural population. See *Código Filipino, ou, Ordenações e Leis do Reino de Portugal: recompiladas por mandado d'el-Rei D. Filipe I*, ed. de Almeida, Livro IV, 43.

This elite was independent of the *sobados*. By controlling activities linked to transatlantic trafficking, its members became closely linked to the elites based in Brazil. According to Beatrix Heintze's description, it consisted of a "quite heterogenous group and hard to define, which included, above all, black Africans (many of them were former slaves) and mestizos, as well as some whites".[34] For Vansina, in turn, a resident was a "wealthy patron" known as *Mwadi*, who led a *sanzala*, that is, a grouping of relatives and subordinates.[35]

In the Portuguese occupation of Africa's eastern coast, the areas allotted to the African chieftains—and, particularly, to the Maraves—are considered by the historiography to be a form of collective property, which no ruler could sell or transfer. This same pattern repeated itself among the Mbundu. In her book *Portugueses e Africanos nos rios de Sena*, Eugénia Rodrigues provides a long inventory of the concessions known as *prazos* in the Zambezi Valley region, which on the Indian Ocean shore provided a distinct legal framework for the partition of lands. The *prazos* were "lease concessions through which the Crown maintained its direct dominion while granting rights of use in exchange for the payment of a fee".[36] This grant was initially designed to last for three generations, after which it could be renewed. Like the Mbundu *sobas*, the rulers of the Sena Rivers conflicted with the colonial residents, who claimed to have purchased their lands.

Rodrigues' work can be helpful in clarifying the basis of the disagreement: did residents really purchase lands from African elites? In Mozambique, the settling of the Portuguese in African territory was sealed with the exchange of textiles. In this transaction, "apparently, only the African ruler remained as the land possessor, even though the river merchants considered that either they had bought these lands, or that they were donated to them". Rodrigues warns that in order to understand this contrast, we must distinguish between the "European concepts of donation and purchase" and the modalities of "gratification of new subjects by the African rulers".[37]

34 Heintze, "A lusofonia no interior da África Central na era pré-colonial", 11. Regarding the 19th century, see: Villas Bôas, *Portugueses, moradores e Sobas em Golungo Alto, Angola*. For Vilas Bôas, residents were a quite distinct group consisting of Africans, *mestizos* and white settlers, who were free and possessed some type of movable or immovable property. "They were active participants of Angola's political life, playing a vital role in trade activities and in bureaucratic positions in the hierarchy of countryside military militias. In a certain way, they were the intermediaries between the colonial administration and African *sobados*" (23, fn. 27).

35 Vansina, "Ambaca Society and the Slave Trade c. 1760–1845", 8.

36 Rodrigues, *Portugueses e Africanos nos rios de Sena*, 25.

37 Rodrigues, *Portugueses e Africanos nos rios de Sena*, 357. Rodrigues also points out that

It is worth considering that similar misunderstandings between the *sobas* and the residents of the villages along the Kwanza River continued to occur, since their relations were based on the supply of products, such as textiles—a common form of currency in West Central Africa.[38] A gesture, a negotiation, or a simple exchange of gifts could all have distinct meanings for the respective parties. We may imagine that what the first settlers believed to be a land purchase, for the Mbundu could well have represented a bid for authorising passage through their territory or the establishment of an alliance. In any case, an interpretation that we must always consider is that of forced seizures of land, for instance, in situations of war. According to Vansina, in the absence of other options, the *sobas* who had been removed from their lands during the conquests, negotiated their resettlement with the colonisers.[39]

Returning to the case at hand, the residents of villages in Luanda's hinterland started providing documents, which are described in the sources only as "titles" capable of proving the possession of the land. Governor Sousa Coutinho even received a list with the names of those who claimed to own lands that were used for the foundry's construction. His order was, then, to compensate those who had parts of their properties unduly annexed to the foundry.[40] However, we do not know if the *sobas* could prove their land tenure.

4 Lineage and Land: The African *Morgados*

According to historian Isabel de Castro Henriques, "the African land is comprehensive; it encompasses all African territories: the land is the cosmos".[41] As such, land contained some "fundamental pillars of African identity", such as kinship and religion, constituting a sacred space: "for Africans, the land has no exchange value, since it does not belong to a group unless mediated by spirits".[42] Elements such as sacred trees, rivers, plants that provided the pigments of sacred colours, the drums that took messages from one *cubata* (house) to another, and the graves of ancestors or founding heroes were all important

merchants obtained lands via military and marital alliances in the territories of the Karanga States, which emerged from the Monomotapa Empire.

38 The term "money object" was first used by Paul Lovejoy in *A escravidão na África*, 169–170.

39 Vansina, "Ambaca Society and the Slave Trade c. 1760–1845", 22.

40 IEB/ USP, AL-083-223.

41 Henriques, "A materialidade do simbólico", 40.

42 Henriques, "A materialidade do simbólico", 40.

markers of this space.[43] For instance, in 1809, the *capitão-mor*[44] of the Pungo Andongo village ordered some *sobas* to inhabit one of the Kwanza River islands. Those rulers did not do so, since it ran against "their rites"—which were translated by the colonial agents as "gentilic laws".[45]

When Governor Sousa Coutinho referred to the *morgado* (entailed estate) to describe the *sobas*' relationship with the lands of Ilamba, he was creating an analogy between the African notions of parentage and transmission of nobility titles and the Portuguese inheritance and succession rights. The key issue to be highlighted in this regard is that, by making an analogy with entailed estates, the governor understood that land possession was ruled by parentage criteria in a kind of African *morgado*. According to Priest Raphael Bluteau's dictionary, entailed estates or *bens de morgado* were a property "that could neither be divested, nor divided, in such a way that a successor shall possess it in the same way and structure that the institutor has declared".[46] The transfer of *morgados* was regulated by the *Ordenações Filipinas*. The *morgado* was usually transmitted to the firstborn male son and was succeeded along his line. In case "the oldest son dies while his father or *morgado* possessor is still alive, if said oldest son has a son, grandson or legitimate descendants, these descendants, following their order, will have precedence over the second oldest son".[47] A *morgado* also had to be confirmed by the heirs through the possession of a document.

Despite the relevant bibliography that exists on other parts of the Portuguese empire, in particular, on Portuguese America, India, and Eastern Africa, the references on land conflicts in the Kingdom of Angola and in West Central Africa, are still scarce and predominantly focused on the 19th and 20th centuries.[48] According to these studies, the rules of access to Mbundu lands experienced a significant change with the decline of the slave trade, as Portuguese coloni-

---

43 Regarding the Africans' multiple meanings for the land, Holly Hanson presents an interesting example in which a system of social relations based on "reciprocal obligations" became the basis for the State of Ganda. Such obligations were linked to the possession of the land (which was, in turn, a payment for the obligation), and embedded an affective meaning that determined the social and political hierarchies. Hanson, *Landed Obligation*. On the importance of non-human entities in the definition of access and distribution of land, see Bastias Saavedra (Chapter 1) in this volume.

44 *Capitão-mor* is the position of commander, a military rank. These commanders were the main authority in the villages and forts of the hinterland.

45 "Seus ritos"; "leis gentílicas". Arquivo Histórico de Angola (AHA), Cód. 3018.

46 Bluteau, *Vocabulário portuguez e latino*, entry "*morgado*".

47 *Código Filipino, ou, Ordenações e Leis do Reino de Portugal. Recompiladas por mandado d'el-Rei D. Filipe I*, Livro IV, Título 100, 'Por que ordem se sucederá nos Morgados e bens vinculados'.

48 Candido's latest book is an important exception: *Wealth, land, and property in Angola*.

alism became predominantly concentrated on agricultural activities, such as the production of cassava, corn, and indigo, in addition to the exploitation of roccella lichen, ivory, and starch. These studies thus argue that the Portuguese only resorted to the exploitation of local labour in West Central Africa to meet the needs of an expanding agriculture.[49] However, as underscored by Candido, since the 16th century, driven by the plans and rights of conquest, and in the name of a "just war", the Portuguese occupation influenced the local politics of land distribution and control.[50] Over time, the expansion to Luanda's hinterland intensified as African rulers' power weakened. Land possession had always been central to Portuguese colonialism in Angola, even though it only became a key issue with the decline of the transatlantic slave trade.

For the areas located to the north of the Kwanza River, the most illustrative studies on land possession were published by Eva Sebestyén on the transmission of land possession among the Ndembu and in N'Dalatando, as well as in the *sobado* of Samba Cajú in the Ambaca-region,[51] located near the place where the Nova Oeiras foundry was built. Sebestyén found documents kept by the local *sobas* on disputes over lands and purchase titles from the 17th century to the 20th century. These records based on the oral tradition were used to legitimise the possession of lands. They follow the narrative thread of Portuguese testaments but cover distinct contents. Their testators do not list their property items or heirs. Instead, they leave a record of the relevant information for their lineage, including instructions for defending their heirs from slavery: "primarily, a declaration validating lineage membership and a record of boundary inspections which codifies lineage landownership".[52] Another relevant piece of information is that the documents of *sobas* from the jurisdiction of the Ambaca fortress were only recognised as genuine if they were registered by the official scribe of its village. Thus, the colonial administration recognised

49 Dias, "Mudanças nos padrões de poder do *hinterland* de Luanda", 42–94; Venâncio, *A economia de Luanda e Hinterland no Século XVIII*; Pantoja, "Donas de '*arimos*'", 35–49; Freudenthal, *Arimos e fazendas*; Ferreira, "A questão das terras na política colonial portuguesa em Angola nos anos de 1880", 261–272. Regarding the Portuguese Empire in America, see Herzog, *Frontiers of Possession*; Mota, "Apropriação econômica da natureza em uma fronteira do império atlântico português", 43–53. On Eastern Africa, see: Rodrigues, *Portugueses e Africanos nos rios de Sena*, 25; Bastião, *Entre a Ilha e a Terra*; Farré, "Regime de terras e cultivo de algodão em dois contextos coloniais", 245–254.

50 Candido, "Conquest, occupation, colonialism and exclusion", 230.

51 Sebestyén found 234 documents. Sebestyén, "*Legitimation through Landcharters in Ambundu Villages*", 363–379; Sebestyén, "Os 'arquivos' de *sobas* Mbundu. Um caso transcultural dos testamentos em Angola", 51–74.

52 Sebestyén, *Legitimation through Landcharters in Ambundu Villages*, 364.

the titles to the land of those lineages if its employees had certified them. Here, we see the dependency of African rulers on the colonial employees, as these officials had the power to register and authenticate their 'testaments'.

For Sebestyén, these titles served two aims. First, they "fulfilled Portuguese demands insofar as they gave detailed accounts of the boundaries of the *sobado* and of the names of neighbouring *sobados*".[53] A *sobado* is a village that can have multiple plantations and productions, where the people dependent on the *soba* live. The number of dependents in a *sobado* is directly proportional to the power of the *soba*. Second, these documents safeguarded the lineage's history: its origin and migrations, as well as its first settlement and the record of local wars and alliances. When a new ruler was elected, a vassalage ceremony was held and the *sobado's* boundaries were confirmed anew, by means of boundary inspections. A symbolic procedure characterised the vassalage rite: a celebration that absorbed the enthronement rituals of the Mbundu culture for a new ruler, named *undamento*. In this ceremony, perpetuated by the Portuguese, the new vassal's *undamento* meant to "lay flour (or white clay) on the shoulders of the African ruler, who would then rub it on his chest and arms".[54] Lineage successors of vassal *sobas* were meant to submit to the investiture as soon as they were selected by the *makota*, lest they would be seen as rebels and, thereby, become liable to punishment.[55] Thus, the *undamento* ceremony became a synonym for vassalage itself.

Sebestyén distinguishes between two groups of issues in connection with these land titles. Conflicts related to lineages, daily life, and politics are prevalent in the documents from Dembos, whereas in the case of Samba Cajú, the prevalent narratives—above all from the 18th and 19th centuries—are linked to land demarcations, disputes, purchases, and sales. In a set of documents kept by the Historical Archives of Angola, the will of Dom Gaspar de Caxinda, dated 1829, reads:

> I, the Testator, declare that with the passing of time, and *seeing that my people were numerous and did not have the means for agricultural activities*, had my Friend the Soba Quitalla Quia Huy help me wage war against the Mucundu Sobas, and another Ndomba. And after being razed, *they left behind the lands* known as Ngando Acaquigy river; my above-mentioned Friend Quittalla shall remain on this side as I, the Testator, shall remain yonder = I, the Testator, declare that by descending along the Carianga

53 Sebestyén, *Legitimation through Landcharters in Ambundu Villages*, 365.
54 Heintze, *Angola nos séculos XVI e XVII*, 398.
55 Sebestyén, *Legitimation through Landcharters in Ambundu Villages*, 365.

stream, as the above-mentioned Friend always remains on this side of the stream, and as I remain on the other side = I declare that by descending along it until the Carianga stream meets the Mussurigi River, and apportioning in two halves the Lake named Quizanga da Branca in the Helho belongs to me the Testator = I declare that the Testator continued, as the two Friends shared the area named Quicembo, having on its left side the Soba Luachy Niandalla Adungo and, on the right side, the Soba Calanga Riaqueta, and, remaining, the initial part of this Area's outlet with the above-mentioned Friend Quittala, while its end reaches me, the Testator, all along to the Zé Ria Cagungo River. This river remained shared by four *sobas*: Calanga Riaqueta, Luachy Luandalla Ndungo, Quitalla Quiahuy by another name, Mucamby Huahuy; *its marks were set in a brotherly way*, with no grievances = I, the Testator, declare that, after, the two companions, *sobas* Quitalla and Luachy, remained on this side of the Zé Riacagungo River, I *went with my companion* Soba Calanga, with the highly named Muxinda Huabúlo and the Calanga descending along the said River to the Spring of the Cubombonuabembe stream, this side-part of which belongs to the said Calanga, whereas the part beyond it belongs to me the Testator = I, the Testator, declare that by moving along the above-said Calombo River until the Cambombo River, known as Cabobmo Caquicuquelle until it meets the Quiongua River. Beyond the Quionga, I demarcated it with my companion Calanga until the Cahissari Stream. Calanga remains on this side of the Quiogua River, and Cahissady, while I, the Testator, remain beyond it up to the Spring of the Quicungulla Stream; I, the Testator, am always beyond, whereas Calanga remains on this side of the said stream, until it meets the river named Cassuissuy = I, the Testator, declare that I went up along the said Cassuissui River, now leaving my companion Calanga on this side of the river. I went on its other side up to its Spring, and demarcated with another, Soba Cámuhóto Cattusu, highly denominated as Calundu Cacumba by another name Quibalanga, *up to the Spring* of the stream known as Quiamifulla, and descending along with it until it meets another stream named Cangulungo, having the Soba Camuhoto taken to himself this side before the stream, and I, the Testator, beyond it, thence to reach Murro Bango's foothill = I, the Testator, declare that, should this deed not be valid as a will, it shall still be valid as a codicil or charitable donation or Lawfully under Better Conditions to Come, and in better expressed terms; and *I revoke any other testament or codicil* I may have established before the present one, even if acting among other *sobas*, regardless of the number of clauses that may contradict the present ones, or of tacit clauses, even if they are

to be intangible and reproachful, and even if they should be compared on a Verbo ad Verbam basis[56] to the way I am now stating and declaring them = And since this is my last and final will, the way in which I have said it was read and explained to me in Mbundu, that [illegible] as I have said, I signed it before the following in-person witnesses: Soba Camuhoto, Soba Quitalla Quiahuy, Soba Juachy Luandalladungo and Soba Calanga Riaqueta, all of whom signed it with a cross, and I request the Justice procedures of Your Majesty, whom God May Guard [satisfy] give full compliance, so that, should this deed not be valid as a will, it may still be valid as a codicil or causa mortis donation, or be Lawfully expressed in better terms to come; may the truth of what I faithfully and personally signed with the Testator at his plea and request = Banza at the location of Mussurigi, on 20 February 1016 = Cross of Testator Dom Gaspar de Caxinda, alias Sabo—Cross of witness Soba Camuhoto Cattusu = Cross of Witness Soba Quitalla Quiahuy = Cross of witness Soba Calanga Riaqueto = *I am the one who produced it at his plea and request as witness* Francisco de Souza Roza = And no other thing was contained in such testament presented to me, which I accurately and faithfully drafted in accordance with the original statement, and which I attest to after having revised and confirmed it, seemingly leaving nothing that may give rise to doubt; written, revised, confirmed and signed in this Banza of Soba Caxinda in conformity with my profession under oath. Cacumby and Canumia, the site where this Banza is located today on 20 February 1829.
[Signatures]
Gaspar Jeronimo
'In ttª G.—Truthfully J.'.[57]

It is certainly difficult to decipher this document, based as it is on oral tradition. Yet, it is worth pointing out how the *soba* described the reasons for his people's migration—"seeing that my people were numerous and did not have the means for agricultural activities"—in addition to the alliances he made with and the wars he waged against other *sobas*, with the aim of occupying new lands, and the streams and rivers that served to demarcate the land, as well as other specific references—"its marks were set". According to Sebestyén, the boundary markers used by locals were specific trees, which she found to have medicinal properties, and other elements: "trees with an incised cross sign [...] pieces of

56 Word by word.
57 I am thankful to Roquinaldo Ferreira for sharing this document with the Cecult/Unicamp researchers. AHA, Caixa 3465 (Avulsos)—Ambaca. Italics added.

crockery [...], pieces of iron, rocks", clay pots and others.[58] In annual rites linked to the land, the *sobas* resorted to the support of their ancestors and water entities "on the banks of bordering rivers, to obtain good harvest by making offerings to mermaids, *quiximbi* who owned the rivers, and protectors of the land".[59]

If we consider that these were not the first written records kept by lineage holders from the region that have reached us today,[60] then it is quite likely that the *sobas* from the ancient province of Ilamba also maintained titles to attest to the possession of lands through their lineages, and that they presented such titles to the governor. There is evidence of such records: in 1860, the Soba Quipola from Moçâmedes claimed the possession of lands that, according to him, were occupied by whites for agricultural activities. He requested the governor to hand him the "land title", so that he could prove the legitimacy of his ownership to anyone who questioned him on the issue. The request supports the reasoning that the lineage's possession had to be attested by the colonial authorities.[61] The evidence strongly indicates that it was due to Governor Sousa Coutinho's knowledge of the documents kept by the *sobas* that he made the *morgado* analogy, since this land could no longer be appropriated. Thus, we find an exchange of legal and cultural practices that must be taken into consideration. Bearing in mind the colonial context, we may also call attention to how Africans, in addition to subordination and/or resistance, conceived new practices and solutions for conflicts, even if this was by resorting to norms and narrative strategies of the Portuguese.[62]

5 *Kilambas* and *Sobas*: The Unfolding of the Conflict in Ilamba

In the consulted documents, we did not find additional allusions to the above-cited Soba Muxixi or to Muxima *sobas*. This indicates that land disputes did

58 Sebestyén, *Legitimation through Landcharters in Ambundu Villages*, 365.

59 Sebestyén, "O contexto cultural dos marcos de terrenos nas aldeias Ambundu/Angola", 93.

60 These records include, at least, the 'Archives of the State of Ndembu Kakulu Kakaenda', which consist of 210 documents exchanged between the *ndembu* and the colonial administration, dating from the 18th century to the 20th century. See Tavares and Santos, *Africae Monumenta*. And an unprecedented set of records is now available online at *Arquivo Histórico Ultramarino, Fundo Dembos: PT/AHU/DEMBOS*—https://digitarq.ahu.arquivos.pt/details?id=1157639.

61 Candido, *Conquest, occupation, colonialism and exclusion*, 224.

62 Mary Louise Pratt employs the concept of transculturation to describe how "subordinated or marginal groups select and invent from materials transmitted to them by a dominant or metropolitan culture". Pratt, *Imperial Eyes*, 7–8.

not only occur among royal officials, residents, and traditional West Central African authorities; the issue of land ownership also produced conflicts among the *sobas* themselves, as well as between *sobas* and other local authorities, such as the *kilamba*. Such reality was confirmed, above all, in regard to the High Ilamba-lands, with their bountiful iron ore mines.

The term *kilamba*, in Kimbundu language, means a person in charge of an activity. It is quite difficult to categorise this title, since, in many contexts, it was linked to black wars and collaboration with colonial initiatives. As mentioned earlier in this Chapter, according to Coelho, it meant a sorcerer "in charge of placating the fury of nature's geniuses". The *kilamba* figure was also described by Antonio de Oliveira Cadornega as a "black war captain". Cadornega associated such rulers to foreign origins and linked their growing political and economic eminence in the region to their military skills. They were "hated" by the *sobas*, since, after settling on *soba* lands, they acted as spies by reporting on the *sobas* to the Portuguese. In the news from the Ambaca village, we find something in this direction: the *kilamba* and the *kimbar*, both of which were seen as black war agents, possessed no lands but were located in a "part of the *soba* lands". Heintze's glossary defines *kilamba* as an "African officer in the black war, who enjoyed special confidence by the Portuguese".[63]

According to Heintze, the *kilamba* were recompensed "for their loyal services with areas in regions of vassal [*sobas*]".[64] The lands where the Novo Belém foundry was built previously belonged to Kilamba Ngongue a Kamukala; the lands around Nova Oeiras, in turn, had belonged to Kilamba Pedro Ambaxi; Soba Muxixi, who claimed lands in Luinha, appears in another set of documents as a *kilamba*.[65] Heintze and Vansina, also suggest that, over time, the *kilamba* could become *sobas*. And there seems to be a consensus among the

63 This interpretation is found in 18th-century sources: see Silva Correa, *História de Angola*, vol. I, 291. In the work *Livro dos Baculamentos*, the *ilamba* appear as tax collectors of the *sobas*. Furthermore, Jan Vansina and Roquinaldo Ferreira identify these chiefs as relevant slave trade agents. See Coelho, *Em busca de Kàbàsà*, 161; Cadornega, *História das Guerras Angolanas (1680)*, ed. Delgado, vol. I, 246. Heintze, *Fontes para a História de Angola do século XVII*, 126–127; Freudenthal and Pantoja (eds.), *Livro dos Baculamentos*, 32; Vansina, "Ambaca Society and the Slave Trade c. 1760–1845", 8; Vansina, *How societies are born*, 59.

64 Heintze, *Angola nos séculos XVI e XVII*, 451. Despite the fact that *ilamba*, the plural of *kilamba*, corresponds to the name of the region (Ilamba), we do not yet know the grounds for such a coincidence. We do know that the *ilamba* received lands in exchange for their participation in the black war. But were all those lands really donated to them? An answer is not currently available for this question, as we do not yet count on new elements to progress in this analysis.

65 AHU_CU_001, Cx. 55, D. 6 and 7.

sources, in that the *kilamba* figure occupied part of the *sobas*' lands by living there, with the intention of spying on them for the Portuguese, but did not possess their own lands. However, the cases mentioned here suggest that at least some of them possessed lands. It was possible that some *ilamba*—in particular, those who first associated with the Portuguese—became possessors of lands, natural resources, and peoples. They may have even been brought into the parentage-based political arrangement to become *sobas*. Others, in turn, may not have been as fortunate and remained based in *soba* lands, like many other secondary *sobas*—the so-called *sobetas*—who clustered over the lands of a more powerful *soba*.[66] But it must be remembered that the *ilamba* were not popular (instead, they were "hated") among the *sobas*, on account of their spying practices and alliances with the Portuguese.[67] Many *sobas* may have been subdued by colonial domination as a result of actions by the *ilamba*, who, as mentioned above, acted as black war captains.

As mentioned, quarrels over land had become "eternal suits". As land disputes in Ilamba unfolded, an additional character appeared on the scene in February 1768 to claim lands: a "black man with shoes" whose name remained unmentioned.[68] This was probably João Correia, who submitted a petition and a "title of lord of the lands on which Nova Oeiras was founded" to the Royal Treasury one year later, in February 1796. In this document, Correia asserted to possess a tobacco field on that spot, as well as profitable activities originating from his access to the Luinha and Lukala Rivers, in the form of canoe rentals to traders and travellers. With the peopling and beginning of the foundry's construction, Correia allegedly lost his businesses and underwent great losses. The orders from Luanda, once again, required "the titles on which the said lordship is based", as well as testimonials of witnesses "truthful and free from any

66 Vansina, "Ambaca Society and the Slave Trade c. 1760–1845", 8.

67 The feeling of hatred described by Cadornega was so evident that in the documents found by Sebestyén, a saying is recurrent: "we are vassals of the Majesty; do not want subjection in a service of *empacaceiro* [hunter], *quilamba* and *quimbar*". The *sobas* seemingly did not want their identity to be associated with those of the *Ilamba* and *Imbari*. Sebestyén, "O contexto cultural dos marcos de terrenos nas aldeias Ambundu/Angola", 92.

68 IEB/USP AL-083-009. In the Angolan hinterland, traders were known as *pumbeiros* or *funadores*, and as "blackmen with shoes". These characters shared cultural and social traits with their victims, and the "success of their business" hinged on the manipulation of these symbols so that they could distinguish themselves from the enslaved. One of their distinctive signs was the use of shoes, whereby traders were called "blackmen with shoes" and considered white. Many of them used their new social status to evade their obligations as vassals of the Portuguese, for instance, by refusing to work as helpers transporting the products of market sellers. Ferreira, *Cross-cultural Exchange in the Atlantic World*, 61–63.

suspicion", to inquire whether the lands were really cultivated, how much they yielded and what the legal grounds for his rights of transit in the rivers were.[69]

Thus, the documents about the lands of Ilamba give us few clues as to how the conflicts involving land possession among the local rulers and other subjects of the Portuguese Crown were solved. The documents are rather fragmentary and filled with contradictions and clashes. In his order of June 1769 to the intendants of iron foundries, Governor Sousa Coutinho instructs how these employees should regulate "doubts regarding the [possession of the] land". The aim of this instruction was to avoid violence and outrage among the Africans, residents, and merchants at the foundry's founding. The governor reiterated that the legitimate owner of a piece of land had to present "his titles". If anyone could prove it, he would be compensated with available lands elsewhere. And in case such "free lands" were not found, then the recent occupant had to pay a tribute to the land's owner.[70]

In the end, a legitimate possession of lands in Ilamba does not seem to have been proved by anyone. What we find is that all the above-mentioned characters used the means within their reach in their attempts to prove their possessions. Inconsistencies indicate how the Luanda government displeased the *sobas* and village residents alike. Since this topic was not addressed again in the correspondence on the construction and peopling of the Nova Oeiras foundry, we may speculate that neither the *sobas*, nor the residents, nor João Correia succeeded in proving that their titles were genuine, thus making it possible for the region to be occupied according to the plans of the Royal Treasury of Angola's government. Another conjecture is that they did have the titles, but not the witnesses to testify to their possessions. Further, royal officials may have performed legal manoeuvres—such as categorising the lands as vacant or requesting the presence of witnesses who either were not found or were not considered "truthful and free from any suspicion"—as measures to expropriate the lands of residents, *sobas* and the *ilamba*, as well as of João Correia, the *Misericórdia* charity institution and, probably, the local *donas* who eventually became large proprietors of *arimos*.[71]

---

69 IEB/USP, AL-083-223.

70 IEB-USP, Al-083–254.

71 Some local women became owners of large *arimos* in Luanda's hinterland after inheriting them as the third part of the possessions of previous lords, or as widows of rich Europeans and Portuguese-Europeans. By associating these properties with others, such as slaves, houses, shops and taverns, these rich ladies were known as *donas*. See Pantoja, "Donas de '*arimos*': um negócio feminino no abastecimento de gêneros alimentícios em Luanda (séculos XVIII e XIX)", 35–49.

6 Final Remarks

Though focusing on other contexts, Sara Berry's studies on the Ashanti Confederation in the Gold Coast help us reflect on some of the topics above. Berry expounds on the influence of the British administration as the confederation was established in the late 19th century. The colonial agents favoured and empowered African rulers aligned to their interests by allotting lands in the region to them. In doing so, they produced a stable basis for controlling the territory. In their land investiture ceremonies, they used black stools—a symbol of traditional Ashanti authority. Berry shows how the colonisers established a legal and administrative apparatus by including and reformulating traditions, as well as inventing new ones to their own benefit, while excluding others, according to what they understood to be "native law and custom".[72]

In Angola, the Portuguese colonial administration also used powerful symbols of African leaders and the local hierarchic structure to exert control over the territory. In a certain way, by harnessing the traditional symbols, such as the *undamento* ceremony, and attesting to the land titles of certain lineages, the Portuguese benefited from the existing African political structures for maintaining their dominion over the *sobados* to the north of the Kwanza River.[73] It is important to point out that other political powers were then just as important as the colonial administration for the maintenance of the Kingdom of Angola. Kristin Mann draws attention to the law-making process on land appropriations in an original way by underscoring the key role played by Africans in Lagos in the transformation of these norms over time. She shows how the Africans reverted impositions of the colonial administration to their favour, for instance, by re-elaborating legal rules to legitimise their property, including lands and slaves, and to uphold the land's status as family property.[74]

In the case of Angola, it is still necessary to reconstitute in detail the elements I have described in this Chapter, as well as the precepts that ruled the occupation of the land for the Mbundus, and how such rules were either incorporated or reformatted in or eliminated by the norms of the colonial agents.

---

72 Berry, *Chiefs Know Their Boundaries*. As colonial states consolidated their power and elaborated the legal and administrative apparatus of their rule, however, officials took steps to formalize conditions of tenure on lands set aside or left for African use—usually according to what they understood to be "native law and custom". Berry, "Debating the Land Question in Africa", 638.

73 Dias, "O Kabuku Kambilu (c. 1850–1900)", 22.

74 According to Mann, the shifts in the uses, meanings and ways of appropriating the land were at the heart of Lagos' emancipation. See Mann, *Slavery and the Birth of an African City*.

Yet, by resorting to the very instruments imposed by the colonial administration, such as land titles and, as seen above, legal testaments, the local chiefdoms found ways to keep the lands of their lineages and sustain their histories and power, even when confronted with successive shifts in the configuration of local powers, driven by the enslaving violence of their days. Such processes did not occur without changes, conflicts, expropriations, and wars. But it is noteworthy how they managed, within the available limits, to ensure their autonomy over time. They did so by using ritualistic emblems and Christian symbols as well as many other ways that deserve further in-depth study. Sebestyén, for instance, only obtained access to the records of her research after participating in a ritual led by local rulers, since they were considered sacred documents.[75] Every year, the records are read to the leaders of the *sobados* and continue to legitimise the rights of their lineages to their lands today.

Despite the striking distinctions found among the Portuguese overseas possessions, in all of them, the royal administration was "unable to maintain large numbers of soldiers and employees in the field"[76] and thus resorted to some expedients in order to safeguard and manage its territories. In Angola, the allegiance of vassal African rulers enabled the control of the territory by means of intermediaries and minimised European costs in the administration of the lands, including those lands that were still unchartered.[77] This reality has ensured both conquest and occupation but has also led to claims and clashes, such as the ones described above. The relations of interdependency that emerged from territorial appropriations in the land of Ilamba stand out and give us a glimpse of several nuances in the exercise of political dominion by *sobas*, *capitães-mores*, residents, and governors alike.

Bibliography

Manuscripts

Arquivo Histórico de Angola (AHA), Cód. 3018.
AHA, Caixa 3465 (Avulsos)—Ambaca.

75 Sebestyén describes that the documents are maintained by African authorities, the *sobas* and *dembos*, as well as their councillors. In the case of the *dembos*, for instance, they are kept along with other power emblems in a specific place under the guardianship of Mene Tandalla, the councillor with links to the local traditions and magic. See Sebestyén, "Os 'arquivos' de sobas Mbundu: um caso transcultural dos testamentos em Angola", 55–56.

76 Rodrigues, *Portugueses e Africanos nos rios de Sena*, 27.

77 Candido, "Conquest, occupation, colonialism and exclusion", 224.

Arquivo Histórico Ultramarino (AHU), AHU_CU_001, Cx. 86, D. 66.
AHU_CU_001, Cx. 52, D. 73.
AHU_CU_001, Cx. 52, Doc. 73.
AHU_CU_001, Cx. 46, D. 4261.
AHU, Códice 544, fl. 8v.
Biblioteca Nacional de Portugal (BNP), C 8742, F6364, fl. 148.
BNP, C 8742, F 6364, fl. 167.
Instituto de Estudos Brasileiros/ Universidade de São Paulo (IEB/USP)—Coleção Alberto Lamego, AL-083-099.
IEB/USP, AL-083-003.
IEB/ USP, AL-083-92.
IEB/ USP, AL-083-223.
IEB/USP AL-083-009.
IEB-USP, Al-083–254.

Printed Sources

Bluteau, Raphael, *Vocabulário portuguez e latino*, 10 vols. Lisboa: Officina de Pascoal da Sylva, 1712–1728.
Cadornega, Antonio de Oliveira, *História das Guerras Angolanas (1680)*, 2 vols., ed. Delgado, José Matias, Lisboa 1972.
[Anon.,] *Código Filipino, ou, Ordenações e Leis do Reino de Portugal: recompiladas por mandado d'el-Rei D. Filipe I*, ed. de Almeida, Cândido Mendes, Brasília 2004.
Montecúccolo, Giovanni Antonio Cavazzi de, *Descrição histórica dos três reinos do Congo, Matamba e Angola*, ed. de Leguzzano, Graciano Maria, Lisboa 1965.
Silva Correa, Elias Alexandre da, *História de Angola*, 2 vols., Lisboa 1937.

Literature

Alfagali, Crislayne, *Blacksmiths of Ilamba. A Social History of Labor at the Nova Oeiras Iron Foundry (Angola, 18th Century)*, Berlin-Boston 2023.
Bastião, Maria Paula Pereira, *Entre a Ilha e a Terra. Processos de construção do continente fronteiro à Ilha de Moçambique (1763—c. 1802)* (Ph.D. Thesis), Lisboa 2013.
Berry, Sara, *Chiefs Know Their Boundaries. Essays on Property, Power, and the Past in Asante, 1896–1996*, Portsmouth-Oxford-Cape Town 2001.
Berry, Sara, "Debating the Land Question in Africa", in *Comparative Studies in Society and History* 44:4 (2002), 638–668.
Candido, Mariana, "Conquest, Occupation, Colonialism and Exclusion. Land Disputes in Angola", in Serrão, José Vicente, Bárbara Direito, Eugénia Rodrigues and Susana Münch Miranda (eds.), *Property Rights, Land and Territory in the European Overseas Empires*, Lisboa 2015, 223–235.
Candido, Mariana, *Wealth, Land, and Property in Angola. A History of Dispossession, Slavery, and Inequality*, Cambridge 2022.

Carvalho, Flávia Maria de, *Sobas e homens do rei: interiorização dos portugueses em Angola (séculos XVII e XVIII)*, Maceió 2015.

Coelho, Virgílio, *Em busca de Kàbàsà. Uma tentativa de explicação da estrutura político-administrativa do reino de Ndòngò*, Luanda 2010.

Delson, Roberta Marx, *Novas Vilas para o Brasil colônia. Planejamento espacial e social no século XVIII*, Brasília 1997.

Dias, Jill, "Mudanças nos padrões de poder do hinterland de Luanda. O impacto da colonização sobre os Mbundu (c; 1845–1920)", in *Penélope: revista de história e ciências sociais* 14 (1994), 42–94.

Dias, Jill, "O Kabuku Kambilu (c. 1850–1900). Uma identidade política ambígua", in Comissão Nacional para as Comemorações dos Descobrimentos Portugueses (ed.), *Actas do Seminário Encontro de povos e culturas em Angola*, Lisboa 1997, 15–52.

Farré, Albert, "Regime de terras e cultivo de algodão em dois contextos coloniais. Uganda e Moçambique (1895–1930)", in Serrão, José Vicente, Bárbara Direito, Eugénia Rodrigues and Susana Münch Miranda (eds.), *Property Rights, Land and Territory in the European Overseas Empires*, Lisboa 2015, 245–254.

Ferreira, Aurora da Fonseca, "A questão das terras na política colonial portuguesa em Angola nos anos de 1880. O caso de um conflito em torno da Kisanga", in Santos, Maria Emília Madeira (ed.), *A África e a instalação do sistema colonial—c. 1885–c. 1930*, Lisboa 2001, 261–272.

Ferreira, Roquinaldo, *Cross-cultural Exchange in the Atlantic World. Angola and Brazil during the Era of the Slave Trade*, Cambridge 2012.

Freudenthal, Aida and Selma Pantoja (eds.), *Livro dos Baculamentos. Que os sobas deste Reino de Angola pagam a Sua Majestade (1630)*, Luanda 2013.

Freudenthal, Aida, *Arimos e fazendas: a transição agrária em Angola, 1850–1880*, Luanda 2005.

Hanson, Holly, *Landed Obligation. The Practice of Power in Buganda*, Portsmouth 2003.

Hespanha, Antonio Manuel and Catarina Madeira Santos, "Os poderes num império oceânico", in José Mattoso (dir.), *O Antigo Regime (1620–1807)*, Lisboa 1993, 395–413.

Herzog, Tamar. *Frontiers of Possession. Spain and Portugal in Europe and the Americas*, Cambridge-Massachusetts 2015.

Kantor, Iris, "Cartografia e diplomacia: usos geopolíticos da informação toponímica (1750–1850)", in *Anais do Museu Paulista* 17: 2 (2009), 39–61.

Heintze, Beatrix, *Fontes para a História de Angola do século XVII. Memórias, relações e outros manuscritos da coletânea documental de Fernão Sousa (1622–1635)*, Stuttgart 1985.

Heintze, Beatrix, *Angola nos séculos XVI e XVII. Estudos sobre Fontes, Métodos e História*, Luanda 2007.

Heintze, Beatriz, "A lusofonia no interior da África Central na era pré-colonial. Um con-tributo para a sua história e compreensão na atualidade", in *Cadernos de Estudos Africanos* 7/8 (2005).

Henriques, Isabel de Castro, "A materialidade do simbólico: marcadores territoriais, marcadores identitários angolanos (1880–1950)", in *Textos de História* 12: 1/2 (2004), 9–41.

Ito, Alec Ichiro, *Uma 'tão pesada cruz'. O governo da Angola portuguesa nos séculos XVI e XVII na perspectiva de Fernão de Sousa (1624–1630)* (Master Thesis), São Paulo 2016.

Lara, Silvia, *Palmares & Cucaú. O aprendizado da dominação*, São Paulo 2022.

Lovejoy, Paul, *A escravidão na África. Uma história de suas transformações*, Rio de Janeiro 2002.

Mann, Kristin, *Slavery and the Birth of an African City. Lagos, 1760–1900*, Bloomington 2007.

Miller, Joseph C., *Poder político e parentesco. Os antigos estados Mbundu em Angola*, Luanda 1995.

Mota, Maria Sarita, "Apropriação econômica da natureza em uma fronteira do império atlântico português. O Rio de Janeiro (século XVII)", in Serrão, José Vicente, Bárbara Direito, Eugénia Rodrigues and Susana Münch Miranda (eds.), *Property Rights, Land and Territory in the European Overseas Empires*, Lisboa 2015, 43–53.

Pantoja, Selma, "Donas de 'arimos': um negócio feminino no abastecimento de gêneros alimentícios em Luanda (séculos XVIII e XIX)", in Pantoja, Selma (ed.), *Entre Áfricas e Brasis*, Brasília 2001, 35–49.

Pratt, Mary Louise, *Imperial Eyes. Travel Writing and Transculturation*, New York 2008.

Rodrigues, Eugénia, *Portugueses e Africanos nos rios de Sena. Os prazos da Coroa em Moçambique nos séculos XVII e XVIII*, Lisboa 2013.

Santos, Catarina Madeira, *Um governo 'polido' para Angola. Reconfigurar dispositivos de domínio (1750–c. 1800)* (Ph.D. Thesis), Lisboa 2005.

Sebestyén, Eva, "Legitimation through Landcharters in Ambundu Villages, Angola", in Bearth, Thomas (ed.). *Perspektiven afrikanistischer Forschung. Beiträge zur Linguistik, Ethnologie, Geschichte, Philosophie und Literatur*, Köln 1993, 363–379.

Sebestyén, Eva, "Os 'arquivos' de sobas Mbundu. Um caso transcultural dos testamentos em Angola", in [Anon.,] (ed.). *População. Encontros e desencontros no espaço português. Actas do IV Curso de Verão da Ericeira*, Ericeira 2003, 51–74.

Sebestyén, Eva, "O contexto cultural dos marcos de terrenos nas aldeias Ambundu/Angola", in *Africana Studia* 24 (2015), 91–106.

Tavares, Ana Paula and Catarina Madeira Santos (eds.), *Africae Monumenta. A Apropriação da escrita pelos africanos*, vol. 1, Lisboa 2002.

Thomaz, Luís Filipe, *De Ceuta a Timor*, Lisboa 1994.

Vansina, Jan, *How Societies are born. Governance in West Central Africa before 1600*, Charlottesville 2004.

Vansina, Jan, "Ambaca Society and the Slave Trade c. 1760–1845", in *The Journal of African History* 46:1 (2005), 1–27.

Venâncio, José Carlos, *A economia de Luanda e Hinterland no Século XVIII. Um estudo de Sociologia Histórica*, Lisboa 1996.

Vilas Bôas, Felipe, *Portugueses, moradores e Sobas em Golungo Alto, Angola. Negociação e conflito em narrativas de militares, (c. 1840–c. 1860)* (Master Thesis), Campinas 2018.

CHAPTER 10

Epilogue: The Necessary De-Westernisation of the Models of Land Ownership

Reflections on the Idea of Feudal Remnants in Spain

Rosa Congost

1 Introduction

The content of this Chapter can be better understood with an introductory note of a personal nature. When Manuel Bastias Saavedra asked me to participate in the workshop that gave rise to this book, I had initial reservations. Not because I was not interested in the subject, but because I found it difficult to contribute something new, that is, something that I had not said on previous occasions, about land ownership in Spain or Latin America. But I also could not help sharing with him the concerns that worried and occupied me at the time, and continue to occupy me, regarding a specific problem: the weight of Western models in the historical analysis of land ownership. He encouraged me to present them in the workshop, and if I did not shy away from this opportunity, it was for two main reasons. Firstly, because the basis of my concerns was the desire to be useful in the historical analysis of land ownership in any geographical area and, therefore, also in the Latin American sphere. Secondly, my reflections were based on my empirical research on Catalonia and Spain, allowing me to weave in certain similarities with the rest of the participants which would have been more difficult to achieve in other contexts. Therefore, the workshop, and now this volume, offered me a unique opportunity, not only to share some new ideas with like-minded researchers, which in itself represents an intellectual stimulus, but also to explain to them the very reason why I decided to investigate supposed model societies. Can this type of reflection be useful for historical research on non-model societies, such as the Spanish, or non-European, such as the Latin American? Readers of this chapter will be able to decide for themselves whether the experience was worthwhile.

DOI:10.1163/9789004722729_011

2 The Necessary De-Westernisation of Our Perception of Land Ownership

The main aim of my text, written in and from Spain, that is, from my experience as a researcher, but in which I will write little about Spain and the Hispanic world and much more about France, England, and the United States, is to contribute to the necessary de-Westernisation of how land ownership is viewed, a step that I consider fully necessary if we are to advance our studies on this subject. Why has this aim led me to address these countries in particular? In fact, since what I am going to present is a small preview of a much broader work, I can make the question a little more specific: why have I decided to devote so many hours of study to these countries in recent years? In this section, I refer to some relatively recent works by authors who have accompanied me in my decision.

The first work I would like to reference is one of Thomas Piketty's latest books, *Capital and Ideology*. In the conclusions, Piketty confesses his fears that he has not sufficiently removed himself from "the limits of de-Westernizing our gaze".[1] And as the main argument in his book, he conducts a self-criticism of the space occupied by France and the United States: "The French Revolution comes up repeatedly, and the experiences of Europe and the United States are constantly cited, much more so than their demogaphic weight".[2] Well, in my case, it could be said that I have followed the exact opposite process; I have decided to deal with countries that have served as universal models for years because it seemed to me the best way to combat some topics that have for decades acted as a kind of linguistic-ideological corset. Returning to Piketty's book, for example, my main criticism would not be that its author talks a lot about France, but that he gives unquestionable importance to France as a model extended to other European countries, without deeming it convenient to stop and explain the real mechanisms of transmission. In my opinion, this is one of the weakest aspects of the dominant historical narrative around "what constitutes feudal", and it serves as the guiding axis for this chapter.

This is the second decision, related to the theme of this book, which perhaps deserves some clarification. Why even write about "feudal" issues? Why not write, for example, about the "commons"? Perhaps because today it is fashionable to speak of the commons and not of the feudal. Perhaps because I have already written about this trend on other occasions. But, above all,

1 Piketty, Capital and Ideology, 1037.
2 Piketty, Capital and Ideology, 1038.

because I think that the word feudal has played an important role in the construction of the Western perspective that we wish to abandon. Jack Goody's reflections in his ouvre, *The Theft of History*, can help us see this. Piketty cites him as a reference for the "de-Westernized" view and, in his work, Goody considers that historians have tended to abuse the concept of "feudalism". Reflecting on this, Goody differentiates between the common meaning of the term and some more technical meanings of the word, to clarify that he uses it to refer to the "period that followed Classical Antiquity in Europe". Goody denounces the view of feudalism as a progressive stage of Western development.[3] It is one which considers the influence of Roman law on feudalism fundamental in explaining "the decisive advance from conditional to absolute private property".[4] Goody criticises the legalistic interpretation hidden behind this view—shared by most historians—and repeatedly cites Henri Summer Maine and, specifically, his work *Ancient Law*, published in 1861, to highlight the fact that all societies actually know "a hierarchy of rights in land, some located in the individual, others in particular groups", which does not match with "the earlier dichotomies of individual and communal, categories that fail adequately to characterize the tenurial system of societies either in the past or in the present".[5]

Throughout this chapter, I will also be drawing on the writings of Maine, and we will therefore have an opportunity to better understand his point of view. For now, let me just point out that the idea highlighted by Goody also fails to fit with the idea of a collectivist *avant la lettre* as promoted by Paolo Grossi.[6] However, I have already said that in this work I am not going to refer to the "common", but rather to the "feudal". In this sense, the use of the word feudalism in the aforementioned work by Maine is interesting: in 1861, he qualified England as "the Herculaneum of feudalism", putting the expression in quotation marks to make it clear that it had an author, which makes it even more interesting because it reveals that it was not an isolated opinion.[7] I have searched for the expression and it was not difficult to find its author: Eduard Gans, a German jurist, disciple of Hegel and professor of Marx at the University of Berlin. Although I have not been able to find the text where Gans used the expression, we know of its authorship thanks to one written by a French jurist, Édouard

3 Goody, *The Theft of History*, 68. This sentence is in Chapter 3: Feudalism: A transition to capitalism or the collapse of Europe and the domination of Asia?

4 Goody, *The Theft of History*, 96.

5 Goody, *The Theft of History*, 59.

6 Grossi, *Un altro modo di possedere*.

7 Maine, *Ancient Law*.

René Lefebvre de Laboulaye, translated into English in 1865.[8] This text contains some interesting reflections on the strength of English feudalism, compared to feudalism on the European continent. Note that these reflections were quite widespread at the beginning of the second half of the 19th century, and I have not found them expounded by any historian of the 20th century. The issue itself is built upon a contradiction: how is it possible that the most economically advanced country in the world could also be a bastion of feudalism?

Now, the common use of the word does not share this progressive view of history. According to dictionaries, "feudalism" means the complete opposite of social progress. How could it be that the same word has served to identify a historical stage of progress and to designate the antithesis of progress today? I think we would be making a mistake if we were to set this paradox to one side. The common meanings that words end up having are not only the result of the dominant historical narratives, but have also contributed to reinforcing that narrative. The word feudalism has two different meanings, but, while the meaning that the dominant historiography has given it, denounced by Goody, has served and can serve to reinforce a unilinear view of history—by representing a more progressive stage than the previous one and less than the following one—the common use of the word combats this view and qualifies as "feudal" all evidence of "anti-progressive" aspects that today's society offers us.

To further develop this last line of reflection, I have found it very useful to read the third contemporary author that I want to mention here: the American legal theorist Joseph Singer. In several of his works, this author does not hesitate to contrast his idea of feudalism with that of democracy and, therefore, with the idea of progress. This is his starting point: "Feudalism was based on the idea of lordship, with the Sovereign as the ultimate lord of the land. This system was premised on inequality, personal loyalty, and landed aristocracy". In this society, a large part of the population lived in undignified conditions: "at the bottom of the feudal hierarchy were the unfree peasants, who lived at the lord's beck and call".[9]

It is clear that Singer has in mind a stereotype of feudal society based on medieval Europe that many medievalists today would refute. But the main question is: why does Singer feel the need to talk about feudalism in a book dedicated to analysing the experience of the subprime crisis of 2008 in the United States? It is here that we find the advantages of mixing the two conceptions. For Singer, the crisis reveals the need to not let our guard down in the face of

8 Laboulaye, "General Reflections upon Feudal Law".

9 Singer, "Property Law as the Infrastructure of Democracy", 3–4.

the threat of significant social regression. To maintain this state of alert, and on this I agree, it is not enough to appeal to a supposed "time's arrow", but rather necessary to recall the social struggles of the past. Thus, in chapter 5 of the book, entitled "Why Conservatives like Regulation and Liberals like Markets", we read:

> Indeed, we remember our history of rebellion against feudalism and our hard-won victory over the institutions of slavery and racial segregation and patriarchal privilege, it becomes clear that our property system has, over time, moved closer to a liberal ideal where each person is secure, free, comfortable.[10]

And in the following chapter, the last in the book, entitled "Democratic Liberty", Singer summarises the achievements for the social progress of the United States through citizen struggle thus:

> We have outlawed feudalism, titles of nobility, slavery, male privileges, racial segregation, and discriminatory denial of access to the market. These laws limit the contracts we can enter into and the property we can create, but they do not take away our freedom; they define what it means to live in a free society that treats each person with dignity.[11]

At this point, I suppose that the reason for the choice of these three countries and the "feudal" theme of my chapter is now clear. In recent years, an economist, an anthropologist, and a jurist have challenged me as a historian. And they have done so based on their vision of France, England, and the United States. The dominant Western thought has presented these three countries as models of economic growth and historical development, and the idea of the "end of feudalism" has played an important role in this model vision. Regarding Spain, which is the case and the example that interests us today, the idea is widespread and accepted both inside and outside of the country that things were not done well; the concept of *supervivencias feudales* (feudal remnants) has contributed to corroborating this image of failure. In fact, everything that has been pointed out as the imperfections of property in Spain, in the sense of not corresponding to ideal types of property, has tended to be seen as 'feudal remnants'. Hence the title of this chapter, in which I will explain that even though we can find the

10 Singer, *No Freedom Without Regulation*, 173.
11 Singer, *No Freedom Without Regulation*, 178.

same type of evidence in rich and therefore developed countries, this has barely provoked the kind of discussion or rejection we see in the Spanish case.

What lessons might we draw from all this? If we limit ourselves to talking about less developed countries, we will always find evidence of multiple 'imperfections'—susceptible of being described as 'feudal remnants'—that will seem to confirm the validity of some ideal models supposedly freed from any historical ballast and will thus continue to feed the dominant models in use. I myself have the feeling of having done so in my work on Spain. This is, in fact, the main reason why I have decided to take a step forward and highlight some misunderstandings at the base of these models. I have already outlined the general lines of my approach. Now we are going to see it in more detail, based on three specific, almost anecdotal, problems, each related to one of the three countries that have served as models and that have been cradles, let us not forget, of the main modern theories on ownership and property rights. These problems differ greatly from one another, but they are all related to certain silences, omissions, uses and abuses regarding the term 'feudal', detected both in history books and in the current mass media, the consultation of which I will not shy away from, because they seem to me to be especially revealing of the pitfalls of a supposedly universal language that can no longer continue to be so.

3 France: The Disappearance of the *Seigneurs Directs* (Direct Lords) from the Scene

I dedicate this section to a vocabulary problem that has had somewhat of an impact internationally. I am referring to the fact of characterising as "eminent lords", or as "lords who possessed eminent domain", those who actually appeared in the texts of the time as direct lords, that is, as holders of direct domain. Undoubtedly, the influence that the French historiography of the 1960s and 1970s exerted on French agrarian historiography as a whole has meant that the same habit has spread to historians from other countries, as is easy to see in the cases of Spain and Italy. The expression "eminent domain" is also found in historical studies on land ownership during the *ancien regime* in these countries to indicate the rights of the lords that in the documents of the time were referred to as "direct lords".

Here, we face a vocabulary problem that I think has affected historical interpretation much more than we could imagine. If we look at the dictionaries of the time, there was no confusion. The texts speak of direct domain, or of *dominium directum* if they are written in Latin. When and why, then, was this

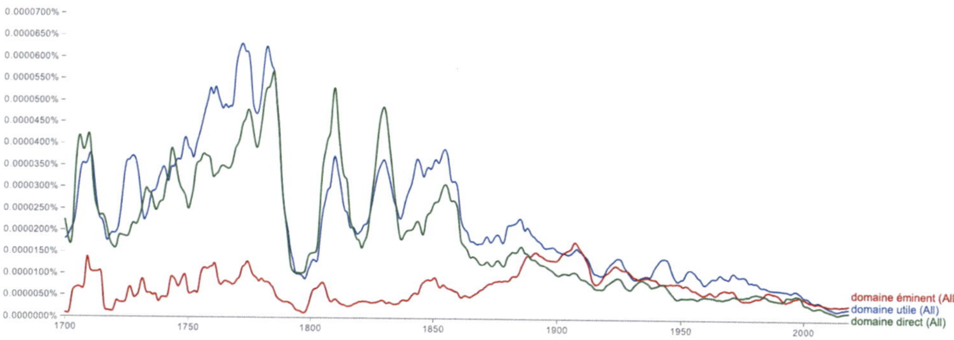

CHART 10.1 "Domaine utile", "domaine direct" and "domaine éminent" in French books (1700–2019) calculated by Ngram Viewer

term substituted for eminent domain? In order not to lose ourselves in quotes, a graphic produced by new digital technologies will suffice to represent this point (see Chart 10.1).

This exercise allows us to observe that in publications written in French, the dominant binomial was clearly *domaine utile/domaine direct*, and that the concept of *domaine éminent* came later. Why, then, have historians and jurists managed to popularise the binomial of useful domain/eminent domain as the authentic one? As an example of this popularisation, it will suffice to reproduce a few paragraphs of the corresponding article from Wikipedia in French:

> Eminent property, also called eminent domain, was a form of property rights in manorial law. It was the case of lordship over lands and cities in the classical Middle Ages, and also of the Spanish Crown over American lands in modern times. Eminent property (or domain) contrasted with useful domain (or property), which was the set of rights of those who exploited goods and collected fruit [...]. The distinction between eminent domain/useful domain disappeared in the revolutionary period in France, which brought an end to many feudal institutions through the abolition of privileges.[12]

12 "La propriété éminente, appelée aussi domaine éminent, est une forme de droits de propriété en droit seigneurial./ C'est le cas de la seigneurie foncière des campagnes et des villes au Moyen Âge classique, ou encore de la Couronne espagnole sur les terres américaines à l'époque moderne./ La propriété (ou le domaine) éminente s'oppose au domaine (ou à la propriété) utile qui est l'ensemble des droits de celui qui exploite le fonds et qui en recueille les fruits/ ... La distinction domaine éminent/domaine utile a disparu en France dans la période révolutionnaire, qui met fin à nombre d'institutions féodales, d'abord par

But the truth is that I have not found any example of historical documentation that corroborates the existence of the binomial eminent domain/useful domain in pre-revolutionary France. It does not appear in *Montesquieu*, nor the *Encyclopedie*, nor in *Pierre-François Boncerf*, nor the different dictionaries I have analysed. It has, nevertheless, long infiltrated the language of law manuals. Thus, in *Les Biens* by J. Carbonnier we read: "The presence of eminent domain hindered exercising of the rights of useful domain: it is useful property that the civil code proclaims as absolute, a concept detached from that of eminent domain".[13] In the *Dictionnaire de l'Ancien Régime*, Jean Gallet, although he has chosen the correct terminology, as he combines domaine utile/domaine direct in a single voice, is still a little ambiguous in the definition of the latter term:

> "Direct domain", domain of superiority, eminent domain, designated the rights that the lord had retained over this same land, especially the right to benefit from the help of the vassal, or the right to collect a *cens* and some other rents, to authorise hereditary sales and transmissions and, on these occasions, to collect some dues.[14]

We would not be giving so much importance to what happened in France if the same substitution process had not spread to other countries, including Spain. Bartolomé Clavero, for example, in his celebrated thesis on the Castilian *Mayorazgo*, published in 1974, defined eminent domain as a form of direct domain.[15] In the current version of Wikipedia, surely due to the influence of the term in English, a distinction is made between the current juridical concept of 'eminent domain', understood as the State's right of expropriation, and the assumed different use of the same term in the past:

> Eminent domain is a legal concept, which in contemporary law is applied to the domain (understood as part of the right to property) that corres-

l'abolition des privilèges". Available at https://fr.wikipedia.org/wiki/Propri%C3%A9t%C3%A9_%C3%A9minente, last consulted on 14 November 2023.

13 Carbonnier, *Les biens*, 116. "La Révolution a abolí le régime féodal, la décomposition du domaine, en domaine éminent et domaine utile. La présence du domaine éminent entravait l'exercice des droits du porpriétaire utile".

14 Gallet, Jean, *Dictionnaire de l'Ancien Régime*, 417: "Domaine direct/domaine utile". "Le 'domaine direct', domaine de supériorité, domaine éminent, désignait les droits que le seigneur avait conservés sur cette même terre, notamment le droit de bénéficier de l'aide du vassal, ou le droit de lever un cens et quelques autres prestations, d'autoriser les ventes et le transmissions par héritage et, a ces ocasions, de lever des redevances".

15 Clavero, *Mayorazgo*, 4–5.

> ponds to the State and is applied in the concept of expropriation. On the other hand, in historical contexts, particularly in medieval feudalism and its extension during the *ancien regime*, land ownership had a peculiar consideration, since it was shared between lord and serf (or, more generically, peasant), that is, between the party that retained that eminent domain and the one that accessed so-called useful domain (in the event that the lands were originally considered to belong to the lord, since the opposite was also possible—that it would have been the lord who attributed rights to lands originally owned by the peasants).[16]

In this same text, which cites some Spanish jurists as authorities, we find clues to interpret the operation we are analysing as one that may have had consequences for the historical analysis of land ownership. This is seen clearly in the following paragraph:

> The lord's "eminent domain" has been interpreted as a mix between property and sovereignty, by means of which the feudal income that he received is identified with the concept of tax and the rest of the rights that he exercised are identified with the concept of jurisdiction.[17]

In my opinion, substituting the concept of 'direct domain' for 'eminent domain' has served to strengthen the idea of the birth of a new concept of ownership in contemporary times, in a way that broke with the past, which has contributed to the idealisation of a certain ownership model. In the French case, this process has served to downplay what was actually a clear process of expropriation. The idea of eminent domain emphasises the idea of the political and blurs the view of lords' rights as particular ownership. However, this was how they

16 "Dominio eminente es un concepto jurídico, que en el Derecho contemporáneo se aplica al dominio (entendido como parte del derecho de propiedad) que corresponde al Estado y se aplica en el concepto de expropiación. En cambio, en contextos históricos, particularmente en el feudalismo medieval y su extensión durante el Antiguo Régimen, la propiedad de la tierra tenía una consideración peculiar, puesto que se compartía entre señor y siervo (o, más genéricamente, campesino), es decir, entre quien retenía ese dominio eminente y quien accedía al denominado dominio útil (en el caso de que las tierras se consideraran originalmente del señor, puesto que también era posible lo contrario—que hubiera sido el señor el que se atribuyera derechos sobre tierras originalmente de los campesinos".

17 "Se ha interpretado el "dominio eminente" del señor como una mezcla entre propiedad y soberanía, con lo que la renta feudal por él percibida se identifica con el concepto de impuesto y el resto de los derechos que ejerce se identifican con el concepto de jurisdicción".

were understood in the context of the Spanish liberal revolution. The Spanish rulers were able to do that type of processing in the name of the sacred right of property. In an economically backward country, such as Spain, calling them eminent, due to the influence and strength of the French model, facilitated their interpretation as 'feudal remnants'. But then, should this same idea not be extended to many other countries, including England, considered one of the countries with the highest level of protection in terms of property rights?

4 England and Scotland: Why Hereditary Practices Ceased to Matter

We could dwell on the subject of copyholders surviving until 1920, but our trip to England will take us down other paths. The conflation of feudalism with a society of unequal inheritance was fairly widespread in many 18th-century writings. Among enlightened 18th-century Spaniards, for example, the feudal institution par excellence was the entail. Adam Smith, John Stuart Mill, and even Maine condemned this practice and saw it as one of the most serious obstacles to the economic development of their country. Let us first consider Smith's words in 1762:

> Upon the whole nothing can be more absurd than perpetual entails. In them the principle of testamentary succession can by no means take place. Piety to the dead can only take place when their memory is fresh in the minds of men: a power to dispose of estates for ever is manifestly absurd. The earth and the fullness of it belongs to every generation, and the preceding one can have no right to bind it up from posterity; such extension of property is quite unnatural. The insensible progress of entails was owing to their not knowing how far the right of the dead might extend, if they had any at all. The utmost extent of entails should be to those who are alive at the person's death, for he can have no affection to those who are unborn. Entails are disadvantageous to the improvement of the country, and those lands where they have never taken place are always best cultivated: heirs of entailed estates have it not in their view to cultivate lands, and often they are not able to do it. A man who buys land has this entirely in view, and in general the new purchasers are the best cultivators.[18]

18 Smith, *Lectures on Jurisprudence*, 401.

Almost a century later, Maine would be of the same opinion. It is in speaking of "entailment", in fact, that he refers to England as the Herculaneum of Feudalism:

> [...] the land-law of England, "the Herculaneum of Feudalism", is certainly much more closely allied to the land-law of the Middle Ages than that of any Continental country, and Wills with us are frequently used to aid or imitate that preference of the eldest son and his line, which is a nearly universal feature in marriage settlements of real property. But nevertheless, feeling and opinion in this country have been profoundly affected by the practice of free Testamentary disposition; and it appears to me that the state of sentiment in a great part of French society, on the subject of the conservation of property in families, is much like that which prevailed through Europe two or three centuries ago than are the current opinions of Englishmen.[19]

In England, unlike in Spain and in many other supposedly more economically backward countries, the great noble fortunes were not questioned by any government or parliament. It comes as no surprise, then, to verify the validity of what is considered feudal in the definition of the word 'entail' in Wikipedia, which redirects the word to the expression 'fee tail':

> In English common law, fee tail or entail is a form of trust established by deed or settlement which restricts the sale or inheritance of an estate in real property and prevents the property from being sold, devised by will, or otherwise alienated by the tenant-in-possession, and instead causes it to pass automatically by operation of law to an heir determined by the settlement deed. The term fee tail is from Medieval Latin *feodum talliatum*, which means "cut(-short) fee" and is in contrast to "fee simple", where no such restriction exists and where the possessor has an absolute title (although subject to the allodial title of the monarch) in the property, which he can bequeath or otherwise dispose of as he wishes. Equivalent legal concepts exist or formerly existed in many other European countries and elsewhere.[20]

The same article highlights the following as being the main opponents of this practice: "the monarchy, the merchant class, and many holders of entailed

19 Maine, *Ancient Law*, 201.

20 Available at https://en.wikipedia.org/wiki/Fee_tail, last consulted on 8 November 2023.

estates themselves who wished to sell or divide their land".[21] It also states that fee tail was abolished as a legal estate in England by the 1925 Law of Property Act. A dozen works of fiction have also been found that deal with this subject, most of them written and published in the 19th century, including the emblematic *Pride and Prejudice*, as well as a reference to the famous 21st-century TV series *Downton Abbey*.

A study of the English case reveals that there was an important break between what was considered emblematic of feudalism in the 18th century and what came to be considered feudal in the 20th century. We have reason to believe that if England had succeeded in regulating those hereditary practices during the 19th century, this would not have happened. The consequences of this may be more important than it would at first appear. Many misgivings regarding those family ties expressed by authors from the time of the *ancien régime* or the first half of the 19th century had a lot to do with the issue of social inequality. The survival of these 'feudal remnants' in England, the country of the industrial revolution, probably contributed to this issue ceasing to be central in debates on economic development and us needing to wait until the 21st century for Piketty's work to become aware of the central role that inheritance has played in the transmission of social inequalities in capitalist societies.

5 The United States: The Anti-Rent Movement, a Little Known War

If this chapter was focused exclusively on the United States, I would certainly not have chosen the subject of feudalism, but rather that of slavery, which seems to me more provocative and effective when it comes to highlighting the contradictions between economic progress and social progress. In the context in which we find ourselves, however, I think it is appropriate to refer to the anti-feudal movement that some US states underwent during the 19th century. We can then link this to the previously mentioned cases. Furthermore, it is a very little known social movement, and it will therefore also be interesting to examine the reasons for it being forgotten in historiographic terms. Let us start by reproducing what Wikipedia says about The Anti-Rent War:

> The Anti-Rent War (also known as the Helderberg War) was a tenants' revolt in upstate New York in the period 1839–1845. The Anti-Renters

21 Available at https://en.wikipedia.org/wiki/Fee_tail, last consulted on 8 November 2023.

> declared their independence from the manor system run by patroons, resisting tax collectors and successfully demanding land reform.[22]

In the same article, at the end of the section entitled "Results", we read: "The New York Constitution of 1846 added provisions for tenants' rights, abolishing feudal tenures and outlawing leases lasting longer than twelve years. The remaining manors dissolved quickly as the patroons sold off the lands".[23]

However, the results were not as clear as this article seems to suggest. One of its main scholars, Charles W. McCurdy, questions the importance of the cited constitutional text:

> Each of the prohibitions spoke to the future and not to the past. For the holder of a lease of two or three lives, the constitution of 1846 merely created a different transaction setting when the existing agreement expired and his family's house, barn, and other improvements reverted to the landlord. For the holder of an existing lease in fee, it changed nothing at all. The tenant and his heirs would remain in "feudal servitude interminable" unless the state government subsequently intervened or a new agreement could be worked out with the landlord.[24]

The book provides numerous pieces of evidence regarding the conflict's continuity and its interrelation with the anti-slavery movement, at least until 1865. The final paragraph is worth reproducing:

> [...] the most appropriate monuments to the Anti-Rent era are buried in county land records. Astonished home buyers sometimes learn that they are required every year to pay a nominal rent charge to some remote assignee of Stephen Van Renselaer III. Their title deeds stand as reminders of how law, politics, and ideology frustrated the achievement of a reform everyone wanted to achieve during a supposed "golden age" of American democracy. We forget them at our peril.[25]

22 Available at https://en.wikipedia.org/wiki/Anti-Rent_War, last consulted on 14 November 2023.

23 Available at https://en.wikipedia.org/wiki/Anti-Rent_War, last consulted on 14 November 2023.

24 McCurdy, 207.

25 McCurdy, 336.

For McCurdy and other scholars of the anti-rent movement, the fact that over the years legislators of different persuasions had left the tenants' demands unprotected, encouraging them to negotiate directly with the landlords, had repercussions on the increasingly individualistic mindset of Americans. But the roots of this individualism can be seen in the movement itself. In reality, many of the leaders of the anti-rent movement were among the wealthiest taxpayers, who may not have felt too comfortable facing acts of anonymous violence perpetrated by young people with little or no land disguised as Indians, who claimed their right to obtain resources from communal lands, which the former were not willing to recognise.

In fact, the anti-rent struggle was not unique to the State of New York. But I am not in a position to pronounce further in this regard, so I will limit myself to pointing out the interest with which Singer has followed a similar movement in New Jersey. Led by Brendan McConville, it had a very different outcome than that of New York. This reference to Singer will allow me to finish this section by linking these historical events with some of the reflections I made at the beginning of this chapter. Singer celebrates the successful struggle of the New Jersey settlers against their feudal lords, who were explicitly referred to as 'proprietors' there, and converts it into a fundamental piece of United States history. We can see this when he cites as a result of that victory a 1971 New Jersey court ruling that a doctor and a lawyer not be denied entry to attend to an immigrant. In a way, as we have said, for Singer the end of feudalism meant the triumph of democracy and the end of absolute property. Thus, although starting from similar historical processes with different outcomes, both McCurdy and Singer warn us of the need to study these cases in order to better understand the present. And this is, I think, the main lesson that we must assimilate from the three reflections that I have shared relating to France, England and the United States.

6 Application to Latin America

To what extent can this be applied to Latin American countries? It is not necessary to change history to argue that it is indeed applicable. Although historiography and historical research has had a decisive weight in the three problems I have addressed, resolving them has required that many elements be rescued from historiographical oblivion.

Let us turn to a practical example to see this. The vision of perfect property has prevailed as the ideal of all liberals in Spanish historiography and in most Latin American countries. And jurists seem to be one of the main transmitters of this vision, both in Spain and in Latin America. But was it really so? We can trace the work of the jurist Joaquín Escriche, considered a progressive liberal, since he was in exile for several years following the Liberal Triennium. In the *Diccionario Razonado de Legislación y Jurisprudencia*, published in Spain, under the word *propiedad* we find: "Property is divided into perfect and imperfect"; and under the word dominion: "Dominion is divided into full and less full, that is, perfect and imperfect. Less full domain is subdivided into direct and useful".[26] In the *Manual del abogado americano*, Escriche recognises the same division of property.

> Domain or property is: the right or power to exclude others from the use of something, according to one's discretion, if not prevented by law, the will of the testator, or any convention. The domain whose effects are divided between two owners is called less full and is divided into direct and useful. Direct is the power either to concur with the disposition of something, or to demand something in recognition of domain; and useful that of perceiving the entire usefulness of the thing. There are innumerable kinds, depending on the convention of the parties.[27]

On the other hand, in the same manual, which addresses an American audience, Escriche does not grant any space to indigenous communal ownership. When he points out that men are subdivided into free men and servants or slaves, he defines the latter category as follows: "Servants are those who are subject to the power of another against nature, so that what they acquire is for their master, and he can do of them what he will, except kill them".[28] He does not seem to feel any need to qualify this definition, as he does when defining nobility. Here Escriche writes one of few footnotes in the *Manual*, to warn

---

26 Escriche, *Diccionario Razonado de Legislación y Jurisprudencia*.

27 Escriche, *Manual del abogado americano*, 45: "Dominio o propiedad es: el derecho o facultad de excluir a los otros del uso de alguna cosa, según su arbitrio, si no lo impide la ley, la voluntad del testador, o alguna convención. El dominio cuyos efectos están repartidos entre dos dueños se llama menos pleno y se divide en directo y útil. Directo es la facultad o de concurrir a la disposición de alguna cosa, o de exigir algo en reconocimiento del dominio; y útil la de percibir toda la utilidad de la cosa. Sus especies pueden ser innumerables según la convención de las partes".

28 Escriche, *Manual del abogado americano*, 13: "Según el estado civil, son los hombres libres o siervos; nobles o plebeyos; eclesiásticos o legos; vecinos o transeuentes; naturales o extranjeros. Siervos son los que están sujetos al poder de otro contra la naturaleza, de modo que cuanto adquieren es para su señor, y este puede hacer de ellos lo que le acomode, menos matarlos".

that in the free states "all of the privileges and prerogatives of the nobles have ceased" because "all citizens are equal before the law". He claims to have left the description of the word so that people remember "such hateful distinctions".[29]

The only other explanatory note refers to entails, where after indicating the damage this institution caused to the members of affected families, he notes the social problem they represent:

> They are ultimately detrimental to society, because by stagnating land properties in a few hands, there are fewer who enjoy them, the improvements that lands usually receive when passing from one hand to another are lost, national wealth is diminished, and the population is reduced. That is why these antisocial establishments have already been abolished in the states governed by good laws, and it would be very advantageous if no trace of them remained anywhere.[30]

Reading this *Manual*, which was of undoubted influence in Latin America, may serve to recreate the prevailing mindset in these countries, but also, as we have just seen, to illustrate many misunderstandings and paradoxes that affect our work as historians. How can we overcome them? The emergence of so-called global history can contribute to doing so, but only if studies carried out on non-European societies are taken into consideration and the concepts on which Western historiography has been built are reviewed. We are not alone, but we are in the minority. And "the voices on the other side are often so dominant, so sure of themselves, that we can perhaps be forgiven for raising ours".[31] These are the final words of Goody's introduction to his book on the theft of history. There he cites Maine, who, as we have seen, in the 1860s regarded England as the European country in which feudalism was most deeply rooted and therefore least weakened. All historiographical schools—including neo-institutionalists and social historians—have tended to convey the opposite idea: that a modern system of property developed in England, and not, for example, in Spain, a country where feudal elements are thought to have survived.

---

29 Escriche, *Manual del abogado americano*, 14.

30 Escriche, *Manual del abogado americano*, 104: "Son en fin perjudiciales á la sociedad, porque estancándose en pocas manos las propiedades territoriales, son menos los que gozan, se pierden las mejoras que suelen recibir las tierras al pasar de unas manos á otras, se disminuye la riqueza nacional, y se va reduciendo la población. Por eso se han abolido ya estos establecimientos antisociales en los Estados gobernados por buenas leyes, y sería muy ventajoso que en ninguna parte quedase vestigio de ellos".

31 Goody, *The Theft of History*, 9.

We are not in a position to blame Spanish and Latin American intellectuals of good faith for adopting the vocabulary that appeared before their ears and eyes as the one that could lead them to progress. It was very difficult to escape this in their times. But today, in the 21st century, we cannot continue to accept this vocabulary as neutral. Goody uses a similar argument when calling for a rereading of Maine:

> Earlier scholars had a paucity of documentation and fanciful notions about the past. Later writers have access to a wealth of studies of recent societies with vaguely similar political economies which demonstrate the validity of Maine's notion of a hierarchy of rights in land, some located in the individual, others in particular groups.[32]

Although Goody cites few works by recent historians, he knows that the historical account cannot remain the same in the 21st century. And he poses a question when he reaches the conclusion that certain supposedly universal terms must be abandoned:

> To affect a valid comparison would involve using not predetermined categories of the kind antiquity, feudalism, capitalism, but abandoning these concepts to construct a sociological grid laying out the possible variations of what is being compared. That is notably lacking from most historical discourse in the West. Instead, historians have simply claimed desirable and "progressive" features for themselves. They have stolen history by imposing their categories and sequences on the rest of the world.[33]

In one way, these may seem like unkind words to a historian's ears. But they can also be stimulating. And there are already a few of us—although we are still, certainly, a minority—who not only do not accept the aforementioned terminological straitjacket, but also fight to remove it as the only way to better understand historical reality. This Chapter is addressed to those who think this is a worthwhile task. Good luck in this exciting adventure!

32 Goody, *The Theft of History*, 59.
33 Goody, *The Theft of History*, 304.

Acknowledgments

This work could be done thanks to Grant PID2022-139652NB-I00 funded by MCIN/AEI/10.13039/501100011033 and by "ERDF A way of making Europe".

Bibliography

Printed Sources

Escriche, Joaquín, *Manual del abogado americano*, Librería de Garnier Hermanos, Paris 1856.

Escriche, Joaquín, *Diccionario Razonado de Legislación y Jurisprudencia*, Madrid 1874–1876.

Laboulaye, "General Reflections upon Feudal Law", *Victoria Magazine* (1865).

Maine, Henri Summer, *Ancient Law. Its connection with the early history of society*, London 1861.

Smith, Adam, *Lectures on Jurisprudence* [1762–1763], Ed. R.L. Meek, D.D. Raphael and P.G. Stein, Oxford 1978.

Literature

Carbonier, Jean, *Les biens*, Paris 1988.

Clavero, Bartolomé, *Mayorazgo. Propiedad feudal en Castilla, 1369–1836*, Madrid 1974.

Gallet, Jean, *Diccionaire de l'Ancien Régime. Royaume de France XVIe–XVIIIe siècle (publié sous la direction de Lucien Bély)*, Paris 1996.

Goody, Jack, *The Theft of History*, Cambridge 2007.

Grossi, Paolo, *Un altro modo di possedere. L'emersione di forme alternative di proprietà alla coscienza giuridica postunitaria*, Milan 1977.

McConville, Brendan, *These Daring Disturbers of the Public Peace. The Struggle for Property and Power in Early New Jersey*, Ithaca 1999.

McCurdy, Charles, *The Anti-Rent Era in New York Law and Politics, 1839–1865*, Chapel Hill 2003

Piketty, Thomas, *Capital and Ideology*, Harvard 2020.

Singer, Joseph, "Property Law as the Infrastructure of Democracy", in: Public Law & Legal Theory Working Paper Series Paper 11–16: 7 (2011).

Singer, Joseph, *No Freedom without Regulation. The hidden Lesson of the subprime Crisis*, New Haven 2015.

Index

Printed in the United States
by Baker & Taylor Publisher Services